Patrimony and Law in Renaissance Italy

Family was a central feature of social life in Italian cities. In the Renaissance, jurists, humanists, and moralists began to theorize on the relations between people and property that formed the 'substance' of the family and what held it together over the years. Family property was a bundle of shared rights. This was most evident when brothers shared a household and enterprise, but it also faced overlapping claims from children and wives which the *paterfamilias* had to recognize. Thomas Kuehn explores patrimony in legal thought, and how property was inherited, managed and shared in Renaissance Italy. Managing a patrimony was not a simple task. This led to a complex and active conceptualization of shared rights, and a conscious application of devices in the law that could override liabilities and preserve the group, or carve out distinct shares for each member. This wide-ranging volume charts the ever-present conflicts that arose and were a constant feature of family life.

Thomas Kuehn is Emeritus Professor of History at Clemson University. His previous publications include five books, three of which have been published with Cambridge University Press. *Heirs, Kin, and Creditors in Renaissance Florence* (2008) was awarded the Marraro Prize of the American Historical Association for the best book on Italian history. He has also published numerous journal articles and book chapters and coedited two volumes of scholarly essays.

T0370956

Patrimony and Law
in Renaissance Italy

Thomas Kuehn

Clemson University

CAMBRIDGE
UNIVERSITY PRESS

Shaftesbury Road, Cambridge CB2 8EA, United Kingdom

One Liberty Plaza, 20th Floor, New York, NY 10006, USA

477 Williamstown Road, Port Melbourne, VIC 3207, Australia

314–321, 3rd Floor, Plot 3, Splendor Forum, Jasola District Centre, New Delhi – 110025, India

103 Penang Road, #05–06/07, Visioncrest Commercial, Singapore 238467

Cambridge University Press is part of Cambridge University Press & Assessment, a department of the University of Cambridge.

We share the University's mission to contribute to society through the pursuit of education, learning and research at the highest international levels of excellence.

www.cambridge.org
Information on this title: www.cambridge.org/9781009073967

DOI: 10.1017/9781009072816

First published 2022
First paperback edition 2024

A catalogue record for this publication is available from the British Library

Library of Congress Cataloging-in-Publication data
Names: Kuehn, Thomas, author.
Title: Patrimony and law in Renaissance Italy / Thomas Kuehn, Clemson University, South Carolina.
Description: Cambridge, United Kingdom ; New York, NY : Cambridge University Press, 2021. | Includes bibliographical references and index.
Identifiers: LCCN 2021041325 (print) | LCCN 2021041326 (ebook) | ISBN 9781316513538 (hardback) | ISBN 9781009072816 (ebook)
Subjects: LCSH: Inheritance and succession – Italy – History – 14th century. | Marital property – Italy – History – 14th century. | Fideicommissum – Italy – History – 14th century. | Inventories of decedents' estates – Italy – History – 14th century. | Wills – Italy – History – 14th century. | Bartolo, of Sassoferrato, 1313–1357. | Albericus, de Rosate, 1290–1360. | Soccini, Bartolommeo, 1436–1507. | Decio, Filippo, 1454-1536 or 1537. | BISAC: HISTORY / Europe / General
Classification: LCC KKH770 .K84 2021 (print) | LCC KKH770 (ebook) | DDC 346.4505/2–dc23
LC record available at https://lccn.loc.gov/2021041325
LC ebook record available at https://lccn.loc.gov/2021041326

ISBN   978-1-316-51353-8   Hardback
ISBN   978-1-009-07396-7   Paperback

Contents

Acknowledgments

To recognize the contributions of everyone to a book that has really been in gestation for decades is impossible. Those decades began with the mentoring and encouragement of Julius Kirshner, so this volume is rightfully dedicated to him. He has always been a source of advice and an example of rigorous scholarship, and I am grateful to have had him as a teacher and a friend for all these years. Others who stepped up with advice, help, or encouragement include Dan Bornstein, Giovanna Benadusi, Nicholas Terpstra, and the late Phil Gavitt. Staffs at the Robbins Collection, University of California Law School Library, the Vatican Microfilm Collection at St. Louis University Library, the Archivio di Stato of Florence, and the Biblioteca Nazionale of Florence were all wonderful to work with. William Caferro and Caroline Castiglione read portions of earlier drafts, and Dan Smail provided incisive and needed criticism of the entire work. This is a much better work for their contributions. Anonymous readers for Cambridge were also effective and searching critics, and I thank them for their interest and energy, and their appreciation of the project. Providing such wonderful readers is just one of the ways in which Liz Friend-Smith put her touches to this book.

Chapter 4 previously appeared, in a version much recast for this context, under the title "Property of Spouses in Law in Renaissance Florence," in *Family Law and Society in Europe from the Middle Ages to the Contemporary Era*, edited by Maria Gigliola di Renzo Villata, fifth volume in the series Studies in the History of Law and Justice, published by Springer International Publishing of Cham, Switzerland, in 2016, pp. 109–34.

As ever, I owe a deep debt to my wife, Teresa, for support and patience, for grounding me, and for keeping me going.

1 Introduction

In the course of the first half of the fourteenth century one of the greatest legal minds of the day, Bartolus of Sassoferrato (1313–57), arrived at a definition of family that rested on the equation of family and property – more particularly, of *familia* and *substantia*. In his words, "familia accipitur in iure pro substantia." Just what was included in *substantia* he did not elaborate. His contemporary, Alberico da Rosciate (1290–1360), came to an identical equation, or, in his terms, "familia, id est substantia."[1] But he revealed more about that *substantia*, specifically including nonmaterial elements, *dignitas* and *memoria*, in that substance.[2] *Dignitas* and *memoria* comprised such things as family name and coat of arms, size and style of dwelling, and all else that contributed to family honor, in other words. Those were all elements that members of a family shared. That sharing may have been most evident at the moments at which it ended or was under some threat, such as the very moment that was Bartolus's focus, namely death and inheritance. The ideal case was that as the nominal owner of the *substantia* died, his son stepped forward and acceded to the *substantia* so seamlessly that in some sense father and son had shared the patrimony together. The tie between father and son was indeed substantial.

What propelled these simultaneous and parallel jurisprudential observations of Bartolus and Alberico? Why the concern about family? And why then? To that point in time there had essentially been no jurisprudential theorizing about family. *Familia*, to be sure, was a term from Roman law, but *familia* had no precise legal definition and was not itself possessed of distinctive rights or legal contours. It was not conceived as a corporate entity. The word was a handy collective noun, useful for certain situations that arose in civic or natural circumstances.[3]

---

[1] For Bartolus, see the references in Chapter 2. Alberico da Rosciate, *Dictionarium iuris tam civilis quam canonici*, s.v. *familia*.

[2] Cf. Andrea Romano, *Famiglie, successioni e patrimonio familiare nell'Italia medievale e moderna*, 2; and Kuehn, "*Memoria* and Family in Law."

[3] Cf. David Herlihy, "Family."

Legal thought had not advanced before that point to concentrate on the ongoing social and political developments, to seek the logic (*ratio*) behind laws and to apply that to new and shifting circumstances.[4] To that point the logical and textual coherence of law (Roman and canon) had been the focus. With the so-called commentators, including Bartolus, an active interest in the relations between society and local laws, on the one hand, and learned academic law, on the other, came to the fore and began to have effects on law in practice. Men like Bartolus and Alberico took direct aim at legal issues that were real and pressing, including those arising from changes in family and in local laws bearing on family affairs and possessions. But what Bartolus and Alberico were addressing was the means, in law, by which property and *dignitas* and *memoria* were preserved, mainly in the management and transmission of *substantia*. They were beginning to think of *familia* as something abstract and corporate, an entity or substance enduring in time.

The timing of this juristic interest in family, however, is indicative of social and economic factors also. It was around the middle of the fourteenth century that, as Cesarina Casanova, among others, has said, "the model of the great horizontal family and its communion of goods began to give way to the emergence of an agnatic and patrilineal conception, which was manifest in the tendency to maintain a unitary patrimony."[5] By the early fourteenth century the large clans in Italian cities that had been prominent in the Guelf and Ghibelline factionalism in the thirteenth century had begun to give way to more elongated, temporally durable configurations, couched in terms of agnatic lineage. Families were more narrowly cast, but also more complex, as they tracked relations over time.[6] Scholars' attention consequently has turned from the accumulation and sharing of resources within a residential and relational group to the passage of families and patrimonies across generations.

It was not an easy or simple task to accord a corporate character to the family. While the ethos of kin sharing and living from a common fund was undoubtedly strong – presumed, in fact, in many realms of activity – it ran up against everyday contingencies that revealed the dark side of shared gains and losses, credits and liabilities. Mismanagement, sudden reversals of fortune, and vagaries of markets always threatened to bring down all those who shared a familial *substantia*. A narrower, temporally extended

---

[4] Ferdinando Treggiari, "Commentaria (Commentaries on Civil Law), Fourteenth Century, Bartolus a Saxoferrato (1313/14–1357/58)."

[5] Cesarina Casanova, *La famiglia italiana in età moderna*, 87. On this theme also Gianna Pomata, "Family and Gender."

[6] Franca Leverotti, *Famiglie e istituzioni nel medioevo italiano: dal tardo antico al rinascimento*, 137.

family was one device to reduce liabilities that might undercut family survival. Even more, for jurists, a more corporate approach to ownership and management ran into conflict with another important premise: that of contractual freedom of legal persons.[7]

The estate itself had qualities of a legal person that emerged mainly when an inheritance was in abeyance (*iacens*). Then an estate had elements of personality, having and meeting obligations, that stood until someone came forth to accept the estate and make it (and its debts) his.[8] The notion of a *haereditas iacens* clarified and allowed the imposition of rights and obligations through the singular person. The legal person is a fiction, but medieval law operated through such devices. As Yan Thomas maintains, looking precisely at the "continuation" of ownership from father to son in inheritance, the law perpetuated fictions that altered the nature of things within the law. In Bartolus's example, the fiction that father and son were somehow one and the same person, in turn, could generate the fiction that family was its substance.[9] In that regard, examined carefully, the law provided space within which the realities of shared domestic existence could proceed alongside concerns to maintain family, substantially, over time. Corporate interests were thus perpetuated through, but also conflicted with, individual prerogatives.

Families were units of production, as Frederik Pedersen has recently noted, that also "shared economic, social, and political resources." Ideally tasks were interchangeable and all family members were supported. The older generation furnished the capital and land; the younger generation the labor. All shared the fruits of that labor and capital.[10] The synchronous sharing of life and resources stood in some contrast, however, to the passage of resources across generations and the personification of rights and obligations in the deceased owner passing to one's heirs. Still, by no means was it the case that the horizontal family and its "communion of goods" (Casanova) had disappeared entirely. In fact, the sharing of goods went on; certainly the ideal and presumption of it did, but now such horizontal solidarity could come to clash with the more vertical emphasis on an intergenerational patrimony. That equation of family and substance that Bartolus and Alberico envisioned so nicely sprang from a perception of a unity of patrimonial elements, of shared resources, under the guiding hand of the single *paterfamilias* directing the

---

[7] Casanova, *La famiglia italiana in età moderna*, 91.

[8] Thomas Kuehn, *Heirs, Kin, and Creditors in Renaissance Florence*, 72–74.

[9] Yan Thomas, Fictio legis: *La funzione romana e i suoi limiti medievali*, 80–82. See also Marta Madero, "Interpreting the Western Legal Tradition: Reading the Work of Yan Thomas," 124–26.

[10] Frederik Pedersen, "The Family Economy," 102, 109, 111.

family, its members and property, to a common well-being and to a prolongation in subsequent generations. *Familia* became a concern, in other words, as the meanings or utilities of *familia* were shifting. Bartolus, as we will see, was struck by the close sharing of the patrimony by father and son, to the extent that during his father's life a son could still be termed a sort of owner (*quodammodo dominus*) of the family's *substantia*, and on his father's death inherited it immediately and automatically in the eyes of the law. This sense of sharing as normative has been lost or at least downplayed in scholarly attention to accounts of patrimonial management, to the strategies employed in moments of transmission, such as marriage or death. The ideal of living together and sharing assets of a patrimony, of surviving lean times and enjoying the good, remained a powerful and persistent force shaping behavior and expectations.

Sharing is not generally seen as an economic activity, if only because it occurs in spaces away from markets and embodies something other than the acquisitive rationality that supposedly governs behavior there. A stark contrast between the home and the market is the expectation of the present. Stephanie Coontz, in a popular book from the 1990s, nicely described those expectations:

The effective adult, at work and in public, is independent, individualistic, rational, and calculative. The effective family member, by contrast, shares, cooperates, sacrifices, and acts nonrationally. The character traits that keep families together are associated in all other arenas of life with immaturity or irrationality; family interdependency is now the only thing that stands in the way of "self-actualization."[11]

This dichotomy continues to shape historical understanding. It is a false dichotomy in many ways, most clearly so when one looks at things like family investments, exploitation of assets, and devolution of wealth across key moments of marriage and death. Wealth as patrimony required more of that sharing, cooperation, sacrifice, and, above all, nonrationality. But the approach to family as *substantia* was not thoroughly beyond the nonrational. There was an interpenetration and combination of the legal and the extralegal, the individual and the collective, the commercial and the inalienable that allowed the equation of family and substance. Patrimony was not incompatible with markets, but both interacted with cultural and political, as well as economic, values. Sharing was not always irrational and it was always meaningful. It was a systematic form of behavior that can be tracked behind and even through the evidence left

---

[11] Stephanie Coontz, *The Way We Never Were: American Families and the Nostalgia Trap*, 155.

by market activities and reciprocities of exchange that formed the core of the economy of gifts. That, again, is what this study seeks to do.

The idea of the patrimony underpinned by a sharing economy is the point of departure for the chapters that follow, beginning with close consideration of Bartolus's formulation. The sharing economy of households can be seen as a third option, between the two conventionally opposed forms of exchange broadly recognized within social sciences – the economy of the commercial market and the economy of the gift. The gift economy was first elaborated by the French anthropologist, Marcel Mauss, and developed and refined by others.[12] It was a notion formulated in clear contrast to relations and exchanges in a market economy (and from that association largely taken as "primitive" in contrast to markets). The market, of course, is broadly taken as indicative of the modern world, which began with commercial markets and then developed industrial and financial markets. The gift is taken as characteristic of earlier forms of exchange and distribution, in tribal or feudal societies, influentially so in the work of the historians Georges Duby and Natalie Zemon Davis.[13]

In both the competitive world of markets and gift-giving, there is a calculated exchange and reciprocity (just not necessarily immediate or precise in the case of gifts). In the market typically the reciprocation (price) is set and the return is made immediately (or credit is extended). A gift, in contrast, set an expectation of reciprocation at some future point, in an as yet undetermined form, and thus put the recipient in the position of debtor to the gift giver. Extension of credit was the essence of gift-giving. In an economy of gift or largesse, reciprocity could present problems of miscalculation, while the norm of reciprocity was real and undeniable. The reciprocal countergift could seem to be a sort of extortion on the person who accepted the initial gift. Reciprocation, imprecise in form and timing, could raise anxiety as to the continuing social relationship between donor and donee.[14]

In the sharing economy, in contrast, there is no reciprocity; there is the "demand" on one side and the accession to or refusal of it on the other. There is no calculation of return. There is no sense of indebtedness or individualistic ownership to acknowledge.[15] As laid out by the

---

[12] Marcel Mauss, *The Gift: Forms and Functions of Exchange in Archaic Societies.* Also interesting is James G. Carrier, *Gifts and Commodities: Exchange and Western Capitalism since 1700.*

[13] Cf. Georges Duby, *The Early Growth of the European Economy: Warriors and Peasants from the Seventh to the Twelfth Century*; Natalie Zemon Davis, *The Gift in Sixteenth-Century France.*

[14] William Ian Miller, *Humiliation: And Other Essays on Honor, Social Discomfort, and Violence*, esp. 5–6, 16–17, 48–50.

[15] Cf. Russell Belk, "Sharing," 716.

anthropologist Thomas Widlok, sharing is not an aspect of gift exchange but a complex social phenomenon in its own right that makes specific demands on those involved in it. Some people share what they value without expecting returns. Sharing is more likely in situations of proximity, though not necessarily face to face, as intermediaries may often be used to convey things. Sharing shelter or food, as with brothers living together (*ad unum panem et vinum*, to use a frequent metaphor from our period), can generate powerful social bonding apart from any sense of blood-relatedness. Sharing helps establish a sense of self as "limited," subject to the demands of others and with possible access to things through them, including the honor shared with others.[16] It does not demand unequivocal ownership as a right to exclude others from access to what is owned.[17] Inequalities and distinctions that are in fact inevitable are muted by sharing.[18]

The centrality of physical presence is one weakness of sharing, as the relationship can be attenuated when presence ends or intervals between appearances lengthen. Claims after a long absence may slide a relationship to a point more akin to gift-giving than sharing, where some expectation of reciprocity and keeping score creeps in.[19] Sharing may also erode when kin relations start to become fixed roles – when those involved stop speaking of and to each other in certain ways, practice different crafts, circulate in different corners of society, and certainly when they take up separate dwellings.[20] Death has extensive effects on sharing, of course, as sharing most often ends at that point, and those not present at the moment might be left out.[21]

Still, as a household mode of living, sharing presents a different option, difficult to reconcile with notions of ownership. In the formulation of some anthropologists, the household economy is more than a set of practices. It is "a way of thinking about those activities, an orientation that sees the household itself as the focus of economic action and that subordinates the economic pursuit of its members to the survival of the house as a social unit."[22] As the business analyst Russell Belk points out,

Within the family, shared things are, de facto if not de jure, joint possessions. Their use requires no invitation, generates no debt, and may entail responsibilities

---

[16] On honor and personality, see William Ian Miller, *Eye for an Eye*, 101.
[17] Cf. Yan Thomas, *Il valore delle cose*.
[18] The foregoing derives from Thomas Widlok, *Anthropology and the Economy of Sharing* and his programmatic essay "Sharing: Allowing Others to Take What Is Valued." Also Belk, "Sharing," 723; and Alfred Gell, "Inter-Tribal Commodity Barter and Reproductive Gift-Exchange in Old Melanesia."
[19] Widlok, *Sharing*, 182.   [20] Widlok, *Sharing*, 83.   [21] Widlok, *Sharing*, 183.
[22] Carrier, *Gifts and Commodities*, 153–54.

as well as rights. The responsibilities may include taking care not to damage shared possessions, not overusing these things to the detriment of other family members, and cleaning up so that others will find these resources in a similar state of readiness for their own use. Such responsibilities underscore a difference between shared possession and sole ownership.[23]

Contrary to the contrasting conditions of seller and buyer or donor and recipient, there is no distinction to be made conceptually between sharers; their ownership, as it were, is mutual.[24] Possessiveness and mastery or control are the sorts of outlooks that threaten the end of sharing.[25] Indeed, sharing is most evident, certainly most apt to fall into the purview of legal documents, at those moments at which individual prerogatives and rights are asserted against those of the group. Sharing, in other words, pops into view when it is threatened (from within or without) or ceases altogether, evidently so at death.[26] We may not always see it from the perspective we adopt as historians dependent on legal records. Indeed, as the anthropologist Marilyn Strathern has demonstrated, perceptions of actions as borrowing or sharing can vary by observers' circumstances – their location in an institutional or social nexus. Sharing within a family can seem something else (e.g., borrowing, theft) from outside. Ownership as a way of negotiating relations and appropriation as a way of acquisition exist in a fluid dynamic.[27] In contrast to a rich line of scholarly investigation, arising from the work of Karl Polanyi and others,[28] which postulates a metahistorical transition from an economy of embedded gift exchange to one of disembedded market exchange, this study wants to insist both on the overlap or persistence of both forms (gift and market) in a given society and, even more importantly, on a third economic model, sharing, which also overlapped the other two.

In an Italian community such as Florence (the principal entry point, but not the only one, for our investigations) all three forms of economy existed and interacted. The borders between them were permeable. One might conceptualize the situation as having a sharing economy at home, a gift economy outside the home with kin and friends, and an exchange economy with all others in the various marketplaces of the city. But calculations went on at all levels, such that there could be and indeed from time to time was individualistic activity with the house and equally nonrational considerations

---

[23] Belk, "Sharing," 717. Also his "You Are What You Can Access: Sharing and Collaborative Consumption Online."
[24] Belk, "Sharing," 720.   [25] Belk, "Sharing," 727.   [26] Widlok, *Sharing*, 187–88.
[27] Marilyn Strathern, "Sharing, Stealing and Borrowing Simultaneously."
[28] Karl Polanyi, *The Great Transformation: The Political and Economic Origins of Our Time*. Also Jens Beckert, "The Great Transformation of Embeddedness: Karl Polanyi and the New Economic Sociology."

that could influence market transactions. Family feelings can also lead to anger or disappointment and produce intergenerational conflict, and as such be essentially ambivalent.[29] In contrast to the clean distinction between market behavior and family that serves Coontz's purposes, the approach here is to insist on the overlaps and interpenetrations between these realms. It is evident, for one thing, in the legal aphorism that the female was the avaricious gender, capable of rational pursuit of desired things even at the expense of other family goals.[30] It was an effective aphorism as it injected market behavior into the family sphere as a negative. Historians have also long recognized that forms of patronage prevalent in Florence were redolent with elements of a gift economy.[31]

The sharing economy was alive mainly in the forms of domestic activity (the monasteries and convents were certainly sharing environments too). People partook of food and shelter, as well as the harder-to-determine emotional life of the group that fed into and from a collective sense of honor and social identity. A strong association of sibling groups could importantly serve to underwrite household solidarity.[32] This collectivity, in turn, interacted through its members in the other economies of market and gift. The presumption of sharing was enthroned in the statutes that made financial liability common among fathers and sons, and brothers living together (though not wives). The markets, as sophisticated as they were, from the public space of the Mercato Vecchio to the scattered stores and workshops throughout a city such as Florence, were also permeated with exchanges of gifts and favors – above all, the extension of credit based on the intangible and tangible qualities of trust. Family members and business partners (not mutually exclusive groups) shared profits and losses.

Florentines, especially those fortunate to command considerable resources, made loans to relatives, neighbors, and business and political associates. Loans expressed and maintained solidarities, based on kinship, neighborhood, or guild. Trust was less of an issue with those people one knew or with whom one had active ties; and personal loans, as opposed to commercial, were often written off, as more was involved than market calculation. Accounts were carefully kept of inter-business credits and debits, while real estate transactions were "almost entirely treated as interpersonal exchanges."[33] Across these relations Florentines

[29] Cf. Aafke E. Komter, *Social Solidarity and the Gift*.
[30] Cf. Thomas Kuehn, *Family and Gender in Renaissance Italy, 1300–1600*, 54, 62, 177.
[31] David Herlihy, "Family and Property in Renaissance Florence," 13.
[32] As Janet Carsten found in Langkawi society (Malaysia): "Houses in Langkawi: Stable Structures or Mobile Homes?".
[33] Paul D. McLean and Neha Gondal, "The Circulation of Interpersonal Credit in Renaissance Florence," esp. 155.

managed to assemble rural estates and move commodities, especially real estate, into a category of items devolving outside output or factor markets. These more personal resources posed less risk to the process of passing property to the young.[34]

Partners in a business venture, a *societas*, in contrast, gave their trust a concrete form in their written partnership agreements. They shared profits and losses according to a contractual formula they had agreed to, although they as often dissolved their partnerships, sorted out the capital and gains, and reentered modified contracts in new, even if essentially the same, partnerships.[35] The marketplace was not secure and thus it was where relations in sharing profit and loss required the most detailed and careful rendering. The patronage exemplified by gifts and favors, in turn, could be at the heart of highly strategic and manipulative thinking, asserting solidarities in the face of the dissolvent forces of the market. And those who lived together and shared unabashedly in a common patrimony, nonetheless, could also keep careful accounts of acquisitions and expenses and seek appropriate returns when the time came. Even for brothers, who could adopt the form of an association nominally more than a mere business *societas*, being rather a *societas omnium bonorum*, there was always an eye on its dissolution, the end of sharing, and the assertion of individual ownership. The family and its substance might then be parceled out, or lost entirely. Against that eventuality it was possible to erect an inheritance device, the fideicommissum (a trust erected around a directed substitution of heirs from the agnatic lineage with the provision that family property not be alienated to outsiders), that took ownership of one person (the founding testator) to an extreme, obliterating the rights of heirs to manage and direct property as they saw fit, and yet it did so to hold collective property for family over generations. Different and at times surprisingly flexible options thus existed across the gamut of economic interactions.[36] Collective ownership could be continued in adverse economic circumstances by turning it legally into individual ownership and asserting a separation of liability from other individual holders (as when a wife retrieved her dowry during marriage on the grounds of her husband's impending bankruptcy) or by giving

[34] Rebecca Jean Emigh, *The Undevelopment of Capitalism: Sectors and Markets in Fifteenth-Century Tuscany*; Bas van Bavel, *The Invisible Hand? How Market Economies Have Emerged and Declined since ad 500*.
[35] On Florence's economy see Richard A. Goldthwaite, *The Economy of Renaissance Florence*; and Goldthwaite with Tim Carter, *Orpheus in the Marketplace: Jacopo Peri and the Economy of Late Renaissance Florence*.
[36] Cf. Diane Scarabotto, "Between: The Hybrid Economies of Collaborative Networks."

property away to someone not liable otherwise.[37] Florentines continued, at least in statutes whose initial formulations went back to the late thirteenth and early fourteenth centuries, to intertwine business and personal activities in an extensive liability for obligations that made little distinction between the substance of a partnership (simple *societas*) and that of a family. Trust resided on such bases.[38] But there was also every reason to forge distinctions in ownership or use when obligations came due, especially when they were so great as to threaten family.

Here, then, is the problem to be investigated in several contexts in the chapters that follow. Although there was a sharing economy of households and their patrimonies, there were in fact and inevitably a variety of personal claims that could burst forth to attenuate sharing or even necessitate an end to sharing. After all, while assets were shared, so were debts and liabilities. To have recourse again to the judicious observations of Casanova, tensions arising from the continuity and pretended unity of the patrimony for individual men and women, seeking to see their rights to property realized, "traversed the histories of many lineages."[39]

Familial substance, or patrimony, was also composite. As Loredana Garlati observes, there was the *patrimonium* of the father (*pater*), but there might also be shares, *peculia*, belonging nominally to the children, and there was the dowry and possibly other property belonging to the wife/mother.[40] To these we can add the conflicting claims of brothers living together on a single patrimony after their father's death. These forms of family property are the focus of Chapters 3 through 5. Issues around these forms of property were real and require investigation.

Of course, the family consisted, at least in most cases, of more than one person; not to deny that a household of one was quite possible, in terms of coresidence and in terms of the law. That family of one, however, unless something was done (marriage, adoption), would die out with the demise of its sole member. As we will see in Chapter 2, it was precisely the continuation of family into subsequent generations that was at the heart of the equation of *familia* and *substantia*. It was also a peculiarity of gender in law that a woman could not begin an enduring family line; rather, she was the beginning and end, it was said, of a family of one – herself.[41]

---

[37] Kuehn, *Family and Gender*, 91–97, 131–39; Kuehn, "Protecting Dowries in Law in Renaissance Florence"; Julius Kirshner, "Wives' Claims against Insolvent Husbands in Late Medieval Italy."

[38] Thomas Kuehn, "Debt and Bankruptcy in Florence: Statutes and Cases."

[39] Casanova, *Famiglia italiana*, 86.

[40] Loredana Garlati, "La famiglia tra passato e presente," 5–6.

[41] Cf. Kuehn, *Family and Gender*, 63.

Those portions of patrimonial *substantia* that were tied to children or wives or siblings became of legal interest on the occasion of breakdown, when outsiders and their claims might impinge on those resources, or simply when someone inside the family wanted to detach him or herself and his or her property from the others. Additionally, at the time of death there might be testamentary bequests to others, possibly including charities or other institutional beneficiaries, in which case making distinctions as to ownership and its prerogatives was a way to bracket off some of the household property from the claims of others. Among those "others" might be the wife-become-widow or the emancipated child.[42] Resisting or limiting such claims was vital to the integrity of the patrimony.[43] Sharing was also about who was denied access; who did not have a share.

Complicating any such individual claims, however, was the fact that among those goods and objects that family members shared were those that were considered inalienable. These were things, including land and buildings, but also "incorporeal" possessions (such as family honor or titles), that were to be enjoyed within a group and also to be passed along to those who would follow.[44] For that purpose property owners seized the option of the early modern fideicommissum, explicitly forbidding alienation of vital properties *extra familiam* (the subject of Chapter 6).[45]

To insist on seeing the patrimonial economy as a sharing economy is, if not perhaps to diminish the role and power of the patriarchal head of family (the *paterfamilias* of civil law), to place it in more nuanced contexts. Scholars such as Isabelle Chabot have cautioned about overemphasis on paternal control of family wealth in light of the actions of wives and daughters in relation to their dowry rights, for one thing (Chapter 4). Less systematically examined, but no less a limiting context for some fathers, were the actions of sons, especially as they came of age and tried to take their place in society. Here indeed, right at the spot where Bartolus found the strong identity of the family, in the substantial tie between fathers and (legitimate) sons, there was bound to be less friction, one assumes. But there too there were tensions and potentially conflicting claims.[46] And there were limits to legal paternal power

---

[42] On these see Kuehn, "Travails of the Widow in Law in Florence at the End of the Fifteenth Century: An Illustrative Case" and *Emancipation in Late Medieval Florence.*

[43] Garlati, "La famiglia tra passato e presente," 9–10.

[44] Foundational is Annette B. Weiner, *Inalienable Possessions: The Paradox of Keeping-While Giving.*

[45] Garlati, "La famiglia tra passato e presente," 11–13, sees this as central to early modern families.

[46] Cf. Kuehn, *Law, Family, and Women: Toward a Legal Anthropology of Renaissance Italy,* 129–42.

(*patria potestas*).[47] Finally, relations between brothers, until quite recently, have largely been left out of account. Their coresidential arrangements are typically taken as temporary. Benedetta Borello's work promises to return attention to sibling relations, made all the more interesting in light of the burgeoning practice of primogeniture (privileging one child against all siblings) as the inheritance norm among mainly elites in some communities.[48] The heir in primogeniture was sole owner, but still had to accede to the rights, however diminished, of siblings to at least basic alimentary support. Conflicts could result, but there were still rights of others to be taken into account.

Here is perhaps where Bartolus's legacy, his linking of *familia* and *substantia*, had its greatest effect. Jurists throughout Italy came to accept a key element of the fideicommissum as it evolved in the fifteenth and sixteenth centuries – namely, the prohibition of the alienation of patrimonial properties *extra familiam*. In that context *familia* came to have legal contours, in that claiming to be part of a *familia* was productive of rights and privileges to share in what the heir could not alienate. The medieval family, conceived in terms of its members, gave way to a patrimonial conception of family, indivisible, tied to male agnatic succession.[49] Chapter 6 displays how some jurists struggled with the contrasts and contradictions between prolonged, shared ownership of property, as spelled out in fideicommissa, and the claims of all singular persons that thereby were trampled upon in the name of enduring *familia*.

The patrimony also required careful management. Its preservation fell to those who inherited and faced the directives in wills or simply the pressures of kin to use all means possible to maintain *substantia*. One of the things an heir by fideicommissary substitution might have to do, for example, was make an inventory of the estate. The inventory could serve to alert subsequent heirs as to what had initially, or at least at some prior point, been in the patrimony. But the inventory was also, first and foremost, a legal device to limit an heir's legal liability for debts on the estate and to guarantee him (or her, more rarely) a requisite minimum portion, the Falcidian quarter of Roman law. These inventories, which survive in profusion for Florence and elsewhere, have proven to be invaluable sources, letting historians in some cases seemingly walk through the rooms of fifteenth- and sixteenth-century houses. Yet these inventories, as legal documents, also had some propensity to conceal or deceive.

[47] Here Kuehn, *Family and Gender*, 71–79. For the legal background, see Yan Thomas, "Il padre, la famiglia e la città: figli e figlie davanti alla giurisdizione domestica a Roma" and Marco Cavina, *Il padre spodestato: l'autorità paterna dall'antichità a oggi*.
[48] Benedetta Borello, *Il posto di ciascuno: fratelli, sorelle e fratellanze (xvi–xix secoli)*.
[49] Romano, *Famiglia, successioni e patrimonio familiare*, 59.

These documents had consequences that people could have every reason to manage or manipulate. For that reason Florence legislated to limit the availability of inventories to the estates of minors (under eighteen), meaning that inventories were mainly the work of legal guardians, who might be the child's mother. Chapter 7 looks carefully at the relevant law and some examples to see how deceptive or merely inept legal inventories could have been, as well as to see what was the *substantia* that some had shared.

Here, as in previous chapters, Florentine sources will be in evidence, though not exclusively, as it is Florence's rich archives with which I am most familiar and which allow access to materials not readily available elsewhere.[50] Also frequently in evidence in the following pages are Florentine domestic accounts. Account books and household fiscal declarations provide unparalleled entree to the handling of family *substantia*. Prominent in these pages too is the humanistic dialogue on family penned by Leon Battista Alberti, a singular monument to the care and attention, if not obsession, for family and domestic life at that time in Florence. As vital as family was in all aspects of life, there was explicit theorizing and strategizing about it. What was said about it and what was at times left unsaid are revealing. These are all sources distinct, though not separate, from the legal discourses on *familia* and *substantia*.

These sources could serve to school and prepare those who would own and manage family property. Whoever managed property, honestly or deceptively, was at some level supposed to be a prudent man. That was the vague legal standard that distinguished the sane from the insane – what Liz Mellyn has called patrimonial rationality.[51] It was prodigality, reckless mismanagement, in contrast, that identified the insane (*furiosus*, *mentecaptus*). Here too it was Bartolus who played a pivotal role, as he laid out the possible qualities of the prudent man, who, as a witness in court, gave testimony that could be taken as reliable. But much as with the well-known qualities of *virtù* (Machiavelli) and *sprezzatura* (Castiglione), there was no clear definition of prudence. It was another form of what Douglas Biow has termed a *nescio quid*, an indefinable something that gave one a measure of individuality, if not of success in general.[52] Chapter 8 directs attention to some cases of insanity and learned discussion of prudence, but now in a context of partible patrimonies and the sharing economies of families. The law assumed the capability of most people to be prudent in

---

[50] Katherine Ludwig Jansen, *Peace and Penance in Late Medieval Italy*, 5.

[51] Elizabeth Mellyn, *Mad Tuscans and Their Families: A History of Mental Disorder in Early Modern Italy*, 17, 21–22, 103–4.

[52] Douglas Biow, *On the Importance of Being an Individual in Renaissance Italy: Men, Their Professions, and Their Beards*.

some sense, and left its determination largely to the discretion of witnesses, and so jurists did not feel compelled to detail what prudence was – or wished to avoid an intellectual quagmire. Much like the notion of the "reasonable man" today, the prudent man of early modern law stood as a hypothetical standard. Though prudence could be a general attribute in some sense, it was not necessarily "shared." The next heir and manager of a patrimony did not necessarily possess it, and there does not seem to have been much hesitation on the part of those who first devised the terms of a fideicommissum to tying the hands of heirs whose prudence could not be assumed. Standards of prudence remained awfully loose and hard to define. The insane were perhaps also those who made unreasonable demands or refused to meet reasonable and appropriate demands of others. The insane did not want to share any longer. They were operating on their own, without reference to the *familia*. Again, it was important that the patrimony, or its management, was divisible – that no individual was truly so autonomous as to waste all his *substantia* to the harm of his own sons.

One type of source plays across all these chapters: the consilium. These were written responses, in technical Latin prose, dense with references to appropriate texts and institutions of the academic *ius commune*, in answer to questions arising for judges and litigants, or even for legislators, coping with legal uncertainties. These unparalleled jurisprudential devices allowed trained experts to try to square local laws, social practices, and the rules of *ius commune*.[53] The consilium represents a creative moment, "providing law where there was none," as I have said elsewhere.[54] They allow us to track law in action. They are the locus where experts in civil and canon law (the essence of the so-called *ius commune*) grappled with the peculiar statutory and customary nexus of a place like Florence, and thus Florentinized the law in some sense, and worked a similar alchemy for Milan, Bologna, Padua, and elsewhere (except Venice).[55] That is another theme that runs through the pages that follow.

Consilia also remind us how much the relevance of legal rules is at play in problem moments, in normatively uncertain circumstances. That again may be most apparent in looking at Bartolus's definition of family. The son was a sort of owner and stepped seamlessly, immediately, into full ownership on the father's death. There was little room for uncertainty, barring a paternal attempt to disinherit the son or simple neglect of him in a will (which made it void in any case). It was when that situation

[53] Here see Kuehn, *Family and Gender*, 12–17.   [54] Kuehn, *Family and Gender*, 15.
[55] For an excellent account of the development of academic law and local legislation in Italy, see Mario Ascheri, *The Laws of Late Medieval Italy (1000–1500): Foundations for a European Legal System*.

failed to materialize that uncertainty reigned, or as Letizia Arcangeli has it, there was some true freedom of maneuver to manage how and to whom one's patrimony passed, to the possible consternation of others who might well bring suit and thus throw the matter into the laps of jurists.[56] We can go further to say that in inheritance practices, especially the fideicommissum, the living were sharing still with the dead and with the yet-to-be-born. A plurality of claims clustered about every patrimony, no matter how unified it pretended to be. Law was indeed "a very flexible instrument" and yet the great variety of actions it encompassed also shows that practice cannot be derived simply from norms.[57]

Finally, before coming to grips with the dimensions and difficulties of patrimony, we might stop to ask what is/was patrimony. There is no better way to approach the issue than to ask what patrimony was to those who had and used it, or hoped to. Here is just one example of insights we can gain from close study of consilia. We can see what patrimony was in a narrative legal context, in which academic terms had to find their effective meaning in the hands of the litigants and legal experts faced with particular pieces of property and specific local customs or laws.

This case arose between 1517 and 1523, for those were the years in which the author of the consilium, the Sienese Mariano Sozzini junior (1482–1556), was teaching at Pisa, where he was asked to take on the legal questions it raised (probably by the heirs of the principal figure). The matter at hand strayed into the arena of a statute of Castro Nuovo di Garfagnana, not far from Pisa, with the rubric De rebus communibus nisi certo modo non alienandis (on not alienating properties except in a certain manner).[58] The law called for a fifteen-day period to intervene if one owner of a common res immobilis wanted to sell his share, so that the other owners were forewarned and could try to buy it themselves. If that format was not followed, any sale was annulled. The law further applied to anyone who wanted to alienate patrimonial or "matrimonial" (here, carrying the sense of coming from the maternal line) real property, requiring the same fifteen-day notice to be given to male relatives to the third degree.

So when a fellow named Francesco sold a house with a shop front, which he had obtained from his brother, as he was about to enter the religious life, to a man named Ercole, with a provision allowing

---

[56] Letizia Arcangeli, "Ragioni di stato e ragioni di famiglia: strategie successorie dell'aristocrazia milanese tra Quattro e Cinquecento (Visconti, Trivulzio, Borromeo)."

[57] David Warren Sabean and Simon Teuscher, "Kinship in Europe: A New Approach to Long-Term Development," in Kinship in Europe: Approaches to Long-Term Development.

[58] Mariano Sozzini junior, Consilia, 1 cons. 20, fols. 32rb–34vb, which opens with a detailed casus.

redemption within a certain time, his heirs invoked their right to repurchase the property (Francesco having died during the intervening fifteen days). This little turn of events left two legal questions that also go to the heart of our interest in defining patrimony: first, as Francesco got the house from his brother and not from his father (directly; that is, as a gift and not as an inheritance), did the statute apply? And second, depending on the answer to the first question, were the heirs freed of the restriction to offer the property first to their *consortes*?

Sozzini proceeded in an uncontroversial manner, rehearsing the pros and cons of each question. He had to start with the statutory language. What did *patrimonialis* and *linea* mean here? A *res patrimonialis* rested on a *patrimonium*, which in turn "is said to be the whole substance of whomever, as if we should say my patrimony, yours, or another's" (vero dicitur uniuscuiusque substantia universa, ut si dixerimus patrimonium meum, tuum, vel alterius). In that regard, dowry was the personal patrimony of a wife (proprium patrimonium mulieris) as it came to her from her natal kin. The house in this case then could be said to be in the patrimony of Francesco, as whatever came to someone was part of his patrimony.[59] But Sozzini declared that this could not be the sense of the statute, because it also differentiated what was *matrimonialis* and what came by maternal line versus the paternal. The statute did not simply see everything one owned as patrimony but looked at where it had come from, what had been accumulated, and what had been inherited, from either line. If the statute meant goods that came in some fashion from one's ancestors, then the house and shop in question could be seen as covered by the statute, because Francesco and his brother obviously got it from their father. Or it meant what came to one directly, by the *linea paterna*, in which case the statute did not apply to what Francesco had received from his brother, rather than his father. In favor of the first reading, that the house and shop were subject to the statute, was the idea that the statutory intent was that the term *patrimonium* meant the same as agnation and that was the meaning of the term *consortes*. Whether in communion of property or not, they were agnate. They were also males, in keeping with the statutes common throughout Italy that excluded dowered women from inheritance in favor of agnate males. But Sozzini determined that the second meaning held, that the property had not come in inheritance (though it had clearly been shared at some level), and thus that Francesco could freely sell his property to anyone without first gaining leave from anyone. To see it the other way would be

---

[59] Sozzini, *Consilia*, 1 *cons.* 20, fol. 32vb, in fact used the first person: "quia undecumque res ad nos pervenerit, dicitur esse de patrimonio nostro."

to condone a "serious harm" to the seller. The first meaning also clearly put the statute in contrast to the *ius commune* – extraordinarily so ("exorbitantissimum"), in fact. The statute thus needed a strict reading according to the interpretive tenets of jurisprudence.[60] In strict terms it seemed that the statute said nothing about the property from a brother, so Francesco was free to sell. We, of course, might look at that as splitting a fine hair, if only because, were there no brother (and his gift to Francesco marked his civil death in entering a monastery[61]), it would all have come to Francesco from his father.

Sozzini therefore followed with another set of arguments, prefaced by the observation that "properly speaking according to experts in Latin vocabulary what comes from the father is called inheritance/estate" (proprie loquendo secundum vocabulorum latinorum explanatores dicitur haereditas a patre proveniens). The statute in fact required not only that something be *patrimonialis* but also that it had come by the paternal or maternal line. There was a difference between brothers, and Sozzini traced it out: "while cousins and uncles and all could be termed descendants of a single father [here, in fact, the paternal grandfather], among those descendants there seemed to be several lines and not just one, because among ourselves we are not of the same line but from our father several [lines] are said to emanate."[62] By this calculus the house had not come to Francesco from the *paterna haereditas*. Sozzini went on,

those words "relatives of the patrimony" could probably be understood in another sense, namely those who would have participation [in the household] without goods, as properly is of the nature of the word according to Baldo. . . . Nor does it matter that it is not required that they must have communion in the object at hand, because it did that; but I say that in other property they have communion, otherwise they are not properly termed relatives of the patrimony.[63]

The relatives who deserved a right of first refusal had to be in a sharing relationship (*communio*) with the seller, even if that did not encompass the

---

[60] Cf. Mario Sbriccoli, *L'interpretazione dello Statuto: Contributo allo studio della funzione dei giuristi nell'età comunale*.

[61] Anne Jacobson Schutte, *By Force and Fear: Taking and Breaking Monastic Vows in Early Modern Europe*.

[62] Sozzini, *Consilia*, 1 cons. 20, fol. 33rb: "advertendum est quod si pater meus habet tres filios et ex quolibet nepotes etc., licet omnes dicantur a patre descendere, et ex linea sua, et suorum genitorum, inter nos tamen non sumus de eadem linea, sed ex patre nostro dicuntur plures lineae emanare."

[63] Sozzini, *Consilia*, 1 cons. 20, fol. 33va: "illa verba consortes de patrimonio possent fortasse aliter intelligi, videlicet de his qui participationem absque bonis haberent, prout proprie est de natura verbi iuxta doctrinam Bal. . . . Nec obstat quod non requiritur quod habeant communionem in re de qua agitur, quia hoc facebat, sed dico quod in alia re debent habere communionem, alias non proprie dicerentur consortes de patrimonio."

specific item put up for sale. Only then were they truly *consortes* – literally, those sharing a common fate.

Sozzini's argument was, in effect, that the legislators had not been thinking of brothers as a source of patrimonial objects (which came neither *per lineam patrimonialem* nor *paternam*). Against the argument that the house had belonged to his father and simply came to him through his brother as an intermediary person, Sozzini asserted that it came from the brother's patrimony, not the father's. Having removed the house from the grasp of the statutory law, Sozzini could proceed to the question of the claims of Francesco's heirs (other brothers). They were not held to have to sell the property on the demand of other agnates, but could keep it. That was the more probable conclusion. The heirs had redeemed the property, which then reverted to its original state, as if the sale had not happened. The statute merely accorded agnates an opportunity to keep an item of property from leaving the lineage if it were sold to outsiders.[64] It did not allow one set of agnates to trump another. The brothers who had shared their existence and assets with Francesco had priority over other agnates who had not.

Clearly, Francesco had gained by his brother's generosity and care for his family, to pass along before his departure for the monastery what had been his father's. This is about as close as possible that something acquired in life could also be seen as inheritance. In keeping with a strict reading of the statute, Sozzini excluded the house and shop from the meaning of *res patrimonialis* in the statute. In the strict sense it came to Francesco as a gift from his brother, not as inheritance from his father. We cannot say if those who drafted the text would have agreed with that narrow construction, but we can see that, in general terms, what one held patrimonially came by inheritance. It, and all one acquired in life, would in turn become patrimony of the heir, and in turn be what came patrimonially to his heirs, for them to pass along, with any acquisitions and, it was to be hoped, no losses.

---

[64] Sozzini, *Consilia*, 1 *cons.* 20, fol. 34va.

2 Bartolus and Family in Law

> The greater surprise for us, in an age when so many things are acquired, consumed, and then disposed of, should not be how little emotion early moderns invested in their children, but rather how much they invested in their property.[1]

Inheritance of family property was the social and economic motor of late medieval Italy. People poured time and attention into arrangements for settlement of their estates. It was property that would serve to link the generations of a family over the years into a sort of transcendent entity. Property, however, is a legal concept, not just an economic fact, and it was necessary for the law, the *ius commune*, based on Roman and canon law and elaborated in the universities, to conceive of property in a manner that would facilitate the aspirations of families to achieve that transcendence.

2.1 Bartolus and *Familia*

In fact, the meaning of *familia* in civil law was a complicated matter, made worse by imprecision in language.[2] At its origins, *familia* referred to the permanent assets one held; and by extension, as those assets could include slaves, it came to mean the group of slaves subject to one master. The assets of one farm were also termed a *familia*, so one master could have several *familiae*. As a family house, the term came to refer to the people who lived there, free or slave. *Familia* was also a term denoting relationships, so it came to be extended to agnate and cognate relations, the former distinguished by the fact of traceable links of paternal power

---

[1] Nicholas Terpstra, "Real and Virtual Families: Forms and Dynamics of Fostering and Adoption in Bologna's Early Modern Hospitals," 147.

[2] For a discussion of issues regarding *familia* in Bartolus's time, see Kuehn, *Family and Gender in Renaissance Italy*, 28–52.

(*patria potestas*). In other terms, those in a household subject to one *potestas* were *familiae iure proprio*, while wider kin descending from a prior *potestas* were *familiae iure communi*.[3] *Familia* could also be seen in legal procedural terms as all those for whom a *pater* spoke in law, for whom he was liable.

In Rome *familia* did not originate in marriage but in civil liability. The family in Roman law was not a creation of marriage and descent only.[4] It arose in civil liability, which was made most apparent in cohabitation. The *lex Pronuntiatio* "stated that a single person had a *familia* and that a woman who managed her own business had a *familia* on her own, independent of that of her husband."[5] When the male head of household (*paterfamilias*) died, his *familia* ended, resulting in a number of new *familiae* around his children and wife. Whereas the *paterfamilias* had been the sole source of liability and legal actions, now each child in turn had to see to constituting and managing his or her own, although sons might also opt to maintain communal living arrangements and pool their resources, at least for a while.[6] Even the wife acquired her own *familia*, though she was its sole member as both its head and its termination.[7] Only men could perpetuate a link to future *familiae*.

The medieval canon law and academic jurisprudence came to conceive of family as an entity arising in the marital union of two people (becoming one flesh by the teaching of canon law and moral theology), though the husband would retain the position of sole administrator as *paterfamilias*.[8] Against this sense of family, then, there was some room to claim a continuance of household in the surviving spouse and a legitimacy resting on birth for heirs (not on cohabitation with the deceased). But there were conceptual limitations to confront before acceptance of such continuation could be achieved. Yan Thomas studied one thirteenth-century gloss that had great difficulty comprehending a fiction by which an incorporeal legal quality, here *proprietas* (ownership), could be said to continue in inheritance. Such continuation was said to occur between *paterfamilias* and *filiusfamilias*, but it could only be termed a fictive continuation (*quasi continuatio*) because incorporeal rights, unlike corporeal things, ceased to exist when the holder of them died or the situation they

[3] Carlos Amunátegui Perelló, "Problems Concerning *Familia* in Early Rome."
[4] Laurent Waelkens, *Amne Adverso: Roman Legal Heritage in European Culture*, 129, 248, 395.
[5] Laurent L. J. M. Waelkens, "Medieval Family and Marriage Law: From Actions of Status to Legal Doctrine," 108.
[6] Waelkens, *Amne Adverso*, 193–256.
[7] Waelkens, *Amne Adverso*, 195–96; "Medieval Family," 108.
[8] Waelkens, *Amne Adverso*, 199–200.

suited came to an end.[9] To that point there was as yet no allowance for throwing blanket terms like *familia* and *substantia* at the issue.

As Laurent Waelkens has noted, "intestacy had to do with the ending of a family and realisation of its assets; so when family was established by matrimony, it was no longer established by cohabitation."[10] The transmission of blood – the sharing of a lineage of blood over time, rather than transmission and sharing of liabilities – became a defining feature of family relationships. The *arbor consanguinitatis* could be conceived on that basis.[11] In parallel David Herlihy put forth the idea of households as commensurable units, compiled into medieval manorial surveys with known quantities of labor and rent due to the manorial lord and prerogatives in the communal agricultural cycle.[12] Continuation of blood, ownership, and productive residence had shifted legal debates. By the fourteenth century the time was ripe for a legal recasting of *familia*.

The crucial figure in adapting medieval senses of family, property ownership, and so much more, to the realities of life in Italian communes, was Bartolus of Sassoferrato (1313–57).[13] To Bartolus the civil law was a living device with myriad social implications. What Bartolus sought was a grasp of underlying premises – points of clarification and insight that went beyond and made sense of ambiguous rules.[14] Perhaps need of such insight was nowhere more pressing than with regard to inheritance and family. Family was, after all, "'more than family': it was the structural morpheme of society of which kindreds and other associations were mimetic extensions."[15]

Historians are well aware of the definition of family Bartolus offered: *familia accipitur in iure pro substantia*.[16] It was a definition that would resonate in subsequent jurisprudence.[17] Rarely, however, has anyone

---

[9] Incorporeal things, in addition to *proprietas*, were such things as servitudes, succession, guardianship, and usufruct. See Yan Thomas, "Les artifices de la verité en droit commun médiéval," 122.

[10] Waelkens, "Medieval Family," 124.

[11] These themes are addressed by Christiane Klapisch-Zuber, "The Genesis of the Family Tree"; Simon Teuscher, "Flesh and Blood in the Treatises on the Arbor Consanguinitatis (Thirteenth to Sixteenth Centuries)."

[12] David Herlihy, *Medieval Households*.

[13] Waelkens, *Amne Adverso*, 105, credits him with seeing Roman law as "a practical system for the administration of justice that could be mixed with local norms."

[14] See the essays of Kees Bezemer, "The Infrastructure of the Early *Ius Commune*: The Formation of *Regulae*, or Its Failure," and of James Gordley, "*Ius Quaerens Intellectum*: The Method of the Medieval Civilians."

[15] Marco Dotti, "Famiglie, istituzioni e comunità," 115, 122.

[16] Romano, *Famiglia, successioni e patrimonio*, 1; Julius Kirshner and Anthony Molho, "The Dowry Fund and the Marriage Market"; Manlio Bellomo, *Problemi di diritto familiare nell'età dei comuni: Beni paterni e "pars filii"*, 36–40.

[17] As Paolo di Castro, to D. 28.2.11, *Commentaria in Digestum infortiatum*, fol. 56ra: "Nam illud verbum 'familias' ponitur pro substantia." Also Jason de Mayno, to l. Suggestioni,

looked closely at the portion of his commentaries in which the definition occurs. The one exception, the legal historian Manlio Bellomo, was engaged in an important examination of the problems of ownership, inheritance, and penal liability between fathers and sons.[18]

Specifically, Bartolus was commenting on the *lex In suis*, in the Digest title *De liberis et posthumis* (D. 28.2.11). *In suis* was an interesting snippet from the Roman jurist Paulus that said:

In one's own heirs there most evidently appears a continuation of ownership to carry forward, such that it seems there were no inheritance, as if these [heirs] were owners who even during the father's life are considered owners in some way [quodammodo domini].

For that reason, after the father's death, sons did not seem to take possession of an inheritance but rather simply to obtain free management of the property, of which they had been a sort of owner already.[19] Paulus here postulated only that some vague legal capacity, a sort of *dominium*, was shared between father and son that could account for the immediate emergence of the *filiusfamilias* as heir to the *paterfamilias* over the same property (or an appropriate share of it). In inheritance there was acquisition not of possession, which in a sense the son as heir already had, but of legal managerial control. Paulus's attention was on the father–son relationship, not on *familia*.

It was in this seamless transition from father to sons that Bartolus found a key to understanding family and inheritance, as ownership persisted in the sons as heirs and there was thus no new inheritance.[20] He continued:

C. De verborum significatione, *In secundam codicis partem commentaria*, fols. 160vb–161ra.

[18] Bellomo, *Problemi*, 36–40. He also mentions Bartolus's introductory remarks calling attention to D. 28.2.11, but in a different context (31).

[19] The classical edition of the *Corpus iuris civilis*, ed. T. H. Mommsen, W. Kroll, P. Krueger, and R. Schoell, 3 vols.

[20] Bartolus to D. 28.2.11, *Opera omnia*, 10 vols. (Venice, 1615), vol. 3, fol. 90va: "In suos heredes dicitur continuare dominium, non nova hereditas obvenire, licet possit exhaeredari. Et sciatis quod audivi bis istum librum sine alia immistione, et nunquid audivi istam legem et Ac<cursius> Doc<tores> et scrib<entes> siccopede eam transeunt, sed ut mihi videtur non posset iste titulus stare sine ista lege. ... Primum dictum est quod in suos heredes dicitur continuari dominium, non nova hereditas obvenire. ... Secundum dictum in quo probatur primum est quod filii et caeteri sui, vivo patre dicuntur quodammodo domini, cum ergo efficiantur heredes, non possunt habere dominium novum, cum ipsi ante haberent. Tertium dictum probat illud quod dictum est supra hoc modo: Familia accipitur in iure pro substantia, l. nam quod ' fin. infra ad Treb<ellianum> [D. 36.1.14–15,8] et l. pronuntiatio de ver<borum> sig<nificatione> [D. 50.16.195]. Sed in usu loquendi et etiam in iure dicitur paterfamilias et filiusfamilias. Est ergo pater istius substantiae dominus, et filius istius substantiae dominus, et sic substantia aliquid tribuit ut<ri>que aequaliter, sed per hoc nomen pater et filius discernitur ut genitor a genito. Quartum dictum est quod ex predictis sequitur verum esse dictum quod nova

"and you should know that I heard this book [taught] twice without any comparison [with others], and never did I hear this law, and Accursius, other doctors, and scribes consistently pass over it, but it seems to me that this title [De liberis et posthumis] cannot stand without this law." The sharing of assets behind the pretended singular title of the *pater* had perhaps been so presumed that no one, by Bartolus's testimony, had bothered to remark on it.

The first two of the six *dicta* he found in Paulus's text simply reinforced the immediate and direct transmission of title to sons who had already been owners "of a sort." So there could be no new ownership by inheritance. It was the third *dictum* that contained Bartolus's singular insight:

> The third dictum proves what is said above in this manner: family is taken in law for substance. ... But in common speech and also in law there is the father of the family and [there is] the son. Therefore the father is owner of this substance and the son is owner of this substance, and so substance concedes something to both equally, but by this term father is distinguished from son as sire from offspring.

The substance that was family continued, making possible the continuity, persistence, and overlap between father and sons (legitimate, it should be stressed). They shared it. This in turn led to the fourth *dictum*, that there was not a new inheritance but provision of direct management by the son(s), which was not the case while the father was alive. It also fed into the fifth *dictum* that filial inheritance was direct on intestacy, even though, in the absence of a testament, the son was not expressly nominated as heir (instituted). Bartolus was comfortable with the legal fiction that extended continuity of *proprietas* from father to son, unlike Yan Thomas's thirteenth-century glossator.

Bartolus had to dedicate concentrated effort to explaining the sixth *dictum*, how it was possible to disinherit a son, as disinheritance "runs counter to that entire matter in law." There was no possibility of denying the existence of disinheritance in the law, so reconciliation of willed

hereditas non dicitur obvenisse filio sed magis administratio libera quam ante non habebat. Quintum dictum est ut ponat illationem ex predictis, quod licet filii non sint instituti, tamen ab intestato domini sunt ex continuatione dominii. Sexto respondet cuidam obiectioni hoc modo. Si filius est dominus vivo patre ergo pater non potest eum exheredare, et sic contra totam istam materiam. Ad hoc respondet, non est mirandum si patri licet eum exheredare et privare bonis: quia eum licebat etiam occidere h.d. Opp. quod duo non possunt esse domini in solidum l. si ut certo ' si duobus vehiculum supra commo. Sol. dicitur filius dominus improprie vivo patre, ut patet ex tex. qui dicit quodammodo. Et hoc est quod dicit glo. quod hoc dominium filii consistit in nudo et puro intellectu, q.d. magis est in imaginatione quadam quam in veritate. ... Quaero, que est ratio, quod preteritio materna habetur pro exheredatione? Respondeo: quia cum dominium a persona matris non continetur in filium, cum non sit suus, non est necesse quod exheredet filium, id est extra dominium ponat, sed si eum pretereat, facit contra officium pietatis, ideo datur querela."

disinheritance of ownership, when it otherwise continued so immediately, had to be worked out.

The conceptual difficulty behind this substantial tie of father and son lay in the legal fact that

two cannot be owners entirely [of the same property]. . . . The solution is the son is said to be owner in an improper manner while the father lives, as it appears in the text, which says "of a sort." And this is what the gloss says, that this ownership of the son consists in a plain and pure conception, which says it is in a type of imagination rather than in truth. The gloss has a similar [finding] about husband and wife, because although the husband is said to be owner, yet the wife is owner [of her property]. . . . But this is not a true equivalent, because in the wife ownership in a thing is said to transfer [to her husband], in the son it is said to be continued, as here.

Bartolus thus posed in close contrast the central relationships in a family – the generational link to children and the marital link to spouses. And he made clear that the sharing of ownership was different in each. It did not apply to the property a wife brought to a marriage, as it did in the patrimony father and sons shared. Along those lines Bartolus continued to draw the contrast between paternal and maternal testaments with regard to the omission of a son from its terms. The father's ties with his son were so close that he could not disinherit his son by a simple omission. He had to expressly, by name and for cause, disinherit. Mere omission of a son from a will meant the son could easily contest the paternal testament and have it judicially voided. With the mother, in contrast, "because ownership is not continued from the person of the mother to the son, as he is not hers, it is not necessary that she disinherit the son, that is place him beyond ownership; but if she should omit him, she acts against the duties of kinship, and so he is given a right to dispute her will."

With the mother too there was a sharing relationship, and though the son was not hers in the way he was his father's child, their relationship deserved legal acknowledgment even to end it, and should not be left simply in oblivion. A son was always his father's, even after emancipation from *patria potestas*, whereas his legal (and possibly residential) tie to his mother ended with the end of the marriage.

Disinheritance caused Bartolus some conceptual problems. As a legal device it was, in fact, resorted to rarely and was only allowed for causes such as the son becoming a heretic or, worse, attempting to kill his father.[21] The son had a firm guarantee in law, moreover, of realizing at least a fractional legitimate portion (*legitima portio*) from the patrimony on

[21] Cf. Julius Kirshner, "Baldus de Ubaldis on Disinheritance: Contexts, Controversies, *Consilia,*" *Ius Commune: Zeitschrift für Europäische Rechtsgeschichte.*

which he "shared" ownership of *substantia* with his father. And that
portion supposedly passed to him immediately, without a formal acceptance (*aditio*) of the estate, although such a formality might be well
advised. What Bartolus essentially found behind these guarantees was
substantia. Whatever all that indistinct term encompassed, it centered on
the legal father–son relationship in all its dimensions of sharing.

By effectively, almost literally reifying the family as *substantia*, Bartolus
"sacralized" it as an enduring institutional composite of property, as
a corporate entity, analogous to the church in all its institutional expressions, and to communes and guilds and other associations.[22] In calling
attention to the automatic and immediate passage of *substantia* from
father to son(s) as *quodammodo domini*, Bartolus was locking into a sense
of family as a quasi-institutional, generational continuity of shared
resources. That was the sense of family that would underwrite the later
widespread use of fideicommissary entails by wealthy and powerful lineages throughout Italy and beyond.[23] That in turn was based on a social
and, thanks to Bartolus, legal sense of family as a set of persons sharing
each other's lives.[24]

It is worth noting that the son's inheritance from his father, while
seamless, was not without actual problems, attested to in the legal archives of Italy's cities. But it is the conceptual issues with which Bartolus
wrestled that require elucidation. The conceptual problem in law lay not
only in the fact that a continuation of ownership (*dominium*) in the son,
and the implication that father and son both had ownership of the
haereditas, flew in the face of the legal maxim that individualized ownership: *duo non possunt esse domini in solidum*. It also raised problems in that
the *pater* held his *filius* in his *potestas* as long as he lived (barring emancipation), and while *in potestate* the son lacked the capacity to own or do
most anything in law.[25] De facto sharing of assets confronted de iure
concentration of ownership in a single pair of hands. Here was the great
paradox about *familia* in law. The sharing of all the various elements of its
substantia by all its members was obscured behind the singularity of

---

[22] Jens Beckert, *Inherited Wealth*, 117, says that entails sacralized feudal noble families,
alongside the church, as property owners.

[23] Rather than rehearse a vast and growing body of work in this area, I direct the reader to
the following recent studies as starting points: Stefano Calonaci, *Dietro lo scudo incantato:
I fedecommessi di famiglia e il trionfo della borghesia fiorentina (1400 ca.–1750)*; Maura
Piccialuti, *L'immortalità dei beni: Fedecommessi e primogeniture a Roma nei secoli xvii
e xviii*; Anna Bellavitis, *Famille, genre, transmission à Venise au xvie siècle.*

[24] The idea of sharing in each other is at the core of Marshall Sahlins's definition of kinship
in *What Kinship Is and Is Not*.

[25] Cf. esp. Bellomo, *Problemi*, 4–7, 9–14. On property law in general the indispensable
works are those of Paolo Grossi, *Le situazioni reali nell'esperienza giuridica medievale* and *Il
dominio e le cose*. On emancipation, see Kuehn, *Emancipation in Late Medieval Florence*.

ownership and control by the *paterfamilias*. *Substantia* was a term suited to encompassing that paradox. There were inevitable distinctions among members of a household, otherwise sharing that very substance that was the essence of *familia*. *Substantia* held people together, though not necessarily strongly; it was malleable and even perishable. One could gain a sense of one's separate self from the situation of sharing with others, though it was a self limited by the demands of others.[26] *Familia* in Bartolus's terms did not ascend to the level of a corporation, with *pater* in the role of CEO, in the manner of the abbot of a monastery.

Bartolus opened a new way to theorizing about family by recognizing, as his teachers twice had not (so he said), the utter centrality of the text of *In suis* to the entire issue of inheritance and children.[27] Bartolus managed to conflate father and son into one substance – which was the essence of family. He confronted historical changes in the law of paternal prerogatives and conceded that the conflation of generations, while having real effects in the law of inheritance, rested on a fiction – *imaginatio*. The substance that was family thus ended up in his treatment as both tangible and imaginary. In that fashion it was on a par with Aristotelian substance, to which different forms of accidents or qualities adhered.[28] Yet there remains something inchoate and imprecise about terms like *substantia* (and *prudentia*, as we will see later) that makes them work so well. How, then, did Bartolus hit on the term?

The text of *In suis* itself did not suggest the term *substantia*, leaving one to suspect Bartolus's own imaginative leap was behind it. The Roman jurist Paulus only posited the continuation of *dominium* in the son as heir, saying that the father's death yielded not a *haereditas* but rather a free administration of the property. Bartolus himself referred to two other texts: *lex Nam quod* (D. 36.1.14–15,8) and *lex Pronuntiatio* (D. 50.16.195). Neither of these used the word *substantia*. They both used *res*. The second, a passage from the third-century jurist Ulpian (d. 228), posed that family "is taken variously as it is deduced both in things and in persons." It further addressed various meanings of *familia* in terms of *personae*. In strictly legal terms, Ulpian had said that *familia* denoted the different persons "who are subject under the power of one by nature or law." The *paterfamilias* then was "he who has things in a house (*domo*)," even if he did not have a son. In a more common mode of speaking, *familia* was legally all the agnates, for, though on the *pater*'s death each

---

[26] Thomas Widlok, *Anthropology and the Economy of Sharing*, 25, on how sharing copes with inequalities and distinctions.

[27] Widlok, *Anthropology and the Economy of Sharing*, 52.

[28] Cf. Lodi Nauta, *In Defense of Common Sense: Lorenzo Valla's Humanist Critique of Scholastic Philosophy*, 13–21.

subject to him thereafter had his own *familia*, "yet all who were under the power of one rightly will be said to be of the same family, who were *proditi* from the same house and people." The link here was the *dominium* still, not a sense of descent.[29]

These texts thus gave Bartolus an opening to put family in terms of possessions, but not the term he settled on. Nor in his commentaries on these texts did Bartolus find occasion to use the term *substantia*. In regard to the *lex Nam quod* he noted only a distinction between a specific item in an estate and the entirety (*universitas*) thereof.[30] The *lex Pronuntiatio* gave rise to an interesting and more obviously related issue of the status of illegitimate children in the house and family. Yet, while the issue of illegitimacy was largely a matter of inheritance rights, Bartolus's commentary to *Pronuntiatio* did not raise that dimension of the matter and did not even use the term *haereditas*, much less *substantia*.[31]

Still, Bartolus did not invent use of the term *substantia* from whole cloth. He could have found the equation of *familia* and *substantia* readily to hand in two locations in the *Corpus iuris civilis*, neither of which he cited in his commentary to *In suis*. A fragment of the jurist Paulus, the initial and defining text in the *Digest* title *De usu fructu* (D. 7.1.1), told him that "usufruct is a right in others' goods of use and enjoyment, save the substance of the things." Here *substantia* carried a simple meaning of the material nature of something, and it was that which was subject to *dominium*, not mere use.[32] That passage at least equated *substantia* with the rights of the owner, as opposed to the usufructuary, and thus was consistent with Bartolus's use of the term in relation to ownership by father and son. Owner and holder of usufruct shared rights over the same thing. More to the point perhaps was the Justinianic decree embodied in the *lex Suggestioni* in the *Codex* title *De verborum et rerum significatione*, where in the third subsection (C. 6.38.5,3), Bartolus would have found the simple statement that "yet in other cases the term family should be understood for substance, because both slaves and other things are reputed to be in the patrimony of a single person."[33] Substance here refers to assets that can be owned. So while the connection between substance and family was overt, it was still a sense of family as the holdings of a singular owner. There was no sense that this substance was shared

---

[29] Waelkens, *Amne Adverso*, 203.
[30] Bartolus to D. 36.1.14–15,8, *Opera*, vol. 4, fol. 143v.
[31] Bartolus to D. 50.16.195, *Opera*, vol. 6, fols. 247vb–48ra.
[32] Waelkens, *Amne Adverso*, 381.
[33] That is, "in aliis autem casibus nomen familiae pro substantia oportet intelligi, quia et servi et aliae res in patrimonio uniuscuiusque esse putantur." For a discussion of various medieval meanings of family, see Herlihy, "Family."

with others of the *familia*, as father and son did in Bartolus's definition. A more immediate source of authority in law for Bartolus was also at hand. Oldrado da Ponte (d. 1335), one of Bartolus's teachers, in commenting on *In suis* (which seems to give the lie to Bartolus's claim that his teachers neglected it), drove a distinction between *substantia* that bound *pater* and *filius* together and an *adiectio* (addition) that made father and son different.[34] The son might increase the holdings left him. Bartolus used *substantia* in the same sense: it is what bound father and son to each other; but he also used it in a more expansive sense as that of which they were equally owners, the patrimony, which was distinct from what a son might add to it in his lifetime.

As Bartolus must have known, the distinction between those terms, *paterfamilias* and *filiusfamilias*, was otherwise precisely not one of biology but of law. The father had the son in his *potestas* by birth from his legal wife, or by adoption, or legitimation, while illegitimate sons were not in *potestas* and not called *filiusfamilias*, nor technically were they emancipated sons.[35] Bartolus himself elsewhere posed that bastards were unworthy of any substance ("filii spurii sunt indigni omni substantia") in civil law.[36] In canon law and local statutes such a situation of illegitimacy might be mitigated.[37]

By turning to *substantia* Bartolus was both returning to an old equation of family and assets and yet passing over the ending of *familia* in the putative continuity of ownership of *substantia* between father and son, who were also linked by marriage/generation. A pragmatic lack of certainty surrounded the term family, but Bartolus was bringing back into it the primacy of property and more. Blood and honor, a family name and coat of arms, were also inherited from father to son, and shared between them before inheritance arose. Bartolus offered a new definition of ownership (*dominium* as a subjective right to goods), as the right to dispose of physical objects within the limits of the law,[38] which was implicated at the heart of his commentary to *In suis*. He was also giving a new cast to *familia*, both as something one had a membership right to by birth and as

---

[34] His statement in a gloss is "unde quantum adiectionem notantem dominium: in substantia non est differentia." Quoted and analyzed in Bellomo, *Problemi*, 34–35 and n. 53. On his teaching Bartolus, see Anna T. Sheedy, *Bartolus on Social Conditions in the Fourteenth Century*, 13, 15, 32, 34.

[35] On these issues and Bartolus's positions regarding them, see Kuehn, *Emancipation*, 11–18, 28–32, and *Illegitimacy*, 33–46.

[36] Bartolus to authentica *Ex complexu*, C. *De incestis nuptiis*, *Opera omnia*, vol. 7, fol. 160vb.

[37] Cf. Kuehn, *Illegitimacy*, 42–43; Lodovico a Sardis Ferrariensis, *Tractatus de naturalibus liberis*, fol. 32rb.

[38] Waelkens, *Amne Adverso*, 294.

something that continued – that could be and was preserved in the passage of property from father to son.

Succession, it should be noted, was the essential element in corporate identity (for monasteries, guilds, and other entities) for Bartolus and other medieval legists or theologians, like Thomas Aquinas. The king was dead but the kingship went on.[39] One mark of perpetual corporation, at least of church and Empire, is that its property was inalienable and imprescriptible ("dead hand").[40] That quality would be given to family property with the elaboration of perpetual trusts (fideicommissi) in law, but there would always be the problem that patrimony changed hands, despite the immediacy of continuity from father to son.

If it is the case that property law is about means and ends, then Bartolus's choice of the term *substantia* was inspired.[41] It focused not on ownership (*dominium*) per se but on the continuity and sharing of the underlying substance, which remained when the son became heir and owner. In Bartolus's eyes it was *substantia* that lay at the heart of family continuity. It made real, in law, the mysterious commingling of fathers and their sons as *quodammodo domini*. *Substantia* encompassed the real and the incorporeal, but leaned on the side of the corporeal, thus getting around the thirteenth-century gloss's uneasiness with the idea of a continuation of incorporeal things.

It is worth considering for a moment what Bartolus did not (but might have) used to define family:

• Familia accipitur in iure pro patria potestate.
• Familia accipitur in iure pro agnatione.
• Familia accipitur in iure pro sanguine.
• Familia accipitur in iure pro honore.
• Familia accipitur in iure pro domo.
• Familia accipitur in iure pro patrimonio/haereditate.

Any of these would have made some sense to him and his contemporaries, and all of them pointed at elements of sharing, but none would have been as effective in expressing continuity across generations. Actions could result in failure; biological continuity could be lost as family lines died out; a particular *domus* could be lost or even just traded off. It was property writ large, as a substance, that would best endure. Yet as *substantia* the property potentially included not just what one inherited from parents or other ancestors; it could also include what was acquired during one's lifetime. The combination of *patrimonium* and acquisitions would become

---

[39] Ernst Kantorowicz, *The King's Two Bodies: A Study in Medieval Political Theology*, 309–10.
[40] Kantorowicz, *The King's Two Bodies*, 176–77.
[41] Cf. Annelise Riles, "Property as Legal Knowledge: Means and Ends."

in turn *haereditas* to the next generation. Or, in the wake of an unfortunate generation, *substantia* might end up being less of a *patrimonium* than before. Nor need *substantia* amount to the entire *haereditas*, let alone things gained in life; it could be just the vital, symbolic, family-identifying pieces of property. And it was real, it was not merely symbolic, for all that symbolic dimensions of property could have real effects.

Before moving off the term *substantia*, we should take account of its resonance outside the law in Bartolus's day. Florentine merchants, for example, used the term *sustanza* to mean more or less the capital of a business, "le sustanze del traffico."[42] But mainly people knew *sustanza* as what was left them by their fathers. Giovanni Rucellai, a Florentine in the fifteenth century, thanked his good fortune "because from the little substance that was left to me I have grown and multiplied it, as today I find myself with nice wealth and with ease and great credit and good faith."[43] Lapo Niccolini, a fellow Florentine, handed to his emancipated son in 1418 that part of his *sustanze* that constituted an appropriate share as a premortem inheritance.[44] Behind that act, given the same son's later financial difficulties, lay the awareness that, in contrast to Rucellai, who had added to his *sustanza* in his life, there were those like this son and like Paolo Morelli, another Florentine, who consumed it.[45] In either case, *sustanza* stood in contrast to but alongside *onore* (honor), a substantial asset next to a symbolic one (mirrored in the placement of a family crest on the facade of a house).[46] From these vernacular senses as well, the term also entered into statutory law, as in an enactment of Florence, for example, that deplored the deleterious effect of merchants' bankruptcies on the *substantia* of its citizens.[47]

It was an imprecise term, but it carried some distinction from other terms applied to kinship and household. In discussing patrimonial ties between mothers and sons, or brothers and sisters, as opposed to fathers and sons, for instance, Bartolus did not use *substantia* but referred instead to the *familiaritas* that bound them.[48] They might thereby come to expect

---

[42] *Giovanni Rucellai e il suo Zibaldone*, vol. 1: *Il Zibaldone quaresimale*, 19. In the vernacular narration in a Florentine *consilium* about a firm's bankruptcy, the basic agreement is depicted "come di sustanza fralli strani" (ASF, Carte strozziane, 3rd ser., 41/2, fol. 437r).

[43] Rucellai, 117: "chè di poche sustanze che mi furno lasciate l'ò acresciute e multiplicate, e al dì d'oggi mi truovo bella richezza chon bello aviamento e chon gran credito e buona fede."

[44] Lapo Niccolini, *Il libro degli affari proprii di casa di Lapo di Giovanni Niccolini de' Sirigatti*, 143.

[45] Giovanni Morelli, *Ricordi*, 144.

[46] Morelli, *Ricordi*, 167, speaking of "quello che richiede e quello che può in quanto all'onore e alla sustanza del tuo valente."

[47] *Statuti della repubblica fiorentina* (1999), 2 vols., vol. 1: *Statuto del capitano del popolo degli anni 1322–25*, 121.

[48] Bartolus to l. *Qui iure fam.* (D. 41.2.41), *Opera omnia*, vol. 5, fol. 88rb.

some access to food and shelter but could claim no immediate right to inheritance or any prerogative in management of resources. Bartolus's employment of *substantia* allowed him to bridge the ever-widening gulf between local laws and the "common" law to which he was wedded by education and profession. He could use terms like *substantia* to keep them both in some sort of single system of law.

A city such as Florence or Perugia, where Bartolus lived, could legislate for itself, as Rome had. But to Bartolus and others Roman law was a living legacy and a standard of reason and justice. Civic statutes that looked to the inheritance of property by males in agnatic relationship (ideally) had to be brought within the ambit of Roman law. Bartolus found a device to that end with *substantia*.

Where he otherwise gave some consistent treatment to *substantia* was in his unfinished treatise on witnesses and testimony. There he followed the scholastic distinction between substance and accidents, the latter being laid out in nine categories. Bartolus, in fact, dealt with substance and only two accidents, quantity and quality (never getting to complete the others). While this organization and definitions he gave show that Bartolus was well versed in the scholastic, even nominalist, treatment of substance, as Susanne Lepsius points out, he was only interested in those dimensions of *substantia* that could come across the notice of judges or jurisconsults.[49] So Bartolus quickly passed over the category of incorporeal substances for corporeal: "a corporeal thing is comprehensible to the senses, so about these it is possible to speak, although a jurisconsult also subdivides corporeal things into many types: yet those subdivisions regard rather the qualities of things than the substance."[50] In the context Bartolus was intent on laying out what and how witnesses knew of the substance of things, beyond their ability to know a negative (that is, to know that something was not wood or a horse, for example).[51] His main concern was with what would persuade a judge to accept a particular fact as such, as when witnesses swore to the identity of person. To Bartolus this meant the witness had seen the person's face, for as the Roman jurist Paulus had said, we recognize someone by his appearance (*imago*).[52] Substance was intimately bound up with qualities (*accidentia*). One can

---

[49] Bartolus, *Tractatus de testibus*; but one must employ the unrivaled edition of Susanne Lepsius, *Der Richter und die Zeugen: Eine Untersuchung anhand des* Tractatus testimoniorum *des Bartolus von Sassoferrato, mit Edition*. Relevant here are her observations, 116–19.

[50] Lepsius, *Der Richter und die Zeugen*, 245–46.

[51] Lepsius, *Der Richter und die Zeugen*, 133–34.

[52] Lepsius, *Der Richter und die Zeugen*, 255: "Si testis dixerit Titium fuisse illum, quia vidit, satis est, idem si dixerit, quia vidit faciem eius, satis exprimit. Nam Paulus respondit, quod per eius imaginem recognoscimur."

see this extended to the substance of the family, its patrimony, unchanged in the flux of different members coming and going over the years. In view of the fact that substance kept father and son linked, and in view of the fact that they were also at times equated as "one flesh," that was in effect the father,[53] Bartolus was placing *substantia* at the heart of *familia*. One did not encounter substance without form. Here, one did not find substance without *familia*. But just as substance mystified the central liturgical moment of the mass (transubstantiation), it mystified what was (ex)changed when ownership changed hands from fathers to sons (that there was no *nova haereditas*).

Another feature, grammatical this time, of Bartolus's use of *substantia* in his commentary to *In suis* is that the word is singular. That a family's patrimony was in fact constructed out of numerous elements was elided into a single entity. Yet not only were there different sorts of assets in any family's wealth – lands and buildings, animals, tools, furnishings and clothing, debts and credits – there were also different provenances and destinations. Bartolus quietly conceded that there would or could be divisions of the *substantia* on the death of a *pater*, but he did not address the differing contributions from a wife/mother or from children to what family could claim and use. Nor did he mention a distinction, familiar and meaningful in other contexts, between goods transmitted in inheritance and goods gained by one's commercial or agricultural activities. *Substantia* was a neat shorthand, but like all such it was much more than that and not so simply grasped in practice.

Bartolus's formulation seems to have been so sensible as to not need frequent recapitulation by all those who followed him. His contemporary, Alberico da Rosciate, in his formulation that "familia, id est substantia," agreed that father and son were so close as to be a single substance and the son could be termed owner (*dominus*) while his father was alive.[54] But Alberico also found defining features of *familia* in the terms *memoria* and *dignitas*, which were preserved for families by keeping *divitiae* within a *proles masculina*.[55] This was Rosciate's formulation of the rationale behind numerous civic statutes that limited the inheritance rights of daughters to what they had been given as dowry at the time of their marriage (*exclusio propter dotem*).[56] Preservation of family and agnation

---

[53] Cf. Kuehn, *Emancipation*, 22, 59, 146.
[54] See his text in translation in Osvaldo Cavallar and Julius Kirshner, eds., *Jurists and Jurisprudence in Medieval Italy: Texts and Contexts*, 605–8.
[55] Giovanni Rossi, "I fedecommessi nella dottrina e nella prassi giuridica di ius commune tra xvi e xvii secolo," 176–77; Kuehn, "*Memoria* and Family in Law."
[56] Cf. Kuehn, "Intestate Inheritance as a Family Matter: Ius Commune, Statutes, and Cases from Florence."

served as the rationale to expansive, as opposed to restrictive, readings of such statutes. It is interesting that Bartolus's most famous student, Baldo degli Ubaldi (1327–1400), in his commentary on *In suis*, and in the expanded *repetitio* on that text, did not repeat the equation of *familia* and *substantia*. He expended his considerable efforts instead on the consequences of emancipation on sons' inheritance claims and on the requirements for and results of disinheritance.[57] His brother Angelo (1323–1400) and later Paolo di Castro (ca. 1360–1441) followed Alberico da Rosciate's formulations and linked the perpetuation of family *dignitas* and *memoria* with preservation of property and its transmission to sons or other agnates.[58]

Around the end of the fifteenth century, the authoritative Milanese jurist, Giason del Maino (1435–1519), found three meanings of *familia*: as a group of relatives, as a collection of servants, and as *substantia bonorum*.[59] In a calculated move of almost perverse dimensions, Filippo Decio (1454–1535) defended the effective disinheritance of more distant agnates (not one's sons) resulting from legitimation of bastard sons with the thought that, had he wanted, the legitimating father could have deprived those agnates by simply tossing all his wealth into the sea.[60] Decio's statement called attention to something Bartolus overlooked in his commentary on *In suis*, namely the conscious management of property; but that was not an issue Bartolus needed to raise in the context of stressing the immediacy of transmission from father to son. It was not the directive hand but the communion of goods among multiple hands, even over time, that was his focus. Shared usage, not strategic management, was the essence of the *familia*.

At least two developments were fostered by such a substantial vision of family. On the one hand, the old Roman device of a trust, fideicommissum, would become a means of substituting heirs from agnate lines and providing continuity of descent in a sense. On the other hand, in future decades the prohibition on alienation of property (by gift, sale, or inheritance) *extra familiam* would constitute the centerpiece of the fideicommissum and would be upheld by jurists and courts, despite the rights of kin and creditors.[61] The *substantia* associated with family was not nebulous; it was the distinct set of holdings that made up the wherewithal of any given

---

[57] Baldo to l. In suis, *Commentaria in primam et secundam infortiati partes*, fols. 50va–b and 50va–55rb.

[58] On them and others, see Kuehn, "*Memoria* and Family in Law."

[59] Giason del Maino, to l. Suggestioni, C. De verborum significatione, fol. 160vb.

[60] On his remark, see Kuehn, *Illegitimacy*, 56 and n. 120.

[61] Mario Caravale, "Fedecommesso (storia)"; Luigi Tria, *Il fedecommesso nella legislazione e nella dottrina dal secolo xvi ai giorni nostri*; and Kuehn, "*Fideicommissum* and Family: The Orsini di Bracciano."

family and was not distinct from it. The fideicommissum would become, in essence, the very *substantia* of the family – what all its members shared in some way, even if *dominium* over it all resided legally in only one person.

There was still an open question. If *substantia* was lost, did family end? The fideicommissum rested on the desire that property not leave the family, which was implicitly also recognition that substance potentially could be lost. Family could persist only in reduced circumstances, if at all. Here one must take note of an idea that arose in the fourteenth and fifteenth centuries of the "shamed poor" (*poveri vergognosi*). These were not people who were destitute. They had some property, but they lacked enough of it, as Baldo degli Ubaldi conceded in his treatment of the matter, to meet social expectations. They could not repay their debts or accumulate suitable dowries for their women. These people were to become the objects of charitable relief that would deny or at least mitigate the downward social mobility experienced by elite families in all communities. Here, then, was admission that *substantia* had to be substantial.[62]

2.2   Practical Law

Doctrines of commentators like Bartolus were devised with an eye to statutes and actual forensic problems. It is interesting to examine how Bartolus and others handled statutes in various surviving consilia. It was this genre of legal writing that was truly coming into its own in this era.[63] It was a genre of expanding use and complexity parallel to the contemporaneous development, by Bartolus and his contemporaries, of academic treatises (*tractatus*).[64]

A first example comes from the pens of two near contemporaries of Bartolus – Tommaso Corsini (d. ca. 1357) of Florence and the fairly obscure Ricco da Muraro. Corsini was the first professor of law hired in the new Florentine *studium generale* in 1349, after the commune was unable to lure Bartolus from Perugia.[65] Corsini had a voice to be heeded, both in law and in the governing bodies of Florence. His son Filippo

---

[62] Richard C. Trexler, "Charity and the Defense of Urban Elites in the Italian Communes"; Giuliana Albini, "Declassamento sociale e povertà vergognosa: uno sguardo sulla società viscontea."

[63] Cf. Franz Wieacker, *Storia del diritto privato moderno*, 1:112–15; Luigi Lombardi, *Saggio sul diritto giurisprudenziale*, 130–31; Adriano Cavanna, "Il ruolo del giurista nell'età del diritto comune."

[64] Cf. Manlio Bellomo, *I fatti e il diritto: tra le certezze e i dubbi dei giuristi medievali (secoli xiii–xiv)*, 562–63, 596–604. On Bartolus's consilia see Mario Ascheri, "Bartolo da Sassoferrato: il 'suo' *tractatus* consiliare e i suoi *consilia*."

[65] Corsini appears among the faculty of the Florentine Studio for 1357–8 but not thereafter, although his sons Piero and Filippo do (hence the dating of his death: see Katherine Park, "The Readers of the Florentine Studio according to Communal Fiscal Records (1357–1380,

(1334–1421) would follow in his father's footsteps as the most prominent native-born legist of Florence in his day.[66] They addressed precisely the problem of the nature of the direct and instantaneous inheritance of a son, though their consilium may well have been composed before Bartolus drew up his commentary to *In suis*. These two jurists began with the *regula* that an estate not formally accepted could not be transmitted to an heir's heir (*haereditas non adita non transmictetur*). Similarly, an heir who had not taken possession (*inmisceat*) could not be called heir. But a son was not just an heir, so the jurists also quickly asserted "in contrarium videt veritas." They determined there was a continuation immediately from father to son, and they cited *In suis* to that effect, but not Bartolus himself. Indeed, they never invoked his name at all. Not that they left jurisprudence out of account. In the course of their consilium they found reason to mention the Glossa ordinaria, Odofredo (d. 1265), Dino del Mugello (d. 1303?), Azzo (d. ca. 1230), Jacopo Buttrigari (d. 1348) several times, and Jacopo de Belviso (1270–1335), not to mention various "magni doctores."[67] Bartolus was seemingly as yet too young or new to claim much *auctoritas*.

In the Florentine case infant heirs had died without formal acceptance, leaving as next in line their maternal uncle Antonio. Corsini and Muraro noted that many jurists had maintained that such deceased infants did transmit their father's estate or the right to deliberate about becoming its heir.[68] But they also noted that there were many other authoritative figures, including Jacopo de Belviso, who took the opposite view: that there was no transmission from sons to an *extraneus* (an heir who did not come from the same *familia* as the deceased). They explored the clear difference between sons and *haeredes extranei*. It was these latter who could not transmit a *ius deliberandi* without accepting an estate left to them. Sons, even infants ignorant of their inheritance, necessarily transmitted it to others. The legal problem, however, rested in Antonio's act as tutor of the infants to accept the estate for them. The uncle Antonio in this case seems to have tried a proactive approach to secure the estate for himself through the sons, acting as a tutor to them. The jurists determined that he had no recourse; the estate did not go to him.[69] They were

---

1413–1446)," 253–54). Also on the Studio, Gene Brucker, "Florence and Its University, 1348–1434."

[66] Cf. Martines, *Lawyers and Statecraft*, 482. Tommaso Corsini took part in an important Florentine ambassadorial mission in 1347 and was on the Signoria of 1353 (Gene Brucker, *Florentine Politics and Society, 1343–1378*, 143, 147), but even as early as 1328 was involved in a crucial electoral commission (John Najemy, *Corporatism and Consensus in Florentine Electoral Politics, 1280–1400*, 100).

[67] Their consilium is in Biblioteca Apostolica Vaticana, Vat. Lat. 8069, fols. 193v–95v.

[68] Vat. Lat. 8069, fol. 194r.   [69] Vat. Lat. 8069, fol. 195v.

enforcing the sense in which the inheritance after the sons did not operate as a continuous and immediate transfer. Though patrimony did indeed pass instantaneously from father to sons, it did not pass that way to the uncle as heir to the children. Instead a court, it seems, would have to determine who was next in line. There would be agnates to the father in all likelihood.

Bartolus's own consilia do not reveal a case precisely on point – a case of father-to-son succession in which the matter of coterminous ownership of family *substantia* arose. That is not so surprising. Father–son succession, even as Bartolus's terms made clear, was more or less automatic, conventionally expected, and unobjectionable. Trouble cases were what came to court and there met with juristic intervention. They typically involved situations in which the seamless transmission from father to son did not arise for some reason. A quick survey of three consilia will allow us, nevertheless, to see Bartolus handle limiting instances and judge how compatible his forensic conclusions were with his teaching.

1. *Exclusion of a dowered daughter.* Perugia, like most every other Italian commune, had an inheritance statute that excluded dowered daughters from inheriting with their brothers, agnate nephews, uncles, and so forth.[70] The statute rested on customs that ran contrary to the rules of civil law. Legal problems tended to arise when there were no male heirs or when a testament seemed to alter this statutory default. Bartolus faced a case in which a man by will left his *haereditas* to his son, who took and used it (*immiscuit*) until his death, when his will in turn directed the property to his wife, having no sons, while leaving his daughters set amounts (doubtless intended as dowry). His sister, Angela, then mounted a claim for half the estate which, she posed, was her father's, not her brother's. Bartolus denied her claim. Her argument rested on the fact that, as her brother was dead, she was no longer excluded by statute. But those who advanced such an argument, said Bartolus, "do not understand the meaning of the term until."[71] Angela had only shared in the patrimony up to the moment she gained her dowry. The estate transferred thereafter to her brother:

---

[70] See Kuehn, "Person and Gender in the Laws"; Manlio Bellomo, *La condizione giuridica della donna in Italia*; *Ricerche sui rapporti patrimoniali tra coniugi: Contributo alla storia della famiglia medievale*; Isabelle Chabot, "La loi du lignage: Notes sur le système successoral florentin (XIVe–XVe, XVIIe siècles)"; Anna Bellavitis, "Dot et richesse des femmes à Venise au XVIe siècle"; Julius Kirshner, "Materials for a Gilded Cage: Non-Dotal Assets in Florence, 1300–1500."

[71] Bartolus, *Opera omnia* (Venice, 1570–1), vol. 11, 1 *cons.* 20, fols. 8va–9ra, at 8va: "non intelligunt significationem dictionis quousque."

Moreover the son was heir of his father, and so by acceptance of the estate it ceased to be the estate of his father. It began to be merged with the estate of the son. So it is a question of the son's estate, not the father's ... and so this daughter wants to enter her father's estate and she cannot because the estate left is that of another.[72]

The statutes of Perugia left the aunt no recourse. The crux of Bartolus's decision was that the wife received the property, though through her it might well pass later to her dowered daughters. He did so notably leaning on the prior, entirely normative, succession of son to father, but also playing up a discontinuity in transfer of the estate rather than some fictive continuation of ownership.

2. *Paternal liability for a criminous son.* It was in the context of paternal liability that Bellomo examined Bartolus's commentary to *In suis.* Bartolus dealt with such a case from Perugia. A ser Cardo saw his son, Bartolomeo, banned for abetting a murder. Bartolus denied that ser Cardo had to divide his property and hand over Bartolomeo's share to be "destroyed" (lost to the family by confiscation). As Bartolomeo's "confession" was fictive, in fact merely inferred from his contumacious placement under ban of the commune, it could only affect Bartolomeo and not anyone else. Nor could his property be subject to destruction, as "the possessive words mine, yours, his, are of present meaning," and at the time in question the property belonged to the father, not the son.[73] Here the substantial and coterminous tie between father and son was not asserted. Instead it was implied that death resulted in a change of ownership, not a continuity at all, beyond any "peculiar" property that may have belonged to the son.[74] Sharing faded into the background; distinct rights and titles took center-stage in order to set, and deny, liabilities. In any case, Bartolus was being consistent in limiting the father's damage from criminous behavior by his son.

3. *Rights of an illegitimate.* Inheritance claims of illegitimates were an element of one text Bartolus cited in support of the *substantia-familia* equation, namely *Pronuntiatio.* In a case from Gubbio, Bartolus encountered a situation in which Filippuccio Giacomelli left to his bastard grandson Marino (son of Francesco) "food, clothing, and shelter in the home of the

---

[72] Bartolus, *Opera omnia*, vol. 11, 1 *cons.* 20, fol. 8vb: "Praeterea filius masculus fuit haeres patris sui, et sic per aditionem desiit esse haereditas patris sui. Coepit enim esse unita cum hereditate filii. Est ergo de hereditate filii tractandum non patris."

[73] Bartolus, *Opera omnia*, vol. 11, 1 *cons.* 116, fol. 30va–vb, at vb: "ista nomina possessiva meum, tuum, suum, sunt significativa presentis temporis."

[74] A major feature of Bellomo's examination of a related *quaestio* of Bartolus in *Problemi del diritto familiare*, 148–55.

testator in the part belonging to his heir, Bartolomeo."[75] Following his
grandfather's death in 1342, Marino lived in the house for six years, and
then for another six years lived on his own and did not seek food or clothing
from his half-brother Bartolomeo. Did Bartolomeo still owe Marino that
sustenance, even in another location than the testator's home? Bartolus went
to the wording of the will and asserted that the phrase "in domo" referred to
the right to shelter, not the rights to food and clothing, and "that Marino be
constrained to stay in the home in order to have support is an absurd
reading" (absurdus intellectus).[76] There did not have to be a sharing of
property in all regards. Rights between a father (or grandfather) and an
illegitimate child were not so automatic as *In suis* pretended, but there were
rights accorded by paternal testament and Bartolus enforced them.[77] The
subjective belonging of the illegitimate Marino was not vitiated by lack of
cohabitation. Right of membership trumped practices of sharing (from
which Marino was seemingly excluded by his absence).

2.3   Concluding Thoughts

Bartolus's idea of a family *substantia* can fit well with the growing sense of
blood-relatedness at the time, with its recourse to genealogical trees.[78]
Substantia, though carrying much more the implication of property, could
also easily stand in for blood. The family tree "has built into it the
assumption that the essence of a person is received, by transmission, at
the point of conception," and that essence precedes growth.[79] As James
Leach argues, however, it is also possible to see land, for example, not as
a mere container for life but as constitutive of identity for those living and
interacting with it. Sharing, in other words. In Bartolus's consilia there
was no sharing. One finds a dowered daughter no longer at home; an
illegitimate son who had not stayed at home; and a criminous son who
had deserted father and city.

It is one of the ironies of law, in its pretense to stand outside the culture
it would regulate, that it calls attention to what it seeks to deny or
obfuscate.[80] The term *substantia* argued for continuity, immediacy even,

---

[75] Bartolus, *Opera omnia*, vol. 11, 2 *cons.* 4, fol. 57va: "victum, et vestitum et habitationem in domo dicti testatoris in parte contingente Bartholomeo heredi suo."

[76] Bartolus, *Opera omnia*, vol. 11, 2 *cons.* 4, fol. 57va.

[77] Cf. Kuehn, *Illegitimacy*, 41–46.

[78] Christiane Klapisch-Zuber, *L'Arbre des familles*; Klapisch-Zuber, "Family Trees and the Construction of Kinship in Renaissance Italy."

[79] James Leach, "Knowledge as Kinship: Mutable Essence and the Significance of Transmission on the Rai Coast of Papua New Guinea," 187–88.

[80] Cf. Karen Crawley, "The Critical Force of Irony: Reframing Photographs in Cultural Legal Studies."

where in fact it was most tenuous and where a real discontinuity (of generations) was taking place. *Substantia* was a term for legal commentaries, for lectures in an academic setting, but it had less utility in litigation, even to the one who creatively employed the term in his lectures. *Substantia* used in connection to family called attention to property and elevated its formative role, as shared. It was when the sharing stopped, or rather when management failed or was at least contested, that the jurists showed up.

In an essay entitled "Family," David Herlihy examined the classical and Christian contributions to modern concepts of family. Herlihy found the classical contribution mainly in juristic texts, which embodied a sense of *familia* as "an authoritarian structure and hierarchical order founded on but not limited to relations of marriage and parenthood." The *potestas* of the Roman father was distinct from his status as *genitor* and it was not coterminous with household. A second sense of *familia* rendered it in terms of possessions. The Christian and medieval contribution gave a central role to *caritas*, seeing *familia* as a "domestic communion" that acquired and shared resources for the good of its members, "who were defined largely in terms of marriage and blood." In the late Middle Ages, the combination of plagues, wars and their accompanying taxes, and far-flung and complex markets made society as a whole seem threatening and, at least in Herlihy's estimation, Florence's families "seem to have developed a stronger sense of internal cohesion and seem to have found, or hoped to find, in their companionship essential rest and refreshment."[81] Perhaps then too it is not an accident that a bastard son of a prominent Florentine lineage, Leon Battista Alberti, would be the first to make *famiglia* the subject of a learned dialogue.

Our examination of Bartolus effectively supplements Herlihy's by returning to the legal heritage after Rome to see that the expansiveness of *patria potestas* and *dominium* had become the basis of an almost institutional continuity not envisioned in Roman sources. When Machiavelli famously advised his prince to contemplate murder, if need be, but to "refrain from seizing the property of others, because a man is quicker to forget the death of his father than the loss of his patrimony," he was not only questioning a moral certitude. He was also giving expression to the realities (dare we say, substance?) of family life for many in Italy, at least among the civic elites and nobility.[82]

Where the paradigm of father-to-son inheritance failed, there were daughters or more distant relatives seeking title to *substantia*. The overt connection between *familia* and *substantia* was broken, or at least murky.

[81] Herlihy, "Family."   [82] Quotation is from *The Essential Writings of Machiavelli*, 65.

Bartolus's sense of family was such that separate residence did not cost even a bastard his rights to food, clothing, and shelter. But it was also a sense of family that strove to limit a father's liability for his son's acts, even in the face of statutes that mapped an extensive liability, especially before the commune's need for civic order. It asserted distinctive individual prerogatives so as to preclude loss of some of the shared resources. But it was also a sense of family that largely excluded the daughters dowered, married, and physically transferred (as or along with their "share") to other households. It was a sense of family open to, if not actively on its way to being, the encompassing patrilineage, rather than the more horizontally extensive consorterie that left their towers about the landscapes of the thirteenth-century communes.[83]

It may be just to say that Bartolus's approach to family through legal problems made "his picture of family life a partial and sharply circumscribed one."[84] But the legal approach necessarily put Bartolus at the nexus of persons and property. Bartolus was imaginative. While imagination was not truth, not even in law (as his use of the term in his commentary on *In suis* shows), it was useful to understanding, to integrating different persons and rights and actions into meaningful wholes, like *familia*.

Over half a century ago Ernst Kantorowicz, in his classic *The King's Two Bodies*, drew attention to the corporate theorizing of medieval civilians. The *universitas* was, of course, a fictive person, but as such it was its persistence in time that set it apart. "The *universitas* thrives on succession," Kantorowicz insisted.[85] Succession was a matter of private law in the first instance, and it was in the presumed continuity of father and son and the fictive continuity of the *haereditas*, as depicted in texts of the *Digest* and *Institutes*, that jurists found a basis to extend to the kingdom the substantial continuity of blood between king and his son (where it was the case that "the king is dead; long live the king").[86] The burgeoning absolutist states (that would have their greatest extent long after Bartolus) would make the most of family as a political metaphor. Paternal power would be reinforced; paternal control of property, career, and marital choices would be expected for the sake of family seen as a collective

---

[83] The pacts of Florentine tower societies were based on synchronous outreach and present purposes and embraced nonkin at times. See Robert Davidsohn, *Storia di Firenze*, vol. 4, *I primordi della civiltà fiorentina*, part 1, *Impulsi interni, influssi esterni e cultura politica*, 393–401.

[84] Sheedy, *Bartolus on Social Conditions*, 77. She does not discuss his commentary to *In suis*.

[85] Kantorowicz, *The King's Two Bodies*, 308.

[86] Notably D. 46.1.22, l. Mortuo, D. de fideiussoribus et mandatoribus: "quia hereditas personae vice fungitur"; and I. 3.1,3: "Et statum morte parentis quasi continuatur dominium."

enterprise. In his commentary to *In suis* Bartolus brought the growing sophistication of scholastic corporate theory back to these roots in the law and elevated *familia* to corporate status (of a sort). That status was not generally at issue in the cases we have examined, where a particular succession was in play, so Bartolus did not need to consider the corporate entity in his opinions. But he engaged in an imaginative extension of law that had an active future.

That said, we might end on an anthropological note, for it is intriguing that the term Bartolus applied to kinship, substance, has lately had great resonance in anthropologists' discussions of kinship. As used in David Schneider's analysis of American kinship, substance is equated with blood and biological matter and thus figures as immutable (substantial in that sense) in contrast to culture or conduct. His analysis ran on a powerful dichotomy of nature vs. nurture. More recently, Marilyn Strathern has deployed the notion of personhood (self and individual) and substance to break down such dichotomies. Instead her work and that of others has drawn out the transformations, conversions, continuities, and flows among previously dichotomous domains. As Janet Carsten has put it, "the analytic vocabulary of kinship apparently lacked a means to express mutability and relationality in terms of flows between persons or between persons and things, and substance neatly filled that gap."[87] Bartolus too was addressing flows between persons (mainly fathers and sons) and the transformation and continuity that both seemed to mark inheritance in direct agnatic line. He too found substance to be an appropriate term because it had a breadth of meanings to express the flow of objects and to stand for the relationships between persons. It was the shared something at the heart of *familia*. It carried continuities and it produced changes. It both destabilized the difference between generations and served to fix the agnatic family in relation to others. Bartolus seems to have been a good anthropologist, as well as jurist.

[87] This discussion relies on Janet Carsten, *After Kinship*, esp. 109–35, quotation 134.

3   The Divisible Patrimony

Legal Property Relations of Fathers and Sons
in Renaissance Florence

The closeness, indeed the very oneness, of fathers and their legitimate sons was not just a legal construct; it was an ideological trope widely celebrated in Italian communities such as Florence. Beyond laws' assumption of effective union of fathers and sons, such personal and material unity is readily apparent in the most well-known work on family life in the fifteenth century, Leon Battista Alberti's *Della famiglia*. There the elder Giannozzo instructs the young Alberti on how to manage property, wife, children, and servants in a household which, if not in fact under one roof, resides at least in the shadow of a single (directing) will – that of the father of the household.[1] It is conceded to be a heavy and difficult task to manage the household, to be a prudent manager (*massaio*), and to know what to delegate to an astute wife (were one fortunate to have found such a woman).[2] The unity of the household was safeguarded materially by closely guarding its assets, even from its members. Giannozzo rails against the idea of even a small sum being entrusted to a son for some trifling expenses.[3]

In his later *Cena familiaris*, Alberti gave voice to another side of familial and patrimonial unity, to the deleterious effects of splitting a patrimony, of giving someone something apart from the common holdings of the group:

I am often amazed when I see in a family such ignorance, and not only that, but inept persistence in competing, especially to accumulate for oneself some part of shared wealth . . . so that when the enterprise is completed they find a greater loss than gain. . . . You contentious ones prefer a small transitory increase to some consistency of all your fortune and goods and you violate the religion and sanctity of the innate brotherhood.[4]

A communion of assets, equally available to all, was "violated" by one family member seeking his portion to the exclusion of others. The sharing

---

[1] Leon Battista Alberti, *The Family in Renaissance Florence*, 186.
[2] Alberti, *The Family in Renaissance Florence*, 230, which also includes the concession that in reality "possessions, family, honor, and friendship are not altogether our belongings."
[3] Alberti, *The Family in Renaissance Florence*, 241–42.
[4] Alberti, *Opere volgari*, 1: 345–56, at 347.

42

of assets, tangible and intangible, was demolished by insistence on what was one's own.

Division of holdings led to the presence of dissension within the family – the worst possible situation. So when Alberti returned to this theme in his *De iciarchia*, he stressed how

> family is a body similar to a republic, composed of yourself and this other [brother] and all of you: and you are to the family like innate instruments and members of this body. The first obligation of anyone in this family will be to make oneself active and attentive that indeed all together form a well united body, in which all the group like a body in motion feel the movement of every one of its parts even the very least, moved by pleasure rather than by pain.[5]

Frequent repetition of the word body (*corpo*) shows how corporate Alberti's sense of family had become since the earlier *Della famiglia*.[6] Family was about living together behind a single *intenzione*. The first care of a father was "that the family be most united without any discord" (senza niuna discordia unitissima).[7] The frequent conjunction of elders and the young at meals functioned as an important means by which the latter might be restrained from following their selfish inclinations.[8] Beyond that, the father had a form of rule over his sons and his wife, whose duty was to obey him.[9]

Alberti's Florentine contemporary, Matteo Palmieri, embraced the same sense of patrimonial unity. Patrimonies were the basis on which civic life rested. So when the father grew old and weak, the sons he had raised well (in accord with Palmieri's advice) would take care of him, by the example he gave them.[10] Continuity would prevail across the generations. Yet the form of expenditure fathers were often discouraged from was precisely that of dividing their patrimony with their sons, ceding control and management to the boys, making themselves vulnerable to them. The early Quattrocento moralist Giovanni Dominici cautioned fathers, "If you make them [sons] proprietors while you live, you make them thieves no less than the abbot [makes] his monk whom he allows to possess property."[11] The equation of family with institutionalized monasticism cannot be ignored. Yet family also clearly was not institutionalized

---

[5] Alberti, *Opere volgari*, 2: 185–286, at 267.
[6] An interesting take on the differences between *De iciarchia* and Alberti's earlier *Della famiglia* is in James Hankins, *Virtue Politics: Soulcraft and Statecraft in Renaissance Italy*, 328–34.
[7] Alberti, *The Family in Renaissance Florence*, 274.
[8] Alberti, *The Family in Renaissance Florence*, 275, 257–58.
[9] Alberti, *The Family in Renaissance Florence*, 279–80.
[10] Matteo Palmieri, *Della vita civile*, 135.
[11] Giovanni Dominici, *On the Education of Children*, 53.

to the same degree. So, while sons were expected to take care of an aged father, the elder was cautioned not to release his control over property to them. Stories appearing in *novelle* purported to reveal the sad fate awaiting a father who foolishly gave his son management of the family patrimony.[12] Despite Palmieri's optimism, retirement was not something to look forward to.[13]

Fathers were the controlling center of the family, managers of its patrimony. Part of that management was training sons to fulfill the same role in their turn. But fears about retirement indicate that there was hesitance and doubt as to the dedication of sons to the singular patrimony of the family. Divisions did happen. Conflicts over management of resources were constant. In a preliminary manner, one can invoke the fairly well-known instance of Michelangelo and his father, whose legal prerogatives in regard to his son's earnings led to complaints that litter Michelangelo's correspondence.[14] How did fathers, then, like the Florentine contemporaries of Alberti and Palmieri or Michelangelo, cope with patrimonial management and possible division of holdings? What tools did law provide to address the claims of sons? What tools did it have to save families from the imprudent decisions of sons, or even fathers? The sharing of patrimony was not a simple matter, to say the least. Claims of parents and children, or even just apprehensions about them, could lead to clashes. The more the family was conceived as an enduring and sharing entity, the more there were difficulties in actually making it so, even for just a while. The instruments of the law and those who wielded and understood them (notaries, attorneys, consultative jurists) intervened. The growing influence of academic jurisprudence and the active intervention of local statutory law inserted into the social order both means to preserve a shared patrimony and multiple means of devising it into individual separate shares, which at times was also how patrimony might be preserved.

3.1   Law and Patrimony

Leaving aside all the religious images and moralistic examples, law too inculcated an image of caring paternalism into every community. Learned jurisprudence, working from the "common" texts of Roman and canon

---

[12] Kuehn, *Emancipation in Late Medieval Florence*, 66–67.
[13] An exception would seem to have been Torquato Tasso, whose 1580 dialogue on the *padre di famiglia* conceded that an aged father who had raised his children well could look forward to retirement (*Dialoghi*, 116–17).
[14] Cf. Alexander Lee, *The Ugly Renaissance: Sex, Greed, Violence and Depravity in an Age of Beauty*, 71–73.

law, developed several tag lines for the father–son relationship that reson-
ated repeatedly in courtrooms and lecture halls throughout Italy. Father
and son were "one flesh" – an echo of the term used for the unity of
husband and wife, as "due in carne una."[15] Alternatively, the father was
called the voice of the son. At other times father and son were said to be
the same person (*eadem persona*). Shared existence could be no more
forcefully put. Such statements, of course, also helped make sense of
legal prohibitions on contracts or obligations between a father and his
son under *patria potestas*.[16] Father and son were so substantially united, as
in blood, that, harkening to biblical imagery, were the father to consume
bitter grapes, his son's teeth would tingle.[17]

The essential union of father and son was carried in the very nature of
legal paternal power (*patria potestas*). This paternal authority was termed
sacred. Its value was inestimable. It invoked a response of *pietas* from the
son, to whom the person of the father "must always seem honorable,
sacred, and holy, even if he is not."[18] And this was not a conception
limited to law. No less a figure than Marsilio Ficino (1433–99) called the
father a second God, who gave his children life itself and sustenance.
Respect, reverence, and obedience were his due. In legalistic terms,
Ficino posed that a son was in his father's debt and owed him
repayment.[19]

This affection, if not reverence, went both ways. A Sienese attorney,
Filippo d'Andrea Balducci da Lucca, argued that a posthumous son not
covered in the paternal will quashed it in all its terms, because, even
though by some happenstance a father may not have known of his wife's
pregnancy, it was presumed "that a father loves his son more than himself" (quia pater magis diligit filium quam se ipsum).[20] He could not
neglect a son in his will. Disinheritance had to be explicit and for cause.
Ficino's Florentine contemporary, Giovanni Rucellai, agreed with
Balducci that it was a father's duty to make his sons his heirs, and that it
was reprehensible to disinherit a son, for "God had bestowed goods on
a father that he might help his son."[21] In practice, disinheritance was
quite rare, unsurprisingly.[22]

---

[15] Laurent Mayali, "*Due erunt in carne una* and the Medieval Canonists."
[16] Kuehn, *Emancipation*, 22.
[17] Kuehn, *Emancipation*, 146, where the image from Jeremiah 31:29 appears in a Florentine
consilium.
[18] Kuehn, *Emancipation*, 30–31.   [19] Marsilio Ficino, "Epistola ad fratres vulgaris."
[20] Mariano and Bartolomeo Sozzini, *Consilia*, 5 *cons*. 108, fols. 146va–47vb.
[21] Quoted in Francis William Kent, *Household and Lineage in Renaissance Florence: The
Family Life of the Capponi, Ginori, and Rucellai*, 72.
[22] Kirshner, "Baldus de Ubaldis on Disinheritance."

While patrimony continued to be what held and kept people together, as a common set of assets it was also increasingly seen as what held them together, in symbolic and substantial unity, with those who had gone before.[23] The heir in one generation has been depicted as simply a steward for generations to come and the link to the generations past, all bound in a lineage described and embodied in testaments and entails (*fideicommissa* in Roman law).[24] Holding property in common and rights to retrieve properties alienated by another member of one's kin (*retrait lignagère*) are important elements of any effective patrimonial economic unity.[25] Included in this patrimonial unity, a prominent component of it, for the entire family, was the symbolic capital of honor. It is an element, as well, that cannot help but strike one as entirely indivisible. All the family reflected the shame of dishonorable deeds of any of its members, and all equally basked in the glow of successes, great deeds, and an honorable reputation.[26] However, honor was so pivotal that it could also provoke moments of conflict and true divisiveness, even among close kindreds.[27] Law furnished concepts, like agnation, that pretended that kinsmen operated as coherent groups and that masked inherent conflicts that could erode familial solidarity. And law was pivotal when patrimonial material and monetary assets were in question, when sharing them was a matter of dispute.

To cite one example, Bartolus's student, Baldo degli Ubaldi (1327–1400), along with a Milanese jurist, Signorello degli Omodei (1308–71), confronted the issue of a son's domicile with his father. Clearly a son followed his father's "original" domicile, and was liable for fiscal duties and enabled for civic offices accordingly, but did he follow his father's "accidental" domicile (where he went on business or for political reasons)? Was the *voluntas* of the son at all relevant in this, even if he lived with his father in this second place? The jurists firmly placed the son's domicile with his father. While it was true that one might choose to move to another city or transfer the bulk of one's fortune elsewhere, and thus change domicile, there was also the case where, beyond the father's decision to change, the local government had conceded the privilege to

---

[23] James Casey, *The History of the Family*, 34, has termed the intergenerational passage of patrimony a "well-nigh universal drive."

[24] Beatrice Gottlieb, *Family in the Western World: From the Black Death to the Industrial Age*, 206–7; J. P. Cooper, "Patterns of Inheritance and Settlement by Great Landowners from the Fifteenth to the Eighteenth Centuries"; Isabelle Chabot, "'Biens de famille': Contrôle des ressources patrimoniales, *gender* et cycle domestique (Italie, XIIIième–XVième siècles)," 90; Gregory Hanlon, *Human Nature in Rural Tuscany: An Early Modern History*, 124–26.

[25] Kent, *Household and Lineage*, 70, 121–27.   [26] See Frank Henderson Stewart, *Honor*.

[27] Kuehn, *Law, Family, and Women*, 129–42.

him. In that case the son was part of the new domicile *irrevocabiliter* and *immutabiliter*, "especially by the infinite qualities that pass from the person of the father to the son."[28] None of this denied that a son might live elsewhere than his father, but his legal domicile otherwise followed his father because he was so legally and substantially attached to him.

In part the shared *substantia* and domicile made sense to Bartolus, Baldo, and so many others, because the *patria potestas* wrapped around it was so extensive in sweep and duration. It did not end when the son came of age. Marriage did not change it; and no Italian community moved to establish legal emancipation at a son's marriage.[29] Paternal legal power lasted as long as the father survived, unless he were to emancipate his son (or daughter) from his control. Because it did not end at some moment of imputed maturity for a child, that showed, said another jurist who had a career in part with great impact in Florence, namely Paolo di Castro (ca. 1360–1441), that *patria potestas* was not devised to protect minor children. Rather, it was invented to the favor of the father "so that he may acquire things through his child and so that he can exercise it on the person of his son in favor of the father himself."[30] The son had no ownership of what he acquired by this description. Rather, it all went into that singular *substantia*, of which the son was only "sort of" owner, as Bartolus said, while the father was still alive.[31] This sense of *potestas* as a unique right and privilege of the (legitimate) father would persist in law, in and beyond Florence, as illustrated in the legal treatise on *patria potestas* by Ascanio Clementini Amerini (1572).[32]

It was also the case, as Isabelle Chabot has demonstrated so thoroughly for Florence, that the seemingly more separate property of the wife/ mother – also in a relationship where two flesh became one – would assimilate into the patrimony when it too passed to the sons.[33] Various legal restrictions on the acts of women, notably those (such as writing a testament) that could most directly prejudice the rights of husband and sons, were geared to the eventual absorption of female patrimony, as we will see more fully in the next chapter.

---

[28] Baldo degli Ubaldi, *Consilia*, 5 *cons.* 415, fol. 110rb–vb: "maxime per infinitas qualitates que ex persona patris transeunt ad filium."

[29] Cf. Cavallar and Kirshner, *Jurists and Jurisprudence*, 586.

[30] Kuehn, *Emancipation*, 31; Paolo di Castro to D. 45.1.141,1, Si servus aut filius extranei, *Commentaria in digesti novi partem secundam*, fol. 56vb.

[31] On these themes also Manlio Bellomo, "La struttura patrimoniale della famiglia italiana nel tardo medioevo."

[32] In *Tractatus universi iuris*, vol. 8, part 2, fols. 98ra–127rb.

[33] Isabelle Chabot, *La dette des familles: femmes, lignage et patrimoine à Florence aux xive et xve siècles*, 69–83.

Fictions and metaphors aside, father and son were two distinct people. And in the agonistic world of Italian cities it was incumbent on the father to raise his son to be assertive and active. Friction between fathers and sons was an endemic feature of the Florentine cityscape.[34] But beyond the spectacular moments when sons revolted from their fathers' management, or fathers found it necessary, though undoubtedly painful, to disinherit sons, there were mundane activities and features of ordinary life that inevitably drew lines between fathers and sons and, by implication, in the family *substantia*. Was it always the case that sons acquired for their fathers? Did sharing a patrimony always go that far? Were there no limits to the ownership fathers had over family property?

There is a curious legal parallel between wives and children *in potestate* in relation to the *vir/pater*. They could not make gifts (that is, the formal transfer of ownership contained in the legal *donatio*) to each other. Husband–wife and father–child relations were conceived of in law as so close that any gift between them was a sort of schizoid giving to oneself. Sharing in a fairly absolute way was assumed. Sons had to be emancipated from *patria potestas* in order to receive a gift from their fathers.[35] Spouses could receive from each other only in death, by means of a testamentary bequest of a *donatio causa mortis*; intestacy gave wives no claim on their husband's patrimony and husbands' rights to wives' dowries were enacted in statutory law only. The issue was that the *familia* in law was a liability group represented by the *paterfamilias*, and allowing gifts and distinct ownership within a *familia* confused and endangered the neat placement of all liability in him.[36] The main substantial difference, and it is an important one, is that wives were generally not liable for their husbands' debts and obligations (and statutes tended to widen and reinforce this), whereas sons *in potestate* were liable for fathers, at least on their common property/*substantia* (and statutes in Florence notoriously widened and reinforced this).[37] Wives might offer to go surety for their husbands or cover their debts, but they could do so only if local law allowed them to explicitly waive their *ius commune* right not to be held liable for another (senatus consultum Velleianum).

Sons might come into possession of property on their own by a number of routes, and, while sons who remained under *potestas* had little legal capacity to manage their goods (whatever their age), they had distinct if often highly ambiguous claims. At some point sons would begin to work in the family enterprise or apprentice or attend school. At some moment

---

[34] See Kuehn, "Honor and Conflict in a Fifteenth-Century Florentine Family."
[35] Cf. Kuehn, *Emancipation*, 18–25.   [36] Waelkens, *Amne Adverso*, 194–95, 198.
[37] See Kuehn, *Family and Gender*, 91–101.

they could start to bring in the sorts of gains that Paolo di Castro envisioned fathers realizing from their sons.

There was indeed a special legal category for property belonging to children *in potestate* – the *peculium* (a term also used for what a master might entrust to a slave). In fact, there were four types of *peculia*. *Peculium castrense* was military pay, which assured the soldier-son had title and some control over what he gained from serving the *res publica*. He could realize the *fructus*, and, although he could not alienate the property, he could have a testament directing where it should go on his death in battle. Later the category of *quasi castrense* was devised to put things like the wages of a civil servant or a priest in the same position. These two categories obviously arose for sons already grown and pursuing important activities which benefited more than their family.

That was not necessarily the case with the other two forms of *peculia*. *Peculium profectitium* was what was allocated to a son from his father. Formal title remained with the father, and he enjoyed the *fructus*. Presumably the father could change his mind, taking back the *profectitium* or alienating it at his pleasure. The overtly gratuitous nature of the *profectitium* gave the son little control over it. The *adventitium* was what came to the son by any other person or means, on which the son's title was a bit firmer, and he might enjoy *fructus*.[38] The father could not just alienate it. *Adventitia* was the grab-bag category, as one Florentine jurist found when looking at the facts of a case: "if therefore it is not profectitia nor is it castrense or quasi, then it is adventitia."[39] Any property coming to a son from his mother, including his inheritance share of her dowry, was *adventitium*, as was anything coming to him from other relatives.

Allowance of *peculia* in the law provided a means of differentiating among children in terms of wealth, thus violating the ideal equality among a father's heirs. That differentiation could be taken further by emancipation, for from that point the emancipatus kept all that he gained, including ownership and active control of *peculia*; and he might additionally gain a gift (known as *praemium*) at the time of emancipation. The singular unity and solidity of a patrimony thus seemed, under closer examination, not to dissolve so much as to be rent by little fissures that might expand.

By and large those fissures were not given recognition in local law, at least in Florence. The expectation was that there was one account, one

---

[38] On the law, see Max Kaser, *Roman Private Law*, 63, 70, 259–60; Andrew Borkowski and Paul du Plessis, *Textbook on Roman Law*, 116–17.

[39] Bartolomeo Sozzini, 1 *cons.* 91, fols. 166vb–68va, at 168rb. This text is identified as belonging to Francesco Pepi (1451–1513) and signed by Alessandro Tartagni (1424–77) and others.

shared patrimony, deeply implicating fathers and sons in the way Bartolus saw. Examination of local statutes from three dozen Italian communities has turned up no real attention anywhere in Italy to *peculia*. Statutes envisioned the unitary patrimony and left its distinct *peculia* to the *ius commune*. And those distinctions certainly did not seem to matter in the central statutory concern about financial liabilities of fathers and sons. By statute in Florence, reaching back to the earliest redaction of 1325, and even well before (1252–86), fathers were declared liable for the debts and obligations of sons or grandsons *in potestate*, and sons and grandsons were equally responsible for their father's debts. That was the baseline. Florentines could operate in the city's markets, shops, and banks, in arenas where the sharing economy was not otherwise in evidence, and assume that their credits were secured against others' entire families and all their shared holdings (at least of males).[40] The markets relied on credit, which rested in turn on trust, and trust in turn resided first and foremost among kin, at the heart of whose *substantia* sat the father–son relationship.[41]

There were two means by which the extensive liability between fathers and sons might be abrogated. One worked only for the father. His liability for his sons rested on their acting publicly as merchants or artisans – on their being matriculated as active members of one of the city's guilds. In that case it was presumed the father was aware of and consented to their activities, which would still gain him title to and use of their incomes. It was allowed that a father not wanting to be bound for his son's business activities could go to the son's guild and formally declare that he refused, from that moment forward, to be held liable. The father–son relationship thus could be refashioned to fit the market economy. For any action, such as purchase or sale, which was not connected to business (that was part of the shared domestic economy, in other words), the son normally could not proceed without paternal consent, so the father's role there would be overt and occasional.[42] Something else needed to sever liability on such interpersonal transactions.

The other device, which severed liability in both directions between father and son, was emancipation. Once emancipated, the son was his own man – he owned and controlled his own property. The problem for everyone else (true also for the denunciation to a guild) was that the statutory presumption of shared liability between father and son still held in the minds of others. It became imperative that others have

---

[40] Goldthwaite, *The Economy of Renaissance Florence*, 67, 76–78, 438. The notion of a limited partnership did not arise in Florence until 1408, and it remained a little-used device in any case.

[41] Kuehn, "Debt and Bankruptcy."   [42] Kuehn, *Emancipation*, 42–45.

a means to be aware of liability-ending emancipations. Florence – and it was not alone or even the first here – hit on the device of registering these in a central, publicly available place, which was the Mercanzia from 1355 and from 1421 also with the Signoria, the central magistracy of the city.[43] Florentines were acutely aware of the potential for fraud striking the unwary, just as they were full of advice on being wary and not heedlessly extending trust, paradoxically but usefully being cautious, secretive, and sharp in one's dealings.[44]

The statutes themselves came off as especially harsh when a debtor had defaulted and as a bankrupt (*cessans*) had fled from the city and its effective jurisdiction, taking with him in effect the property of others (his creditors). Such a debtor was no better than a thief.[45] Then his son might be jailed and his property seized. These statutory provisions went well beyond what was allowable in Roman law. Jurists throughout Italy would find the terms of these statutes difficult to swallow, even as they conceded the deterrent value of their tough provisions. These rested, however, on the sense that a bankrupt was effectively a thief and subject to legal infamy (including a defamatory portrait on the wall of the Podestà's palace).[46]

Another statute that caused interpretive problems and is related to father–son property relations was the provision dealing with filial obligations on a paternal estate. When the father died and the son became true owner and not just a "sort of" owner, the son had to pay off all his father's debts, even if they exceeded the value of the estate. Sons could repudiate such an onerous estate, but in Florence by law they had only fifteen days to do so and could not be resident in or using the estate after that. But here too there were legal rights that a son might have on family property that did not come from his father. Most notably a son was also heir to his mother; and her dowry, secured against the family home or other asset, would give the son a right to stay there, though it was a *ius familiaritatis* and not a right of ownership, if the mother were still alive.[47] *Ius familiaritatis* served as a legal recognition of a right to share in the household, a right that demanded recognition by others while seemingly excluding any obligation to them. The Florentine jurist, Tommaso Salvetti (1390–1472), in an extensive commentary on Florence's statutes, added that

---

[43] Kuehn, *Emancipation*, 35–42.   [44] Kuehn, "Debt and Bankruptcy."

[45] Indeed, Alberti's chief interlocutor, Giannozzo, charterizes all debtors as potential thieves. Cf. McLean and Gondal, "The Circulation of Interpersonal Credit in Renaissance Florence," 135–36.

[46] Samuel Y. Edgerton, Jr., *Pictures and Punishment: Art and Criminal Prosecution during the Florentine Renaissance*; Gherardo Ortalli, *La pittura infamante, secoli xii–xvi*.

[47] On repudiation, see Kuehn, *Heirs, Kin, and Creditors*.

sons could also gain the property that came to a mother from her family (*adventitium* to the son).[48]

Florentines proved adept at getting around the statutes, and their success in turn fired off further revisions of the laws. The 1470s seem to have seen especially difficult challenges in this regard. On 20 March 1476 the priors addressed the "molte fraude" that they perceived in the city, due to the "occulti contracti" by which people concealed assets and successfully resisted claims and lawsuits, to the effect – it was said – that "girls quite often lose their dowries" (le fanciulle ne perdono molte volte le loro dote) and "many men withdraw from business" (molti si ritraggono dal trafficare). Instances of sharp practices and their attendant lawsuits are not hard to find, though it was probably an exaggeration (but a popular perception) to say that people were withdrawing from commerce.[49] The remedy, in any case, was an overly ambitious scheme to record in an alphabetical arrangement for public consultation all forms of contract, including arbitrations and wills, that alienated or obligated property.[50]

That measure was, in fact, only an opening salvo, as a week later the priors dealt with the property actions of fathers and sons:

it is doubted whether a son [under *potestas*] obligating himself with his father's consent in a matter or utility which is or can be said to be his father's can validly obligate himself. . . . Therefore it is provided that from henceforth sons of the age of twenty-five years can obligate themselves in the matter and utility of their father with paternal consent.[51]

This and the issue of the shady use of a wife's dowry by bankrupts and those who repudiated a bankrupt's estate (which would be *peculium adventitium* for sons) arose, according to the legislative preamble, in good part from the constantly varying and confusing sentences of doctors of law.[52] The legislation was keen on restating and reinforcing the presumptive sharing of a patrimony, including its liabilities, in the face of legal professionals' sense of individual rights and prerogatives.[53] It was

---

[48] BNF, Principale, II, iv, 434, fols. 69v–70r.

[49] For an example, see Kuehn, *Heirs, Kin, and Creditors*, 193–96.

[50] ASF, Provvisioni registri 168, fols. 4v–5v.

[51] ASF, Provvisioni registri 168, fols. 4v–5v: "dubitatur an filius familias se obligans cum consensu patris in rem sive utilitatem que sit aut dici possit esse patris valeat se iure obligare. . . . Propterea providetur quod deinceps filii familias etatis annorum vigintiquinque completorum possint in rem et utilitatem patris se obligare interveniente consensu patris."

[52] Provvisioni registri 168, fols. 12v–13v (29 March 1477).

[53] A powerful presentation regarding liabilities and avoiding them is William Ian Miller, *Bloodtaking and Peacemaking: Feud, Law, and Society in Saga Iceland*.

also intent on modifying the situation in *ius commune* by allowing ad hoc consensual obligation and liability.

The larger Consiglio del Cento subsequently took up a number of prudent revisions to statutes, concerned, among other things, with the rising expenses of litigation in the city. That body set penalties on those who took sureties from *filiifamilias* without paternal consent, and fined such sons 200 *lire*. If the surety was expressed in notarized form, then it could stand if the father came forth to express his consent.[54] The assumptions of familial economic solidarity could dupe even shrewd merchants in the face of legal avenues for avoidance.

3.2   Florentine Fathers and Their Property

For Florence there survives the unparalleled fiscal source, the catasto. Among other things, it allows us to see how households listed their belongings, at least for the benefit of civic officials. The catasto was based on the shared patrimonies of citizens as the meaningful units for fiscal purposes, which is testimony to the fundamental position of shared arrangements in Florence, for all that there were differences between the fiscal and physical household.[55] The listings of household property rarely designated a specific property in a son's name. This state of affairs relates to the fact that "neither in the city nor in the countryside did the father abandon his powers or pass on his authority to a son living at home."[56] As a fiscal register of domestic holdings the catasto was organized around the presumption of patrimonial unity. The father/head of household was presented as the owner of all that was listed. But at times the distinct property of sons or even daughters leaked through. Niccolò di messer Donato Barbadori in 1427, as one example, was a rich man who turned in a lengthy listing of properties, assets, debts, and credits, along with his married son, who lived with him with his wife and children, as well as the other sons. Included in all they had were some things ascribed to the older son, Lionardo. Not designated as separate was anything pledged for his daughter-in-law's dowry, let alone for any *peculia* of Niccolò's younger sons.[57] In a more distinct example, Niccolò da Uzzano, one of Florence's wealthiest and most politically active citizens, designated the separate house of his illegitimate son with his own wife and children. It still appeared under the father's account, not as a separate holding of the

---

[54] ASF, Consiglio del Cento 2, fol. 18r (23 July 1477).
[55] Cf. the classic analysis by David Herlihy and Christiane Klapisch-Zuber, *Tuscans and Their Families*, 11–13.
[56] Herlihy and Klapisch-Zuber, *Tuscans and Their Families*, 312.
[57] ASF, Catasto 65, fols. 475r–78r.

son, even though as an illegitimate he was not subject to his father's legal *potestas*.[58] He was also not his father's heir, so the catasto declaration specified what was his out of the patrimony, intended otherwise for Niccolò's brother.

Other situations reveal a mental, if not legal, accounting, such as would not have appeared in a source such as the catasto. Testaments, like that of Cristoforo d'Andrea Rapetti, might disclose that a son had acquired property on his own, though it had seemed to others that the father owned it. So Cristoforo indicated that his son and heir, Simone, purchased several goods from his own money, which he took to be his own, and on which Cristoforo had only usufruct.[59] Where Cristoforo had waited until his will to make sure his son got his due, Matteo di Francesco Lapucci of Ripoli delivered their due to his sons on emancipation, "considering how ... they had aided him in his needs and with money from their labor and sweat had acquired the most part of all the household furnishings and mobile goods."[60] The sons then turned around and gave it all to their mother, so in effect the husband had given property to his wife, which he otherwise could not legally do, by way of his newly emancipated sons, and perhaps saved all that for the household against creditors, though it was a deceptive step that was open to challenge.[61] Were that indeed the case, the separate ownership in law would have been used to the effect of continued integrity of household belongings in fact.

There were some parallels with the annotation in his records by Bartolomeo di Tommaso Sassetti to the effect that the man he rented land to had divided property among his four sons equally, but with an extra 50 florins for one son "because he had promised to pay their debts" (che avea promesso di pagare per loro debiti).[62] Here, it appears, was a father who wanted to direct division in detail. This instance varies in its way from that affected by Niccolò di Giovanni Giraldi from his father, which he worked out through Florence's legislative councils with the goal of resolving fiscal debts and finding his way into civic offices, for which he was otherwise qualified. Niccolò made clear that he did not want to be held liable for his father's fiscal obligations, lest he find himself listed in

---

[58] ASF, Catasto 64, fols. 65v–75v. He later gave his son that same house in testamentary inheritance (Notarile antecosimiano 9040 [1422–30], fols. 168r–71v, 172r–74r, and 174r–75r [22 December 1430, 3 March, 7 April]).

[59] ASF, Notarile Antecosimiano, 9041 (testamenti), fols. 21r–22r (3 May 1459).

[60] ASF, Notarile Antecosimiano 9041 (testamenti), fols. 21r–22r: "considerans qualiter ... eum in eius necessitatibus subvenerunt et cum eorum industria et sudore lucrati sunt pro maiori parte omnium masseritiarum et bonorum mobilium."

[61] ASF, NA 14722, fol. 151v (5 February 1488).

[62] ASF, Carte strozziane, 5th ser., 1750, fol. 198v.

the speculum (a list of those disqualified for civic offices for failure to meet fiscal obligations), "although he lives commonly with him and inhabits the house" (quamvis comuniter cum ipso convivat et cohabitet domi).[63] His petition met with a favorable response. This all belied what would have appeared to be patrimonial, financial, and fiscal unity in the household in the catasto of five years earlier.

The realities of household management in Florence show us the substance, such as it was, of the various *pecula* – of the sense that sons, even *in potestate*, had some substance of their own. A good example can be found in the fulsome *ricordanze* of Luca di Matteo da Panzano (ca. 1393–1461), who lived long enough to deal with grown-up sons across the process of their growth and education.[64]

Luca's oldest was Antonio, born in November 1426. In a testament drawn up when Antonio was six and his younger brother Niccolò was two (19 April 1432), Luca named the boys his universal heirs. Luca later presented these boys and their brother, Francesco, then barely four months old (born 26 September 1434), for matriculation in the arte of Por Santa Maria (he did the same in 1453 with the later-born Salvadore and Michele, ages eighteen and sixteen, respectively). Luca's second testament of 1449, when Antonio was twenty-four or so, named all five sons as universal heirs.[65] In all this Luca seems to have been an unexceptional manager of the family's holdings.

In 1454 Luca permitted his sons to claim each their one-fifth share in the dowry of their mother, who had passed away in 1445. In law these shares were *peculia adventitia*, though Luca did not employ that term. Also *adventitia* was property that came to his sons from a family friend. Back in 1449 Luca had witnessed the will of the widow of a good friend from San Gimignano, Bartolomea, which made his sons her heirs but left Luca with "administration" as long as he lived. The upshot of these infusions of resources was that in 1457 Michele, with Antonio and Salvadore, rented a small farm at Panzano.[66] The boys had resources and were of an age at which they could undertake some limited management. The next year Antonio was married at the insistence of Cosimo de' Medici. Luca duly recorded wedding expenses for his wife (mainly articles of clothing), but chiefly he assigned Antonio his *roba* and emancipated him.[67] The dowry was received in two installments, 800 and 200

---

[63] ASF, Provvisioni registri 176, fols. 47v–48r (17 June 1485).
[64] *"Brighe, affanni, volgimenti di stato": le ricordanze quattrocentesche di Luca di Matteo di messer Luca dei Firidolfi da Panzano.*
[65] *"Brighe, affanni, volgimenti di stato,"* 174, 281.
[66] *"Brighe, affanni, volgimenti di stato,"* 283–86, 375.
[67] *"Brighe, affanni, volgimenti di stato,"* 383–90.

florins. The eldest was now distinct, legal separate from his father, though still part of the household.

Luca and Antonio, moreover, had already divided their holdings, intending that there was no more that Antonio could seek from his father, his mother, or the generous Bartolomea. Division was worked out by means of an arbitration, and a list of what fell to Antonio was subsequently entered in his father's accounts, followed by a list of monte credits that served to capitalize his new wife's dowry, and finally a listing of the *alimenta* due the couple, in Florence or Panzano, for the next two years.[68] From that point Antonio did not exactly disappear from the pages of Luca's records, but his appearances were sporadic: an arbitration between him and his father-in-law about his wife's dowry; taxes on a mill; rental of the same small farm in Panzano; Antonio's gain of a small house (*casolare*) when Luca divided with his brother, Tommaso.[69]

Salvadore died only a month before Antonio's wedding. The next year Luca took his share of Salvadore's estate – a fifth, splitting with the other four sons. Salvadore's estate was in fact the fifth he had gained of Bartolomea's property, as nothing more is mentioned. Luca and the other four sons in 1460 sold a house and a *casolare* in San Niccolò; at least the sons were surety (*sodare*).[70] Standing surety gave reality to the shared patrimony. For Francesco there were also entries for the purchase of cloth, for wages, for a bit of land on which a cousin who gave it to them kept usufruct, for other rentals, and for Francesco's role in buying a house with his sister's dowry.[71]

Luca's son Niccolò had a more adventurous existence, at least in that it is indicated that he traveled, for which a secure piece of luggage was purchased. Luca involved Niccolò and Antonio in an arbitration regarding rent of a farm from a Peruzzi widow and her son for five years, and a similar transaction with another widow two years later. And Niccolò and Francesco were involved in a five-year rental of a farm from a nun. Purchase of some lands near Radda was ascribed to Antonio and Niccolò, and record of a payment of a small sum by Niccolò was recorded.[72] The main difference regarding Niccolò is that his father felt compelled to copy an entry from the *ricordi* of Niccolò di Schiatta Ridolfi, a business partner. This entry relayed that Luca's Niccolò had been lifting

---

[68] Luca's *catasto* report of 1458 (397–403) was completed earlier in the year and does not reflect the results of Antonio's marriage and emancipation.
[69] *"Brighe, affanni, volgimenti di stato,"* 416, 422, 428, 444, 432.
[70] *"Brighe, affanni, volgimenti di stato,"* 434.
[71] *"Brighe, affanni, volgimenti di stato,"* 443, 322, 328, 324, 379, 418, 425.
[72] *"Brighe, affanni, volgimenti di stato,"* 250, 291, 319, 373, 327, 329.

amounts of cash from Ridolfi's locked chest, to which he had a key. Luca, of course, had to make good these bits of theft.[73]

Peeking through Luca's pages then, from time to time, were dealings with his sons. The boys emerge largely as passive figures, if only because they did not get to write the accounts. Antonio, the eldest, received different treatment, though maybe not any more of the patrimony. He was married, and his marriage occasioned his emancipation and division of property. Luca, unlike many other Florentines, appears to have decided to let his son handle his dowry and its attendant headaches himself.[74] Antonio took his share as separate, but his father and brothers continued to share, and to act together, though in differing combinations at times.

The *ricordanze* of the tradesman Bartolomeo di Bernardo Masi some decades later give us two different perspectives. For one thing, here we have records kept by a son while his father was still alive. For another, this was a man who was not possessed of near the wealth da Panzano had. Masi recorded some incidents from his father's life and thus generated some continuity to his own life. An early entry concerned guild matriculation at age seven.[75] At age ten Bartolomeo was taken from abacus school and began his career in the family shop, and the following year he began to keep an account book "in which I made record of all the money that was gained or spent in the shop's accounts."[76] It was thus a commercial, not patrimonial, set of accounts; but as such it kept track of what Bartolomeo could claim to own or have earned, separate from his father.

Bartolomeo reported his mother's death (at age fifteen for him) and his father's remarriage barely two months later, along with details of the second wife's dowry of 300 florins, of which 250 florins were in monte shares and the rest in cash and trousseau. We also learn of his emancipation, with his brother, at age thirty-five, "so that we could obligate ourselves and have credit, to be able to make some profit or utility, to gain on our own account and not have to participate with others, as much for profit as of loss, that we might make."[77] There was also a carefully equal division of a room in the house and furnishings for each son (said to be worth 25 florins each). The following day, father, newly emancipated sons, and the shop's two *garzoni* evaluated all stock and

---

[73] *"Brighe, affanni, volgimenti di stato,"* 238–39.   [74] Kuehn, *Emancipation*, 110–11.

[75] *Ricordanze di Bartolomeo Masi calderaio fiorentino dal 1478 al 1526*, 12.

[76] Masi, *Ricordanze*, 15.

[77] Masi, *Ricordanze*: "a causa che noi ci potessimo ubrigare et avere credito, per potere fare qualche profitto o utile di guadagniare per nostro conto proprio e non l'avere a participare con altri, così d'utile come di danno che noi faciessimo" (148–49).

implements therein, agreeing on a final balance of almost 4000 *lire*.[78] The next day Bartolomeo and his father hammered out a partnership agreement. The father posted one debt of 179 florins to the shop, but all other credits and debits were his own ("per se proprio"). Because the father owned everything they had appraised the previous day, he was to receive two-thirds of the profits (or loss), as long as he continued to meet his sons' living expenses. The sons split the rest, otherwise contributing their labor to the enterprise. Each month the father could extract eight florins from the shop, the sons one and a half florins each. As we will see in Chapter 4, this did not amount to the legal status of a *societas omnium bonorum* because of the careful accounting of each member's portion, which fell short of the extreme sharing of the *omnium bonorum*. Still, it shows a considerable degree of sharing, a commingling of their acts and efforts. But these arrangements with the eldest sons also clearly excluded all the other children Bernardo had. Not everyone in the house was directly involved in the family business.

Bartolomeo and his brother were clearly junior partners, even though Bartolomeo had already been active in the Arte de' chiavaiuoli and just the next month began a four-month term as a consul of the guild.[79] But the firm did well. A rendering of accounts after a year showed they had gained 190 florins, which was split up as they had agreed.[80]

Bernardo died in 1526, having thirteen surviving children by his two wives. None of the eight sons was married. Three months later all the sons submitted to an arbitration propelled by the three older boys. The arbitrators were given a month to hit on the eventual division of the household items (*masserizie*) into two lots, one for the sons of each wife. A few more of the items were allocated to the younger set of brothers, so they were held to be in debt to the older brothers for the difference (61 *lire*).[81] Again, what sharing there was among offspring of different mothers was not deep and ended almost immediately on the father's death.

As none of the Masi boys married, there were no dowries and other uxorial properties to keep separate, which would have complicated all their neat arrangements. There is no mention even of returning the maternal dowries or of accounting for them against the value of the household furnishings. The 50 florins given Bartolomeo and his brother Piero at their emancipation (the two furnished rooms) did not account for their mother's 200-florin dowry, although six months after contracting and consummating the marriage Bernardo was able to rent his first shop

---

[78] For insight into the process by which individuals and/or their chosen arbitrators could arrive at monetized estimates, see Giovanni Ceccarelli, "Stime senza probabilità: assicurazione e rischio nella Firenze rinascimentale."
[79] Masi, *Ricordanze*, 152.   [80] Masi, *Ricordanze*, 200.   [81] Masi, *Ricordanze*, 287–88.

and open the business his sons would later join. One suspects the 15-florin rent was at least initially paid from the dowry. Still, simply put, there is no tracking of dowry and securing it in real estate or government securities, as da Panzano did. With the Masi, however, we see the end of sharing. They did not take from and contribute to a common pot. Instead there was careful accounting so that each received his *proprio*. True, the boys had taken precisely equilibrated shares, but they had been taken and were no longer *comune*.

Lastly, it is worth noting that both the Masi and da Panzano accounts, especially in the treatment of emancipated sons in their cases, bear out the conclusion reached by David Herlihy and Christiane Klapisch-Zuber that with mature sons fathers became creditors to the sons and family capital began to bankroll the actions and careers of the young.[82]

A final, different set of accounts comes from the Ciurianni family, mainly from an earlier period. Here several generations kept the same accounts, so it is possible to a degree to trace the passage of patrimony.[83] There were considerable paternal debts that became an issue. The *ricordi* themselves began with an entry in the name of father (Lapo) and son (Valorino) regarding a partnership of 1326 with four others, including another son. Valorino soon took over and continued his father's book. In 1329 Valorino emancipated his two sons and gave them a piece of land, later having them renounce the *retaggio* of his father.[84] When his wife died, Barna Ciurianni, a later heir to the patrimony, wrote that "she left her sons in words and by reason heirs of her dowry and all her goods" (sua dota e d'angni suoi beni).[85] As usual, the dowry sum and its formal reception had already been carefully set forth. Barna also kept account of lands purchased in his mother's name, presumably from the dowry.[86] He did the same as he began buying other pieces in the name of his son Valorino through the good offices of the Frescobaldi, kin to his second wife.[87] This wife, despite her twelve-year-old son, left the house and took her dowry (which had been converted into a farm in Valdelsa) with her, ignoring Barna's will directing her to stay and raise Borgognone.[88] Later concerns about the value of the farm and especially its livestock were amicably put to an arbitrator.[89]

---

[82] Herlihy and Klapisch-Zuber, *Tuscans and Their Families*, 304.
[83] *Ricostruzione di una famiglia: i Ciurianni di Firenze tra xii e xv secolo, con l'edizione critica del "Libro proprio" di Lapo di Valore Ciurianni e successori (1326–1429)*.
[84] *Ricostruzione*, 109. [85] *Ricostruzione*, 116. [86] *Ricostruzione*, 128, 131.
[87] *Ricostruzione*, 135–37. [88] *Ricostruzione*, 146.
[89] *Ricostruzione*, 152. On the arbitrators in such situations, see Miller, *An Eye for an Eye*, 180.

One project Valorino di Barna pursued was to reacquire a fractional ownership in the Torre di Lione, which had been in the family until a division of holdings back in 1339. Having bought back portions, in 1399 he emancipated his three sons and gave them each one-eighteenth of the tower (reserving another eighteenth to the youngest son who had not been emancipated).[90] They were ordered not to sell or alienate, except to one of the others. By any legal reckoning, these shares were *peculium profectitium*, but the term appears nowhere. There consequently seems no need or interest to be legally precise about the ownership of such property (prior to the father's death).

In 1409, his sons now grown, Valorino had to engage in legal adjustments with them. First, with Lapozzo, acting as agent for Barna (both emancipated years before), son and father entered an arbitration. There was a real conflict between them, and Valorino had worries about the patrimony in consequence. After a few days the arbitrator ruled that Barna could not demand his share or take his mother's dowry, and even what he had been given at his emancipation had to be returned to his father.[91] The next day the youngest, Bernardo, then twenty-two, departed for Ferrara to work with a relative (affinal), with the blessing of both parents – quite the opposite of Barna being ordered to return home and to the true status of son. But Barna would always be a disappointment to Valorino, as he made clear in recording Barna's death in 1418 in Pisa: "From him there remain neither goods nor family but debts. ... God grant him peace and give me more consolation from the others, as from him I never had other than loss and trouble."[92] Here the statutory liability of fathers for sons took on a reality, though by emancipation Valorino had no obligation to Barna's creditors. The arbitration returned any property he could claim to his father, and thus, it was hoped, he was immune to his creditors. The Ciurianni were not a wealthy or successful lineage in the end. Nurturing their *substantia* across the generations did not work out.

The disparate *ricordanze* show us no examples of military or civic income, *castrense* or *quasi*. The main sources of separate property were either inheritance from someone (friends, relatives, mothers) or earnings of and by their effort in business. At times, a dowry might come in, even as dowries for daughters or sisters might leave. But there were doubts about these earnings, insofar as they were enabled by paternal money. These doubts and others landed at the feet of doctors of law; otherwise

---

[90] *Ricostruzione*, 164.   [91] *Ricostruzione*, 181.

[92] *Ricostruzione*, 187: "Di lui non rimase né avere né persona ma debiti. ... Dio gli facca pace e a me dia più consolazioni degli altri, che di lui non ebbi mai altro che danno e brigha."

arbitrators stepped in to award precise amounts or titles. The legists had to confront the actions, documents, and statutory language with the terms they had acquired in their professional training. Those terms encompassed both the substantial unity of father and son and the individuality of rights and intents.

3.3 Cases

Basic distinctions between fathers and sons with regard to property were not simple. In that regard it is interesting that relatively early on Francesco di Baldo degli Ubaldi (d. 1426) crafted a hypothetical case so that his resulting consilium could clarify some of the issues of property between fathers and sons.[93] If a man had two sons and one of them, Martino, were to leave home "discurrendo per mundum," realizing some gain both from money he had invested and from the fruits of his own labor ("ex stipendio et ex sua industria"), and then return to his native city but live apart from his parents, what could his brother, Giovanni, who had stayed at home, expect from him regarding his portion of the inheritance from their father? If the property Martino held was classifiable as *profectitium*, coming from the father, the other son might claim an equal share. But was it *profectitium*?

If a son realized gain from paternal funds with no particular labor on his part (presumably by being handed something like rental property), then there was no doubt that the gain was *profectitium* and was to be shared with one's brother in the division of the estate. The problem was if gain resulted from a combination of paternal capital and filial effort. There were jurists, such as Jacopo de Belviso (1270–1335) and Guglielmo Durante (d. 1295), who said this too was *profectitium*; but Bartolus had demurred, declaring "that all gain coming from the person of the son is adventitium."[94] So Francesco Ubaldi's answer was that gain attributable to paternal funds was to be shared with one's brother, but one kept what was attributable to his efforts. But that easy resolution did not work because the case before the jurist, he said, was yet a third type. Rather than a combination of paternal capital and filial labor, all gain was the result of the "opera" and "arte" of Martino. In case of doubt on this, the jurist offered a distinction – if the son was known as "industriosus et artifex," gain came from his work. If he had no such commercial reputation from the economy of the market, then presumably any gains came

---

[93] Baldo degli Ubaldi, *Consilia*, 5 *cons.* 259, fols. 64vb–65ra. It is signed Francesco.

[94] Ubaldi, *Consilia*, "Item certum est quod omne lucrum proveniens ex persona filii est adventitium."

from paternal reputation. Martino had gone off on his own to distant lands, so he fit the profile of the industrious merchant. Indeed, letting a son keep what came from his effort was widely accepted in and beyond the law. Florentines, like Luca da Panzano, kept some account of such things and attempted to strike a balance, when emancipating, a son, for example.[95] Rare provision of separate fiscal accounts for sons in the catasto demonstrates some separation and room for maneuver by sons.[96]

In contrast to that situation, in a consilium of Baldo, it was apparent that anything given by a father to a son *in potestate* was considered *profectitium* and thus to be shared with all heirs. If the son were emancipated, then property was treated as a gift to him (no longer a shared portion of the patrimony but having to be calculated into the entire patrimony if the emancipated son wanted his share along with his brothers). Equally, if a father supported the living expenses of a married son, it was considered that the father enjoyed the *fructus* of the son's wife's dowry. The father would have to renounce his right of use for the revenue to be treated as *adventitium* of a son *in potestate*.[97] There was no question of possible contribution coming from a son's *industria* on his wife's dowry.

Another seeming elementary issue for the law was the status of property that a father purchased for himself and his sons. Angelo degli Ubaldi (1325–1400) had a case where that had been done, with an express declaration in the deed of purchase that the sons' money gained from maritime trade had been used to buy the house in which they all lived "promiscue." Was this then *adventitium*? Angelo in fact faced the assertion that the purchase was fraudulent, attributing ownership to a son to keep the property from being claimed by the father's creditors. He determined that the notarial document's testimony that it had been the son's money, on its own, was not enough. In fact, in this case there was even a question about the validity of the notarial instrument. The presumption against gifts and deals between fathers and sons was a powerful one.[98] Potential for fraud lurked just below the surface, in many cases because of the indistinct nature of the shared patrimony. These consilia from the late fourteenth century show us jurists struggling with the means to distinguish son's property from paternal.

In another consilium Angelo degli Ubaldi encountered the fact that a father, with several sons "diligent and skilled at trade and negotiation" (ad mercaturam et ad negotiationes diligentes et aptos), had given them

[95] Kuehn, *Emancipation*, 32, 102–3, 106, 112.

[96] Kent, 71–72; Hanlon, *Human Nature*, 125–26; Herlihy and Klapisch-Zuber, *Tuscans and Their Families*, 312.

[97] Baldo, 3 *cons.* 394, fols. 111vb–12ra.

[98] Angelo degli Ubaldi, *Consilia, cons.* 341, fols. 241vb–42rb.

money to begin their careers. What they gained over the years was attributed to their father, following whose death they continued to transact
business while living with their other brother – not a merchant, but
a minor. There was thus a shared patrimony and largely shared business
enterprises. Finally arriving at the point of dividing their holdings, the
younger brother demanded a full share. Angelo found three forms of
assets to be determined: the profits made with paternal money, profits
attributable to the sons' own efforts, and the gains realized in common
after their father's death. Angelo noted that the profits could be said to
reside with the brothers who had run the risks and did the work, citing (1)
St. Paul (that sons should not be the ones to enrich their parents); (2) civil
law "by which it is provided that profits coming to the sons by good
fortune or their industry is adventitia for the sons, while the father lives,
as far as ownership"; and (3) equity (because the sons had experienced
"misfortunes and storms both maritime and terrestrial, perhaps they
feared also an incursion of thieves or pirates and perhaps many dangers
of death"). But Angelo turned around and said that the sons had in fact
simply been their father's agents, acting with his money and his approval,
so that all profit and loss lodged with the father, to whom they had
consistently credited their gains. By his exercise of his *patria potestas* the
father could expect his sons to work for him, and they could expect to be
fed and supported.[99] A father exercising his *potestas* could force his sons to
live with him, "unless they resist the father's will because of his vicious-
ness or because his well meant marriage perhaps would be disturbing
their habitation."[100] What they had gained with paternal money clearly
fell into the category of *profectitia*, to which the father had full title and to
which the younger brother had a claim. What they had gained by their
labor fell into the category of *adventitia*, and that belonged to the sons and
was not to be shared with the other son. But the father enjoyed use of
adventitia and all subsequent profits and that was to be divided. How
much was *profectitium* and how much *adventitium* was to be determined by
the *consuetudo regionis*. Leaving it to custom (presumably in the person of
an arbitrator) allowed Angelo to duck the difficult decision as to how
much was due to the older brothers. As to the third form of property, what
the older sons had earned in their enterprise after their father's death was
clearly their own. The younger son not in business with the others was
assumed not to share in their profits and losses. Nothing was said about

---

[99] Ubaldi, *Consilia*, *cons*. 85, fols. 55ra–vb, at 55va.
[100] Ubaldi, *Consilia*, *cons*. 85, fols. 55ra–vb, at 55va: "nisi patris voluntati resistant propter
eius faevitiam vel quia matrimonium suum bene concordatum ex tali habitatione forsan
turbaretur."

him not sharing, if only as a minor, in other patrimonial resources not implicated in the business activities of his older brothers.

Resolving claims between brothers when complicated by business associations with their father became a consistent problem. Part of that was involved in the father's potential liability for his sons. In the consilia of the Sienese jurist Mariano Sozzini senior (1397–1467), there is a Florentine case to which in fact four jurists subscribed.[101] The first, Francesco Accolti of Arezzo (ca. 1418–85/6), inspected statutory wording obligating a father for a son active in business (an implied consent), but held it did not hold for contracts made outside the jurisdiction of Florence. Among other things, to avoid liability the father could renounce such debts through formal means of sending a herald to appropriate points in town, which showed the law did not contemplate obligations contracted elsewhere, out of reach of such heralds. Mainly, although the law made sense with regard to public utility, it was "unreasonable, contrary to the weight of law and natural equity" (irrationabile, gravi iuri et aequitati naturali contrarium). Sozzini was only willing to take sharing so far.

Sozzini himself made clear that simply holding the father liable for not stopping his son's business dealings, as opposed to consenting expressly to them, was unfair. So at the least this father should not be held liable for debts contracted outside Florentine territory. Two others, Tommaso Docci and Gregorio Lolli, also chimed in with their concern about the irrational unfairness of the statute.[102] They were in line with so many others who argued to restrict statutes whose sense of shared liabilities was quite extensive.[103] So we have seen jurists quick to consider sons' properties to be their fathers' for purposes of dividing an inheritance among sons, but equally quick to consider fathers' property separate from sons' when it was a question of meeting liabilities to outsiders.

The "turbata possessio" of a house from the town of Montalcino, subject to Siena, concerned two brothers. At the heart of this case was Donato's attempt to forbid Antonio and his wife from inhabiting the house in question. Donato claimed it was his alone. But an instrument of division among his sons by Donato's father did not establish a clear right of possession, as it was *profectitium* and done before the father's death. Then it might be seen as a gift, and gifts to sons *in potestate* were not valid. A deed of purchase showing father and son both contributing to the price also did not establish the son's right, as by rule "whatever a son sought he sought for his father" (quidquid quaerit filius quaerit patri).

---

[101] On him, see Paolo Nardi, *Mariano Sozzini: giureconsulto senese del Quattrocento*.
[102] Sozzini, 5 *cons.* 87, fols. 106va–8va.   [103] Kuehn, *Emancipation*, 146–52.

Part, at least, was still the father's and thus in his estate, so Antonio had a right to inhabit there. The brothers were going to have to live there together, or not, and divide up things in any case.[104]

Pierfilippo da Corgna (1420–92) was another jurist who lived and worked in Tuscany and dealt with Florentine cases from time to time. In one instance, in which a Lorenzo had bought a fourth of a farm in his own name, but with money from his father, it seemed there was little question that this was *profectitium* and therefore to be shared by Lorenzo with his brother Bernardino as part of the paternal estate. This Lorenzo was in fact a *iuris doctor* and so could not have been ignorant of the law. His continued possession of that property apart from his brother had to be considered an act in bad faith (*mala fides*). Corgna, however, defended his colleague's title, first as a gift from his father, of which there had been a true *traditio* of the farm, and as "the son possessed it up to the father's death, and the father knowing and suffering it to be so, it is presumed that the father had a desire to give it."[105] Such a gift was confirmed by the father's death, as it otherwise was precluded as a gift from father to son. Bernardino's argument that, if not the farm itself, then the sum of 375 *lire* loaned to Lorenzo for its purchase should be shared with him was also brushed aside – again as a paternal gift that, even if repayment were expected, did not give rise to an action for Bernardino, as there was no civil obligation between father and son on *profectitia*.[106] This son, a jurist, knew full well that division of patrimony need not be equal. Lorenzo and Bernardino, by the factual terms recoverable from the case, seem not to have been in much of a sharing arrangement even when their father was alive.

Antonio Strozzi (1455–1523) was Florentine and so was the case that raised the problem that Francesco had served as a male guardian, *mundualdus*, when his wife gave some property to his sons. As that property then became *adventitium* in title to his sons, it could be argued he had consented to an act in his own interest, as he acquired usufruct by that, and so the donation should be invalidated. Strozzi's opinion had to begin with discussion of the purpose of a *mundualdus* as male guardian of a woman in Florence.[107] Because any male could be *mundualdus*, that showed that the purpose was not to allay any ill effects of a woman's legal acts for the man. Otherwise the guardian would have been restricted to husband or kin or other interested party. Instead, the guardian was to

---

[104] Sozzini, 5 *cons.* 87, fols. 5vb–7rb.

[105] Sozzini, 5 *cons.* 87, fols. 5vb–7rb: "et filius possedit usque ad mortem patris sciente et patiente patre presumitur quod pater habuerit animum donandi."

[106] Pierfilippo da Corgna, *Consilia*, 1 *cons.* 235, fol. 178ra–va.

[107] On this, see Kuehn, *Law, Family, and Women*, 212–37.

make up for the supposed "imbecillitas intellectus" of the woman, to alert her to the utility of the contract she would execute. The *mundualdus* served to fill out the insufficient legal weight of the woman ("ad integrandam personam mulieris"). So the guardian in effect provided more than consent to that act; he provided *auctoritas*, *solemnitas*, and *forma*. It was licit for any guardian, including a *tutor* of minors, to consent to an act that benefited him, if that benefit were merely a secondary effect. In the case at hand the acquisition of usufruct by the father could be termed an indirect result of the acquisition of title for the sons, as would also be the case if a father as *tutor* approved of his sons' acceptance of an inheritance. So the donation stood, and might have even without a *mundualdus*, as, following Francesco Accolti, his teacher, Strozzi added that a woman might be deceived and weak but would be perfectly aware of the costs and consequences of giving something away, "cum mulierum genus sit avarissimum."[108] Francesco had taken advantage of the law's distinction between father and sons, and the wife, to fashion a more solid patrimonial basis for his family by embedding ownership (not use) of his wife's dowry with their sons.

The son of Mariano Sozzini, Bartolomeo (1436–1506), teacher and frequent co-consultor with Antonio Strozzi, came to be involved in several interesting bits of litigation. Among his published consilia are some that belonged to the Florentine jurist Francesco Pepi (1451–1513).[109] This case again threw into relief how jurists could generate conclusions that fostered a sharing of resources. A man named Jacopo had realized an inheritance that passed to him by fideicommissum when his father, Galgano, had refused it. By the terms of the trust, it went next to Jacopo. As his father thus had never held title to the property, it could be argued that with regard to Jacopo it was then not *profectitium* but *adventitium* (because "non videantur profecta ex substantia patris"). That being the case, Jacopo could argue that he did not have to share it with his brothers when it came time to split Galgano's estate. Sozzini argued otherwise. One line of attack was that Jacopo, by terms of the fideicommissum, freed his father from obligations he had on the estate to the testator (Cristoforo) who had made him heir, and Jacopo after him. Secondly, Galgano had directed the inheritance to Jacopo in his renunciation and in that way had seemingly donated to him.[110] Sozzini was not going to flinch at the technicalities but saw that the property came to Jacopo from his father.

[108] ASF, Carte strozziane, 3rd series, 41/14, fols. 337r–39r.
[109] Sozzini, 1 *cons.* 91, fols. 166vb–68va.   [110] Sozzini, 1 *cons.* 91, fol. 167va.

When two Florentines stood surety for their father, Bartolomeo Sozzini was forced to consider the effects of Florence's statutes. He poked into Florentine legislation and cases, noting a law of 1471, which addressed the involvement of sons in *potestate* "making dishonest contracts, by which sons are induced to pursue games and other dishonest activities," and that thus "declared the intention of the statute was that it be provided for the weakness and protection of sons."[111] So the law was protective of sons, not of paternal interests. Even though the statute enjoined fathers to cover sons' debts, and thus seemed to give fathers a reason to protect themselves, Sozzini said the statute sought to protect against frauds perpetrated on unwitting sons. That stretch of logic was followed by another, when Sozzini noted that it could be argued that "the statute simply speaks of sons and so in whatever age, so that the statute could not have respect for the weakness of intellect of a fifty year old, who can be in *potestate*, so it seems to require consent of the father with respect to the prejudice that could result for him."[112] He brushed this away as conjecture, as many *filiifamilias* were *iuvenes* and entered into bad contracts. And beyond age "sons who do not have administration of goods are easily led to this rather than fathers who have administration." The fact that the statute nullified acts done without paternal consent meant it took consent as a formal requirement and not a mere protection for the father. The intent of the father in this case could be alleged to be fraudulent, moreover, as he had let his sons assert emancipation. Finally, Sozzini alleged weight of opinion among local jurists. He declared that a host of Florentine doctors of law (Salustio Buonguglielmi [1373–1461], Benedetto Barzi [1379–1459], Orlando Bonarli [1399–1461], Otto Niccolini [1410–70], Giovanni Buongirolami da Gubbio [1381–1454], and Benedetto Accolti [1415–64]) had all said the statute voided filial contracts.

The accumulation of case experiences across the fifteenth century serves to give clearer determination to ownership between father and son. When Sozzini looked into whether a son's acquisitions were his own or his father's, he dubbed the matter "trite." If the son operated without any *substantia patris*, there was no acquisition for the father (except usufruct). If the son administered property but lived with his father, then the way was open to conjecture, seeing how industrious the son was or how relatively

---

[111] Sozzini, 4 *cons.* 23, fols. 26va–28va: "quibus filiifamilias inducebantur ut ludis et aliis inhonestatibus intenderent, habemus ergo statuentes declarantes intentionem dicti statuti quod fuit ut provideretur fragiliati et indemnitati filiorumfamilias."

[112] Sozzini, 4 *cons.* 23, fols. 26va–28va: "statutum simpliciter loquitur de filiisfamilias et sic in quacunque etate constitutis, non ergo potuit statutum habere respectum ad fragilitatem intellectus in homine quinquagenario, qui potest esse filiusfamilias, ergo videtur requirere consensum patris respectu praeiudicii quod posset sibi inferri."

wealthy or poor the father was. If the father's money was involved it was his, except for allowance for the son's labor, that was up to judicial discretion. Whatever might exceed common estimation of the worth of a son's *labor et industria*, as by *prospera fortuna* (the unpredictable gyrations of market prices) fell to the father. For the case in hand, the lands the son, Cristoforo, had acquired in transactions with Tommaso belonged to the father, messer Gasparre, even though the notarial bill of sale attributed it to Cristoforo by using his money. The assertions rested on additions to the notarial protocol but were not in the notary's hand.[113]

In another case Sozzini found a need to distinguish three periods in the business and family life of a man named Girolamo: first, from the day he left for London to work with the Salviati; second, after he left the Salviati and began to trade in his own name up to his father's death; third, up to the point the legal questions arose.[114] His father had arranged his sojourn with the Salviati and furnished Girolamo with a total of 320 florins. The profits gained in that period were *profectitium* and belonged to the father, but were also generated by the son's *industria*, so it was left to the *arbitrium iudicis* to determine how much weight to give the two factors, paternal money and son's labor. There were, in addition, two circumstances Sozzini believed the judge should consider. The first was that if the son gained more than seemed reasonably possible, by the combination of money and labor, then that seemed due to great good fortune. Should the father get that or the son?[115] Baldo had maintained that such gains were to be shared fifty-fifty, but Bartolus had said, after a proper estimate of the son's contribution, the rest should go to his father. Bartolus's position seemed to be authoritative in terms of the number of others who supported it. Angelo degli Ubaldi had said that when "in doubt the son's gains are presumed to derive from the paternal substance unless the proportional input of industry of the son leads to and persuades otherwise."[116] Bartolomeo da Saliceto (d. 1412) had pointed to the problem of envy between brothers if one gained from his industry, so he entrusted the judge to keep down any *occasio malignandi*. Angelo, again, had pointed to possible problems among brothers in attributing to the father all gains, as all was done with the father's money and with his direction and permission. Sons "from the reverence owed their father were constrained to obey licit and honest orders of their father."[117]

---

[113] Sozzini, 2 *cons.* 192, fols. 50va–52rb.   [114] Sozzini, 2 *cons.* 162, fols. 19va–21rb.

[115] Sozzini, 2 *cons.* 162, fol. 19vb.

[116] Sozzini, 2 *cons.* 162, fol. 19vb: "in dubio lucrum filii praesumitur procedere a paterna substantia, nisi ratio industriae filii aliud inducat et persuadeat."

[117] Sozzini, 2 *cons.* 162, fol. 20ra.

Sozzini concluded that the father had it all, but also that he had no problem if arbitrators engineered a settlement.

As for the second period, after leaving the Salviati, with Girolamo operating ostensibly in his own name, Sozzini produced arguments to the effect that really nothing was changed. The son was still using his father's money and conducting business with his knowledge and approval. There were letters between father and son demonstrating their continual interaction.[118] As Girolamo had no known partners, his assertion that he negotiated for partners must have been meant to include his father. In 1471 Girolamo had sent for his brother, Bartolomeo, to join him in London, which added up to a tacit business partnership (*societas*) between the brothers. Then in 1475 Girolamo returned to Florence and lived with his father and brothers and took part in their business affairs. Even after Girolamo had been emancipated, there was still the common enterprise and reliance on paternal funds – a true sharing. That continued among the brothers after their father's death (the "partners" referred to in Girolamo's ledgers had to be his brothers). They continued in that manner at least into 1480. Girolamo labored in his brothers' names and they did in his. It was only right, as a consilium of Pietro d'Ancarano (ca. 1330–1416) had argued, that a brother using family funds share his gains with his brothers.

Girolamo had written letters detailing his view of division of property (for that was clearly the occasion for the legal discussion). He had not wanted a division of fiscal obligations (*gravedines*), which showed that they had been considered common. He had also claimed to have reported all gains; he had called transactions in London *res nostras*. Letters and common account books presented an image of partnership and shared substance. Sozzini could only conclude that Girolamo's London profits were to be shared with his brothers, and that arbitrators affecting the division of assets should take that into account and could demand to see the account books to do so.

A place to draw things to a close is a consilium of Francesco Guicciardini rendered for a judge but with, as he noted, a vague set of facts and a poorly posed question, forcing him to a more hypothetical and general response. The case involved a Florentine *fiiusfamilias*, Raffaele di Jacopo da Prato, who was nonetheless an adult who was tried for homicide and had his property confiscated.[119] But was the property truly his or

---

[118] Sozzini, 2 *cons*. 162, fol. 20rb: "verisimiliter pater habuit literas a filio de his que a filio gerebantur, iuxta consuetudinem mercatorum, maxime cum esset filius et haberet pecuniam paternam in manibus, et ex voluntate paterna negociaretur, in quibus non arbitror."

[119] The case is nicely discussed in Julius Kirshner, "Custom, Customary Law and *Ius Commune* in Francesco Guicciardini," 156–63; and in Cavallar and Kirshner, *Jurists and Jurisprudence*, 608–12, where the text is translated.

did it belong to his father on account of his *potestas*? Guicciardini rehashed the distinction between *profectitia* and *adventitia*, for it was the latter that were liable for confiscation. If the son gained by his own industry and labor, and he did not merely act as his father's agent and subordinate, then at least a portion of any profits were his and thus open to confiscation. Guicciardini found no evidence that any capital transacted by Raffaele was his; it all seemed to be his father's. So even though Raffaele had conducted business in his own name, and profitably, Guicciardini held that all profits were the father's. It relied on his sense that it was a known custom for Florentines to put things in their sons' names to help build their reputation and honor, but they truly intended to remain owner of it all – an interesting revelation that has to remind us to be wary of assertions of ownership in notarial records. The son's reputation derived from his father, but otherwise fathers were notoriously loath to free their sons from *potestas*, barring some economic or legal need. Still, custom only proffered a supposition, not proof. Guicciardini urged the judge to examine the father's and son's records and use his discretion (a prominent term in Guicciardini's thought) to determine who owned what or how much. Guicciardini knew these issues firsthand from his own family experience and looked to a set of pragmatic solutions. But clearly there could be a distinction between property of the father and that of his son, even one in *potestas*.

3.4   Conclusion

The passage of property across the generations, a primary goal of the provident householder, was always fraught with difficulties. Crippling losses could come at any moment – in daily market transactions, periodic disasters, or the moment of death. Advice books and careful keeping of accounts were intended to cope with the dangers, as best they might. The property relations in life between fathers and sons were themselves too moments of danger or mechanisms for coping. So it was that in his brief dialogue on the *padre di famiglia*, published in 1580, Torquato Tasso utilized the figure of a *buon padre di famiglia*, who purported to pass along the advice his father had given him. He told his young listener how to treat wife, children, and servants, but he was especially admonished to work with his wife, who was well placed to aid with the conservation of family wealth, as parsimony was a particular female virtue that helped keep order with things like foodstuffs and family linens (and nonetheless sounded like a nicer way to say that women were the greedy gender). Without conservation it was impossible to gain more, and seeking gain too avidly – acting like a greedy merchant rather than like a father who sees an end to mere accumulation, being away from home too long and too far – was a danger.[120] Preservation to pass on to inheritance was preferable. There is a bit more of a nod to shared management of patrimony with Tasso in comparison to Alberti.

The law gave them instruments and strategies, though, as we have seen, courts and doctors of law were capable of upholding rules as they understood them. These issues were not peculiar to the fourteenth and fifteenth centuries. We still see them later, as in a case before Marcantonio Pellegrini (1530–1616). Vincenzo wanted to have overturned an alienation by his father, Matteo, of maternal goods, on which Matteo had usufruct. Pellegrini denied the son any action for recovery. One reason he gave was calculated to worry a son who had doubts about his father's management:

for in adventitia alienation is permitted a father without a court decree because law has great confidence in the administration of the father than otherwise is the case in other administrators, for it is not allowed them to alienate, even for a necessary reason, without a judge's decree.[121]

A father also did not have to render an account of his management, even though the son was nominal owner. In this instance, Pellegrini pointed out, Matteo had not damaged or dissipated the property; he had simply let it out in an emphyteotic lease at an appropriate rent, just like any careful father. The jurist was going to let a perfectly good, seemingly prudent, legal act of management stand, even if the son seems to have wanted to dispose of the property by some device other than emphyteosis. Certainly here there was no question of father and son colluding to somehow defraud the renters. He perhaps brushed aside too easily the father's alienation of effective title in such a long-term rental and not just his right of usufruct, but he referred to an analogy by which a subsequent generation could not revoke an alienation by a prior generation of property subject to a trust (fideicommissum) and expressly prohibited from alienation. This is an opinion Florentines like Luca da Panzano could have understood quite well.

The bottom line is that the patrimony, while seemingly managed by the head of household, was itself made up of parts on which sons might have some rights more direct than merely being *sui heredes* in waiting. There

---

[120] Torquato Tasso, *I discorsi dell'arte, poetica, Il padre di famiglia, e L'Aminta*, esp. 105–16. On this and similar treatises of the era, Daniela Frigo, *Il padre di famiglia: governo della casa e governo civile nella tradizione dell' 'economica' tra Cinque e Seicento.*

[121] Marcantonio Pellegrini, *Consilia*, cons. 96, fols. 259rb–60va: "nam in adventitiis patri permittitur alienatio, absque decreto, quia lex plurimum confidit de patris administratione quamvis secus sit in aliis administratoribus, nam non licet iis valide alienare, etiam ex causa necessaria, absque iudicis decreto."

were things that came into the patrimony by way of or in the name of sons. Such resources may well have been shared, and used as needed without an immediate accounting or compensatory maneuver. But in the end they had to be accounted for. The unity of patrimony broke down eventually, at least at inheritance, and the subsequent accounting distinguished sons and their claims. If only then, the distinctions mattered in law and in fact against the presumption of sharing.

Anthropologists have shown that ownership (in the sense of appropriation) and the type of personhood it enables varies across different societies.[122] Processes of inheritance and exchange formed the ways in which people gained goods. But sharing too was a primary way in which goods were appropriated and social and political relations were transacted. Sharing was also the means by which sons gained from their fathers and perceived how to proceed themselves in turn. Sons, as we have seen, were expected to obey their fathers and trust in their management, because they were united in substance, shared honor and name, and a common fate. They came forward to help as they could and were needed. They also attempted to draw lines when necessary and cut their losses in adverse circumstances. What was shared in the context of family had to be distinguished in the presence of outsiders, even in the face of family who would set up their own sharing network in which they could continue to appropriate goods. Market and family intersected fluidly. Ownership was negotiated and reconfigured across social situations. And they formed relations, as in marriage.

---

[122] Cf. Mark Busse and Veronica Strang, "Introduction: Ownership and Appropriation."

4   Property of Spouses in Law in Renaissance Florence

Piero di Luigi Guicciardini (d. 1441), great-grandfather of the well-known Florentine lawyer and statesman, Francesco Guicciardini (1483–1540), found himself in financial straits at several points in his life. At one of those moments, determined to meet his obligations and satisfy his creditors, Piero arranged to sell various of his possessions, including his house in Florence. Then things took an unexpected turn, as Francesco noted in his book of family *memorie*:

and because [the house] was pledged for his wife's dowry, who was a Buondelmonti ... he could not sell it without her consent. And having already reached agreement with the purchaser, he took him to his house with a notary to record the contract and take down his wife's consent, [but] she did not ever intend to say yes, rather she chased from the house the notary and the one who was set to buy; and seeing the obstinacy of his wife, and perhaps her resistance pleased him, he had patience [with her].[1]

Guicciardini's story ends there, so we do not know how Piero resolved his debts, though Francesco also described Piero's state at his death as one of great civic reputation but relative poverty ("because he did not leave what amounted to 5000 florins").

This story confounds on several levels. Here a head of household – an honorable, powerful, and still rather wealthy household, at that – was unable to execute his strategy to get through a bad patch and hold the family and its property together. And the snag came from within his house and from his wife, of all people. This hardly seems to be what one would expect from a reading of the substantial body of historical work on women and family life in Florence. The many perceptive and careful scholars who have traversed the field have stressed the subordination of Florentine women, especially daughters and wives, even in comparison to those of other cities, like Venice.[2] Nor does this instance of wifely obstinance seem

---

[1] Francesco Guicciardini, *Ricordi, diari, memorie*, 39.
[2] See Heather Gregory, "Daughters, Dowries and Family in Fifteenth-Century Florence"; Maria Fubini Leuzzi, *"Condurre a onore": Famiglia, matrimonio e assistenza a Firenze in età moderna*. On Venice, see Stanley Chojnacki, *Women and Men in Renaissance Venice: Twelve*

to square with the idealized account of married property relations famously recounted by an earlier Florentine, Leon Battista Alberti, a man who was not himself married or head of a household. In his dialogue on family, the character of Giannozzo Alberti discusses household management. On his terms, whether in the more intimate context of "children, wife, and other members of the household, both relatives and servants" or the larger family, separately lodged but still "in the shadow of a single will," there was a sole manager of property.[3] That will was not to be opposed, least of all by a wife. There might be sharing of resources, but not of command over them.

Giannozzo describes his wife as young, illiterate, humble, and obedient; someone from whom he kept hidden various secrets of his affairs, while revealing to her in confidence what he deemed she needed to know to play her role for the good of the entire household. Much of what he told her was about maintaining a modest and honorable bearing to avoid bringing shame to him and the family, but it also included how to treat the family's possessions:

This property, this family, and the children to be born to us will belong to us both, to you as much as to me, to me as much as to you. It behooves us, therefore, not to think how much each of us has brought into our marriage, but how we can best maintain all that belongs to both of us. I shall try to obtain outside what you need inside the house; you must see that none of it is wasted.[4]

This was not a statement of the legal state of affairs of a married couple. It was a sense of the quotidian sharing of space, food, and more, including the separate spheres of their labor (inside and outside). The sense of sharing was overt and complete. Spouses shared the same bed. They had in common children, household furnishings, and honor. Yet as an outsider and relative newcomer to the group, the wife had to be instructed in her new role.

It also must be affirmed at the outset that women, as wives and especially as widows, were active in urban and rural markets. They were not nearly as secluded as Alberti's portrait of marital relations can make it seem, as Alberto Luongo has affirmed.[5] Simona Feci has offered a sparkling account of women's activities and legal standing as merchants and paid workers, noting that though their legal abilities were carefully

---

Essays on Patrician Society, but see also Anna Bellavitis and Isabelle Chabot, "A propositio di 'Men and Women in Renaissance Venice' di Stanley Chojnacki."

[3] Alberti, *The Family in Renaissance Florence*, 180, 186. On Alberti in a civic context, see Luca Boschetto, *Leon Battista Alberti e Firenze*.

[4] Alberti, *The Family in Renaissance Florence*, 211.

[5] Alberto Luongo, "Relativamente marginali: la condizione social delle donne nella Gubbio trecentesca."

circumscribed in the laws of many communities, they were not banned from all activities. At least, "once the consent of husband had been obtained, a woman engaging in economic activities and having an acknowledged trading status could conclude necessary agreements with complete autonomy."[6] Women may have had to exercise their rights to property through men, as we will see, and they may have let their legally separate property take a conspicuous place in overall household resources, but they could be fully part of a domestic partnership. Wives' management of household accounts was vital (as Giannozzo Alberti's advice to his wife tacitly conceded). They were often trusted to be executors and guardians in their husbands' wills. As James Shaw has concluded, women were fundamentally creditors: "to their husbands in the form of dowry, to sons in their business ventures, to governments through investing in public debt, and to merchants, shopkeepers and craftsmen as equity investors."[7] All this rested on their distinct property rights (no matter how passively exercised) and their role of sharing and caring wife and mother.

These were not sentiments peculiar to Alberti, by any means. One need only cite the Venetian Francesco Barbaro (1390–1454) and his letter on the duties of a wife, addressed to the Florentine Lorenzo de' Medici, brother of Cosimo. A similar image of modest household management was in play there.[8] The point of this chapter is that, when it came to spouses, there was limited intermingling of property in law, as opposed to the day-to-day behaviors of a household. There was not a single patrimony, but at least two. And while at times, in some houses, there may have been one effective manager of all, that was not always the case. And the academic "common law" and local statutes did little to simplify matters.

There was no room in Alberti's schema for someone like Piero Guicciardini's wife. A man like Piero might rather have expected behavior like that of Giovanni Morelli's (another Florentine, 1371–1444) sister, who consented to her husband's deals, eventually losing all her dowry in order to meet household debts. Her husband too, like Piero Guicciardini, worked out his deals and then appeared at home with a notary in tow, thus

<hr />

[6] Simona Feci, "Exceptional Women: Female Merchants and Working Women in Italy in the Early Modern Period." See also Giovanna Petti Balbi and Paola Guglielmotti, eds., *Dare credito alle donne: presenze femminile nell'economia tra medioevo ed età moderna.*
[7] Cf. James E. Shaw, "Women, Credit, and Dowry in Early Modern Italy." See also Anna Bellavitis, "Dare credito, fiducia e responsabilità alle donne (Venezia, sec. xvi)"; Elena Brizio, "In the Shadow of the Campo: Sienese Women and Their Families (c. 1400–1600)"; and William Chester Jordan, *Women and Credit in Pre-Industrial and Developing Societies.*
[8] Francesco Barbaro, "On Wifely Duties," 215–20.

pressuring his wife to give in.[9] Morelli's sister perhaps did not have the haughty self-assurance of Guicciardini's wife, born to one of the most illustrious magnate lineages of the Arno city. But both women certainly faced parallel presumptions about sharing in and contributing to the household's needs. The historically interesting issue, to my mind, is not the differences of temperament among Florentine wives such as these, or of their husbands, for that matter. Rather, the element on which I wish to focus is the fact that uxorial consent had a role to play at all in these incidents.

4.1   Spousal Property in *Ius Commune*

In his now classic evocation of property relations between spouses, Manlio Bellomo detected in the opinions of medieval glossators a tendency to restrict a wife's capacity to act against an alienation of dotal property by her husband – a tendency, in other words, "aimed at freeing the husband from all links that constrained his powers in the management and governance of the family and the patrimony and leaving the wife on the margins of a position of command." This control over property lay at the heart of "a new type of family," a "broader organism" and "rigidly organized," able to take its place and pursue its interests in the rough and tumble of politics in the late medieval Italian commune.[10] Against this picture we are again faced with moments such as the Guicciardini example that seem to indicate that the situation was perhaps a bit more complex, at least in practice.

It is not that we are unaware of the material contributions of both spouses to their marital life and household. It is not that we cannot see and anticipate the contributions of women to property management. Law settled certain rights and powers on women that were real and belied any simple sense of household or patrimonial material unity. Indeed, those rights and powers might make such unity harder to achieve, although they could and did also serve that purpose on occasion. As Renata Ago concluded years ago, women were in fact quite frequently engaged in acts brought before notaries (thus having some legal significance for families), though notaries were able to shape their texts into "a form compatible with the principle of the unity of the family patrimony under the responsibility of the husband, that is to say to cloak them in a 'corporative' logic."[11] When the wife was acting legally at the behest

<hr />

[9] Morelli, *Ricordi*, 187–88. See also Kuehn, *Law, Family, and Women*, 223–24.

[10] Bellomo, *Ricerche sui rapporti patrimoniali tra coniugi*, 108, 246–47.

[11] Renata Ago, "Ruoli familiari e statuto giuridico," 126; and her "Oltre la dote: i beni femminili."

of her husband and for his benefit, she was in a real way sharing the burdens of the household and family.

There was an uneasy, ambiguous relationship between the separate pieces of a family's patrimony and the drive or need to see the patrimony as a shared unit subject to singular, male control. The main element in that uneasy relationship was the dowry the wife brought to the household, but it was not the only piece of the puzzle.

Baldo degli Ubaldi laid out in a brief consilium that there were broadly three types of property that wives might have.[12] There were those things "in dominio mariti."[13] Such property was subject to his control and he enjoyed the *fructus*. These were mainly the *res dotales*. They could be used to "sustain the burdens of marriage." The husband was restrained only in that he could not alienate title to dowry without his wife's consent – as with Guicciardini.

Secondly, there were items "in dominio uxoris" but subject to the husband's *administratio*, largely because they were brought into the marital home; and these were the *res paraphernales*, for which the husband's property was tacitly obligated, as it was expressly and powerfully obligated for return of dowry. Jurisprudence treated the husband's management of *parapherna* as dependent on his wife's consent, which, as we will see, was not necessarily the way local statutes looked at it. But even learned law took her consent as tacit in the simple act of bringing things into the house with him.[14] The *fructus* of these second sorts of goods were to be consumed for the wife and the "communem familiam," but they also served to compensate the husband for the risk he ran in managing them. The wife was due only the *fructus* not consumed for her benefit or that of the family.

Finally, there might be things in the wife's ownership and control. These were *res extra dotem*, generally remaining outside and apart from the marital home. These were to be shared, if at all, only on the wife's initiative. Their *fructus* went to the wife, and any of that used by or for the husband was considered a debt that had to be returned to her. Here is where the prevailing ideology behind marriage was most apparent, in Baldo's treatment of marital property:

truly it seems that either a wife does this [allow her husband to use her property] to assist with the husband's needs, and she does not seek return, for she is required to assist him in cases of need. . . . For they are partners of a divine and human house

---

[12] These issues and Baldo's consilium have been insightfully analyzed in Kirshner, "Materials for a Gilded Cage."

[13] See Jacques Anthony Pluss, "Baldus de Ubaldis of Perugia on Dominium over Dotal Property."

[14] Kirshner, "Materials," 77–78.

and one flesh, and one should bear the burdens of the other, but the husband for his wife, because wives always seem to be in need ... or she for her husband rarely and contrary to what commonly occurs. But if in fact a husband toils in poverty and his wife is wealthy, she must support him, unless indeed the husband fell into such a state by his own malfeasance.[15]

From this reasoning Baldo arrived at a decision in his case, which was that a widow's mourning dress should come at the husband's expense. But a widow's clothing was just another piece in the tripartite division of women's property.

In fact, Baldo's opinion was offered following an opening consilium on the case by Francesco di Bici Albergotti (1304–76). The suit arose somewhere between 1358 and 1364 at or near Florence. A widow had sought restitution of what her husband had appropriated from her *bona non dotalia*. She claimed she had been a young and respectful bride, so there was no extraneous reason to deny her recovery. Albergotti worked with the same tripartite division of property, adding that if the wife had voluntarily conceded the *fructus* to her husband or if the returns on the property were not the result of *natura* but of the labor and effort of the husband, he was entitled to the revenues. There were at least four reasons her consent to his appropriation was not to be presumed, including the particularly avaricious nature posited by law of all women and the husband's greater obligation to support his wife (than vice versa). Perhaps most telling was the fact that reverence for the husband was expected from the wife, "because of which from her patience results a presumption of dissent or of forced acceptance."[16] Albergotti looked for the meekness Giovanni Morelli's sister had exhibited.

Baldo's student, Andrea Alfeo da Corte, adding his opinion on the same case, utilized the same basic scheme of a wife's *patrimonium* and the husband's varying rights to enjoy *fructus*. A wife, he conceded, could voluntarily give *fructus* to her mate, but such could not be presumed:

---

[15] Baldo, *Consilia*, 5 *cons.* 478, fol. 128va: "sed verius videtur quod aut mulier hoc facit pro subveniendo necessitati viri, et non repetit, nam tenetur ei subvenire posito in necessitate C unde vir et uxor l. i et Authen. preterea et in corpore unde summitur. Sunt enim socii divinae et humanae domus et una caro, et alter alteri onera debet portare sed vir uxoris, quia semper mulieres semper videntur in necessitate ff de donatio. inter virum et uxorem l. quin uxor autem viri pro raro et contra communiter accidentia. Sed si tamen de facto vir laborat inopia et uxor sit dives virum tenetur alere: nisi forte vir in eadem inciderit propter suum maleficium." His text has received a critical edition in Julius Kirshner and Jacques Pluss, "Two Fourteenth-Century Opinions on Dowries, Paraphernalia and Non-Dotal Goods," 76–77. Also Gabriela Signori, "Similitude, égalité et réciprocité: l'économie matrimoniale dans les sociétés urbaines de l'Empire à la fin du Moyen Âge."

[16] Kirshner and Pluss, "Two Fourteenth-Century Opinions," 70, 75.

the common nature of both sexes is that when there is any doubt no one is presumed to throw away his money ... but to give is to lose ... so it should not be presumed it was a gift. Moreover it is proven by the special nature of the female sex, which is that all are most avaricious, so that they are not presumed to give something away.[17]

The ideologized "avarice" of women became a powerful argument for the separateness of their property. They were not assumed to share things easily, even with their children or other loved ones. Further, the law did not condone gifts between spouses, unless later confirmed on death (as a bequest). Gifts were not indicative of a sharing environment, though they certainly were indicative of meaningful relationships.[18] The husband was effectively his wife's debtor for the dowry, and although he had ownership and administration of moveable and immoveable property of his wife, he could not alienate anything without his wife's consent, as in the Guicciardini family. A bright line separated spousal property and women were well advised to make an inventory of their belongings on entering their husband's home.[19] In essence, in the eyes of the law, spouses existed in a world of two complementary property regimes: "a regime of separate spousal property pertaining to ownership and a regime of community use and enjoyment of the property each spouse owned."[20] They could get around the prohibition on gifts by recourse to third parties, while the running objection to spousal gifts was the idea that one spouse should not be enriched at the expense of the other.[21] Sharing of food and other daily expenses was excluded from the prohibition of gifts, and by a bit of legal sleight of hand, drawing a distinction between giving a gift (*donare*) and more generalized giving (*dare*), Bartolus managed to excuse the provision of clothing and jewelry to a wife. She gained use, not ownership. Husbands clearly considered such gifts to still be their property.[22] The prohibition on gifts would seem to be the ultimate expression of the separateness of spousal patrimonies, to preclude one gaining at the expense of the other (with some exceptions).[23] Such unequal reciprocity

---

[17] Kirshner and Pluss, "Two Fourteenth-Century Opinions": "communis utriusque sexus natura est ut nemo in dubio presumatur pecunias suas iactare l. cum in debito ff de prob. Sed donare est perdere ut l. contra iuris ff de pac. ergo non est presumendum quod fuerit donatio. Preterea probatur ex speciali foeminei sexus natura, quae est ut omnes sint avarissime, adeo quod donare non praesumantur."

[18] Ideological positioning of greed as a female failing may also open up the accusation that a man acting greedily was being effeminate, as Dan Smail perceptively remarked to me.

[19] Cavallar and Kirshner, *Jurists and Jurisprudence*, 694 and 698.

[20] Cavallar and Kirshner, *Jurists and Jurisprudence*, 740.

[21] Cavallar and Kirshner, *Jurists and Jurisprudence*, 742.

[22] Cavallar and Kirshner, *Jurists and Jurisprudence*, 730 and 746.

[23] Kaser, *Roman Private Law*, 250–51.

violated the sharing partnership that jurists saw marriage to be. Parallel in the Roman law was the fact that spouses fell last in the order of intestate succession, after all other blood relations, agnatic and cognatic.[24] Again, one did not gain at the expense of the other. But these norms were also in effect when the couple was otherwise sharing resources, not to mention lives. These basic legal points of the relations of husband and wife were in the mind of Baldo's student. He went on to declare gifts from a wife to her husband to be "incongruens et monstruosum." So, lacking clear proof that there was a voluntary gift or any concession of administration of her *res extra dotales* to her husband, the woman, whose case was before him, was due restitution of the *fructus* by her husband's heirs.[25]

So, whatever the corporate sense of family that figures like Alberti might have embraced and propounded, there was in law a female patrimony, and the capacity of women to dispose of it by contracts or testaments had to be recognized (if only to try to limit it). As Andrée Courtemanche found for a southern French community, women were able to direct property to relatives in their family of origin, indicating that marriage did not result in "definitively integrating" a woman and her property into the patrimony. The shared environment of the household for couples rested on work, income, and cohabitation, which were all susceptible to contractual revision.[26] Separate female property was perhaps most apparent after a husband's death, when the widow could seek return of her dowry and restitution of the *fructus* on her other property (if she had any) within the terms of the law.[27] That was when what was owed her – the "debt of the family," to use Isabelle Chabot's term – came due.[28] But, though it is clear, as Chabot, among others, demonstrates, that widows were more active as legal players in various markets, married women too had reason to enter contracts or write wills, even if only to bail out their husbands, as in the Guicciardini and Morelli cases. A woman's patrimony was not limited to dowry, as she could receive property more directly in the form of gifts or bequests, emanating from among her natal kin. These would be the basis especially of what Baldo termed *res extra dotem*.

4.2   Women's Property in Statutes

In his account of spousal property, Bellomo places weight on statutes, such as that of Verona in 1276, that equated all goods *extra dotem* with

[24] Kaser, *Roman Private Law*, 287; Borkowski and du Plessis, *Textbook on Roman Law*, 213.
[25] This consilium is 2 *cons*. 366, fol. 100rb–vb.
[26] Andrée Courtemanche, *La richesse des femmes: patrimoines et gestion à Manosque au xive siècle*, 51, 171–81.
[27] Ago, "Ruoli familiari," 126.   [28] Chabot, *La dette des familles*.

parapherna. He goes on to say that all goods brought into the marital home were to be considered as if they were part of the dowry.[29] Florence too, as Bellomo points out, treated *parapherna* as dotal property in the statutes of 1325, placing all usufruct in the hands of the husband for whatever a wife acquired during marriage. Yet, just as clearly, the same statute specified that any such property "is property of the wife and her heirs." Further, the statute said that what came to a wife by inheritance, or otherwise from her paternal or maternal line, belonged to her, not her husband, and that what came to her "as a result of any succession she can defend that against all creditors of her husband from every person and place, as a result of the husband."[30] Still, such statutes, says Bellomo, yield "an image of the medieval family founded on the figure of the husband, head of the family, and characterized by the tendency to identify with the husband the right to receive all the fruits, civil and natural, from the dotal goods as much as those that were paraphernal."[31]

Because of her tacit hypothec on her husband's property for return of her dowry and her nominal ownership of *paraphernalia* and *res extra dotem*, a wife's kin, most notably her father (were he still alive, especially were she also unemancipated), had an interest in her and her property. Morelli certainly expressed interest, if also disappointment, in his sister's disposal of her property. Such interest could demand return of control and a rendering of payments that ran counter to the interests of the husband, or his heirs, mainly sons (who were also possibly her children).[32] Guarantees for return of dowry were a continuing legal obsession, and the veto of transactions by a wife like Piero Guicciardini's was one part of that. Even more particular steps were possible. Luca da Panzano and many other Florentine husbands purchased monte shares in their wives' names, thus setting aside an income-earning fund for dowry. Transaction of any such shares required approval from her family, if they availed themselves of the opportunity to place encumbrances on such shares.[33] There were instances of Florentines who gave property to their married daughters or sisters on condition that no benefit accrue to the woman's husband. At some level such measures reeked of distrust of the husband, but they also expressed some trust and support for a wife by her family of origin.[34] Such bequests, from parents or any other kin, were a prime source of women's nondotal property.[35]

---

[29] Bellomo, *Ricerche*, 139.
[30] "Occasione alicuius successionis possit ea defendere contra omnes creditores viri ab omni persona et loco, occasione viri" (quoted in Bellomo, *Ricerche*, 140–41).
[31] Bellomo, *Ricerche*, 142.   [32] Chabot, *La dette des familles*, 146–62.
[33] Kirshner, "The Seven Percent Fund of Renaissance Florence," in *Marriage, Dowry, and Citizenship*, 114–30, at 127.
[34] Kuehn, *Law, Family, and Women*, 206.   [35] Kirshner, "Materials," 87–90.

Between the situation in the learned common law and the practices of women and their kin regarding dowry and other property, there was room for the play of local statutes, which tended in some regards to rein in the separateness of female property. Florence's statutes, as an example, addressed spousal property relations at a couple of points. One was the restitution of dowry on ecclesiastically sanctioned separations or, more regularly, death of the husband. In the earliest redaction (1325), the statutes simply mandated summary procedure to resolve the problems more rapidly, within no more than two months, making clear that in the eyes of civic authorities, such as the podestà, the obligation to return dowry (and any bequests to a wife beyond dowry) was a real debt that could even incur incarceration to coerce payment.[36] The more precise and long-winded version of the same provision in the redaction of 1415 essentially added nothing, except for the brief remark that restitution of dowry (other than on ecclesiastical separation) was to be allowed "on account of the natural death of the other spouse only, and for no other reason."[37]

The legal logic for such a specification was to preclude, or at least distinguish, a legal measure that arose in the course of the fourteenth century, mainly as a result of juristic interpretation, that some litigants in Florence were attempting to use in the late fourteenth and early fifteenth centuries. This was the surrender to the wife of control of her dowry from the hands of a husband verging on insolvency (*consignatio dotis*).[38] There was some resistance to allowing this recourse in Florence (and elsewhere), as it brought into focus both the failings of men and the unwonted prospect of a woman actually controlling her dowry. As Julie Hardwick has remarked, on the basis of judicial settlements involving nonelite propertied Frenchmen,

Separate property alone muddied the categories of husband and wife, along with the rights, privileges, and reputations they bestowed. Separate property came with a price for both spouses. Men lost the right to manage household property, and saw news of their financial difficulties publicized in their parish and marketplace. Wives' separate property eroded a defining pillar of adult masculinity, and effectively emasculated married men for whom the link between property and potency was severed, as well as damaging their credit. Moreover, while honourable failure could happen to anyone, separate property carried the slap of mismanagement, and not just bad luck or hard times.[39]

[36] *Statuti della repubblica fiorentina*, vol. 2: *Statuti del podestà dell'anno 1325*, 91–93.
[37] *Statuta communis Florentiae anno salutis mccccxv*, 3 vols. 1: 156–59.
[38] Kirshner, "Wives' Claims against Insolvent Husbands"; Kuehn, "Protecting Dowries in Law in Renaissance Florence."
[39] Julie Hardwick, *Family Business: Litigation and the Political Economies of Daily Life in Early Modern France*, 49. See also Courtemanche, *La richesse des femmes*, 123–41, 184–93.

Hardwick is concerned more with actual separation of holdings, including by means of a legal marital separation, but she is alive to the effects of a "merely" legal separation of property. After all, husband and wife probably continued to live together after *consignatio* and thus effectively to share the wife's property. And given the legal distinctions among categories of spousal property as laid out by Baldo, it was mainly the dowry and *parapherna* that were affected by a judicially ordered separation of assets.

Eventually such *consignatio dotis* was accepted in Florence and other communities, with the provision (in Florence) that such reversions be recorded and registered with civic authorities to provide some means of protection to a husband's other creditors in the face of the powerful hypothec being enforced for wives' dowries. *Consignatio*, after all, violated the presumptive sharing of household assets, under the husband's control. Such thorough distinction between husband's and wife's patrimonies during marriage was about the most extreme statement of the force of the hypothec for dowry. In fact, the statutes of 1415 went so far as to affirm that the hypothec remained in force and was not hurt by any consensual renunciation a woman might make to sale or alienation of her dowry (the Morelli problem).[40] All pretense of sharing patrimony seems to have come into question, if not broken totally, when a woman sought to exercise her title to her dowry or other property.

That statutory reassurance that dowries were protected fed into another feature of Florence's laws: a prohibition on wives coming to the financial rescue of their husbands. The rubric "Quod nulla mulier vivente viro possit defendere bona viri" said it all. The statutory exception, of course, was to protect the wife's dowry, which was amorphously part of her husband's property if her dowry was "inextimata" (not given a precise value in monetary terms).[41] The sole substantial addition to that statute in 1415 was to concede the right to protect one's dowry from the husband "vergente ad inopiam."[42] There was also a statute precluding wives from being held liable for taxes and forced loans falling on their husbands, directly exempting their nondotal goods.[43] In another statute that broadly equated women and minors, alienation of dotal property by a woman could not be upheld, on suspicion it was done from fear or to defraud, unless it was very formally taken before communal judges, with father or guardian present. Hence also no such oath would be accepted if supposedly made outside Florentine territory.[44]

---

[40] *Statuta* (1415), 1: 160. [41] *Statuti* (1325), 93. [42] *Statuta* (1415), 1: 161.
[43] Kirshner, "Materials," 84. [44] *Statuta* (1415), 1: 206.

A third area of concern was property a wife might acquire during marriage. In the 1325 statutes any objects, lands, houses, or vineyards that might come to a wife generated a right for the husband to *fructus*, with or without his wife's leave, unless he were to mistreat her or expel her from the house or proved to be an incompetent manager. Anything the wife gained by way of succession from her paternal or maternal kin was understood to be her property, however, and she could defend it from claims of any creditors. The only exception to the husband's claims to enjoy and use his wife's property was if it came to her with the express condition that no *fructus* come to him, and Florentines were willing to use such conditions.[45] In 1415 a specification was added that the wife could not alienate her property without her husband's consent, and the distinction regarding inherited property coming to her disappeared.[46] In effect, this measure reduced such extra-dotal property to the status of *parapherna* (again, a term not found in Florence's statutes), eliminating Ubaldi's and Albergotti's third form of female patrimony.[47] In essence, Florence's statutes (more systematically from 1415) helped husbands exercise some control over nondotal properties and *fructus*, with or without their spouses' consent, keeping clear only that title to such properties lay with the wife.[48] Shared property under spousal control remained the norm.

Chabot has concluded that this statutory equation of a wife's nondotal property to dowry, under the husband's control, "consecrated the concentration in the husband's hands of the entirety of female goods acquired during marriage," and that, in turn, "participated in a vaster design to guarantee the incorporation of the spouse's property in an axis of succession of her husband."[49] At least by statute, then, Florentine husbands gained the same sort of control they had nominally over property brought into the home by their sons.

As the wife held nominal *dominium* on her property, one mode of disposition of it, in which her husband's control might be limited or even undercut, was by her testament, which might direct portions of her belongings to those she chose. Florence's statutes moved to limit the damage that might strike the husband, and affect the trust and credit he could hope to have in the community, from his wife's testament. As was the case in some other cities, in Florence a husband gained his wife's dowry on her predecease, while remaining *fructus* on nondotal assets were recoverable by her heirs. If there were children, they got the dowry, though he retained usufruct. If she made a will, he still gained a third of

[45] *Statuti* (1325), 103; Kirshner, "Materials," 82–83.   [46] *Statuta* (1415), 1: 161–62.
[47] Kirshner, "Materials," 75.   [48] Kirshner, "Materials," 79.
[49] Chabot, *La dette des familles*, 176–77.

her nondotal property, unless there were children; and if she died intestate, he still got a third.[50] Children of any prior marriage were left out. In 1415 a simple definition was added of what was dowry (what had been "confessed" as such), along with the proviso that no woman could concoct a testament that harmed the rights of her husband or children or their descendants in her property.[51] As Julius Kirshner has concluded, "although no rationale accompanied the innovation that made the Florentine husband part successor to his wife's nondotal assets, it should be understood as a calculated extension of the legislation that had permitted husbands to enjoy usufruct of nondotal fruits in an ongoing marriage."[52]

Women in Florence, as elsewhere, exercised their right to have a testament and direct property to a variety of relatives and pious causes. Isabelle Chabot has located a number of examples from the Trecento and Quattrocento.[53] Women's testaments could advantage different family groups – their marital family, their family of origin, other families, or nubile young women in any of those in particular.[54] While the statutes reveal a concern that women would direct their testaments to the benefit of others than their husbands and children, their activities as testators could also work to the family's benefit.[55] Of course, as widows, women, and their natal family kin, could play an important role in the guardianship of minors.[56]

Another mode to limit a wife's attempts to manage and control her property, although it was also a potentially porous mode, was the peculiar Florentine requirement that any woman conducting a legal transaction needed a male guardian, a *mundualdus*. If a married woman entered a contract with her husband's consent, he was held to be her *mundualdus* and her act was valid and could not be revoked. Her right to protect her interests in the face of payments to her husband's creditors was upheld in the same statute. The wife could not cede a right to her dowry to someone other than her husband. If he gave away the property that was originally in her dowry and the creditor who had received it wanted to keep it, she had to be content with what was repaid her as an equivalent value.[57] But her consent to any alienation of property obligated for her dowry or any

---

[50] *Statuti* (1325), 130.   [51] *Statuta* (1415), 1: 222–23; Chabot, 51–56.
[52] Kirshner, "Materials," 83.   [53] Chabot, *La dette des familles*, 54–60.
[54] A typology laid out by Stefano Calonaci, "Gli angeli del testamento: Donne fedecommissarie e fedecommittente nella Toscana moderna," 90–91.
[55] Calonaci, "Gli angeli del testament," 94 n. 95.
[56] Giulia Calvi, "Rights and Ties That Bind: Mothers, Children, and the State in Tuscany during the Early Modern Period."
[57] *Statuti* (1325), 107; *Statuta* (1415), 1: 203–4.

renunciation of her hypothecary rights did not hold unless, at the time, there were sufficient *immobilia* to cover her dowry.

While it was thus the case that a woman would always have to have a male guardian (*mundualdus*), Florentine law – except for the presumption in favor of the spouse – allowed that any adult male could be that guardian. This was not a form of guardianship that included management of assets and corresponding liability for that, as with the guardian of a minor (*tutor, curator*), who was appointed by a testament or a civic body. The *mundualdus* was "electus" by the woman, in theory. Such a guardian had no real or personal liability for the consequences of the woman's acts, so any real control, guidance, or concern about any woman's acts may have been minimal.[58] For widows, lacking a husband and quite probably a father, that seems especially to have been the case. But married women transacting nondotal goods were more than likely to employ husbands as *mundualdi* (the statutes assumed as much), though there were instances when others, including a kinsman of the husband, might serve as guardian.[59]

While it was the case that a husband was presumed to be his wife's legal guardian, it was also the case that a woman's acts could be voided on the basis of overwhelming fear (*metus*) of her husband. But it was also the case in law, as Bartolus made clear, that such fear was not to be presumed. It had to be proven by witness testimony and other evidence.[60]

The effective "abuse" of the *mundualdus* in employing men with no real interest in the actions being undertaken by women led to grandducal intervention in 1568 from concern that women's interests were not being sufficiently protected. A judicial decree was thereafter necessary for women's transactions, while alienation of dotal goods remained under the supervision of Orsanmichele.[61] Husbands and relatives were left out of account, replaced by the benevolent monarch, or rather his official, who had to look to the nature of the legal act in course and the interests of the woman involved. Behind him were the legists active in Tuscany, who would act as advisers to the judge or one of the parties to a suit.

Statutes refined and "Florentinized" the rules of law, but they hardly erased all ambiguities of the two spousal patrimonies. In some regards they made them more opaque. If they did not, the ever-changing and

---

[58] Kuehn, *Law, Family, and Women*, 212–37. See also Simona Feci, *Pesci fuor d'acqua: Donne a Roma in età moderna: diritti e patrimoni.*
[59] Kirshner, "Materials," 86.
[60] See Paolo Mari, "Bartolo e la condizione femminile: brevi appunti dalle *lecturae* bartoliane," 249–50.
[61] Daniele Edigati, "Ut mulier non circumveniatur: La capacità di agire della donna in età moderna fra *ius commune* e *ius proprium*," 63.

inventive acts of residents of Florence complicated things inevitably. Whatever the dictates of law, surely the unity of the patrimony was most apparent in the way Florentines saw women's property and treated it. In that regard it has to be noted that the officials entrusted with compilation of the first Florentine catasto declared that "wives were not allowed to declare separately from their husbands; husbands had to assume fiscal responsibility for their wives."[62] Husbands' declarations rarely distinguished wifely property from any other household assets for fiscal purposes. But husbands were otherwise highly aware of their obligations in regard to the property wives brought into the marital home and took steps to cover those obligations.

4.3 A Florentine Householder

The distinctness of spousal patrimonies and the blurred edges around them are apparent in that most Florentine of sources, *ricordanze*. We will concentrate on one for now, but it is rich in references to dowries in a number of contexts – the *ricordanze* of Luca da Panzano.[63] Dowries figured into his text at many points, from mother, wife, daughters, and others, beginning with an early reference to his mother, Mattea, making her will in the plague year of 1400, in which she left her 1,200-florin dowry to her sons; but if they all died without legitimate children, it was to go to her brothers. Luca's mother, with his help as legal agent, also succeeded in lodging a claim on Antonio's property for 400 florins still owed her for her dowry and ended up with a farm.[64] Striking also is Luca's account of maneuvers by his cousins, Totto and Mea d'Antonio, such that Mea took possession of her mother's dowry as her heir (Totto having refused it), despite her father still being alive, "in truth to defend the goods of her father Antonio because the conditions of his bank were bad."[65] Here there was deliberate use of the distinctness of female titles to protect men and the family as a whole.

Luca was involved as surety on dowries received by others, relatives and associates, including in restoring dowries to widows. But for our purposes the more interesting points concern dowries that came to him or that he arranged. His wife, Lucrezia di Salvadore del Caccia, brought him a dowry of 1,018 florins in 1425. And that is how Luca saw it: "I should

---

[62] Herlihy and Klapisch-Zuber, *Tuscans and Their Families*, 12.
[63] *"Brighe, affanni, volgimenti di stato."*
[64] *"Brighe, affanni, volgimenti di stato,"* 7, 144–45.
[65] *"Brighe, affanni, volgimenti di stato,"* 6: "in verità per difendere i beni d'Antonio suo padre perch'e fatti del suo bancho istavano male."

have my dowry of said Lucrezia."[66] His text next records the children he had from her. Like so many other Florentines who kept such registers of their doings, Luca da Panzano nowhere noted any other property, including the contents of her trousseau, that his wife may have brought into the home. There was no category of *parapherna* to keep track of in his mind.[67] Later he jotted down that he had taken his own money and bought shares in Florence's public debt (monte) in Lucrezia's name, at 6 percent interest. He added: "should it happen that my wife want her dowry after my death, my sons may not have to unload all their possessions and that it remain to support them."[68] In 1432 he moved the sum to another fund, still as security for her dowry, while he enjoyed the interest.[69] Other Florentines similarly converted dowries into annuities based on shares in the public debt. Of course, he also remembered to accord her dowry and *alimenta* when he made his will, but he added no other (nondotal) assets to it.

Luca also fashioned an agreement with Michele de' Benenati da San Gimignano and his wife Bartolomea that once both of them had died Luca would receive 1,500 florins in monte holdings in return for a payment of 360 florins to the Innocenti and the Arte di Por Santa Maria. Benenati was a fellow silk merchant and business associate, after whom Luca named one of his sons. Bartolomea designated Luca's sons as her heirs years later. A house in San Gimignano was bought in Bartolomea's name with the condition that after Bartolomea's death it go to Lucrezia, with the condition that she not remarry. If she did, it went to her sons by Luca.[70]

In 1436 Luca scrupulously recorded that, though he and his brothers held properties in common, his wife's dowry "and clothes that I have expended from my money or from money of the dowry that I have had are mine, Luca, and that the dowry cannot be demanded by them."[71] Her death led him to remark that she was a "valente e buona donna," "dolcie," and "costumata," and he saw to appropriate obsequies.[72] He waited nine years to designate his five sons as his wife's intestate heirs and dispatch them to retrieve the credits in her name in the monte.[73] There is no mention of any nondotal goods coming to him.

---

[66] *"Brighe, affanni, volgimenti di stato,"* 52: "debbo avere per *mia* [emphasis added] dota di detta Luchrezia."

[67] Kirshner, "Materials," 75.

[68] "ischadendo che detta mia donna volesse suo dota manchando io, ch'e miei figliuoli non s'abino a ischorporare tutte loro possisione e che rimanghi loro da vivere" (Panzano, 82–83).

[69] Panzano, 120.   [70] Panzano, 190.

[71] "e' panni che io avessi ispesi di miei danari o di danari di dota che abbi auti si sieno di me Lucha, e che la dota non possi loro adomandare" (Panzano, 199).

[72] Panzano, 225, 241–42.   [73] Panzano, 330.

When Luca's son Antonio married, the dowry amount and payments they received were set forth, along with other legal adjustments between father and son. The monte credits to indemnify this dowry were also set down, as well as amounts of grain, oil, wine, and other victuals.[74] Mattea's husband, who did not immediately realize the 1,000 florins in the monte, bought a farm near Pistoia, declaring that he used his wife's dowry (400 *lire* of it, at any rate), "and he designated the buyer as Gualterotto and that it stood for part of my Mattea's dowry." It was purchased from a woman with the consent of her male guardian and her mother.[75]

Yes, Luca called his wife's dowry "mia," just as he called his children "mia." But that did not define how he could and did act in so many situations. This was a man, given all the legal transactions he compiled in his records, who was keenly aware of the impact of law and its procedures.[76] Still, while dowry was a distinct protected asset, it remained a source of common use.

4.4 Cases

Statutes gave a man like Luca da Panzano a great deal of latitude, but they did not free him of all the complications engendered by the legal distinctions. Title to uxorial property could be uncertain. Interesting on this score is a fairly rare division of property between two sisters, both married, whose husbands were present and involved. Francesca and Dianora, daughters of the late Lapo Orlanducci, went to arbitration to divide a large piece of land, mainly vineyard, and two pieces of woodland, located at San Romolo a Colonata, that they held "communiter et pro indiviso." The two arbitrators took the highly unusual step of drawing up a plat, identifying the contiguous parcels, its neighbors, and its common approach (*viactola*), and dividing it by drawing lines in red ink. From the looks of the drawing, they seem to have been as fair and evenhanded in allotting surface area as they could have been. The woodlands were allocated in thirds, two to Dianora and one to Francesca. That discrepant inequality seems to have been the result of the fact that Francesca had initially brought the land as dowry to her husband, with Dianora nominally holding the other half. As her husband was a notary who acted as her attorney in this division, it is possible that Dianora acceded to his insistence behind the division, although there was also the expressed concern of the arbitrators that "because of the aforesaid communion of goods

[74] Panzano, 383–85, 389–90.   [75] Panzano, 425.
[76] In parallel, see Hardwick, *Family Business*, 71–72.

several differences and scandals have arisen between the parties and an even greater one might arise over the cultivation of said property unless a division happens."[77] The immediate move to the final sentence with the carefully drawn figure indicates that the settlement was worked out amicably, whatever the previous differences. This was an event involving women and their coextensive property rights and scrupulous safeguarding of them. Husbands and wives worked together here, as sharing partners, but also overtly on the distinct rights of the wives.

Of course, many divisions led to counterclaims and even animosities that could not be easily unraveled by the parties. These divisions escalated from arbitration to litigation. At Trieste a statute gave husbands usufruct on all their wives' property "those given in dowry as well as acquired [during marriage]." On a husband's death it was all to revert to his wife. In view of that statute a widow fell into conflict with her husband's heirs. Trieste's statute also attributed ownership of goods acquired during marriage to both husband and wife, though only he had direct use. He could dispose of them with her consent, and so for a long time the customary sense of the statute was that he was free to do so. Could he give it away, as opposed to exchange? Here Baldo equivocated a bit, but embraced the view that the interpretation of the statute generally held to by jurists returned the situation to that of common law: "the husbands do not acquire for the wife but the wives for the husbands." Husbands could alienate only their share of the property. As things might be gained by testamentary bequest or full-out inheritance by one or the other spouse, husbands were not free to alienate what wives brought in by those means. Acquisitions of other sorts in the course of marriage, such as earnings of a shop, were his in full by his presumed industry, but not if use of their common money was seen as the source of gains, for then some part of it was hers.[78] So this wife could claim her due from the heirs of her husband.

Baldo's brother Angelo faced a similar case in hypothetical form and determined that the statutes of Florence advantaged husbands. If a woman received two houses as bequests from her mother, could her husband appropriate the rents obtained from them? Florence's statutes of 1355 had given women operative custody of property inherited from either parent. Angelo saw the statutes otherwise, as trying to give control of nondotal assets to the husband. As the distinction about inherited property contradicted the statute's first assertion about spousal control, and landed the statutes back in line with *ius commune*, Angelo had to work

---

[77] ASF, NA 9037, fols. 369v–72v (30 January 1412): "propter comunionem predictam pluries orte sunt differentie et scandala inter ipsas partes et maiores etiam oriri possent ex cultivatione dictorum bonorum nisi dividantur."

[78] Baldo, 2 *cons.* 234 and 235, fol. 66rb–vb.

hard to find a coherent line of interpretation. He hit on a strange distinction. The husband, he said, received usufruct on bequests from the wife's paternal line, but not on bequests from her maternal line.[79] In the case before him the property came from the maternal line, so the rents it generated were to stay with the wife. Whatever her husband had appropriated had to be returned.[80] In reaction, the statutes of 1415 later removed the distinction about bequests as paternal or maternal, and it should have firmly ended any doubt about the husband's active *administratio* of his wife's assets acquired during marriage. The Florentine law seemed to see effective sharing going on when things were in the husband's control; the wife might be too individualistic (greedy) of what was in her control. That seems to be the way Angelo took it too.

Curiously, in a closely similar case from Bologna, Angelo offered more direct support of the wife's right to dispose of property acquired in marriage, though this time in effect securing a house to the person who bought it from the wife. The statute protected *immobilia* given in the dowry. A woman who during marriage acquired a house by succession, who treated it as her home (*inquilinum suum*) and kept it in her own name, later sold it; and the purchaser wanted to know that his title was secure despite the statute, which varied greatly from common law, which did not so easily assume dowry and attribute it to the husband. Angelo aimed to bring both laws into conformity, beginning with the observation that "at the time of the marriage the wife had her property, so that the husband believed he would possess that as dowry, otherwise he would in no way have contracted the marriage."[81] Goods acquired during marriage did not answer to that logic, by which individual title and sharing of assets coincided, so the statute did not apply to them. Either acquired goods were common to both spouses or they were part of dowry. The exception was if the wife knew and allowed her husband to behave like the owner. In this case the purchaser was secure because the house had never been in the husband's hands; the wife acted as owner and received the rents and sold it in her name alone.[82] It was seemingly never part of a shared endowment to sustain the burdens of marriage.

The impetus behind these cases seems to have been the wife's desire to recover all she could on the end of the marriage. In that case her property

---

[79] Married women were expressly exempted by statute from liability for their fathers' debts, unless they were heirs to their fathers (*Statuta* [1415], 1: 205).

[80] Angelo degli Ubaldi, *Consilia, cons.* 62, fols. 40rb–41ra.

[81] Ubaldi, *Consilia, cons.* 62, fol. 40va: "cum tempore matrimonii mulier bona sua stabilia habet, ut sic illa vir se credat possessurum pro dote, aliter matrimonium nullatenus contracturus fuisset."

[82] Ubaldi, *Consilia, cons.* 335, fol. 236ra–va.

rights were about her needs and uses in widowhood. In other instances her rights might act as a cover to help retain some property when faced with the demands of creditors. The commune of Prato, near Florence, was the creditor in a suit against a wife whose dowry had supposedly been increased by 200 florins during marriage. Though Florentine law clearly privileged the wife's dowry credit against her husband's other creditors, that did not apply to a later increase, declared the jurist Paolo di Castro.[83] He compared Prato's statute to a new revision of Florence's. The key point was that an increase to dowry during marriage was suspicious: "one presumes fraud and machinations against creditors, because then as conjugal affection is contracted, it is easily presumed that fraud is thought of."[84] Sharing developed over time and might even result in conniving. Proofs that the increase was somehow genuine were rejected out of hand. There was no notarized *confessio* of the increase, let alone one dating from before the point the husband began to slide into insolvency. The only guarantee to the wife was that she receive sufficient resources, even against claims of prior creditors, to sustain herself and her husband and children.[85] Fraudulent intentions too could be shared.

A parallel case, and a similar jurisprudential distrust, arose later and came before Bartolomeo Sozzini.[86] A Sienese Jew named Jacob Consilii, after his marriage began, in a publicly notarized instrument, gave Dulce 500 florins for her "great benefits and merits and gain and convenience" (magna beneficia et merita et lucra et commoda), and "lest she suffer some shame in going bankrupt or having to flee or in capture of her person" (ne verecundiam aliquam in cessando, vel fugiendo, vel in captura personae pateretur). Further, over the previous three years, "by industry, care, and diligence of said Dulce" another 100 florins had been realized for the family. Jacob swore by Mosaic law, on the Hebrew bible, to abide by the gift and *fructus*. This was posed as a gift between spouses, which was something generally precluded in Roman law, and thus was easy for Sozzini to dismiss. But he did not make it easy. He pedantically offered no fewer than twenty-three reasons such a gift did not hold. Behind the cascade of textual references he marshaled, the simple fact was that, no matter the assertion of merit to validate the gift, there was

[83] On him, see Martines, *Lawyers and Statecraft*, 499–500; Giuseppe Biscione, *Statuti del Comune di Firenze nell'Archivio di State: Tradizione archivistica e ordinamenti*, 661–74; Lorenzo Tanzini, *Statuti e legislazione a Firenze dal 1355 al 1415: Lo statuto cittadino del 1409*, 280–310.
[84] Ubaldi, *Consilia, cons.* 325, fol. 236va: "praesumit fraudem et machinationem contra creditores, quia tunc cum sit contracta affectio coniugalis, faciliter praesumitur fraudem excogitatam."
[85] Paolo di Castro, *Consilia*, 3 vols., 3 *cons.* 37, fols. 42va–44rb.
[86] On him, Roberta Bargagli, *Bartolomeo Sozzini: giurista e politico (1436–1506)*.

only the husband's word on that. His assertion seemed rather a feigned act of deceit (colore fictitie simulationis). Sozzini also dismissed the oath on Jewish scripture, as canon law's prescriptions regarding oaths did not affect Jews, who were outside the church. As the gift was not real, then, there was no need to explore in depth the question whether Jacob could revoke the gift following Dulce's death. Were the gift real, a true *donatio causa mortis*, he could revoke it at any point in his life, were his wife alive or dead.[87]

Acting as attorney for a Sienese man named Tommaso in another case, Sozzini argued that seizure of the household furnishings and utensils (*massaritia*) for a father's debts should be overturned. The fact was that those objects belonged not to the father but to his wife, and thus passed to Tommaso, their son, without obligation for the paternal debts. Here the father and mother had moved in with her mother and continued to live there with their children after the mother-in-law's death, and the father and children resided there after the mother's death. But all that sharing did not mean that the property belonged to the husband. Whereas usually "when husband and wife live in the same house the furnishings are presumed to be the husband's" (quando vir et uxor habitant in eadem domo massaritiae praesumantur esse viri), the presumption here had to be that they belonged to the wife, whose mother's house it was. Sozzini also took note of a teaching of Angelo degli Ubaldi that cohabiting spouses were to be understood to each possess half.[88] In Sozzini's eyes, at least in this instance, both wife's and son's ownership stood separate from that of the husband/father.

Filippo Decio caught a case from Ferrara that was in fact emblematic of legal problems of women's contracts. Could a woman contract about dowry when local statute forbade women to make contracts without the consent of certain male relatives? Dowry seemed a special contract, enjoying favor in law to encourage marriage, so a general statute about contracts might well not have applied to it. Decio, however, gave force to the very generality of the statute as applying universally to all contracts, including dowry. That was particularly the case given the intent of the statute:

it appears that this statute was made to preclude fraud, lest wives be deceived out of their assets, because the statute presumes and keeps constant that without formalities [set out by] the statute wives obligating themselves would be seduced on account of the shame of their sex and reverential fear, which sex and nature

---

[87] Sozzini, *Consilia*, 1 *cons.* 56, fols. 121vb–25ra.
[88] Sozzini, 1 cons. 128, fols. 216vb–17rb.

induces in them. As a statute for removing frauds, such a statute must be amplified and liberally interpreted.[89]

This last flourish indeed pointed to the direction from which a counter-argument might be launched, to the effect that the law was harmful to women and against the common law, which usually required a restrictive interpretation. In any case, Decio went on to state that fraud and deception might as easily be perpetrated on a woman regarding dowry as anything else. Dowry was not accorded privileged status by the Ferrarese statute. Indeed, concluded Decio, "I advised otherwise at Florence and so at Florence was it judged at the time I was teaching there."

His treatment was similar in a Pisan case. Decio concurred with a prior ruling. The statute that forbade a married woman from entering a contract about her dowry also covered a gift following and confirmed by death. It was true that prior to death such a gift could simply be revoked, but Decio pointed to the obvious loss to her children, as her heirs, and to the fact that the same female *fragilitas* that led the law to forbid contracts on dowry would also be at work in any gift. Further, "in reality it cannot be judged otherwise that a gift made to the stepmother by Cornelia seems made in contemplation of her father consenting and not on account of the stepmother herself, because a stepmother is hateful to a stepson or stepdaughter."[90] Invoking such stereotypes made it more a gift to the father, and through him to his wife. So the gift was invalid, as the father, who had been the male giving consent to Cornelia's act, was in fact acting to his own benefit.[91]

The separateness of marital patrimonies was perhaps most on display precisely when it was violated, when a wife stepped up and used her property to meet her husband's debts, which would require her, in thus obligating herself, to renounce the privilege under the civil law text, the s. c. Velleianum, protecting women from obligating themselves for others. Otherwise she might invoke it to dissolve any such obligation for a third party. The problem Bartolomeo Sozzini once faced revolved around the

[89] Filippo Decio, *Consilia*, 1 *cons.* 301, fols. 329vb–30vb: "ex proemio statuti apparet quod tale statutum fuit factum ad obviandum fraudibus ne mulieres eorum facilitate deciperentur, quia statutum presumit et habet pro constante quod absque solennitate statuti mulieres se obligantes seductae fuerint propter verecundiam sexus et timorem reverentialem, quem eis sexus et natura induxit, ut statutum ad removendum fraudes, tale statutum debet ampliari et late interpretari."
[90] Decio, 1 *cons.* 279, fols. 304rb–5rb: "quia veritate et ratione consonat, adeo quod verisimiliter aliter iudicari non possit quod donatio facta novercae per dictam Corneliam videtur facta contemplatione patris consentientis, et non propter ipsam novercam, quia noverca odiosa est privigno vel privignae."
[91] Decio, 1 *cons.* 279, fols. 304rb–5rb.

question whether the contract a woman had entered was in fact simulated. Regularly one assumed that a contract was what it said it was. One did not begin presuming a fiction. At least reasonable conjectures had to be available to conclude the contrary. A fictive contract meant her oath not to invoke Velleianum did not stand. But in his case that oath was not simply to uphold the contract but to substantiate the transfer of assets; and the Velleianum had been specifically waived, so it could not now be invoked (probably not by the wife, in any case, but possibly by her husband or her heir, seeking to get the property back or escape the obligation). The woman in question, a monna Giovanna, had sold off her property "so that she might save the house" (ut conservaret domum) and it "otherwise not to be sold" (alias non venditura). In fact, within a year, it seems, the couple were evicted from the home, but that had not been the doing of the creditors she had paid off but of others. Nor was preservation of the home the singular *causa* behind the wife's intervention:

that greater principle [helping the husband] has to be considered, therefore saving the house was not in the end the final cause and consequently the contract must not be settled ... and especially because, as I said, she seems to have been moved by love of her husband ... and that she wanted rather to save his person than his goods.[92]

Here then he ended up with an argument about affection, the oneness of the couple, to uphold the wife's acts, which, given the later eviction, seemed to have come a bit late. Shared patrimony backed up that love. But their sharing was here not to be allowed to prejudice the rights of creditors.

The opposite of a wife's contributing to pay off her husband's debts was her suit to retrieve her dowry from him lest it be lost to creditors as he verged on insolvency. This legal device gave the lie to any sense of patrimonial solidarity in a household or between spouses. But it also gave rise to valid fears of fraud. Paolo di Castro was involved in the 1415 revision of Florence's statutes, and he handled cases arising from *consignatio dotis*. Among them was one in which Mattea, whose husband, Andrea, was clearly in difficulty, could invoke her hypothec against her mother-in-law, Antonia, and brother-in-law, Lorenzo, who had pledged themselves for return of her dowry in a *confessio*. Certainly the husband

---

[92] Sozzini, 3 *cons.* 83, fol. 98ra–va: "causa liberandi maritum ne caperetur ultra causam conservando domum, immo illa magis principalis in contractu videtur consideranda, igitur conservatio domus non fuit in totum causa finalis et per consequens non debet contractus resolvi ... et maxime quia, ut dixi, videtur quod mota fuerit amore viri ... et quod potius vellet personam conservare quam bona."

was on the hook for the dowry, and so was any of his property in his mother's possession. But was the mother's property in jeopardy? Paolo di Castro faced the objection that her oath to return the dowry on the occasion of *restitutio* did not cover *consignatio*. He also addressed the statutory language, which allowed broad action by a wife, though he admitted that creditors might have a claim to see demonstration of the husband's true circumstances and the wife's exigencies. In the end he insisted that the mother-in-law's pledge on the dowry her son received did not include *consignatio*. He concluded she was not liable for a claim on the hypothec in her property or that of her sons already hypothecated for her own dowry, which was a prior and more powerful claim.[93]

Effectively di Castro was not going to save one dowry with another. Mariano Sozzini also placed one dowry ahead of another. The heirs of monna Ginevra, he said, had a better claim to the dowry of Niccolosa, Ginevra's mother, than did the heirs of Bianco, who were creditors of Bernardo and in possession. The story began back in 1407 when Bernardo formally acknowledged a 600-florin dowry. Twenty years later his difficulties provoked *consignatio*, and possession of a farm went to Niccolosa. Niccolosa held the land for the rest of her life, and importantly Sozzini affirmed that *consignatio* vested ownership (*dominium*) in her. So her husband living with her, while he too enjoyed the *fructus*, had only a *ius familiaritatis* (no real ownership). The son, Corrado, thus also had only *familiaritas*. *Consignatio*, furthermore, was not vitiated by a subsequent recovery of wealth. Once consigned to her, the dowry stayed with her (presumably unless she relented freely and there was another *confessio*). *Consignatio* was a legitimate act that was not retracted. *Ius familiaritatis* nicely indicated a claim to share without ownership.

Corrado was also not his father's heir, as he had repudiated the estate formally and had not taken possession of his father's property (as the house belonged to the mother, Niccolosa).[94] He thus escaped the terms of Florence's statute on the obligations of heirs. Niccolosa's heir was Ginevra by her will (though she had taken care to institute Corrado also, so the will stood for not passing him over unmentioned). Ginevra had accepted this maternal inheritance (presumably Corrado had not), so it passed from her to Girolamo and her other children. These heirs, however, faced the argument of Bianco's heirs that no right passed to them from Ginevra because, by the terms of Niccolosa's will, no rights were to go to Ginevra's husband or children. Donors did on occasion add restrictions against husbands, so that was not an unheard-of stipulation.

---

[93] Di Castro, 3 *cons.* 6, fols. 9va–10va.
[94] Cf. Kuehn, *Heirs, Kin, and Creditors*, 68–69, 165.

Bianco's heirs also claimed that Ginevra had not in fact accepted (*adita*) the estate of her mother. Sozzini countered that Ginevra's heirs had their right through her, and that Niccolosa's property had become a single patrimony with Ginevra's. He also said that there had indeed been *aditio*, as Ginevra acted as agent of her dead mother, at least tacitly agreeing to the inheritance's terms. *Aditio* could also be presumed from the fact that the maternal estate was *lucrosa*. Who would turn down something of real value? She transmitted right of inheritance to her children, but she tried to make sure her husband did not get ownership or use.[95]

Bianco's heirs were also precluded by the passage of time. As it had been decades since Bernardo's death, and as Corrado had not been his father's heir, his knowledge of the debts and the estate did not prevent the clock from beginning to run. The son was not subject to the father's obligations in all regards. Thus, as Domenico da San Gimignano (d. 1424) had said, though heir and deceased "are considered the same person," in fact they were different in person and soul, so what struck one did not strike the other (at least in canon law). Sharing ended at the death of one party.

In another instance, when *consignatio* retrieved the dowries of Francesca and her daughter-in-law Antonia from ser Lodovico, his other creditors sought to exchange cash for the properties assigned to the two women. There were several reasons that option seemed licit, including that *consignatio* "is done to the effect that a wife can support herself, her husband and children ... and that the dowry in entirety be situated so that it may easily provide for this effect, placing the dowry with honest merchants."[96] Sozzini, however, sided with the women, though ordinarily creditors might offer the swap of cash for real dotal assets. *Consignatio* was not like restitution, as it had the limited end of furnishing *alimenta* to a woman otherwise in danger of losing wherewithal to her husband's debts. That was not the case when a marriage ended and restitution was at issue. Above all, the properties were safer than cash, as "it is not easily found one with whom money lies in safety and who may realize fructus, as often these merchants become bankrupt, as experience teaches."[97] It would hardly seem that a woman having *consignatio* due to her own husband's insolvency needed reminding that merchants often

---

[95] Sozzini, 1 *cons.* 61, fols. 113rb–15va.
[96] Sozzini, 3 *cons.* 111, fols. 142va–43ra: "fiat ad effectum ut mulier alere possit se, maritum, et liberos ... et ut dos ponatur in tuto ad finem, poterit faciliter provideri huic effectui, ponendo dotem apud mercatores ad honestum lucrum."
[97] Sozzini, 3 *cons.* 111, fols. 142va–43ra: "non de facili invenitur apud quem pecuniae sint in tuto et possit fructus percipere cum saepe isti mercatores efficiantur falliti, ut experientia docet."

went bankrupt. It is interesting that the case of *consignatio*, when the woman was still married and living with her husband, was treated as distinct. Creditors could not simply buy them out of home, shop, farm, vineyard, or whatever. When it was a matter of restitution and inheritance at the end of marriage, it was different, perhaps because the household then was necessarily being reconstituted, as sharing was at an end.

4.5   Conclusion

In all these situations marital patrimonial separation was maintained, though in some instances augmented and in others decreased. There was a functioning household to keep in mind, or that certainly was in the minds of legislators and litigants, and that household was assumed to function on the basis of shared assets, including the use of a wife's dowry to help "sustain the burdens of marriage." Suits were about keeping households more or less together, or letting them come apart on the basis of individual legal rights and claims.

Luca da Panzano was one such householder. He kept careful accounts of his mother's, wife's, and daughters' dowries. While these sums were recorded in the same ledgers with his business deals and contracts on family holdings, they were always separately ascribed. Except for a few weak hints about input or concurrence from his wife and the desires of his mother, there is little sense in his pages that the women around his house were active in managing property or influencing his management. But he also dealt with widows who seemed to have an active command of their resources, and he had to know, as with his mother and one daughter, that they had to be able to rely on resources.

The jurists, who themselves lived in such households, upheld property distinctions, even while aware that female patrimony might help preserve households, and male patrimony more generally. Though statutes seem intent at times on amalgamating wives' assets with their husbands', and account books centered on the figure of the husband and father as property manager, the patrimony was in fact fractured. "What remains beyond doubt is the rarity of the phenomenon of assets held jointly by spouses, which confirms that, in harmony with Roman law, the patri-monies of wife and husband continued to be reckoned as distinct legal entities."[98] That legal distinction could be vital when legal issues pressed. But that continued legal distinction also made sense against a presumed sharing of assets, at least in meeting the mundane and daily expenses of a household – against social realities, in other words.

[98] Kirshner, "Materials," 87.

Wives, then, contributed to and shared in the household economy, but in a different way than did sons, who, after all, had not been part of any other household previously (unlike their mother). The wife, as mother, did not stand in the same substantial relationship with her sons that her husband did as their father. Her sharing was a bit tentative. She could look to move objects and belongings to others, notably to her kin, by gifts or bequests. What she left to her sons, for all that statutes might demand that she leave all or the bulk of her wealth to them, came off as more voluntary than obligatory. Conversely, she could opt to retain her wealth in her marital relations, as Piero Guicciardini's wife did when she chased the creditor and notary from her house.

5   *Societas* and *Fraterna* of Brothers

We have seen how Alberti cautioned against splitting a patrimony and advised that family members should always work to maintain a "well united body." If there was anywhere that the sharing domestic economy was more evident, it would seem to be where brothers were coresident and sharing. Brothers came to such an arrangement, a *fraterna*, as equals, at least in comparison to the unequal relations of father and child, or husband and wife.

Inheritance laws just about everywhere in Italy specified equal division of property among heirs of the same class or degree – in most places with men of the class, excluding dowered women, even those of a closer degree of relationship to the deceased. All of a man's sons, in other words, had legal claims to equal shares of the patrimony. Were there to be the same situation arising at the next point of generational transmission, and the next, the consequence would be the successive fractioning of a patrimony and the relative impoverishment of its owners. The sole exception was that of feudal properties, which by their nature passed as wholes, generally to one heir in primogeniture.[1] The countervailing tendency to such potential fractioning of a patrimony across generations was the widely held expectation and preference for brothers as coheirs to live together, pooling their resources and efforts. Alberti's discussions of family spoke to this expectation. We have also seen the example of the Masi brothers, who stayed together after their father's death but also separated themselves legally from their half-brothers.

Paradoxically, it has been later patterns of unequal inheritance, especially the employment of primogeniture among elites in various regions, that has sparked historical interest recently in sibling relationships. Systemic inequalities in distribution of patrimony resulting from norms regarding dowry and primogeniture, when closely examined in a broad

---

[1] Leverotti, *Famiglie e istituzioni*; Cooper, "Patterns of Inheritance"; Clavero, "Dictum beati: a proposito della cultura del lignaggio."

context of relationships evolving over time, turn out to be less unequal than one suspected. Dowries were recycled over generations, serving to forge alliances of families in marital exchanges.[2] The supposed rules of inheritance, especially primogeniture, were in fact circumvented and relaxed. The family palace could still be and often remained a place of shared living arrangements.[3] Behind primogeniture was supposed to be a continuation of the sharing economy of the household, in contrast to the distinctive ownership and agency of the marketplace and the gift economy, which were bestowed on the eldest son. Still, animosities among siblings, markedly so around the division of patrimony, could become legendary. Exhortations, like that of Alberti, that brothers stay together spoke to the live possibilities that they would not. Exchanges among siblings could also be the key to the survival of a family line.

In essence, there were three possibilities. An inheritance could be divided among multiple heirs; or they could attempt to hold the estate together, undivided; or they could fashion a mixed set of holdings, some divided among them and other discrete properties remaining in common, as much for their symbolic as economic value.[4] The latter two options might still lead eventually to full, real, formal division.

The long-term effects of partible inheritance were apparent to all. The problem was finding some way around them. Clearly, one could limit the number of children and thus reduce the actual claims on patrimony in each generation. But in an era of plagues and other mortality factors, demographic continuity was tenuous at best, especially over the long term.[5] Family strategies in addition had to center around legal devices that preserved ownership and defined its transmission across generations, including customs and expectations with regard to the treatment of property during and immediately after its transmission to the heirs.

The fractioning of patrimonies could also, of course, be countered by the acquisition of further holdings in the next generation, by at least some if not all the heirs. The rebuilt patrimony would pass to the next generation, whose turn it would be similarly to build back the size of the family holdings. Markets, transportation, politics, and weather being what they

---

[2] Cf. Bernard Derouet, "Dowry: Sharing Inheritance or Exclusion? Timing, Destination, and Contents of Transmission in Late Medieval and Early Modern France" and Sophie Ruppel, "Subordinates, Patrons, and Most Beloved: Sibling Relationships in Seventeenth-Century German Court Society."

[3] Benedetta Borello, "Prossimi e lontani: fratelli aristocratici a Roma e Siena (secoli xvii–xix)."

[4] Marta Gravela, "Parentela e finanziamento dello stato: Percorsi di mobilità sociale nella Torino del Tre-Quattrocento," 158–60.

[5] Herlihy and Klapisch-Zuber, *Tuscans and Their Families*, 189–204.

were, however, nothing was assured even to the most conscientious and prudent manager of a patrimony.

The law presented another area in which to look for a remedy to patrimonial division. Testaments could be shaped so as to preclude division among heirs or simply to encourage cohabitation and pooling of assets, or, contrarily, to single out one heir to hold the bulk of the patrimony. The popularity of fideicommissa – teaming substitutions of heirs with blanket and perpetual prohibitions on alienating inherited property outside the family (*extra familiam*) – was one widespread result. We will examine this in the next chapter.

Another means of countering patrimonial erosion – the one of interest here – was to have the multiple heirs continue to hold their shares in common. After all, the real danger to the patrimony was not multiple owners per se but the possibility that they would move to actualize their shares as separate holdings under sole control. The whole was greater than the sum of its parts. The wealthiest families, as revealed by a source like the Florentine catasto, were also almost invariably among the largest.[6] As Benedetta Borello points out, membership in such families did not mean just coresidence but also a daily exchange of views and sentiments to that effect.[7] Identities were forged in that daily experience of a shared patrimony. So in Florence and elsewhere, something like the custom of patrilocal residence of a son upon marriage encouraged sons to remain together with their father. That pattern carried over even after his demise. As Herlihy and Klapisch-Zuber have it, "the rule of patrilocality and the tendency toward keeping the patrimony undivided, which responds to the custom of equal division among male heirs, work to limit the effects of the natural family cycle-expansion as long as children are born and are reared, and contraction when they reach the age when they can set up their own families."[8] A fraternal household was a relatively frequent feature. The existence of more complex, laterally extended households, at least for Florence and Tuscany, which Herlihy and Klapisch-Zuber found already noticeable in the fourteenth century, became more statistically significant in the course of the fifteenth century.[9] Marta Gravela likewise points to the fifteenth century as pivotal in the spread of practices of keeping property undivided.[10]

Still, Herlihy and Klapisch-Zuber also recognize that the cohesion of such brotherly assemblages was weak. Many did not long survive the

[6] Herlihy and Klapisch-Zuber, *Tuscans and Their Families*, 319–25.
[7] Borello, *Il posto di ciascuno: Fratelli, sorelle e fratellanze (xvi–xix secolo)*, 18.
[8] Herlihy and Klapisch-Zuber, *Tuscans and Their Families*, 311–12.
[9] Herlihy and Klapisch-Zuber, *Tuscans and Their Families*, 512–22.
[10] Marta Gravela, *Il corpo della città: politica e parentela a Torino nel tardo Medioevo*, 94.

death of the father. It might be a number of years, but eventually the demand for a division of assets would come. Any greater authority that might fall to the oldest would yield in time as the younger brothers grew up.[11] The household was a process, both in its acquisition and loss of people and of property. If nothing else, as Francis William Kent pointed out, the physical capacity of even a large *palazzo* might be reached, and then it became necessary for at least some of the inhabitants to move out, even if only next door or across the street.[12] As Borello remarks, brothers managing property could act as a cohesive domestic unit or fall out into controversies which, while apparently about lending of goods and services, in reality "were conflicts over the place that each of them occupied and might have had to occupy in family activities with respect to those principles of reciprocity and redistribution on which the enterprises of brothers were founded."[13]

Such reciprocity and redistribution came about when sharing was weakening. There were deeper issues than availability of space. There were questions of status that signaled full belonging in a family and household and standing in the wider community (or failed to). As much as there were reasons for siblings to stay together in a brotherhood (*fraterna*, *fratellanza*), there were reasons to terminate such arrangements. How long such households would last was always in doubt. Gravela points to three areas: conflicts among brothers, between sons and their mother, and with other kin such as uncles and cousins.[14] What is remarkable in view of the frequency of division is that in the fifteenth century commitments to living together and keeping property undivided tended to reduce contentious divisions. The strong presence of landed property in those holdings served as well to furnish a family with a social identity, as "the goods, beyond being an economic investment, became the means to construct social relations, to demonstrate one's economic reliability, to insert oneself actively into the *civitas*."[15] A shared living arrangement among brothers was more than something interior to the home, and supposedly not part of the external, competitive, and visible world of production and markets.[16]

Brothers could position themselves at various points along a continuum. They could base their relationship on a form of gift economy – offering gifts or loans with no expectation of immediate return in order to express and maintain their solidarity (as they might with wider kin relations, neighbors, or associates). Or they could plunge themselves

[11] Herlihy and Klapisch-Zuber, *Tuscans and Their Families*, 322–23, 335.
[12] Kent, *Household and Lineage*, 31.   [13] Borello, *Posto di ciascuno*, 19.
[14] Gravela, *Corpo*, 237.   [15] Gravela, *Corpo*, 250, quote 264.
[16] Cf. Belk, "Sharing," 716.

fully into a sharing of assets and activities on a daily basis, alternately contributing and enjoying as able or needed. There was no calculation of return. There was no sense of indebtedness or individualistic ownership to acknowledge. Sharing shelter or food, as with brothers living *ad unum panem et vinum* (to use a common metaphor of the time), can generate powerful social bonding apart from any sense of blood-relatedness. Inequalities and distinctions that are in fact inevitable were dealt with by sharing.[17]

The goal of this chapter is to examine the sharing economy of the late medieval *fraterna*, or the *societas omnium bonorum*, as we will encounter it in law. We will find that the learned academic law became more accommodating to such *societates*, in the sense of finding them a conceptual space in the law. But the law would also set the bar high, demanding that sharing be total (at least as long as it lasted). The key issue was the sharing of liabilities toward those outside the group, where markets and politics might work their dissolvent magic on family solidarity. How could *familia* be saved by the arrangement of a *societas*? Or how could it be undermined? Would *substantia* be lost? And *familia* with it? As Siglinde Clementi has found for the Tyrolese nobility, "individual property allowed ambivalence that could be used to one's advantage but which also could lead to a high degree of conflict."[18]

5.1   Problems of Division

Physical presence of sharing partners not only lies at the core of sharing; it can also be a weakness of sharing, for, when presence ends or intervals between appearances lengthen, sharing can come to an end. Claims after a long absence may slide a relationship more to gift-giving than sharing.[19] Sharing may also erode when kin relations start to become fixed roles, when those involved stop speaking of and to each other in certain ways, and certainly when they take up separate dwellings.[20]

Possessiveness and mastery or control are the sorts of outlooks that threaten the end of sharing.[21] Or, as assessment of singular interests are not solely individualistic (as per Clementi), things can slip apart on conflicting views of what is good or needed for the group. Then we see the division of the patrimony between or among inheriting brothers.

---

[17] The foregoing derives from Widlok, *Anthropology and the Economy of Sharing*; also on the self, Belk, "Sharing," 723.

[18] Siglinde Clementi, "Undivided Brothers-Renouncing Sisters: Family Strategies of Low Nobility in Sixteenth- and Seventeenth-Century Tyrol," 156.

[19] Widlok, *Anthropology and the Economy of Sharing*, 182.

[20] Widlok, *Anthropology and the Economy of Sharing*, 83.   [21] Belk, "Sharing," 727.

Division of patrimony did not necessarily signal an end to affection and respect among brothers, let alone to an end of cooperation and coordination of patrimonial strategies; but it could. It seems from various statutory provisions that a good number of Italian communities had very real concerns about conflicts arising disturbingly at the heart of domestic relations – conflicts that became most obviously manifest in the division of property among brothers, whether at the moment of inheritance or later. Divisions of patrimony were certainly among the situations in mind when Florence, for example, demanded in law that kin take their disputes to binding arbitration, at least to keep them from more prolonged and presumably more maddening judicial processes.[22]

Laws from a number of communities show that the division of shares in real property, *res immobiles*, were seen as an especially touchy moment that might generate rancor and outright conflict among people who should not be in conflict. Bologna's statutes of 1288, for example, ordered that three neighbors or three trusted friends determine the *pretium competens* when one brother (or cousin or nephew) wanted to liquidate his share. The seller could offer to another common owner only at the price subsequently determined.[23] Venice in 1242 regulated specifically divisions among brothers, desiring that division be equal and that the eldest not cheat the younger. The next statute simply instructed anyone who had a share in an "undivided possession" to notify all the other shareholders if he wanted to sell off his share. If they could not all come to agreement, a judge was to step in. For Venice, a busy commercial port, complications arose over getting all the holders physically together.[24] The early occurrence of such measures in the thirteenth century shows both how common and how pressing were such matters of division. They also certainly lingered on. Bologna found it necessary to repeat its corresponding statute in later redactions – a tribute perhaps to its success but also to its continued need.[25]

In the fourteenth century the Tuscan cities of Cortona, Arezzo, and Montepulciano all enacted statutes declaring that if one common owner wanted to sell off his share, the other holders had to agree, and that a communal judicial official should step in to determine the price and see that the sale occurred.[26] These places obviously sided with the party wanting out of common ownership as a way of obviating conflict, while

---

[22] See Kuehn, *Law, Family, and Women*, 19–74.
[23] *Statuti di Bologna dell'anno 1288*, 2: 65–66.
[24] *Gli statuti veneziani di Jacopo Tiepolo del 1242 e le loro glosse*, 125–27.
[25] *Lo statuto del Comune di Bologna dell'anno 1335*, 2: 530–31.
[26] *Statuto del Comune di Cortona (1325–1380)*, 344–45; *Statuto di Arezzo (1327)*, 178–80; *Statuto del comune di Montepulciano (1337)*, 143.

also respecting other holders who wished to retain their common economy. Siena took the same stance in its statute in the late redaction of 1545.[27] Florence reenacted as late as 1415 a statute that was very complete on the matter of intrafamilial arbitrations.[28] That city was intent on resolving quickly and fairly any disputes among kin arising over patrimonial division.[29] And matters of fair price of goods or fair evaluation of value were not easily resolved. Some people were considered experts and were relied on at such moments.

Difficulties arising during divisions between brothers are evident in one intriguing Florentine example involving the sons of ser Viviano di Neri Viviani.[30] A prolonged litigation was needed to forge some sort of accommodation among eight surviving sons and their progeny. There was conflict not only between the two sets of siblings ser Viviano left by different mothers but also within the set of older brothers. These brothers presented separate inventories of household assets to communal officials in 1427 (the Florentine fiscal device of the catasto, enacted in that year, quite possibly being the occasion for the brothers to divide property and take on separate fiscal identities). But those documents also reveal that the division among them was not simple. The most prestigious of them, the lawyer messer Francesco Viviani (1379–1430), revealed that he held shared ownership of a house with his brother Neri, but also part of an "albergho" with his other brothers, Lodovico and Giovanni.[31] For his part Neri revealed that he was also part owner of the *albergo*, as well as the houses, about which he complained of Francesco that he had not shared with him. Neri also listed some debts he had in common with his brothers. The assertion of sole ownership signaled the end to sharing, though by Neri's testimony there was never any sharing with Francesco.

Lodovico and Giovanni also shared a second house, where Giovanni lived, and Lodovico told of another two houses split four ways and a seventh of another house (also split four ways, meaning he had one twenty-eighth). For his part Giovanni disclosed that Lodovico owed him for the expenses of their brother Andrea, a professed religious left out of the paternal will. That obligation was in fact subject to arbitration that had yet to conclude.[32] In a subsequent catasto almost twenty years later (1446), Giovanni reported holding five pieces of land and a house in

---

[27] *L'ultimo statuto della Repubblica di Siena (1545)*, 180–81.

[28] *Statuta populi et communis Florentiae, anno salutis mccccxv*, 1: 162–64.

[29] Kuehn, *Law, Family, and Women*, 26–30.

[30] Cf. Kuehn, "'Nemo mortalis cognitus vivit in evo': Moral and Legal Conflicts in a Florence Inheritance Case of 1442."

[31] On Francesco, cf. Martines, *Lawyers and Statecraft*, 492.

[32] The above comes from the catasto declarations of the four brothers, each entered separately in ASF, Catasto 74, fols. 30r–31v, 67v, 69v, 54r–56v, 49v–50v.

Santa Maria Novella a Peretola that had been Lodovico's.[33] These two brothers remained closer to each other than to their other brothers, and Lodovico, who seems to have died without sons or daughters, advantaged his favorite brother in inheritance over the other two, Francesco and Neri. With these brothers any real sharing gave way to individualized holdings, even as fractions of title to some things.

A less messy, less complicated, more typical example is that of Corso and Sandro de' Ricci, who seem amicably to have settled their division through an arbitrator. Sandro came away with a rural estate at Pozzolatico, keeping all credits in the public debt that were posted in his name. Corso had a few days to pay him an additional 116 florins, plus twenty staia of grain, and faced the obligation to meet all fiscal exactions of his brother for five years, to a total of 300 florins. Any debts of Sandro in Corso's bank were to be canceled. For his part Corso kept the house in Florence on via de' Balestieri where they both lived, a rural holding at Montici, and all his capital in his bank. Except for the bank and monte shares, the brothers had held their property "communiter" to that point. Corso, in fact, was not present when the arbitration settlement was described and set down, but the notary's marginal notation reveals that he ratified it all over three months later.[34]

These examples remind us that brothers were also capable of getting along for prolonged periods, in living together and pooling their assets for the good of the household. The Florentine catasto is replete with examples of joint fiscal declarations by cohabiting brothers. While many of these were indeed young and had only recently lost their father, not being in a position yet to manage property and earn a living on their own, that was not so in all cases.[35] There are plenty of examples of brothers being older, married and with children, continuing to live together. For example, we find in the catasto of 1427 that Bernardo Bardi, age forty-two and just married, and Vieri di Bartolo Bardi, as yet unmarried and away in Valencia, reported their holdings in common, including a business debt for 800 florins.[36] No return obligation was ascribed to one brother alone. Three other Bardi (Giovanni, Simone, and Arnolfo) men in their forties and sixties, the elder two having married and sired children (Arnolfo, the youngest, had a bastard daughter), held their relatively modest patrimony

---

[33] ASF, Catasto 667, fol. 131v.   [34] ASF, NA 9037, fols. 359v–62v (31 December 1411).
[35] E.g., six Alberti brothers, the oldest not yet sixteen, in 1480 (Catasto 1020, fols. 9r–12r); two Bardi in 1427 (Catasto 64, fols. 394r–94v); three Machiavelli (Catasto 65, fols. 195r–97r); a married and an unmarried brother of the Viviani (Franco and Lionardo) in 1427 (Catasto 69, fols. 281v–84v); five Benvenuti (Catasto 69, fols. 281v–85r); three Angiolini in 1457 (Catasto 790, fols. 23r–24v); two Bini (Catasto 790, fols. 399r–402r); and three Rinuccini (Catasto 800, fols. 408r–12v).
[36] Catasto 64, fols. 43r–45r.

in common.[37] Three Gianfigliazzi in their fifties, sons of messer Rinaldo, had a similar arrangement that included the son of their dead brother.[38] Two pairs of Tornabuoni brothers, Francesco and Niccolò di messer Simone, and Simone and Filippo di Filippo (men in their forties and twenties), managed a household of twenty souls, including their mother, wives (of Francesco and Niccolò), and Francesco's large brood. Here there was some distinction drawn as to what belonged to one pair or the other, given the unevenness in marital and familial situations.[39] But the brothers were jointly responsible for household fiscal duties, no matter how they might account that all out among themselves.

In the 1457 catasto one comes across the household of Luigi and Giovanni Quaratesi, in their forties, with their wives, a sister aged fifty, and fifteen children between them, not counting an eighteen-year-old bastard son of Giovanni and one in utero. Paternity of each child was attributed, but not separate ownership of any objects or credits.[40] In another example, four sons of Stefano di Filippo Porechi – ranging in age from eighteen to forty – lived together and pooled their property. The two oldest were married and one had an infant daughter.[41] The eight sons of Giovanni Capponi lived together with their mother, who was in fact described as head of household. The eldest had married, but the youngest was only fourteen. As the mother was still around, this *fraterna compagnia* would survive in some form a few more years at least.[42] Carlo, Lorenzo, and Francesco Biliotti, ranging in age from forty to fifty-three, resided together. Carlo was married with seven children; Lorenzo married with two. Their wives were also part of the household.[43] Such examples can be found throughout Florentine records. Brothers differentiated relationships, marriage, and paternity, but little else. To be sure, the catasto officials did not care about a breakdown of internal ownership; they held all brothers equally liable on all the holdings. But time and again brothers living together accepted that joint fiscal liability by the form their disclosures took. Both on their part and that of officials the presumption of sharing was immediate and unquestioned.

5.2   Brothers and Business in Law

Klapisch-Zuber has brought out the fact that such joint ownership did not merely counter the threat of division of inheritance but rested as well on presumptions about obligations and acquisitions. There was an economy

---

[37] Catasto 74, fols. 157r–58v.   [38] Catasto 75, fols. 141v–45v.
[39] Catasto 77, fols. 383r–90r.   [40] Catasto 785, fols. 287r–90r.
[41] Catasto 785, fols. 571r–73r.   [42] Catasto 795, fols. 448r–50v.
[43] Catasto 1003, fols. 230r–31r.

in which to operate and there was law behind that.[44] Angelo Verga, who has conducted the most thorough yet now dated study, sees the "comunione di famiglie" as essentially a Germanic legal import, and mainly of use in rural areas with the common enterprise of agriculture. The absolute ownership of the Roman *pater* seemed to preclude any such communion, though the equation of sons subject to his power did level them into a common position.[45] A good number of Italian communes, including Florence, enacted into statutes the presumption of solidarity of coresident kin for liabilities, but this ran up against (according to Verga) the utter silence of doctrine on this.

The academic law, in fact, made some crucial distinctions. These began with the fact of living together, as per Borello: "it is always residence that, jurists maintain ... gives rise to the presumption of a brotherly tie between individuals."[46] Even the presence or absence of architectural dividing walls or separate entrances told whether there was exclusive or "promiscuous" use of household space – of what kind of relationship brothers had.[47] Brothers merely living together – presumably continuing their fraternal affection or gaining the economies of shared living arrangements – were termed a *fraterna communio*. Those who were also in business together, with their domestic life an extension of their financial life, constituted something more, a *societas*.

Societas was essentially a commercial partnership. As defined by Laurent Waelkens, it was a

legal concept by means of which two or more people who were *sui iuris* joined part of their assets or *familia* in order to reach a commercial goal. All of the assets which they devoted to the *societas* belonged to all *socii* in the same way and could be revendicated by each *socius*. The co-ownership that had been agreed upon was full ownership of the assets by each *socius*.[48]

The *societas* could end at any time, if a partner died or simply demanded liquidation of the assets. The commercial partnership was something less than the full sharing *societas omnium bonorum*, which also began with coresidence.

Starting from the premise that business partnerships paradigmatically began with associations of brothers, Max Weber, referencing Orazio Carpano's (fl. 1595) commentary on the Milanese statutes, noted that

---

[44] Christiane Klapisch-Zuber and Michel Demonet, "'A uno pane e uno vino': The Rural Tuscan Family at the Beginning of the Fifteenth Century," 47–48. On the law see Camillo Fumagalli, *Il diritto di fraterna nella giurisprudenza da Accursio alla codificazione* and more recently Umberto Santarelli, *Mercanti e società tra mercanti: Lezioni di storia del diritto*.
[45] Angelo Verga, *Le comunioni tacite familiari*, 14–31.   [46] Borello, *Posto di ciascuno*, 67.
[47] Borello, *Posto di ciascuno*, 81–82.   [48] Waelkens, *Amne Adverso*.

the *societas* for business purposes had to have distinct elements in order to trigger full joint liability for partners. Only contracts made on behalf of the *societas* could be taken as involving partners. A partner acting alone was presumed to be acting on his behalf only, and thus obligating himself alone. Otherwise, as Carpano noted, brothers living together could face disaster. Those dealing with people in such a fraternal union had to watch out for it "as much as for fire."[49]

Such fires may have been more pronounced in Florence than anywhere else, at least in that Florence, unlike most everywhere else, went beyond the principles of the *lex mercatoria* holding partners liable for each other, and enacted statutes explicitly to that effect. These laws, in fact, involved more than brothers. Their main concern seems to have been the mutual liability of fathers and their unemancipated sons, where the legal tie of *patria potestas*, more than the fact of coresidence, underwrote such liability. But coresidence was easy to spot and served as the basis for imputing collective liabilities, even though the appearances of coresidence could be deceiving as to underlying legal realities. For those in the community, who were potential clients and customers, the evident fact of coresidence implied common involvement in economic and legal affairs of the household. Legal steps that might undercut the fact of coresidence – like emancipation or the repudiation of inheritance – were carefully controlled and even registered.[50] These steps attempted to make the underlying legal situation public knowledge.

There was a different statutory attitude toward cohabiting kin, in contrast to unrelated and noncohabiting partners. With regard to brothers specifically, the statutes declared that those living with a brother who went into default, sharing a common craft or shop, were liable for his debts.[51] This principle of fraternal liability, first emerging in law in the statutes of the Mercanzia of 1309, and repeated in guild statutes, reappearing in the communal statues of 1325 and 1355, saw only the minor clarification in the redaction of 1415. The later statute obligated brothers, if "they lived commonly in the same house and practiced the same craft or trade according to the public opinion of neighbors."[52] Here the appearances of coresidence and economic activity were obviously telling. Other than posing that neighborhood opinion bore probative

---

[49] Orazio Carpano, *Statuta ducatus mediolanensis collecta et commentarius illustrata* [quoted in Max Weber, *The History of Commercial Partnerships in the Middle Ages*, 176].

[50] See Kuehn, *Emancipation in Late Medieval Italy*, 42–46; *Heirs, Kin, and Creditors*, 61–65; and "Debt and Bankruptcy in Florence."

[51] *Statuta del Capitano del Popolo degli anni 1322–25*, 105–6: "stabant simul et vocabant indivisi in eadem domo, comuniter faciendo eandem artem vel alia negotia."

[52] Statuta 1415, 1: 520–21: "viverent in eadem domo comuniter et eadem artem vel mercantiam exerceat secundum publicam opinionem vicinorum."

weight, there is nothing in this statute that specifies what practicing the same *mercantia* meant.

The device of a limited liability partnership, brought into effect at the insistence of the Mercanzia in 1408, in fact was little used.[53] What Florentines at least tended to do instead, keeping an essential family basis to their partnerships, was to devise not a single, all-embracing partnership, but diverse commercial *societates* for different places and purposes. This is what the Medici famously did, fashioning what Raymond de Roover referred to as a holding company.[54] Richard Goldthwaite has speculated that this practice offered better prospects of attracting partners and capital from outside one's family; but he also importantly notes that a principal investor, implicated in many different partnerships, was still liable to the full extent of his patrimony.[55] Bankruptcies and liabilities were thus spread across several entities and did not have a systemic, catastrophic impact on family and patrimony.[56] This behavior has been taken as indicative of a capitalistic individualism.[57]

What is remarkable is the fact that Florentines and others continued to form expansive and total *societates omnium bonorum*, which seemed to accept extended liability otherwise avoided in interlocked but specific business partnerships. People continued to believe and act in such a way that they still projected common and shared interests, such "that there remained into the Renaissance period some feeling that a *consors* had a common economic interest, that *consorti* were especially to be trusted in delicate questions concerning property."[58] It is hard to give a statistical picture of such *societates*, for, whereas one could count fraternal associations from a source like the catasto, it is not possible from that evidence alone to say if the brotherly arrangements rose to the legal level of a *societas*, let alone a *societas omnium bonorum*.

Business may over time have become more individualistic, separate from family management of real estate, but the separation could also be very porous.[59] The enforcement of extended liabilities, filial and fraternal, was often swift and harsh, especially when the primary debtor who had

---

[53] Thomas Kuehn, "Multorum Fraudibus Occurrere: Litigation and Jurisprudential Interpretation Concerning Fraud and Liability in Quattrocento Florence," 317; Goldthwaite, *The Economy of Renaissance Florence*, 64–79. An example from a guild is found in Saverio Lasorsa, *L'organizzazione dei cambiatori fiorentini nel medio evo*, 138.

[54] Raymond de Roover, *The Rise and Decline of the Medici Bank, 1397–1494*, 77–86.

[55] Goldthwaite, *The Economy of Renaissance Florence*, 77.

[56] Cf. Lorenzo Tanzini, *1345, la bancarotta di Firenze: una storia di banchieri, fallimenti e finanza*, 103 and 105.

[57] Cf. William Caferro, *Contesting the Renaissance*, 130–31.

[58] Kent, *Household and Lineage*, 132.   [59] Kent, *Household and Lineage*, 122.

effectively become bankrupt had fled the city. Florence had a whole raft of statutes dealing with such notorious *cessantes et fugitivi*, treating them as thieves of others' property, which included the measure of painting their likeness on the walls of the palace of the podestà as a very public act of disgrace. There was some protection in another statute that allowed a father, son, brother, and so forth of someone who was mismanaging his affairs (male gesserit sua negotia) to move that the podestà banish or jail the prodigal.[60] Clearly, the embrace of collective liability in a partnership of cohabiting brothers in financial good times could give way to distinct interests and claims in a scramble to limit liability when times became bad.

A few other cities exhibited similar concern to hold brothers liable so as to assure those active in the markets that they would have some legal and economic recourse against an absent creditor. Cortona's statute said that, if a brother received a dowry for his wife and used it for the benefit of all, on his decease his brothers were liable for return of the dowry.[61] This did not directly deal with markets and common business ventures, but another law did, when it absolved brothers of those who had gone surety for another, but not the brothers of the principal debtor himself.[62] On a related matter Arezzo clarified that brothers were responsible for taxes, even if only one of them was actually listed in the fiscal registers (*alibratus*), when they lived together.[63] Broadly, a solidarity and shared liability were imputed to members of a fraternal company – the very expression of the unity among a plurality of persons. This imputation, in turn, rested on the extraction of family from the usual norms of markets and market relations, as coalescing around feelings of *caritas* and sharing.[64]

5.3   Jurisprudence

While Florence's statutes were nonchalant about what counted as fraternal business, jurisprudence was seeking precision. The scattered texts of civil law that could relate to the problem of brothers cohabiting fairly begged for more systematic treatment. An early attempt in that direction was the treatise of Jacopo Balduini (fl. 1210–35), whose survival in a single manuscript speaks to its limited professional impact.[65] That

---

[60] Edgerton, *Pictures and Punishment*; Ortalli, *La pittura infamante, secoli xii–xvi*.
[61] *Statuto del Comune di Cortona (1325–1380)*, 326.
[62] *Statuto del Comune di Cortona (1325–1380)*, 281.   [63] *Statuto di Arezzo (1327)*, 185.
[64] Borello, *Posto di ciascuno*, 203–6.
[65] Andrea Romano, "La summula de fratribus simul habitantibus di Jacopo Balduini," which has been translated in Cavallar and Kirshner, *Jurists and Jurisprudence in Medieval Italy: Texts and Contexts*, 803–6.

may be because Balduini was only interested in the issues of coresidence and not the problem of business activities and consequent liabilities. Later jurists, Riccardo Malombra (d. 1334) and Oldrado da Ponte (d. 1335), ventured the first conjectures on the tacit business partnership (*societas tacita*) that might arise between brothers living together with undivided ownership of their patrimony.[66] But it was Bartolus of Sassoferrato who truly first addressed the *materia duorum fratrum simul habitantium* in a treatise. Unfortunately, death overtook him before he completed the second part. So his treatise was limited to the issues of division among brothers when one of them had realized gains from activities underwritten by paternal funds.[67] Still, in distinguishing among situations in which neither brother conducted business, or only one did, or both did, Bartolus concluded that only in the third case could it be said that one might presume that a partnership (*societas*) had been contracted.

Bartolus was notably reluctant to construe the existence of a partnership merely from the fact of brothers living together. He required that they both conduct the same business. In that way he could concede a *societas* as tacitly contracted.[68] As Elvira Contino determines, Bartolus "was inclined to recognize the existence of a tacit partnership in the family only when the cohabiting brothers engaged in a commercial activity (*negotiatio*) that could also embrace different trade operations (*negotiationes diversae illarum*)."[69] He even drew the distinction between sharing and gift, as sharing did not demand reciprocity: "It cannot be called a gift, as it is not done from generosity, such that I confer on you so that you will confer on me."[70] The *societas* of all goods was distinct, with all gains, personal as well as commercial, being involved, and it could not be tacit; it had to be formal, according to Bartolus.[71] It was not about generosity. If anything, it was about a sense of duty or obligation.

It was Bartolus's student, Baldo degli Ubaldi, who stepped forward to complete Bartolus's unfinished work, and who followed that up with comments not only in his academic lectures but also in a number of case opinions (consilia) addressing real issues arising from the tangled

---

[66] Elvira Contino, "Societas e famiglia nel pensiero di Baldo degli Ubaldi," 34.
[67] Contino, "Societas e famiglia nel pensiero di Baldo degli Ubaldi," 34–36.
[68] Verga, *Le comunioni tacite familiari*, 48–50.
[69] Contino, "Societas e famiglia nel pensiero di Baldo degli Ubaldi," 37–38.
[70] "Non potest dici donatio, cum non fiat ex liberalitate, ideo enim tibi confero ut tu conferas mihi" (quoted in Verga, *Le comunioni tacite familiari*, 50–51). See also Ferdinando Treggiari, "La società di fatto: Sondaggi di dottrina giuridica medievale," 2239.
[71] Contino, "Societas e famiglia nel pensiero di Baldo degli Ubaldi," 39.

and often secretive dealings of brothers.[72] Baldo thus also addressed other issues than those arising on division of assets among brothers.

In contrast to Bartolus, Baldo was more liberal in construing active co-involvement in communal life. At its core, there had to be an acceptance of risk to all parties.[73] He posited also a certain affection among brothers such that they would pool and share their gains coming from whatever source, and not just from common business activities – revenue from a fief or benefice, dowry, salary.[74] Above all, the plain fact of living together on an undivided inheritance was not of itself sufficient to conclude that there was a *societas* between two brothers. But Baldo also conceded that there was doubt in that situation, to be clarified by how brothers used resources that were common or personal. If no gains or losses were shared (implying some sort of separate accounting was going on), there was no *societas*. The opposite was the *societas omnium bonorum* with obligation of conferral of all gains from whatever source, including one's singular labors (*industria*), whether the obligation was entered into explicitly or tacitly. Similarly, all expenses, losses, and debts were in common, whatever their source.[75] Brothers did not have to be business partners to be in a *societas omnium bonorum* by Baldo's reasoning. He invoked the example where one brother was in commerce while the other was a lawyer or notary, but they brought their profits and losses into a single common pool.[76] That approach coincided with the tendency of Florentines in practice to engage in different occupations and not have all sons in the same business – a diversification that was probably a good precaution.[77] The third, inter-mediate, option was an express *societas* for lucrative purposes – a true business partnership that did not cover certain more personal activities (such as receiving or paying out a dowry, covering educational expenses, and so forth). Baldo maintained a wider sense of such partnerships, covering not just commercial affairs but also agricultural, artisanal, or professional activities.[78] In that regard more jurists seem to have endorsed his formulation than Bartolus's more restrictive one.[79]

---

[72] Baldo was a continuator at least in the sense that the great sixteenth-century compendium of Bartolo's writings included Baldo's treatise as the second half of Bartolo's. See Bartolo, *Consilia, Quaestiones et Tractatus*.

[73] Treggiari, "La società di fatto: Sondaggi di dottrina giuridica medievale," 2240.

[74] Contino, "Societas e famiglia nel pensiero di Baldo degli Ubaldi," 39–47.

[75] Contino, "Societas e famiglia nel pensiero di Baldo degli Ubaldi," 49–51.

[76] Verga, *Le comunioni tacite familiari*, 53.

[77] A pattern noticed years ago by Gene Brucker, *Florentine Politics and Society, 1343–1378*, 26–27.

[78] Contino, "Societas e famiglia nel pensiero di Baldo degli Ubaldi," 58.

[79] Verga, *Le comunioni tacite familiari*, 54–55.

Dowries were a difficult matter. Each brother's wife would come with a different dowry. They could not be simply equated. They broached a real distinction in the nominal holdings of each brother, both to establish dowry for one's daughter and to return the dowry of one's wife following the end of the marriage, even if his brother had been co-guarantor for return of the dowry in the notarial instrument creating it. To Baldo dowries were not commercial acts but personal, arising in natural law, incumbent on a girl's father, first of all, but also on brothers or others in his absence. Educational costs and other family expenses were also things that were incumbent typically on one brother alone for his children. But these things did not preclude that there was a *societas negotiativa*. In a *societas omnium bonorum*, however, even such personal expenses were common, as there was no separate fund in effect for each brother. Thus it was that Baldo, according to Contino, was well aware that a *fraterna* "might not be in condition to satisfy completely the needs of its individual members" and so he devised a solution in "the possible subsistence, within the domestic situation, of an associative agreement aimed at reaching a common aim."[80] Baldo gave full play to an idea of family united by more than blood, by an identity forged in the formation and growth of common patrimony and personal gain. He gave the domestic sharing economy a place in law. He made way for a family that could pour vitality into its actions and "overcome the rigid structure of the patriarchal family."[81] But it is also clear that patriarchal concerns, expressed prior to a *pater*'s death and carrying continual force in his will, still had weight.

5.4   Cases

Many of the problems faced by cohabiting brothers came to jurists, who approached them with the tools available to them as a result of the efforts of Baldo, if without his talent and incisive mind. The issues for them were practical and immediate, even if being treated hypothetically at times. It is to them we now turn to complete our sense of the dynamics of late medieval and Renaissance *fraterna*. There were broadly two avenues of concern in cases: (1) division of property among brothers, and (2) provision for liability arising from the actions of one partner (which might also lead to division).

---

[80] Contino, "Societas e famiglia nel pensiero di Baldo degli Ubaldi," 89.
[81] Contino, "Societas e famiglia nel pensiero di Baldo degli Ubaldi," 90.

5.4.1   *Division*

In a case from the early sixteenth century, a phalanx of Florentine jurists faced complicated issues. In this instance it required six pages to relate all the details.[82] The brothers Francesco and Domenico Naldini in May 1502 made an explicit *societas* of all their property, even to the extent that neither could draw up a testament without the other's participation, except for donations to "pious causes" not to exceed 100 scudi. They modified the agreement the following February with more specific terms to cover all *mobilia* and *immobilia*, credits and debts, and the right of succession to one brother or his children, if the deceased left no children. The exception for donations doubled to 200 scudi. The amount to go to one brother's children was to be at least half the other brother's share (thus a quarter of the whole), and dowries were to be provided to any daughters. Neither brother could "sell, alienate, pawn, give, cede, trans-port" or otherwise dispose of anything without the consent of the other. This all seemed a total and carefully contrived explicit *societas omnium bonorum*.

Yet in November 1516 Francesco had a notary draw up an assertion that the *conventio* with Domenico was not valid, because it restricted his free capacity to testate and effectively made a gift (a transfer of title, not a simple sharing) of all his property to his brother. On that ground he "revoked, broke, and annulled" his agreement with Domenico. Seemingly, something had arisen after more than a decade to sour the relationship between the brothers. Later Domenico Naldini and Francesco Belcarii, Francesco's agent, drew up an agreement ending the *societas* between the brothers. The very legalistic and detailed nature of the agreement of *societas* makes one wonder how sharing (in the sense of not calculating reciprocities) the entire arrangement ever was.

In September 1517 Francesco drew up a will containing a number of bequests to both religious and lay recipients. A year later, in September 1518, Francesco, said to be ill and away in Milan, added codicils, including the bequest to an Andrea Baldantie and his wife of 100 scudi annually for life. Francesco died a few days later. Domenico was still his brother's heir, but in the face of all the bequests in the testament and codicil, the value of the estate was greatly diminished, at the least. He decided to repudiate the estate, which then fell to his children (next in line), for whom he then accepted the estate with benefit of inventory, so as to reduce his exposure to Francesco's debts, including all those bequests. He could do this with the pretense of the children as

---

[82] ASF, Carte strozziane, 3rd ser., 42, fols. 89r–109v (hereafter Strozzi et al.).

heirs, because they were minors for whom inventory was available in Florence.[83] Thereafter Domenico refused to pay any bequests as he asserted that there was nothing in the inheritance, other than 200 scudi for *pias causas*, "because his brother's property belonged to him by virtue of the donation made to him in the contract of partnership" (virtute donationis sibi facte in contractu societatis omnium bonorum), which he claimed remained in effect despite the renunciation two years earlier. It was the beneficiaries of Francesco's generosity who opposed Domenico's claims and argued that the 1502 *conventio* between the brothers was properly quashed because it limited freedom of testation and generally was "contra bonos mores."[84] They noted that Domenico himself had renounced the *societas*. The beneficiaries further alleged that there never had been a true *societas*, because the brothers had in fact operated independently and without informing each other of their interests and activities.[85] That pattern may have been behind Francesco's demand to terminate the partnership.

Three legal issues thus emerged – did the succession still fall to the survivor and his sons? Was the renunciation valid? Were Domenico's assertions of continued validity of the *societas* valid? These questions were addressed seriatim by seven Florentine jurists, of whose opinions four survive.[86] The lengthy opening positions were those of Antonio Strozzi (1455–1523), in 1518 a venerable figure on Florence's legal scene and senior of those involved in the case. In fact, the others dared add little to his fulsome treatment. Proceeding pro-et-contra, he noted a number of commentaries and consilia that could be taken as upholding the *societas* and its stipulations about inheritance, thereby supporting Domenico's position. The effective *donatio* of all one's present and future goods in the second contract could be construed to be equivalent to free

---

[83] On these legal maneuvers, see Kuehn, *Heirs, Kin, and Creditors*, 55–59, 166. There is no record of the repudiation in the surviving Florentine registry.

[84] In this case, providing an excellent example of the observations of Angelo Torre and Riccardo Rossolino about the involvement of legatees of *piae causae* working to affect all the intentions of the testators who had included them in their testaments. Cf. Angelo Torre, "'Cause pie': riflessioni su lasciti e benefici in antico regime"; Riccardo Rossolino, *Credito e morte a Palermo nel Seicento*.

[85] Strozzi et al., fol. 91v: "societas predicta non habuit effectum quia dicte partes nihil ut socii egerunt sed omnia eorum negocia separatim egerunt Aretium."

[86] The beginning of the fifth, Antonio Bonsi's (1490–1533), occurs at the end of the manuscript. Nothing remains of the consilia of Alessandro Malegonnelli (1491–1555) and Bernardo Gualterotti (b. 1491), who were also said to have "subscribed," according to the note inserted at the very beginning (fol. 83r). These three were all of a younger generation than the other four and their opinions may well have been brief, and lightly prized by other practicing jurists. On all the signatories, see Lauro Martines, *Lawyers and Statecraft*, 486–87, 489–90, 497.

testation. And right of testation certainly remained on the 200 scudi stipulated in the agreement.

Yet in Strozzi's thinking it was the legatees (some of whom were religious institutions) who gained. The *societas* agreement either set up a succession pact that was not valid or it made a gift of all present and future belongings, which also could not hold. The vital argument was that, by the common opinion in jurisprudence, a gift of all present and future possessions was illegal, as it impeded the making of a testament "because there would be nothing to be gained from the estate."[87] First of all, such a "common opinion" was not to be set aside "in consulendo et iudicando." What it declared was that by its nature the gift of all left nothing in the estate for an heir. The reservation of 200 scudi did not vindicate freedom of testation because it had to go to *pias causas*. No amount of sworn intent to uphold such an agreement could make it valid both for present and future possessions. Domenico's claims did not stand against his brother's will.

Though the contract between the brothers was certainly valid at its beginning, the fact that they operated independently of each other (separatim) created a situation "as if they had not contracted a partnership."[88] Domenico had conducted business without reference to his brother many times. Furthermore, while it took two to agree to form a partnership, it took only one to end it. So it was at least ended by Francesco in 1516. Nor could Domenico, who by his actions effectively agreed to abrogate the partnership, try to allege it to his benefit. In any case, he had renounced the *societas* and the partners had resolved their issues in a formal settlement (*finis*). Domenico could not argue either that he had been seriously harmed (*laesus*) by the dissolution of the *societas* or that he acted under fear. That Francesco had threatened to disperse his goods if Domenico did not agree to end their *societas* did not rise to the level of fear that justified overturning a legal act.[89]

Secondly because a prudent man would not be fearful of such threats because of doubt at least as to which of the contracting parties would predecease, likewise Francesco might not fulfill what he threatened. For he could not know he would go first and therefore he would not diminish his property lest it pass to Domenico.[90]

---

[87] Strozzi et al., fol. 95v: "quantum ad effectum heredem habendi, quia nullus adiret hereditatem nil lucraturus ex ea."

[88] Strozzi et al., fol. 102r.   [89] Strozzi et al., fol. 105r.

[90] Strozzi et al., fol. 105v: "Secundo quid vir prudens non timuisset huiusmodi comminationes eo quia propter dubium saltem predecedente alterius ex contrahentibus verisimile non adimplvisset Franciscus ea que comminabatur. Non enim scire poterat quia eorum predecessurus foret et propterea bona sua ne in Dominicum pervenirent non dilapidasset."

Even if fear of such consequences was what motivated Domenico, a "constant man" was not felled by such fear. He could make nothing of the *societas* agreement to try to shut out beneficiaries.

Matteo Niccolini (1473–1542) and Marco degli Asini (ca. 1484–1575) both briefly signed Strozzi's opinion, admitting to have exchanged views and arguments (*communicato colloquio*) with him. Giovanvettorio Soderini (1460–1528) added three pages of argument against Domenico's attempt to rescind his closing of the *societas*, even in the face of Francesco's threats to dissipate all his property, and despite his ignorance of Francesco's holdings and their adequacy to meet all the bequests he threw into his will. There was nothing here "as must stop a constant man."[91] That fear (*metus*) rose to the level of physical threats, arms in hand, or even some physical harm with threat of more.[92]

The reality of the *societas*, rather than its formal terms, was what came to matter. Intriguingly, nothing is included in this case about cohabitation or about the pooling of assets and expenses on personal and domestic matters, rather than on business. Failure to find those elements, the essence of true sharing, would also seem to be pertinent to arguments against the *societas omnium bonorum* every bit as much as to say that the brothers conducted business apart from each other.

It is worth noting in this context too a position staked out by Strozzi in a legal glossary, thus not in the back-and-forth of a case, but seemingly in a dispassionate moment:

Two or more brothers, while their father is alive, if they have goods in common and have not yet made a division of goods, and one lives on his own, that which one of the brothers acquires is not shared with the others, because while the father is alive there is no presumption of a tacit partnership among the brothers possessing goods in common even if they live together and do business.[93]

Needless to say, a host of citations supported that position.

In the consilium we encountered in Chapter 3, Bartolomeo Sozzini had to determine whether Cristoforo had been in a relationship of full sharing with his brother Giovanni, a matter, said Sozzini, that was subject to

[91] Strozzi et al., fol. 109r: "ideo non debet censeri hic metus talis ut cadere debeat in constantem virum."
[92] On *metus* see Jacobson Schutte, *By Force and Fear*, 144–46, 155–57; James A. Brundage, *Law, Sex, and Christian Society in Medieval Europe*, 335, 345; Daniela Hacke, "'Non lo volevo per marito in modo alcuno': Forced Marriages, Generational Conflicts, and the Limits of Patriarchy in Early Modern Venice, c. 1580–1680."
[93] ASF, Carte strozziane, 3rd ser., 41/17, fol. 466r: "Fratres duo vel plures vivente patre si habeant bona in comuni et nondum fecerunt divisionem bonorum et unus habitet seorsum ab aliis, illud quod unus ex fratribus acquirit non venit comunicandum cum alteris, quia patre vivente non presumitur inter fratres bona comuniter possidentes tacita societas contracts etiam si simul habitarent et negociarent."

varying judgments every day.[94] Sozzini argued for a strong but tacit *societas omnium bonorum*. It rose to the standards of proof of a *societas omnium bonorum* urged by jurists like Bartolus and Baldo: "when brothers live in common in the same house, have business under a common name, act 'promiscuously,' share profits and take no accounting of profits between them and stay that way for a long time."[95] Cristoforo's absence while living in Ferrara did not end that, as expenses were still covered by the common holdings. The sale of a *hospitium* by Giovanni to Cristoforo, an act of separate ownership, did not end that *societas* either. No single act like that meant the end of partnership.

Cristoforo's *peculium quasi castrense* raised a thornier problem. This was money that had come to him from the *princeps*. But Sozzini said that in a situation of tacit communion of goods, it too became part of the common pot. As the brothers were in fact on the verge of dividing their holdings, there were questions about dowries and other expenses for wives and children to be squared and other credits to litigate. Time was needed for that process. What Sozzini saw as a very sharing domestic situation, beginning with the father, was finally coming to an end.

There were many other issues between brothers. Three jurists took on a case from Pisa. This text has no detailed *punctus* of facts, and only a limited amount can be gleaned serially under the heading whether there was a *societas* between an uncle and nephew (a carryover from a partnership of brothers), especially in view of the testament of the nephew's father, and whether in a *societas omnium bonorum* one partner could dower his daughter from the common holdings. If he could, that sum was simply to be ignored in division of the common holdings; if he could not, the sum was charged against his share, thus leaving that much more to the other's share. These opinions are found in a printed edition of the consilia of the second jurist on the case, Bartolomeo Sozzini.[96]

The first jurist, whose identity is never revealed, noted that, whether expressed or tacit, a *societas* rested on consent. The *societas* in this case could be taken as expressed, because the testator in his will "condemned" (damnavit) his heirs to the partnership, which the heirs accepted along with the estate. The testator used language that in more than one way indicated a fraternal communion of all property. The burden of being

[94] Sozzini, 2 *cons.* 192, fol. 51ra.
[95] Sozzini, 2 *cons.* 192, fol. 51ra: "quando fratres vivunt in communione in eadem domo, negocia communi nomine et promiscue gerunt, lucra communicant, et nulla inter eos lucrorum ratio redditur, et ita longo tempore steterunt, omnium bonorum societas tacite contracta censeatur."
[96] This is the edition of his and his father's, Mariano the elder, Venice, 1579–94, 5 vols., 4 *cons.* 4–6, fols. 5ra–11vb.

in communion with the uncle meant the nephew had to share (communicare) all gain, expenses, loss, and burdens of any sort. This was from a desire to prevent inequality, which arose if the heirs did not stay in common or if they sought division; and it was conceded that there could be a lack of sharing, even if there was no formal division of the estate or vice versa.[97] The testator wanted neither of these states of affairs to come about. In parallel, there were no fewer than fourteen reasons that stood to make the father of a girl liable for her dowry from his own share and not a communal charge falling on the goods in common.[98] But the jurist overturned them all, as "whatever one partner expends in honor of his children is imputed to the whole." That was the sharing nature of the *societas omnium bonorum*. It was not a partnership or brotherhood if gains only were to be shared, while losses were kept apart for the particular person. The results of honor to the whole mattered and were realized even if one partner had many more children than the other. Such burdens were usually personal, but they fell on all in a communal partnership. Fifteen arguments were marshaled to this effect, backed by many consilia of prominent jurists. Among the conclusions reached was that the nature of the *societas omnium bonorum* was "that all fortune, good and bad, be shared among partners."[99] The jurist gave no names or particulars in the case and in the printed edition there is not even his name.

Sozzini took off from a position that the sharing of all assets also meant the sharing of all burdens. Implicitly he saw that reciprocity did not apply with true sharing. He built his case and demolished arguments to the opposite effect with his customary thoroughness of citation, including to the first jurist who spoke to the case and to Paolo di Castro (ca. 1360–1441) "in recollectis Florentinis." As long as the terms of the contract were equitable (e.g., that all daughters would be thus dowered), it was not iniquitous and stood as valid. Nor were the portions of a dowry contributed by brothers, other than the girl's father, to be considered gifts from them. They were shared obligations, even if Sozzini had to conclude from his lengthy treatment that "lest I am mistaken, Paolo di Castro erred in this regard."[100]

A relatively brief third opinion came from the pen of Hieronymo Sanetti of Bologna, teaching canon law in Pisa, who filled in nonetheless the practical dimension of this *societas*: "they lived together for quite

---

[97] Sozzini, 2 *cons.* 192, fol. 6rb.
[98] Sozzini, 2 *cons.* 192, fols. 6vb–7ra: "quicquid unus ex sociis expendit in honorem liberorum suorum societati imputatur."
[99] Sozzini, 2 *cons.* 192, fol. 9ra: "ex capite societatis omnium bonorum, de cuius natura est omnem fortunam prosperam et adversam inter socios communicari."
[100] Sozzini, 4 *cons.* 5, fol. 10vb.

a long time and shared all gains and all revenues, that together they also had a trade, all of which acts point to *societas omnium bonorum*, even if they practiced different trades."[101]

He added that girls whose dowries were set up in shares of the Florentine dowry monte,[102] but who were never married and thus never actually received a dowry (it had never been paid to their husbands), saw the ownership of those shares remain in the *societas*. Finally, he agreed with the other two that the dowry was communally established; it was not to be imputed solely to the share of the girls' father. Even if one assumed cohabiting brothers kept separate accounts, that presumption was not proved by the facts in this case.Another jurist who was active in Tuscany was Pierfilippo da Corgna (1420–92). He too had a case in which not only dowry was concerned, but also the educational expenses of apprenticeship involving a certain maestro Pietro *pictor* and his brothers Marco and Antonio.[103] Here and elsewhere, unlike those jurists we have seen up to this point, Corgna proved himself to be tough on anything purporting to be a *societas omnium bonorum*.

He began with the distinction that these three brothers had a tacit *societas lucri et quesitus et fructuum bonorum* but not *omnium bonorum*. There was a limit to their partnership. They would have the latter only if they specified that it concerned absolutely everything. Turning to an observation that served as something of a mantra in cases on *societas* for him, Corgna stated that "the contract of partnership arises from the closeness of any brotherhood" (contractus societatis contrahitur instar cuiusdam fraternitatis). A *societas* should be just and equitable, with the parties being equal. A limited *societas* would recognize divergent contributions, as if one partner put in twice as much cash as the other, or one put in more effort. There was a calculation of returns, just as in businesses. The truly hard-working, industrious man could find a partner willing to provide a thousand florins in business capital; one less industrious would find partners willing to furnish only more modest amounts.[104] Any profit found on dissolution of the business was split among partners, though it might take the kind offices of an arbitrator to make it happen (according to Paolo di Castro, the reigning common custom was to see

---

[101] Sozzini, 4 *cons.* 6, fol. 11ra: "vixerunt longissimo tempore insimul, et communicaverunt omnia lucra et omnes redditus, quod etiam insimul fecerunt unam artem, qui omnes actus inducunt societatem omnium bonorum, imo et si exercuissent diversas artes."
[102] On this see Kirshner and Molho, "The Dowry Fund and the Marriage Market in Early *Quattrocento* Florence'; and Molho, *Marriage Alliance in Late Medieval Florence*, 27–79.
[103] Corgna, *Consilia*, 4 *cons.* 58, fols. 57vb–58va.
[104] Corgna, *Consilia*, 4 *cons.* 58, fol. 58ra: "si unus erit homo multum industriosus contrahere volet societatem cum alio qui ponet pecuniam inveniet ponentem forte mille, et si opere sue erunt magis viles non inveniet ponentem tantam quantitatem."

half as due to capital and half to labor). Corgna said he had so counseled differently, along with the jurists Filippo di Francesco and Baldo de' Bartolini (1409–90), in a case from Monte Falcone, and he mentioned six or seven other instances, where more profit had to be assigned to the more industrious brother for his more lucrative efforts. How industriousness was to be measured was left undefined, or assumed. In this uncertain legal landscape, in the case before him, Corgna believed one brother had contributed more to the profits than had his brothers. Similarly, he asserted that there were differences in dowries, such that even

if they were partners of all goods, expenses for daughters' dowries should be ascribed to their fathers, and at the end of the partnership said parents should be held to place the dowries paid from the common holdings into their share and make their partners whole in proportion to their shares to each one.[105]

Similarly also, adjustments could be made for the costs of a doctorate or for books. In a *societas omnium bonorum*, Corgna concluded, "all should participate in the expenses of food and clothing of a son in school, even though the son's clothing be expensive." The same held for medicinal expenses, which otherwise did not contribute to a partnership's profits. Expenses for the common honor were not something undertaken with the idea of claiming them back. Baldo, however, had taught that for a rural *fraternitas*, in which one brother had several children and the other none, what had been extracted from the common assets for those children could be reclaimed at division.

So the one brother, Pietro, had no obligation to share in the expenses of Antonio's son who had done nothing "notable," or in the medical expenses of Marco, as they were not in a *societas omnium bonorum*. Funeral and related expenses fell on the heirs. Contributions of children had to be recognized insofar as they contributed to profits. These were the conditions as they went, it seems, to division of the estate. There was no real sharing here, on Corgna's construction of the facts, just a delay in reckoning, which was now going forward.

Corgna's strict reading of fraternal *societas* extended to another case. There he began by noting that by a number of indices there was an expressly contracted *societas* between brothers. They lived together, "possessing common property in common" (possedendo communiter bona communia). Even *bona propria* like dowries were held in common. The

---

[105] Corgna, *Consilia*, 4 *cons.* 58, fol. 58rb: "videtur itaque etiam ad presens quod etiam si fuissent socii omnium bonorum expensas factas pro dotibus filiarum debeant ascribi patribus earum et finita societate teneantur dicti parentes dictas dotes solutas de communi ponere ad eorum computum et reficere alios socios pro rata ad eos spectante singula singulis referendo."

elder brother's purchases in his own name were tacitly for the others as well. But all that was not enough: "although several brothers possessed property in common, undivided, and lived together," and that admittedly seemed to meet the tests set out by several authoritative jurisconsults, a contract required consent and corresponding actions of both parties. As some of these brothers were minors, they had effectively contributed nothing.[106] Common possession was not sufficient, as it could be seen not as a contractual matter but merely as a result of "iure familiaritatis," as resting on simple kinship and nothing more functionally substantial – even as a result of inertia more than active choice. So brothers had the right to seek their own separate share of *fructus* from purchases and sales, and dowries belonged to each married brother separately. *Ius familiaritatis* denoted sharing, but it also was not a real legal obligation, so Corgna did not see fit to rest an argument on it.

Corgna was similarly hard-nosed about another fraternal arrangement. A man named Evangelista lived with his brothers and "lucrabatur sua industria," which he put to common use, mainly for building houses held in common. Again, there seemed to be a *societas* by virtue of cohabitation. To his brothers' way of thinking, Evangelista was fully cognizant of the situation and that he was forfeiting his earnings to the common house, so he could not now come forward and demand his contribution be returned. But Corgna said he could, again for a lack of acts that would indicate a tacit *societas* on the part of the brothers.[107] In fact, it would seem that his contribution to construction costs would be a good indicator of partnership. But in Corgna's eyes the facts of the case did not indicate that Evangelista always put his earnings at the disposal of the brothers. It was a fact that the brothers had their own wives and families and did not dispose of funds to dedicate to the structure, at least not to the extent Evangelista did, "who did not have a family" and was more industrious and fortunate in his affairs. Division of assets in this *fraterna* should not then be in equal shares. Evangelista was due a greater share, including in the house, even if there was a *societas*, but, as Corgna doubted that there was one, Evangelista had the right to recover all that he had expended.

In this instance Corgna also turned to undercutting jurisprudential arguments in favor of *societas*. Expenses for illness or for marriages or food and clothing in Evangelista's absence were considered a donation (not a sharing) to the brothers, if these were deemed "parve." If they were, however, "magne," one had to consider that during his prolonged absence Evangelista had consumed nothing from the common holdings,

---

[106] Corgna, 4 *cons.* 251, fol. 210ra–vb.   [107] Corgna, 4 *cons.* 214, fol. 176ra–vb.

which were consumed by the brothers, and "seeing how Evangelista living abroad did not use his property and so there did not occur the common habitation and common table and promiscuous use of goods that seem to be considered by jurists," his brothers used it all for their wives and children.[108] A "good man" could determine how much could be seen as a gift to the brothers and how much could be reclaimed by Evangelista for his own uses.

In another case Corgna followed on the opinion of the Milanese jurist Filippo Decio.[109] Decio had determined that there was a *societas* between brothers even though one was a minor. There was a line of thinking that a *tutor* or *tutrix* could approve sales and all *actus promiscuos* that made for a *societas omnium bonorum*. While a lack of such a *tutor* meant there could be no *societas*, because a minor could not consent to such acts, Decio had argued that "still with respect to his use he can ratify it when he grows up."

Corgna had to go to some lengths to convince himself, despite "reverence" for such an esteemed colleague. Corgna found a way to distance himself from any determination that there had been a full partnership implying sharing of all assets. While the *punctus* disclosed no *actus reciproci* on which to base a finding that there was a *societas*, there were two issues "not much discussed by the lord counselor [Decio]." Antonio was said to have 200 florins from the sale of the house he shared with Martino, the minor. Antonio was also said to "diligently" ply the *arte mercantie*. Among other things, he went to Rome with 100 florins "de bonis patrimonialibus" and came back with 400, gains partly due to the capital and partly to his industry. Martino was due some of that, even if not an equal share, but Antonio had operated in his name only and was not his brother's guardian. So Decio had decided that all gains made by Antonio by his industry, although common money also helped, were not to be shared with the brother: "but the greater part is to be attributed to Antonio by reason of his industry and actions that he, and not Martino, placed in partnership."[110]

The second issue Decio had left untouched was that the 400 florins fell into a fiscal liability for both brothers. Whatever had been said about title in contracts of acquisition, title was clearly treated as collective in communal tax records, even though Antonio had otherwise described the funds as his own for business ("per mio capitale"). But Corgna found

---

[108] Corgna, 4 *cons.* 214, fol. 176ra–vb, "attento quod ipse Evangelista foris permanens non utebatur bonis suis et sic non concurrebat communis habitatio et communis mensa et promisuus usus bonorum que videntur per doctores ponderari."
[109] Corgna, 3 *cons.* 213, fols. 225va–26va.
[110] Corgna, 3 *cons.* 213, fol. 226ra: "sed maior portio esset attribuenda Antonio ratione sue industrie quam et operarum quas ipse et non Martinus posuit in societate."

with Decio that the 400 belonged to Antonio and were not to be shared with Martino, given their "patrimonio et industria." In sum, "it must not be presumed that said Antonio wanted to toss his money away."[111] His *industria* had gained him the money. He had only separated out the 400 florins for the common fiscal obligations and had not signaled a desire to share all his property. Sienese statute did not tell against Antonio, as it simply wanted to "designate someone to pay the tax." By asserting his ownership of 400, Antonio was making sure no one else could claim it, short of an entry in another account. Beyond that, Corgna said, "I agree in the aforesaid lord jurist's decisions that I judge clear and solid." There is a curious diffidence on Corgna's part toward his younger but already quite illustrious colleague.

Decio in fact seems not to have found the legal problems of a *societas* near as intriguing and engaging as Corgna. He opened his treatment of one case with the observation that the subject was "trite and raised little doubt." This case was in fact much like the one we have just considered. The same progression of arguments was given: prolonged cohabitation, a mother as *tutrix* to enable the acts of the minor, and even were there no *tutor*, the minor could ratify it all on coming of age and continuing to live together in the same circumstances.[112] But instead Decio decided there was no *societas*, especially not one *omnium bonorum*, as there were not the requisite sorts of acts. There were three indices needed to construe a *societas*: "that they lived together with the estate undivided after the father's death and that all profits they shared and of what remained they render no account to each other."[113] There had to be an *animum contra-hendi societatis* in words and deeds. In this case there had been no sharing of *lucra*, although the *haereditas* was still shared *indivisa*. They did not live together, at least once the older brother went to Rome. The brothers did not act together; even had there been sharing of *lucrum*, there had been no declaration of willingness to share all wealth. Decio was holding *societas* to a very strict standard in keeping, it seems, with market practices.

Giason del Maino (1435–1519) handled two cases that add some perspective. The first is fairly brief.[114] Four brothers continued after their father's death to live together, undivided, and commonly meeting expenses, while two also ran an apothecary, one studied medicine, and

---

[111] Corgna, 3 *cons.* 213, fol. 226rb: "monet presumendum quod dictus Antonius voluerit iactare suum."

[112] Filippo Decio, *Consilia*, 1 *cons.* 21, fols. 26va–28va.

[113] Decio, *Consilia*, 1 *cons.* 21, fol. 27ra: "quod simul cum haereditate indivisa post mortem patris vixerunt et quod omnia lucra communicaverunt et de eo quod superlucratur adinvicem rationem non reddant."

[114] Giason del Maino, *Consilia*, 1 *cons.* 5, pp. 28–30.

the fourth became a notary. Three of them married and faced the expenses of bringing their brides into the home. Two of them had children in addition. When it came time finally to divide their shares, the unmarried brother, the medical student, whose educational expenses had already been figured in his share, argued that the expenses of his married brothers (wedding expenses, daily expenditures, wet-nursing) now had to be calculated into their shares.

Resolving this division rested, Maino said, on determining if there had been a tacit *societas omnium bonorum*. Of course, as Bartolus had long since established, mere living together did not constitute a *societas*, especially when there was no common mercantile or other enterprise. Two brothers in the same business meant only that they had a *societas* with each other for that purpose, and that did not include the other two brothers. The brother who was a notary notably did not put his earnings at the service of all. Dowries were not treated as a shared responsibility. So the three brothers with children and wives had to calculate their expenses against their quarter shares of the patrimony, with adequate compensation thus going to the fourth, unmarried brother. That might not have been easy.

That such a case could come up speaks to the powerful presumption that brothers living together shared gains and losses, credits and debts, such that at the moment of division they could try to argue that certain expenses were common and not to be computed into their shares. But, as we have seen, these jurists also insisted that a true *societas omnium bonorum* meant a sharing of profits and expenses from continued common activity, not just a sharing of *haereditas*. They had a fairly rigorous and absolute standard of a sharing economy and were ready to back the claims of any one member of a *fraterna* against the other(s).

In another instance, there was doubt about a *societas omnium bonorum* between the medical doctors and brothers, Francesco and Bernardino of Castello Ferrariense, given that while over twenty-five years of age they had continued to live "simul in comunione" for over sixteen years. No express contract of *societas* existed, so one was thrown into a realm of conjectures and presumptions that was "ambiguous" and "difficult." Their simple continuance in cohabitation after the father's death was not sufficient proof of *societas*. Even sharing the expenses of being "ad unum panem et unum vinum" was not enough, if in all else each remained a separate owner of his own property. The bone of contention was the "domum excelsam et superbam" recently completed. In fact, Francesco had become a familiar face at the ducal court of Ercole d'Este (1431–1505) and often spent the night there (saepius dormiebat). Francesco kept an active trade, while Bernardino had not. And Francesco had dealt in his own name and with partners other than his brother in different *societates*, as witnesses for him and general repute (*publica fama*) demonstrated. A resulting difference in the relative wealth of the two brothers likewise spoke to a lack of *societas* between them. "Although these brothers living together shared with each other fruits and revenues and also profits," nevertheless "they are not deemed to have shared ownership of goods from which said fruits and revenues arose, and so for this they are not deemed to have communicated ownership, such that there is thought to have tacitly been contracted a *societas omnium bonorum*."[115] Even if the brothers carried a common business, that did not rise to the level of *societas omnium bonorum*. For another thing, Bernardino had sought to have a *societas* with his brother, even conceding Francesco 3,000 ducats from the start, but Francesco "recused himself as seems proven by three witnesses." And Bernardino elsewhere admitted to owing Francesco an amount of money, which again showed a lack of *societas*. And this lack of partnership seems to come to a head with the new *palazzo*. Francesco in his own name had hired the various tradesmen who in fact built the house and the materials they required to do so. Bernardino's attempt to bring a formal lawsuit was deemed "repugnant" and "inept."

In all, by his numeration, Maino thus ran through twelve compelling reasons that there should not be judged to have been a *societas* between these brothers. This thoroughness was in fact a set-up to his reversal to arguing for Bernardino. The force of his arguments could seem to be all the greater for being so exhaustive. But on what basis could he find for a *societas omnium bonorum*, which always seemed to demand a high degree of mutual engagement? He even began with a lengthy recitation of all the many elements of mutual existence that lay behind any *societas omnium bonorum* – not only living together and sharing those expenses for sixteen years, but also sharing property, debtors and creditors, *fructus*, *redditus*, and salaries, with no accounting, and collectively meeting fiscal demands. Francesco and Bernardino shared not only their father's estate but also those of their brother Lorenzo and their paternal grandmother Margarita. They had separated as one party from another brother, messer Giovanbattista, *decretorum doctor*. Bernardino's wife's 2,000-*lire* dowry "was shared by the brothers," as were the proceeds (3,800 *lire*) from selling their father's house as a prelude to building their sumptuous new abode. Francesco, the elder, was always manager of everything, "and all was referred to him." So *societas omnium bonorum* was considered to exist between them: "for living together, sharing of gains from one and what

---

[115] Maino, 3 *cons.* 2, pp. 6–14, at 8: "per hoc non censentur communicasse proprietatem bonorum ex quibus dicti fructus et redditus percipiuntur, et sic per hoc non censentur communicasse proprietatem adeo quod censeatur tacite contracta societas omnium bonorum."

the other gains to each other [and] not rendering an accounting makes for a presumption of partnership."[116] Whatever the different sources of income, if brothers brought that into a common holding, they could be seen to have a *societas omnium bonorum*. And purchase of a farm or house by one was to be communicated to the other. The conjectures for Bernardino, in favor of a *societas omnium bonorum*, were said to be greatly preponderant "in number, weight, and measure" compared with those for Francesco; but no reason was given as to why that was so. Further, there were all the moments Francesco seemingly indicated that there was a *societas* prior to Bernardino's marriage to Corona di messer Giovanmaria Riminaldi, her father, a doctor of law.

In a *societas* it did not matter that one brother outearned or outspent the other. All acquisitions came to the partnership, even if in the act of acquiring it was asserted that it was "suo proprio nomine." It was in the terms of the *societas omnium bonorum* that gains would be shared, even if secretly acquired. In essence, in these arguments Maino was reducing or eliminating any volitional elements, while elevating the legal demands of a valid, if tacit, *societas omnium bonorum*. He invoked as a rule that "by reason of *fraterna* and communion it is forbidden for one brother to buy for himself alone" (ex ratione fraternitatis et communionis est interdictum uni fratrum ne emat pro se solo). As for the family home, it was commonly built using the proceeds from the sale of the paternal residence, Bernardino's wife's dowry, and other common funds. Even if only one brother lived in a house, there was still undivided ownership. There were also two letters written in master Francesco's hand which called the house common.[117] Bernardino too had contracted with tradesmen and purchased for the house. No one "sane capitis" could conclude that this was not a common holding of a *societas omnium bonorum*.

So Maino mounted twelve arguments to the opposite effect for Bernardino. He then rounded back on the twelve he had conjured up for Francesco to dismiss or at least diminish those. That Francesco ate and slept in the ducal palace did not matter, at least in that he did so while "with respect to servants, maids, horses and mules, they were fed in the same common home." Lack of a common trade did not overshadow the many *actus sociales* of Bernardino, nor could witnesses truly testify to

---

[116] Maino, 3 *cons.* 2, p. 9: "Sed magister Franciscus grandior natu omnium dictorum bonorum semper fuit administrator; omnia passim et domi et foris administrabat et omnia ad eum referebantur. Ex istis tot et tanquam simul concurrentibus proculdubio causata est inter eos societas universalis omnium bonorum. Nam insimul habitatio lucrorum in unam collatio et eius quod alter superlucratur invicem non reddita ratio facit praesumi societatem."

[117] Maino, 3 *cons.* 2, p. 12.

Francesco's dealings. It did not matter that the brothers shared only *fructus* and not *proprietas*. Bernardino's statements that he was in debt to his brother sprang from Francesco's longstanding role as administrator of the holdings. The expenses Francesco put into the house had been met secretly without informing Bernardino, whom he was otherwise obliged to inform. What witnesses attested to in this case as to what Bernardino knew, especially once the house was evidently completed or at least much further along in construction, did not alleviate Francesco's obligations within a *societas omnium bonorum* to inform his brother. Certainly, it could not be maintained that the greater share of the cost of the house had been met by Francesco alone. Any implications that Francesco took advantage of his role as administrator, however "repugnant," pointed to the need to account for all assets in order to have a truly equal division.

One wonders how persuasive Maino's opinion was before a court. His position as a Milanese arguing in Ferrara may have had an effect, but it may also have been a concession to the fact that Francesco had status in Ferrara that his brother lacked. There was indeed a complex and ambiguous situation with these brothers. Bernardino's claim to his share of the estate and to recover his wife's dowry does not come to grips with Francesco's greater income and standing in the community. Francesco was the one who hung around the ducal court and had the social need for an appropriately grandiose *palazzo* of his own. The previous paternal house (which was no hovel at a value of 3,800 *lire*) was obviously not enough. The *palazzo* in the "terra nova" of Ferrara was, in fact, part of a ducal design to make Ferrara a showcase as capital of the Este world, in which the duke was deeply personally involved from 1493. Messer Francesco da Castello, as Ercole's physician, was the first mentioned owner and builder of a *palazzo* in this new part of town (now known as Palazzo Prosperi Sacrati). Nothing is recorded of any participation by Bernardino in this venture.[118] It is hard to see that there was a *societas* with these brothers. Bernardino was not going to end up with the new dwelling, even if he could hope Francesco had to fork over some money to buy him out.

5.4.2   Debts and Liability

One of Baldo's consilia dealing with *fraterna* was hypothetical in that the persons concerned were labeled A, B, and C. Hypotheticals could be structured to preclude certain issues and thus sharpen the focus on others.

---

[118] Thomas Tuohy, *Herculean Ferrara: Ercole d'Este (1471–1505) and the Invention of a Ducal Capital*, 128–30.

A good example comes from the collective efforts of four Perugian jurists, including Baldo's son Francesco (fl. 1391–1432). The sealed originals survive in a Florentine manuscript.[119] The "facts" postulated that a man named Titius (a common Roman-law equivalent to John Doe) had a wife, Berta, whose dowry was the only property he was said to have acquired in his life.[120] So there was no question of any resources of his funneling to his four sons. There were no complications about industriousness or the provenance of paternal capital. In any case, the sons Pietro and Paolo went off into the world to make their fortunes – the first to Lombardy and the second to the Papal States, to see "if they could gain anything by their effort" (si aliquid lucrari possent ex eorum industria). Meanwhile, Jacopo entered holy orders and Giovanni, the youngest, stayed at home with his parents. Pietro was singularly unfortunate and constantly in debt.[121] Paolo succeeded where his brother failed and acquired some wealth in the fifteen years that he and Pietro were away from their father's house before Titius's death, and another four years thereafter. During that nineteen-year period they had not shared a meal or seen each other for two days running, as the document put it.[122] Pietro died at that point and shortly thereafter so did Berta. Paolo had been separate from his unfortunate brother then in total for thirty years, but Pietro's creditors in Lombardy tried to see if Paolo was liable for his brother's debts, or perhaps Berta's property was (there was no question of a real liability of the father in this situation in which he was said to be destitute). As part of the hypothetical, it was also asked if the stay-at-home son Giovanni was entitled to any of Paolo's earnings.

This scenario pared things down to a simple liability by kinship alone, as no household or other form of resource was shared by Pietro and Paolo once they left the paternal home, and not with their mother or younger brother. The lead opinion is that of Pietro da Perugia, a fairly obscure relative of Baldo who wrote a *Libellus de duobus fratribus*.[123] His point of departure was that someone who had business by himself and in his own name only gained for himself and not for anyone else, unless he was a "socius omnium bonorum," in which case he had to share with his brothers. Paolo was not. In keeping with the nature of a hypothetical, the jurist noted that there were also other possibilities – one acquired for

[119] BNF, Landau Finaly 98, fols. 3r–6v.
[120] BNF, Landau Finaly 98, fol. 3r: "usque ad tempus et tempore sue mortis nulla bona habuit vel acquisivit nisi bona dotalia."
[121] Landau Finaly 98, fol. 3r: "et nicchil unquam potuit lucrari sed semper fecit et contraxit debitum cum diversis et variis hominibus et personis."
[122] Landau Finaly 98, fol. 3r: "non commorati fuerunt in simul nec se viderunt ad invicem per spatium duorum dierum continuorum."
[123] Published in Venice in 1487, 1490, and 1500.

oneself and another, one acquired only for another, one acquired neither for oneself nor another (impediments or disqualifications intervened), one acquired ownership (*proprietas*) for oneself and usufruct for another, or one acquired both ownership and usufruct for another. Paolo had only acquired for himself, so there was no obligation to or through another. Pietro's creditors could not go after the mother's property, as mothers had no liability for sons, nor could Giovanni seek a part of Paolo's property.

Francesco degli Ubaldi was more long-winded, advancing three possibilities regarding profits, debts, and expenses. If a father's assets had been involved in a son's business profits, they could be termed to have come from the father and taken the form of *peculium profectitium* for the son. Thus they were to be shared with brothers in inheritance. But what came from the labor of the son remained his alone (*peculium adventitium*). In this case there was no claim for Giovanni on Paolo's earnings, as it had all seemingly come from his labors. There was no *societas* "as it is presupposed in the facts that these brothers lived apart and Paolo made gains for himself and acted alone and did not place them in common."[124]

Onofri Bartolini (1350–1415) reemphasized the crucial missing element of cohabitation: the lack of both express and tacit proofs of any form of *societas* between brothers. Similarly, Marco Angelelli (1383–1464) noted a lack of any words indicating partnership, and a lack of sharing debts, profits, and expenses. These jurists effectively said that brothers as such did not share ownership and liability and indicated that even had they lived together, more was required, though that was a moot point in their situation. The other thing this collective consilium alerts us to is that the issues of ownership and liability were not immediate but came into play when a division of assets was at hand, and especially at the death of a brother, which brought into focus his gains and losses and the interests of creditors from outside the family. In this case they had nothing to lose in pursuing the long shot that the law might find them recourse in the holdings of a brother they had never even met, let alone did business with.

It seems from what we have seen that by and large jurists were loath to tag with liabilities family members who were not the principal debtors, no matter what statutes specified. There was often some way to argue around extensive liability, even though that was also a key element in trust and credit in the markets. Certainly, demanding a total *societas omnium bonorum* set a high standard for imputing liability among cohabiting brothers. In a Florentine case involving members of the prestigious Bardi lineage, three local jurists, Bernardo di messer Giovanni

---

[124] BNF, Landau Finaly 98, fol. 5r: "isti fratres seorsum habitaverunt et lucra Paulus frater pro se faciebat et gerebat nec in communi ponebat."

Buongirolami (d. 1484), Piero Ambrosini da Iesi (1403–77), and Michele di Piero Strozzi (1428–98), argued that the brothers of Antonio di Mariotto Bardi were not liable for the debts he had incurred during his twenty-two years away from Florence, largely in Portugal.[125] The key finding for Buongirolami was that the brothers did not formally have a *societas*, for which it was necessary that all should share equally income and expenditures, and although one might have a larger family than another, he was not made to contribute more. These brothers failed that test, because they kept precise accounts on what each earned and spent, and two of them were not so much partners as employees of their brother. Michele Strozzi added the fact that Antonio had earned everything he had by his own *industria* and was not held to share any of that with his brothers. In any case, the statute extending liability to cohabiting brothers was declared irrational, odious, and exorbitant. The presumption behind statutory liability was systematically dismantled by these three, and they were able to cite a range of juristic opinions in line with theirs.

Finally, we also might note the different perspective on kinship taken here. At least there was no sort of (to be anachronistic) genetic argument in view. Rather, as Borello has it, here "it was in sum acting *fraternamente* every day that constituted the essence of the bond: the 'tractatus' [treatment] to which judges attached a greater importance among the proofs in lawsuits about recognition of paternity than with respect to physical resemblance."[126] In the hypothetical we have just examined there was no question of treatment like a brother, of shared intent, or even of shared residence. Treating one as a brother was a necessary but not sufficient indicator of a brotherhood or shared property, shared activities and aspirations, and shared liability.

5.5   Conclusions

Fraternal living was always in tension with business arrangements. As Borello remarks, individual dignity within the house and household (by no means lessened by recourse to primogeniture) "was anything but fixed and measurable in rigid parameters."[127] The consequence was a multitude of interpretive approaches to ever-arising controversies. It is also Borello's sense that the *fraterna compagnia*, as *societas*, was more likely to crop up a bit lower down the social scale from the true elites.[128] These

---

[125] This case is covered in Kuehn, "Debt and Bankruptcy," 375–77.
[126] Borello, *Posto di ciascuno*, 225.   [127] Borello, *Posto di ciascuno*, 88.
[128] Borello, *Posto di ciascuno*, 189.

latter had more resources to hold things together, though probably no less reason for resentments and animosities to flare up. It is also importantly the case that the patrimonies brothers tried to hold together were also immaterial, so that honor and reputation were spendable commodities, shared by all. Persistence in sharing honor and enhancing its collective weight was a goal of keeping an undivided patrimony.[129] We could take Bernardino da Castello's suit against his brother as trying to maintain honor and social respectability, rather than see his brother, well connected at court, march away with it.

In the law some of the truly common dimensions of a shared family life did not come into play. Cases do not revolve around coats of arms, family names and titles, or honor. To the law, for which, as Bartolus and Alberico said, *familia* was *substantia*, it was communal property, its acquisition and loss, that truly mattered. Symbolic assets and reputation counted, but they were not susceptible to the kind of accounting that law could muster.

Simple *fraterna* of brothers cohabiting usually for a period following their father's death did not pose much legal difficulty. These had their problems, to be sure, as one might anticipate from the process of division among brothers; but those problems fell largely to arbitrators (trusted kin, friends, neighbors), not to jurists. What exercised juristic talents, as we have seen from a number of examples, was the possibility or reality of true partnership, *societas*. As Domenico Toschi (1535–1620) would refine the doctrine in the early seventeenth century, simply living together and not dividing the patrimony qualified only as particular, rather than universal, *societas*. A truly all-encompassing accommodation (*universalis*) required sharing of profits and losses without accounting among the brothers.[130]

Thanks to Bartolus, Baldo degli Ubaldi, and others, the *societas omnium bonorum* rose to the level of a pooling of all incomes, assets, expenses, and obligations, encompassing all areas of existence, not just business. In that situation responsibility for things like business debts does not seem to have raised serious problems. The cases we have encountered, with a few exceptions, revolved not around paying debts to outsiders but around working out an equitable division of property once the *societas omnium bonorum* dissolved; and this division paralleled that which occurred whenever any business partnership ended. Accounting for dowries paid out loomed large, as potentially did other expenses from brothers' modes of

---

[129] Cf. Stella Leprai, "Ai confini del ducato: Forme di mobilità sociale nelle comunità dell'Appennino tosco-ligure-emiliano."

[130] Domenico Toschi, *Practicarum conclusionum iuris in omni foro*, vol. 7, 353: "quia ut debeat praesumi universalis requiruntur iura, quod simul cohabitaverint, lucra omnia communicaverint, et eius quod quis superlucratus fuerit non sit inter eos habita ratio."

living for things like educational expenses, costs of childrearing, and so forth. But dowry was a more urgent and thorny matter, as it involved contributions to a daughter's marriage to another family or a charge on the family possessions in the name of a wife who had married in.[131]

What is also striking about the juristic treatment of *societates* is how insistent they were about equality. That part of sharing that operated over and despite inequalities, that allowed Francesco and Bernardino da Castello, for example, to maintain their common arrangement for years, escaped the jurists. As they generally engaged the issue of *societas* only when it was ending, or at least under serious stress and questioning, and as statutes and so much else in and around law were fixated on equalities and peace, perhaps it is only natural that someone like Pierfilippo da Corgna was so absolutist in his reckoning of what was, and was not, a *societas omnium bonorum*. But the jurists, and possibly the plaintiffs in their cases, were inserting reciprocity as a rule where it had not previously governed.

The essence of *fraterna* or its form as *societas* lay in cohabitation. That was where the benefits and problems all lay. Within that it was highly unlikely that brothers would not see inequities emerge in their domestic and commercial lives. Some married and had children, others did not. Some worked hard and prospered; others not so much. In order to make a division, for whatever reason and at whatever time, there had to be some accounting of what had been spent, when, by whom, for what. There had to be some keeping of accounts, even if not precise and not written down. Tensions on these scores were not far below the surface in many instances.

It was rare to have an explicit written contract to prove existence of a *societas*, as the Naldini brothers did for fourteen years. More likely was a tacit pattern of sharing and interaction, with perhaps common account books and receipts. Jurisconsults looked for evidence of *actus sociales* and might dispute whether patterns of interaction were indicative of partnership. In searching out such patterns from the evidence of accounts or witnesses, consultative jurists were following a route laid out by Baldo that gave weight to the voluntary associations and agreements among brothers.[132] Equally voluntary were moves to avoid or terminate any form of *societas* and cohabitation. But there were also constraints, as there were to any contract that one had agreed to. The jurists were clearly looking past local repute, generally termed *fama* in law, beyond presumptions of partnership arising from cohabitation, to actual arrangement and

---

[131] Here, above all, see Chabot, *La dette des familles*.
[132] Contino, "Societas e famiglia nel pensiero di Baldo degli Ubaldi," 90–91.

management of family substance. At least it was possible for someone such as Giason del Maino to maintain that Francesco da Castello still had associative obligations and commitments to a brother otherwise not near as active and successful as he was. His relationship with Bernardino, including selling the paternal house and building a sumptuous new palace, was at least more active than mere inertial cohabitation following the death of the father, for all seem to have agreed that cohabitation alone did not amount to *societas*.

A broader lesson may be that these fraternal arrangements, and their dissolution, point out, however obliquely at times, that kinship was not just a given (genealogy); it was also about lives and changing experiences in households, where kinship was made (or unmade) and where *substantia* was shared.[133] Relations between brothers were certainly subject to change, much of it centrifugal, as careers and marriages were pursued. What is intriguing is not that such arrangements broke up over time but that there seem to have been so many of them and that they lasted as long as they did. The sense of shared substance, material but also symbolic (honor) was indeed powerful.

[133] See Carsten, *After Kinship*, 35.

6 Fideicommissum and Law
Consilia of Bartolomeo Sozzini and Filippo Decio

The fideicommissum was a pervasive legal institution in early modern Europe. It served to preserve property (mainly *immobilia*) in the hands of those whose inheritance it governed, as its use was intended to prevent loss of patrimony, fragmentation of holdings, or other disasters. The linchpin of inheritance strategies among nobilities, but also among others with substantial property interests, the fideicommissum flourished in varying forms throughout those areas in which the Roman civil law served as the basis of the legal culture and courts. So successful was it that progressive thinkers of the Enlightenment, eager to see a more rationalistic commercial economy and a society free of most forms of inherited privilege, singled the fideicommissum out for systematic criticism. In a memorable phrase coined by Ludovico Antonio Muratori (1672–1750), the fideicommissum served as an "enchanted shield" that protected noble property, thwarting creditors and even younger sons and daughters, while seemingly enriching only the lawyers who handled countless lawsuits the fideicommissum generated.[1] There was no more powerful and concise expression of a sense of patrimonial unity and sharing than an enduring fideicommissum.

The enlightened views of Muratori and others ultimately won out in law in Europe and the United States. In the latter, which ruled out noble titles in its constitution, there was enthusiastic adoption of the common law rule against perpetuities. By and large the rule sought to preclude dynastic trusts that aimed to keep property in the control of the "dead hand" across generations. The rule was that property could vest for the lifetime of the recipient plus twenty-one years. Past that point, control had to return to the living. In the eyes of critics of perpetuities, after a limited period of enjoyment property should return to the realm of markets, where creditors and others could hope for access to property that had been otherwise isolated under the control of a trustee for the term of the trust.[2] The rule was intent on avoiding the vesting of contingent future interests.

---

[1] Ludovico Antonio Muratori, *Dei difetti della giurisprudenza*, ed. Arrigo Solmi, chap. 17.

[2] Cf. "Dynasty Trusts and the Rule of Perpetuities"; Angela M. Vallario, "Death by a Thousand Cuts: The Rule against Perpetuities"; and Lawrence M. Friedman, *Dead Hands: A Social History of Wills, Trusts, and Inheritance Law*, 115–39.

The nature of markets and the existence of corporations and their ownership of property have greatly changed to the present, to the point that a number of states have moved to abolish the rule against perpetuities. There is controversy over these moves, which also seem to make sense because property is no longer rendered discrete from marketability. Removal of property from the markets into the shared interests of the beneficiaries over generations – agreement rather than conflict of inter-generational interests – was what the fideicommissum intended.

We now have some careful studies of its enforcement in laws and courts and its effects over the generations. Maura Piccialuti's research on Rome and Stefano Calonaci's for Florence has unmasked the working of the fideicommissum in great detail.[3] There is also a valuable study of Lombard inheritance practices by Maria Carla Zorzoli, and works by Gerard Delille and Maria Antonietta Visceglia for Naples.[4] They have confirmed what other studies were only suggestively able to assert.[5] In the words of Calonaci,

fideicommissary substitution served to transform a patrician aristocracy into a sedentary nobility, ancient of descent and memory, inscribed in civic history, rich in substance as in its own archives, clear testimony to a scrupulous keeping of accounts, enterprises, and factories from a strong sense of family identity and continuity.[6]

Still, the spread of fideicommissa in practice and their evident success in preserving patrimonies in agnatic lines over generations was not a simple, let alone inevitable, process. It rested, in fact, on a weak basis in Roman law that had to be strengthened in doctrine, statutes, and practice, though the fideicommissum had a venerable place in the civil law tradition. Its Roman and Justinianic forms simply did not contemplate the early modern adaptation. Nor were the statutes of cities or principalities, outside a feudal context at least, necessarily hospitable ground for the flourishing and elaboration of fideicommissa in law.

What was called the fideicommissum by late medieval and early modern lawyers, notaries, judges, and laymen, even dubbed at times fideicommissum familiae, was in fact a combination of two chief elements.

---

[3] Piccialuti, *L'immortalità dei beni*; Calonaci, *Dietro lo scudo incantato*; and Kuehn, "*Fideicommissum* and Family: The Orsini di Bracciano."

[4] Maria Carla Zorzoli, "Della famiglia e del suo patrimonio: riflessioni sull'uso del fedecommesso in lombardia tra cinque e seicento"; Maria Antonietta Visceglia, *Il bisogno di eternità: i comportamenti aristocratici a Napoli in età moderna*; Gérard Delille, *Famille et propriété dans le Royaume de Naples, xve–xixe siècle*.

[5] Litchfield, *Emergence of a Bureaucracy: The Florentine Patricians*; Cooper, "Patterns of Inheritance and Settlement by Great Landowners"; Cohn, *The Cult of Remembrance and the Black Death* and *Death and Property in Siena, 1200–1800: Strategies for the Afterlife*.

[6] Calonaci, *Dietro lo scudo incantato*, 3–4.

United with an inheritance trust, by which one person received property with the duty to pass it to another – in other words, a substitution – was an unlimited prohibition on the alienation of that property to anyone *extra familiam* (the *familia* in Bartolus's sense). It asserted the nonmarket status of a shared, inalienable entity that lasted in perpetuity.

It was, as Piccialuti succinctly puts it, the "dynastic sense of the family" that drove the use of fideicommissa.[7] More specifically, it was distrust of the future – the disappearance of lines of descent and/or loss of central properties (including titles, coats of arms, and other symbols) – that animated individuals, most frequently at the moment of composing their last will and testament, to demand a continuity of ownership in the family and to devise a set of substitutions of heirs to vital properties. These individuals operated from a distinct, yet shared sense of family as an enduring collective entity, a vertically arrayed agnatic lineage. In the words of Calonaci,

From the end of the Middle Ages family became ever more perceived in an agnatic and patrilinear sense, without that coming to preclude a continual renegotiation between the transmission of patrimony and the needs of the family nucleus … and shaped, in the case of the Florentine nobility, to a self-legitimation of family identity, but also "to create a dynasty where there was not one before."[8]

In its way, the fideicommissum was also a means of enforcing a sharing familial solidarity, seemingly precluding divisions of patrimony. Where there were multiple equal heirs, it served to push them into some sort of fraternal sharing, but largely also without the possibility of contentious and threatening divisions among heirs. Fathers could begin educating their sons quite early to expect to remain together as long as possible, and a fideicommissum could seek to lock property up and avoid division of the patrimony for any number of reasons.[9] Where primogeniture came to hold sway as testamentary practice, it kept property under one name while enforcing some sort of sharing, however unequal, with siblings. Easily imagined tensions in that situation could further impel the search for ecclesiastical roles for siblings to reduce their call on family patrimony and its single nominal possessor.

These enduring schemes of inheritance, captured on notarized pages, became the core of a family archive that itself became a powerful symbol of the dynasty that kept it.[10] The fideicommissum could violate the usual

---

[7] Piccialuti, *L'immortalità dei beni*, 10.   [8] Calonaci, *Dietro lo scudo incantato*, 54.

[9] Cf. Joanne M. Ferraro, *Family and Public Life in Brescia, 1580–1650: The Foundations of Power in the Venetian State*, 108–9.

[10] Piccialuti, *L'immortalità dei beni*, 7; Calonaci, *Dietro lo scudo incantato*, 54–55. See also Kent, *Household and Lineage in Renaissance Florence*, 136–40.

rules of inheritance by designating one heir out of several equally qualified recipients (usually by primogeniture), and it tied the hands of heirs as owners of estates, and subsequently as testators themselves, as they were bound to transmit the estate intact to the next generation, as well as to share some of it with siblings and other kin, if needed.

This sense of family arose toward the end of the Middle Ages according to those who have studied the fideicommissum. Then this peculiar institution of Roman legal provenance began to appear in testaments, though also on occasion in deeds of gift, dowries, and other devices for transmission of property. But in the eyes of many, the real heyday of the fideicommissum came even later. Muratori pegged the upswing in its use after 1600. Calonaci and Piccialuti point to the first decades of the sixteenth century.[11] But others look somewhat earlier and take into account local conditions and not just academic legal developments accommodating fideicommissa.[12] Calonaci particularly attributes the increased use of fideicommissa to a shift from a fifteenth-century concern to reaffirm familial prestige, as captured symbolically in a palazzo or other property of distinction, to a sixteenth-century concern more overtly with preservation of patrimony and a practical strategy of investment.[13] So in the sixteenth century he finds some 4,000 Florentine testators employed fideicommissa for their families, although he hastens to add that it was still a small proportion of the Florentine population across that century.[14] The timing of this expansion in the use of fideicommissa points to factors beyond just a growing dynastic sense of family. The political and economic chaos of the Italian Wars beginning in 1494, the consequent solidification of more centralizing regimes, reliant on a dependent nobility, and the growing economic importance of landed investments were all factors impelling concerns for families' futures.[15] All that is to say nothing of disease or other factors driving mortality. It had long seemed too that real estate was a safer investment, and transactions of real estate were almost always treated as interpersonal, rather than commercial.[16] The otherwise extensive liabilities, by which commercial misfortunes might be

---

[11] Piccialuti, *L'immortalità dei beni*, 97; Calonaci, *Dietro lo scudo incantato*, 54; Cooper, "Patterns of Inheritance and Settlement by Great Landowners," 315–21.

[12] Cf. the introduction to a journal issue dedicated to the issues of fideicommissa: Jean-François Chauvard, Anna Bellavitis, and Paola Lanaro, "De l'usage du fidéicommis à l'âge moderne: État des lieux."

[13] Calonaci, *Dietro lo scudo incantato*, 104.

[14] Calonaci, *Dietro lo scudo incantato*, 88–89.

[15] On economic conditions, see Goldthwaite, *The Economy of Renaissance Florence*.

[16] Emigh, *The Undevelopment of Capitalism: Sectors and Markets in Fifteenth-Century Tuscany*, 95–96; McLean and Gondal, "The Correlation of Interpersonal Credit in Renaissance Florence," 155.

held against noncommercial, patrimonial assets, might be effectively attenuated by the use of countervailing legal devices, but mainly fideicommissa attached to testaments, removing lineage devolution from the market economy.

In fact, in Florence the crucial change in the conception of family and inheritance probably began in the late fourteenth century. The city's elite in the aftermath of the first plagues, but especially after the Ciompi Revolt and the last efflorescence of the guild republic (1378–82), began to reform and entrench itself with marriage alliances and business partnerships, as well as officeholding. In this regard, the research of John Padgett and Paul McLean has put a statistical edge to the intuitions of political historians such as Gene Brucker, Lauro Martines, Anthony Molho, and John Najemy.[17] Marital *parentado* with other lineages became distinct from, but also vied with, a genealogical memory of lineage that traced descent in agnatic ties through men.[18]

Family and state came to intertwine, and with the assistance of Florence's erudite humanists, the homology of familial and state paternalism entered the culture and law. In a flurry of legislative and institutional measures, what Isabelle Chabot has called the "government of the fathers" came into being in Florence.[19] Among the features of this paternalistic regime (beyond exalting paternal power and benevolence) lay a preoccupation with the preservation of patrimonies that in turn rested on two prongs: the careful restriction of marriages and the employment of fideicommissary substitutions.[20]

These were being employed, then, in Florence well before 1500, if not as frequently as later. In contrast to those in other Italian regions, it must be said, Florentines did not practice primogeniture; they tended to hold property in common even among several heirs and pass it to the next generation, also in common. Above all they placed city palaces and extensive rural holdings subject to testamentary substitutions and prohibitions of alienation.[21] These testaments, of course, could modify the reigning local rules of intestacy in regard to succession, while they also

---

[17] Padgett and McLean, "Organizational Invention and Elite Transformation: The Birth of Partnership Systems in Renaissance Florence"; Padgett, "Open Elite? Social Mobility, Marriage, and Family in Florence, 1282–1494"; Brucker, *The Civic World of Early Renaissance Florence*, 248–318; Lauro Martines, *The Social World of the Florentine Humanists, 1390–1460*; Najemy, *A History of Florence, 1200–1575*, 156–218. Cf. also Molho, *Marriage Alliance in Late Medieval Florence*, 338–48.

[18] Anthony Molho, Roberto Barducci, Gabriella Battista, and Francesco Donnini, "Genealogy and Marriage Alliance: Memories of Power in Late Medieval Florence."

[19] Isabelle Chabot, "Le gouvernement des pères: l'État florentin et la famille (xive–xve siècles)." Also Najemy, *A History of Florence, 1200–1575*, 211–18.

[20] Chabot, *La dette des familles*.   [21] Kent, *Household and Lineage*, 136–41.

reduced for the heirs the otherwise wide latitude given testators in law that might have been available to them had they not inherited under a - fideicommissum.[22] Certainly, partible inheritance practices could foster the volatile fluidity of wealth that characterized Florence's fourteenth-century elites, as Richard Goldthwaite has noted; but adoption of testamentary devices to hold onto key properties did not need to await greater investments in land in the sixteenth century.[23] A dynastic sense of family was in place early enough to move some Florentines to begin exploiting some of the potential of fideicommissa, as Calonaci shows, by at least the fifteenth century.[24] By this point the increasing "verticalization" and complexity of households in Florence and Tuscany in general was clear.[25]

Indeed, Florentines had sufficiently regular recourse to fideicommissa that by 1477 they were cited as a source of legal and economic difficulty from use in fraudulent transactions.[26] Property subject to fideicommissa could not be alienated for any reason (except to constitute a dowry if there were no other property available for that purpose), so there were clear consequences in law to employment of this device.[27] Fideicommissa could keep property in the hands of kin and out of the hands of creditors. There were economic consequences too, as the law of 1477 worried over the state of markets and the withdrawal of some merchants from commerce from fear of being defrauded by devices such as fideicommissa. Again, in the face of hostility to fideicommissa on this front, one has to wonder where and how acceptance of the device was possible, if not by Florentine householders, then by the city's legislators and courts, which took an active interest in Florence's markets. There was, after all, an unresolvable tension, what Casanova terms an unresolved fundamental ambiguity in the fideicommissum, which both posed the union of the whole against the desires of individual family members and placed the family property in opposition to the more fluid, if not less personal, ownership transacted in markets.[28] The sharing economy of the family whose substance lay under a fideicommissum was underwritten, in fact, by bracketing rights of ownership with severe restrictions, in the hands of

---

[22] A succinct appreciation of these features can be found in Renzo Sabbatini, "Famiglie e potere nella Lucca moderna."

[23] Goldthwaite, *The Economy of Renaissance Florence*, 550, 557–58, 570.

[24] Calonaci, *Dietro lo scudo incantato*, 104, claims one anomaly as early as 1343, but finds others before 1500, clustering between 1450 and 1498.

[25] Franca Leverotti, "Strutture familiari nel tardo medioevo italiano."

[26] Cf. Kuehn, "Multorum Fraudibus Occurrere," 320–21 and "Debt and Bankruptcy in Florence."

[27] As an example of this doctrine, see the legal glossary of the Florentine lawyer, Antonio di Vanni Strozzi (1454–1523), ASF, Carte strozziane, 3rd ser., 41/17, fol. 72v.

[28] Casanova, *La famiglia italiana in età moderna*, 86.

a few heirs or even just one by decree of the dead hand that established it in the first place. The fideicommissum worked a permanent devolution of patrimony to the benefit of future generations, perpetuating family at the cost of individual rights to alienate or otherwise manage their property.[29] The acceptance of fideicommissa as a broad familial trust in law was not easy. Law and its practitioners had to devise new notarial devices embodying fideicommissa. They had to cope with the "agnaticization" of family in treatises on dowry and fideicommissa, and they turned increased attention in juristic consilia to related issues.[30] In sum, the fideicommissum did not take on the legal dimensions and substance needed to make it a powerful part of family strategies until around 1500. Even then, as we will see, it was not easy for jurists to assimilate what was happening in practice, for all that as fathers and householders they could sympathize with and share the agnatic sense of lineage that lay behind the increasing use of fideicommissa.

6.1   Fideicommissa in Practice

We can capture the characteristic language of a fideicommissum from examples Calonaci provides. In a testament of 1598, count Pandolfo Bardi, following clauses about his burial and certain pious bequests, divided his holdings between his nephews (Alberto and Carlo d'Ottavio Bardi), leaving them some other assets to be held in common (chiefly the Contea di Vernio). If the male lines of both nephews died out, Vernio was to pass to *parenti* "in infinito." Pandolfo's heirs were to be his unborn male children, or girls if there were no sons. If he died without any such heirs, his nephews became heirs (and not just handsomely endowed legatees), substituting one for the other, and their legitimate male descendants in infinity. Then, expressing his "will" (*volontà*) "that said properties might be conserved by said instrument in perpetuity," he prohibited the nephews and their descendants from making any sale or other form of alienation (such as a gift), except to assemble a dowry. He declared that subject to this "fidecommisso perpetuo" fell all the properties he had enumerated, cautioning that no bit of Vernio could be alienated, even for a dowry. Any alienated property had to be retrieved; its alienation annulled. If his line died out and the final holder made no will, in intestacy the patrimony should go to male heirs in the line of Cosimo di Gualterotto Bardi. This was a more elaborate statement than found in other,

---

[29] Katia Béguin, Pierre-Charles Pradier, and Elena Avellino, "Nascondere il valore dei titoli pubblici per truccare i bilanci patrimoniali: il caso delle rendite dell'Hotel de Ville (Parigi xvii secolo)," 715.
[30] Leverotti, "Strutture familiari nel tardo medioevo italiano," 255–56.

especially earlier examples, and it was highly self-conscious of being a "fedecommesso perpetuo," but precisely for that reason it gives us sufficient sense of all the elements of a fideicommissum.[31] The idea of heirs sharing the patrimony in perpetuity, thus preserving the family over generations, lay at the heart of provisions of testators, like Pandolfo Bardi.

The process by which learned law came to grips with such inheritance practices and needs of families and elaborated interpretations of the texts of Roman and canon law in that regard has been studied by legal historians to a limited extent.[32] The fideicommissum began in Rome as a device by which a testator committed to a trusted friend, relative, or other associate some property for the benefit of yet others designated by him. Such trusts circumvented the strict rules of civil law succession, directing property to others than direct heirs, who thus held it under the trust, not as inheritance. A Roman testator might try to preserve property in a family for generations, but it was not allowed to dispose a trust in favor of unnamed persons. A partial way around that ban was for a testator to bind his successors not to let specified property leave the family. Justinian limited any such trusts to four generations (those conceivably known to a person in one lifetime).[33] This situation was well short of the early modern example we have just seen, in which such trusts were perpetual and bound to an unnamable succession of heirs in a series of contingent lines, should the direct line fail.[34]

The legal transactional essence of the early modern fideicommissum seems easy to spell out. Heirs were not to sell or otherwise alienate the designated familial substance, most notably urban palaces and productive rural estates. They were not to separate out the legitimate portions otherwise guaranteed to each heir by the terms of *ius commune*. There was to be a precise order of succession imagined well into the future.[35] The legality of that marriage of substitution and prohibition of alienation

---

[31] Calonaci, *Dietro lo scudo incantato*, 236–41.

[32] On the law in this area generally, see Caravale, "Fedecommesso (storia); Trifone, *Il fedecommesso: Storia dell'istituto dal diritto romano all'inizio del xvi secolo*; Tria, *Il fedecommesso nella legislazione e nella dottrina dal secolo xvi ai giorni nostri*; Johnston, *The Roman Law of Trusts*; Padovani, *Studi storici sulla dottrina delle sostituzioni*; Treggiari, *Minister ultimae voluntatis*, vol. 1: *Le premesse romane e l'età del diritto comune*; Rossi, "I fedecommessi nella dottrina e nella prassi giuridica di ius commune."

[33] For an incisive, brief treatment see Borkowski and de Plessis, *Textbook on Roman Law*, 243–48; and Tria, *fedecommesso nella legislazione e nella dottrina dal secolo xvi ai giorni nostri*, 5–9; Alan Watson, *The Law of Succession in the Later Roman Republic*; Treggiari, *Minister ultimae voluntatis*, 1: 78–102; Franciszek Longchamps de Berier, *Il fedecommesso universale nel diritto romano classico*.

[34] For this sense, cf. ASF, Carte strozziane, 3rd ser., 41/18 (legal glossary of Antonio Strozzi), fol. 234r–v.

[35] Calonaci, *Dietro lo scudo incantato*, 8–9.

against the prerogatives of heirs and creditors was forged only with careful effort. That process has been sporadically studied or merely taken for granted.

Calonaci himself, intent on systematic analysis of the wealth of families from Florence's archive, spends little time with the law and seems to see it as unproblematic, until the eighteenth-century legislation to limit and ultimately abolish fideicommissa (1782). He finds preliminary traces of the institution in the Florentine statutes of 1415, when in fact it was present in essentially the same statute back in 1325.[36] In fact, that statute was not particularly accommodating to fideicommissa, as it specified that an heir in possession of the deceased's property was liable to the estate's creditors, despite even formal repudiation, including property left "pro legatis et fideicommissis."[37] As we saw earlier, in 1477 fideicommissa were identified in legislation as a source of fraud.

In essence, fideicommissum was an institution of civil law and its doctrinal development had to occur there. Other than its acceptance into the statutes, usually tacit, as with so much else of civil law, fideicommissum did not necessarily feature positively in local norms, as opposed to practices.[38] The central problem is to understand how the institution gained legal support from university-trained jurists, who were, at various points in their lives, heirs, testators, and householders. They knew and understood what a shared domestic economy was (as we have seen especially in the previous chapter). But they also dwelled intellectually in a realm of highly individualized rights and agency that was the persona of the *paterfamilias*, *dominus* of the family *substantia*. They had to find ways to reconcile the individualism of ownership in the law with the actual sharing of resources that could be the essence of family life and preservation.

In an important study, Bartolomé Clavero tried to account for the acceptance into law of the Spanish equivalent of the fideicommissum, the *mayorazgo*. Although he was more intent on explaining the practice of primogeniture and consequent effective disinheritance of younger children, an immoral practice in the eyes of the law, he noted that law was also hostile to tying patrimony to lineage with no limits.[39] It was an apocryphal text attributed to St. Bernard that became the vehicle by which moral and legal acceptance of a principle, primogeniture, contrary to the *favor*

---

[36] Calonaci, *Dietro lo scudo incantato*, 69; but see *Statuti della repubblica fiorentina*, vol. 2: *Statuto del Podestà dell'anno 1325*, 123–24, rubric De heredibus conveniendis pro debito defuncti.

[37] Cf. Kuehn, *Heirs, Kin, and Creditors*, 54, 75.

[38] Calonaci, *Dietro lo scudo incantato*, 69–70, discusses sixteenth-century legislation.

[39] Clavero, "Dictum beati."

legitimorum, found its way into civil law. It was much easier to concede perpetual patrimonies without the addition of primogeniture. And it was certainly possible to retain property over many generations in a male line without demanding primogeniture.

Zorzoli, whose Lombard sources were no more insistent on primogeniture than the Tuscan, recognizes also that a shifting sense of *favor* was applied in law. The key behind fideicommissum became the intent of the testator (*mens testatoris*). A favorable take allowed for expansive reading of the testator's intentions. A finding that a fideicommissum was "odiosum," to the contrary, led to a restrictive interpretation. If the focus was on the interest of the heir, whose free disposition of property was interfered with by a fideicommissum, then it certainly seemed to be "odiosum." However, if the focus were the family, transcending any single person, then a *favor agnationis* came into play that could expansively validate testaments seeking to protect the agnatic family.[40] Fideicommissum became the heart of inheritance practices, "as an instrument of conservation of wealth at the interior of the family."[41] If the testator made mention of family, the interpretive door was open. Especially efficacious was a testator's prohibition on alienation "extra familiam."[42] Here the echoes of Bartolus's equation of *familia* and *substantia* came home to roost.

The papacy was a more active legislative entity than civic boards and princely councils. And it had a more authoritative court in the Roman Rota. Piccialuti necessarily devotes much more attention to the legislation and the establishment of judicial precedents. She notes that civil law was in its roots hostile to holding patrimony in a unit or even to directing all of it by will. Portions were reserved for all legitimate heirs, the so-called *legitima portio*, which were theirs by individual title. Of course, that insistence of Roman law on legitimate portions had long since been elided for dowered daughters, so that they did not share equally with their brothers. But the device by which that occurred back in the twelfth and thirteenth centuries was local custom and legislation.[43] Learned law continued to raise exceptions and offer restrictive interpretations to the so-called *exclusio propter dotem*, as it also remained notably hostile to disinheritance (effectively the result for sons and daughters if the fideicommissum insisted on primogeniture).[44] In any case, daughters' rights

---

[40] For all the preceding, Zorzoli, "Della famiglia e del suo patrimonio," 158–60.
[41] Zorzoli, "Della famiglia e del suo patrimonio," 162.
[42] Zorzoli, "Della famiglia e del suo patrimonio," 166.
[43] Cf. Romano, *Famiglia, successioni e patrimonio familiare*, 42–49. The classic work remains Bellomo, *Ricerche sui rapporti patrimoniali tra coniugi*, and see Mayali, *Droit savant et coutumes: L'exclusion des filles dotées, xiième-xvème siècles*.
[44] On disinheritance see Kirshner, "Baldus de Ubaldis on Disinheritance."

to dowries were broadly protected in law, including statutes, even being an exception to provisions against alienation of family property subject to fideicommissum, so those portions were constantly being broken away from existing patrimonies.[45] There were also myriad exhortations to dispose of parts of a patrimony to *pias causas,* and that option might be precluded to those who inherited under the dead hand of a fideicommissum.

There was much theoretical discussion of fideicommissa, especially as they began to be more widely used after 1500. Opinions varied by cases, as Zorzoli has also noted, but there remained an undercurrent of hostility to current practices and "a certain attachment on the part of the jurists to the figure, surpassed in practice, of the Justinianic fideicommisssary substitution: from it followed the unfavorable consideration of the contemporary fideicommissum, defined as *odiosum.*"[46] Despite a long tradition of commentary on the many dense texts touching on fideicommissa in the *Corpus iuris civilis,* systematic treatises did not appear until the sixteenth century, when they were keyed to practices. Piccialuti attributes the first to Marco Antonio Pellegrini in 1595.[47]

There was a measure of egotistical arrogance at the center of the fideicommissum. The expression of a corporate dynastic sense of family and the means of its preservation lay in the hands of a single individual who first set the terms of a fideicommissum. His *voluntas testatoris* overrode what jurists saw as natural law, by which each child received an equal share in full ownership to dispose of in turn by his own testament.[48] Another dimension of the individual-as-bearer-of-rights within the family was the designation of collateral lines of descent in substitution should the direct line fail. It was never the family as a vague whole, a lineage, that inherited; it was lines of descent within it (or one person in the line). The agnatic family as a whole only marked the limits of the prohibition of alienation and ultimate descent, should all other lines fail. Otherwise it was generally some first cousin who was favored over another in the absence of sons.[49] Property was always in someone's name, which meant it was not in others'. Florentines and Milanese, at least outside a limited nobility, tended to use a "dividual" fideicommissum in which all sons (or cousins of the same line) shared equal portions but held them in

[45] Cf. Kuehn, "Protecting Dowries in Law in Renaissance Florence."
[46] Piccialuti, *L'immortalità dei beni,* 97.   [47] Piccialuti, *L'immortalità dei beni,* 76–77.
[48] Romano, *Famiglia, successioni e patrimonio familiare,* 68, and Calonaci, *Dietro lo scudo incantato,* 55.
[49] An example is the 1648 testament of Niccolò Panciatichi (Calonaci, *Dietro lo scudo incantato,* 253–58), who designated, in order, the line of Bandino Panciatichi, then that of Giovanni Panciatichi, and in final substitution that of Cavalier Filippo Panciatichi.

common.[50] Presumably there were no problems with legitima in such cases, other than forbidding their separation from the rest of the patrimony as a unit. In any case, it is not beyond reason to see the fideicommissum as enacting an enforced form of familial sharing, without calculating returns or debts, without assertions of individual ownership beyond a tacit fractional entitlement. As we have seen, however, these common sharing households also often came sooner or later to division of holdings and to fine lines of reckoning what was inherited and what was earned, what was common and what individual. The fideicommissum aimed to obviate any such divisions, both by removing the legitimate portion each heir could claim and by demanding the preservation of holdings to go to the next in line, across generations. Sharing became perpetual (where there were coheirs). One problem for the heirs was to find a balance between the properties rendered inalienable by the fideicommissum and some sort of free and mobile capital that could be employed for market transactions or for such things as return of a dowry.[51] The shared inalienable possessions sat at the heart of a lasting but possibly stifling patrimony.

6.2   Construing a Fideicommissum

Given the limited range of fideicommissum in the civil law heritage and the relative neglect or even hostility in civic statutes,[52] how did the early modern fideicommissum gain legal traction? The only answer can be the jurists, who generally had two spheres in which to expand the law of trusts into an entail of property. One was academic. In the lecture hall and in disputations they could address questions and interpret texts. The other was in the courtroom, in the guise of expert consultants to courts and litigants raising real questions of the meaning and scope of fideicommissa and substitutions encapsulated in testaments, codicils, gifts, and other instruments, as well as interpreting local statutes of inheritance that touched on these. Jurists like Bartolus of Sassoferrato (1313–57), Baldo degli Ubaldi (1323–1400), Paolo di Castro (1360–1441), Alessandro Tartagni (1423–77), and Giason del Maino (1435–1519) contributed to a process of minimizing the *haeres fiduciarius*, turning him into a *nudus minister* to carry out the testator's desire to hold property for the benefit of another.[53] But jurists also found a number of

---

[50] Calonaci, *Dietro lo scudo incantato*, 46.

[51] Paola Lanaro, "La restituzione della dote: il gioco ambiguo della stima tra beni mobili e beni immobili (Venezia tra Cinque e Settecento)."

[52] Franco Niccolai, *La formazione del diritto successorio negli statuti comunali del territorio lombardo-tosco.*

[53] Treggiari, *Minister ultimae voluntatis*, 524–48.

problems and inconsistencies in construing substitutions with the logical and grammatical tools at their disposal.[54] They also examined problems and attempted at times to restrict the reach of fideicommissa, to preserve legitimate portions and the need of a *haereditas* to meet bequests and other obligations.

Jurists had to work out some accommodations to the subsuming of legitima into an enduring *patrimonium* in order to allow fideicommissa to work. Incontestably there were high levels of litigation, as Muratori later decried.[55] Those who lost out to a fideicommissum were the source of countless suits, not all of them by any means unsuccessful. Even those who accepted fideicommissa and their accompanying restrictions on the management and disposal of property had reasons to chafe at those restrictions and hope for ways around them. Notably the Senate of Milan granted dispensations from fideicommissa, especially to allow the putting together of a dowry.[56]

Litigation regarding fideicommissa would generally have arisen from one of two sorts of people: either from prospective (by intestacy) heirs whose rights were postponed or subverted by the trust or substitutions; or from creditors whose rights were jeopardized by the fideicommissum's hold on property (the situation raised by the Florentine legislation of 1477). They would raise what challenges they could to the scope and validity of the otherwise revered *mens* of the original possessor/testator.

To Piccialuti, who deals predominantly with primogeniture common among Roman nobility, the main legal obstacle to the fideicommissum was its lack of provision of shares for all heirs. However, that was not the only obstacle, especially in Tuscany, where primogeniture, though used, was rarer. There legitima and even provision of dowries for girls were handled with relative ease.[57] The problem instead, one that Bartolomeo Sozzini resolved with celebrated clarity, was construing the testator's intent so as to allow a conditional substitution and transmission of a patrimony in its entirety over many generations, effectively indefinitely, when law envisioned the fideicommissum as a transaction limited to three parties (the institutor, the heir, and the fideicommissarius [trustee]). Against the seemingly "solid" imaginary geometry of descent as laid out in a fideicommissum, there were intricate conjectures and unexpected deaths (or failures of births).[58] There were variant senses of family

---

[54] See, broadly, Padovani, *Studi storici sulla dottrina delle sostituzioni.*
[55] Piccialuti, *L'immortalità dei beni*, 93–95.
[56] Annamaria Monti, "Fedecommessi lombardi: profili giuridici e riflessi private delle dispense senatorie" and Albane Cogné, "Le fidéicommis: un instrument d'immobilisation des patrimoines? Le cas de la Lombardie durant la période moderne."
[57] Calonaci, *Dietro lo scudo incantato*, 15.   [58] Piccialuti, *L'immortalità dei beni*, 180.

embraced by litigants in opposition, and uncertainties about testators' wishes.

The typical testator, for all that law spoke of freedom of testation and his ability to inscribe his *voluntas* in his testament, was in fact quite constrained. As Letizia Arcangeli incisively puts it,

> the freedom of the testator in regard to succession was very limited: it was possible, but risky, not to take account of the dispositions of *ius commune* in regard to legitimate portion, falcidia and trebellianica; one could not be excessive with bequests, and bequests to one's wife, nor "improve" the situation of one son at the expense of the others, and we are not talking about instituting primogeniture. In substance to decide the fate of one's own patrimony was truly possible only in the absence of male descendants: then one could leave daughters as heirs or dower them and exclude them from succession; one could even choose heirs from outside one's own relatives.[59]

It might be that the resulting dissipation of the patrimony ultimately was less an issue than the shame of seeing a property so closely associated with family fall into the hands of others as a result of failed business activities. Perhaps better to have the family line die out than to survive to witness such a shameful loss. A "dividual" fideicommissum could not serve to preserve house and patrimony.[60]

Several jurists are often cited as crucial in the development of the fideicommissum in law. One was a Sienese, also active in Florence and a professor at the law school in Pisa, Bartolomeo Sozzini. Piccialuti cites him as a source of a "cautela del Soccino" by which, with the insertion of an appropriate clause into a testament, the fideicommissary heir relinquished his right to a legitimate portion all his own. The legitima that remained with the patrimony was shared with all who came before and after.[61] It was, in effect, an expression of patrimonial unity.

Another jurist of importance for fideicommissa was Filippo Decio, a Milanese, cited by his contemporary, Antonio Strozzi, a student and colleague of Sozzini, for important consilia on aspects of fideicommissa.[62] Decio took his doctorate at Pisa and taught there from 1475 to 1502, returning in 1516. He was acquainted with Sozzini. We will examine important examples from both men. But first, to offer an earlier stance on the issue, we will look at a Florentine case that involved Sozzini's

---

[59] Arcangeli, "Ragion di stato e ragioni di famiglia."

[60] Arcangeli, "Ragion di stato e ragioni di famiglia," para. 10.

[61] Piccialuti, *L'immortalità dei beni*, 132, though it is also conceded that this could be termed *cautela Angeli* from the earlier Angelo degli Ubaldi. Sozzini's consilia are also mentioned by Romano, *Famiglia, successioni e patrimonio familiare*, 62. Tria, *Il fedecommesso nella legislazione e nella dottrina dal secolo xvi ai giorni nostri*, 11, mentions Sozzini's argument in favor of an undivided patrimony and primogeniture.

[62] ASF, Carte strozziane, 3rd ser., 41/17, fol. 434r; and 41/18, fol. 236r–v.

father, Mariano (1397–1467), along with a phalanx of other legists, mainly Florentine. This case can give us purchase on some important preliminary issues in jurisprudence as it came to grips with practices that became vital to the later perpetual fideicommissum. A man named Antonio di Francesco, in a testament composed more than seventy years before the lawsuit (situating it even into the later fourteenth century), had left daughters 100-florin dowries, and then established that if all his sons should die without legitimate issue, he wanted his two sisters to have lifelong usufruct in equal portions. Otherwise he designated as his heirs his sons Bianco, Francesco, and Matteo, with substitution to each other. If these sons all died *sine liberis*, then Antonio substituted the legitimate sons of Geri, Baronzio, and Vito, sons of his brother Bianco. In fact, following Antonio's death, his three sons became heirs. Subsequently, Antonio's sisters all died, as did all the sons of Geri, Baronzio, and Vito, although they had sons of their own (but there was no mention of the sons of sons in Antonio's testament). Meanwhile, Francesco was the only surviving son of Antonio, having become heir also to his brothers, Bianco and Matteo. The problem was: if Francesco died without issue, did his property revert to the sons of the sons of Geri, Baronzio, and Vito, or were they unable to "aspire" to the fideicommissum (and hence leave Francesco free to make a will and devise the property according to his lights)?

No fewer than a dozen Florentine and other jurists offered comments or at least signatures on the case, beginning with Otto di Lapo Niccolini (1410–70).[63] He noted that he was not faced with a new problem. It had perplexed glosses and commentaries, past and present, whether the term *filius* meant only son or also encompassed *nepos* (grandson).[64] Niccolini, despite some distinctions made by Bartolus that included grandsons in a testator's meaning of the term sons (in situations favorable to the sons as heirs), fell in line with jurists such as Francesco Accursio that *filius* did not include grandson in any will that also made provision for any *extranei* (heirs from outside direct *potestas* of the testator). In the end it was also a matter of the common usage (*communis usus loquendi*), by which the word sons did not include grandsons. The sons of the sons, furthermore, had not been born when the testator drew up his will, or even when he died. It was not probable (*verisimile*) that the testator would want to burden his sons in perpetuity with restoring the estate to persons so distant.[65] The heirs, under the specific term *liberi*,

[63] Martines, *Lawyers and Statecraft*, 493.
[64] Sozzini, *Consilia*, 1 *cons.* 152, fols. 258rb–63vb, at 258va.
[65] Sozzini, *Consilia*, 1 *cons.* 152, fol. 259ra.

could be taken to include grandsons, but the testator had employed the more specific word *filius* that designated someone in the first degree of relationship. The notary who drew up the will had been precise. So Francesco was free to direct his property as he wished, for the substitution had expired.[66]

Salustio Buonguglielmi (ca. 1373–1461) followed and emphasized that as the grandsons had not been born, and were thus unknown to the testator, they could not have been included in his thinking. Even if it were alleged that he may have thought generally of descendants, and that he harbored a general affection for the male line of descent from Bianco, that did not carry weight "because no one seems to think of those he did not know" (quia nemo videtur cogitare de his quae ignorabat). More to the point,

if it were true that the testator had regard for consanguinity and line of descent, the same testator would have made the substitution of fathers rather than of their sons, because the one is greater and includes such sons. It is therefore to be said and presumed the testator rather had regard for the persons of those sons than for the relation (*parentela*) which he had with their parents on account of the friendship and knowledge he had of those sons.[67]

Buonguglielmi construed Antonio's testamentary provision as an act of personal regard for the sons and not an act of agnatic consciousness for the family.

Mariano Sozzini was merely the third to address the issues, and he largely only rehashed previous arguments. Andrea Barbazza da Sicilia (d. 1480) again made reference to the nonexistence of these grandsons at the time of the will. Then followed a brief subscription by Angelo Gambiglioni from Ferrara (d. 1465) and a long one by Francesco Accolti (1416–88), again arguing time of birth against the fact of lineal blood descent.[68] Tommaso Salvetti (1390–1472) came next and pointed to the specificity of terms required in *scientia legis* as opposed to the imprecise speech of the unlearned (*idiota*).

Along the same lines were the opinions and affirmations of Piero Ambrosini da Iesi (1403–73), Benedetto di Michele Accolti (1415–64), Bernardo Buongirolami (d. 1484), and Zanobi Guasconi (1397–1464).

[66] Sozzini, *Consilia*, 1 *cons.* 152, fol. 259rb.
[67] Sozzini, *Consilia*, 1 *cons.* 152, fol. 259rb: "Nam si hoc foret verum, quod habuisset testator respectum ad consanguinitatem et stirpem, potius fecisset substitutionem ipse testator filius eius de ipsis patribus quam de filiis eorum: quia propterea quod unum quoque tale, et illud magis, dicendum est ergo et praesumendum testatorem potius fabuisse respectum ad personas ipsorum filiorum quam ad parentelam quam haebat cum eorum parentibus propter amicitiam et notitiam quam de ipsis filiis habebat."
[68] Sozzini, *Consilia*, 1 *cons.* 152, fol. 260rb–va.

The last to look at the case, the Sienese Giovanbattista Caccialupi (1420–96), who was also the youngest of the dozen jurists, took the testator as not interested in simple agnation but in the sons who were known to him. Therefore he found the strongest argument, the one all the others had cited, to lie in the fact that the grandsons were unborn and thus unknown to the testator.[69]

It is striking how at least this generation of mainly Tuscan jurists (twelve in total) could not easily extend a line of descent in a substitution. They were struck instead by the horizontal extension of knowledge and interaction with others, something that could not have happened with the young men that were born after the testator's death and thus shared the patrimony with an entirely different set of family members. They were hardly of a mind to allow the extension of substitution to one generation, let alone to untold generations to come, which lay at the heart of the perpetual fideicommissum. They were certainly aware of such extension, but they were unwilling to make it where there was no precise language to that effect and where the extension of kinship over time had been attenuated by so many childless heirs – where, in short, there could never have been a sharing of substance or affection such as they could imagine with Antonio and the sons of Geri, Baronzio, and Vito whom he knew. We are not yet in the presence of a fideicommissum in line with those Calonaci examines.

Let us move forward a generation to Bartolomeo Sozzini. Sozzini's consilium, as is true of most of his that survive in manuscript as well as in print, is devoid of factual detail and narrative context. We can give it no firm date. At the heart of the case were the possible claims of the daughters (Cornelia and Margherita) of a man named Guglielmo, and thus the claims of their children in turn, which were opposed by an Antonmaria (presumably a cousin). It seems that Guglielmo had inherited under a fideicommissum ordering substitution if the heir had no sons. The original heir had been Guglielmo's father, Battista. The fideicommissum also carried a prohibition on alienation of patrimonial properties outside the family. Reference to a statute of Bologna leads to the inference that the case arose there. The lack of specificity and the thorough treatment of the issues in a complex geometry of arguments gives Sozzini's opinion an authoritative aura, though civil law did not have the capacity to make such a judicial opinion a precedent.[70] His opinion carried weight. With many other of Sozzini's opinions, it was printed.[71] But even in manuscript

---

[69] Sozzini, *Consilia*, 1 *cons*. 152, fol. 263rb.
[70] See here Julius Kirshner, "*Consilia* as Authority in Late Medieval Italy: The Case of Florence."
[71] Sozzini, 2 *cons*. 227, fols. 84rb–88rb.

among the papers of Sozzini's eminent Florentine pupil, Antonio Strozzi (1454–1523), it was given the number of its first printing, as consilium 227, and copied more than once.[72] The copies are also heavily annotated with marginal references and summaries of content (thirty-four in the one used here), showing active and constant reading. This opinion was cited by others, including Filippo Decio.

Right away Sozzini indicated his fascination with the issues the case raised: "the present consultation is beautiful and subtle and so must be diligently investigated."[73] It was clear to him that the first substitution in the will had lapsed, because the heir died with sons. Battista had sired Guglielmo, who, in turn, had no sons and left the estate to his two girls. The substitution and succession of heirs was not problematic here. The problem lay with construing the prohibition of alienation of *immobilia*, the other key feature of a fideicommissum as perpetual family trust, which had been justified as the testator's desire. There were four questions to resolve: (1) whether this was an absolute fideicommissum that fell on family members, or one that came into play only if there were an alienation of property outside the family, which was the major problem; (2) whether Guglielmo's institution of his daughters as his heirs violated the prohibition on alienation *extra familiam*; (3) whether the daughters' children succeeded them; and (4) if the fideicommissum were absolute, what rights fell to the daughters or their children. The consilium was arranged around these four questions, with the first taking up, as advertised, about half the opinion.[74]

That half had its own elaborate structure. The initial assertion that the fideicommissum was indeed absolute was backed up by no fewer than nine arguments based on civil law texts and jurisprudential commentaries, though following the lengthy presentation Sozzini asserted that the contrary was in fact true. The fideicommissum was not absolute but arose only if a forbidden alienation occurred. On that score he assembled four arguments. Obviously, it was the force of the arguments, not their number, that he considered telling. He began his discussion by noting that he had been pressured by other legal practitioners to declare such a fideicommissum absolute and he had refused.[75]

---

[72] The analysis here will rely on ASF, Carte strozziane, 3rd ser., 41/2, fols. 216r–26r (hereafter Consilium 1).

[73] Consilium 1, fol. 216r: "presens consultatio pulcra est et subtilis, ideo diligenter investiganda."

[74] Consilium 1, fols. 216r–20v.

[75] Consilium 1, fol. 218r: "quidam consulentes diebus elapsis per ea conati sunt me in hanc sententiam adducere, sed mihi non placuerunt, unde requisitus, ut consulerem, recusavi."

What did it matter if the fideicommissum were absolute or not? If absolute, it left an order of succession and a prohibition touching all in the same degree of relationship and was triggered by the death of the previous holder.[76] Sozzini's nine pro arguments first took the testator's intent (*mens*) as imposing a fideicommissum. Behind this line of thinking ran a fairly continual stream of references to commentaries of Bartolus of Sassoferrato. The motive that property remain in the *familia* justified the prohibition of alienation, which otherwise was ineffective, without some such rationale,[77] and, according to the ninth argument, the contribution of the prohibition and rationale for it was that "inducatur fideicommissum."[78] As Sozzini summed up the thrust of the nine arguments, the combination of prohibition and its rationale showed the testator did not simply want to preclude ways property might not reach his heirs, but he wanted it to go to them, seemingly precluding not only *inter vivos* alienation but also institution of any heirs from outside the family.[79]

But for all this, Sozzini's conclusion fell on the other side of the issue. The fideicommissum, he declared, was not absolute, to come into play simply on the death of the previous heir, but arose only in the case of a prohibited alienation. The key text, *lex Peto fratre*, of the Digest's second book dealing with *legata* and fideicommissa (D. 31.[1].69,3) raised the example of a testator instituting his brother as heir with a prohibition on alienation of the house beyond the family. Sozzini saw the parallel words in the testament in his case as equally suited to construe a fideicommissum (mainly the difference between the verbs "peto" and "volo" and "relinquere" and "permanere"). But as he put it, "the difficulty is what type of fideicommissum is produced."[80] The testator's desire that family members step forth and stop an alienation could proceed only at the moment of alienation or of a death enabling an outsider as heir, and not immediately or absolutely, "and in this I find a fixed necessity and I marvel that anyone would understand that there an absolute fideicommissum is produced because it is quite false."[81] The justification about family was simply there to validate the prohibition on alienation. It was not itself a clause to be applied in interpreting the testament.

At this point, Sozzini made a revealing move. He further supported his sense that the fideicommissum was not absolute, but invoked when

---

[76] Tria, *Il fedecommesso nella legislazione e nella dottrina dal secolo xvi ai giorni nostri*, 29.

[77] As Antonio Strozzi noted in his glossary, under the heading *prohibitio alienationis*, "sine causa non valet" (ASF, CS, 3rd, 41/18, fol. 234r).

[78] Consilium 1, fol. 217r. [79] Consilium 1, fol. 217v.

[80] Consilium 1, fol. 218r: "difficultas stat que species fideicommissi inducatur."

[81] Consilium 1, fol. 219r: "et in hoc necessitatem reperio condicentem, et miror quod aliquis intelligat quod ibi inducatur fideicommissum absolute quia falsissimum est."

a prohibited alienation occurred. It was the desire that property remain in the family that gained affirmation in the fideicommissum, which would also last beyond the fourth degree.[82] He posed the possibility of the fideicommissum being, if not absolute, at least perpetual, well beyond the Justinianic limitation to four degrees, because it was *favorabile*. In contrast, limitation of the fideicommissum would seem to rest on finding it not *favorabile* but *odiosum*. He did not take the step of then declaring the fideicommissum "odiosum," though it seems he easily could have. He was conceding that by certain lights (at least the testator's intent) a fideicommissum that was absolute could be taken as favorable. But this was not an absolute fideicommissum intent on keeping property in the family. Instead, there was not a simple fideicommissum along degrees of descent but an exclusion of outsiders, carried most forcefully because the testator gave as a reason "lest something leave the family."[83]

Sozzini finally turned to the second major issue before him – given that the fideicommissum came into play only on alienation, did Guglielmo's will in favor of his married daughters mark such a point? Various statements of both Bartolus and Baldo degli Ubaldi led to the sense that a married woman left her father's family and entered that of her husband, that she lost her original domicile and entered her husband's, and that she was thus "extra familiam patris." Sozzini argued the contrary on the basis of *lex Voluntas* Codex *De fideicommissis* (C. 6.42.4), a simple text that said "the desire of a father to prohibit children to sell farms outside the family or place at pawn does not seem to have prohibited a brother from giving to his sister."[84] By that text the daughter seemed to be "de familia," married or not. Marriage, after all, did not remove agnation. Daughters were still *de familia* and subject to *patria potestas*.

Then he backtracked. If the disposition of the testator could be shown to have been to exclude women, that he effectively did not consider them part of his family, then "servanda est voluntas." In fact, in a *legatum* in his testament Battista, Guglielmo's father, had left his brother and other males some property. Not to women. He had also declared that were his brother to die without male heirs, a *collegium* would be his heir, in seeming preference to any daughters. It could also be argued that his desires were in accord with Bologna's statutes declaring that dowered girls were excluded from paternal and grandpaternal estates. In doubt the

---

[82] Consilium 1, fol. 219v.

[83] Consilium 1, fols. 219v–20r: "tanquam finalem intendebat ad hunc effectum ne res extra familiam exiret, ex qua adiectione causa de necessitate resultat fideicommissum si fiat alienatio in casu non permisso."

[84] Consilium 1, fols. 219v–20r: "voluntas patris prohibentis liberos fundos extra familiam vendere vel pignori dare fratrem sorori donare prohibuisse non videtur."

testator's intent should be seen as conforming to statute. To all this too Sozzini then reversed course again and defended the status of the daughters as part of the family, "from the proper meaning and according to the disposition of the law" (de proprietate sermonis et secundum iuris dispositionem).[85] While men were clearly preferred to women in inheritance, it was also the case that where sons were lacking women were able to succeed as part of the family. Had the fideicommissum been absolute, there would be a question of its limitation to males, but not in the instance where alienation activated the fideicommissum. And the will of the testator, in the absence of direct male heirs, was in conformity with Bologna's statute that in that case also allowed inheritance to daughters.

Inheritance by daughters' children, male or female, in turn, was another matter. Daughters were agnate to their fathers and brothers, but their children were not. A set of citations in their favor was quickly pushed aside. The "common opinion," which was not lightly to be set aside, drew an effective distinction between a prohibition of alienation and a *ratio* that property remain in the family. The second meant that the daughters' children could not succeed them on intestacy to the property of their grandfather. True, those who succeeded on intestacy were necessarily in some way "de familia," and from their perspective the prohibition could seem *exorbitans* and thus merit a strict interpretation, but just as conventionally children were not of the family of their mother. By that, the married daughters could not testate to their children as heirs, because that would result in alienation *extra familiam*. But their children could be their intestate heirs.

After all this, the fourth issue seemed to be another regression, because it approached the case on the supposition that the first long argument had lost, and that the fideicommissum was absolute, for then women as next in degree would be admitted. Any substitution requiring the heir to direct property within the family had to be understood as based on the condition "si sine liberis decessit." As the testator had inserted a *collegium* as heir if his sons died without male heirs, and thus preferred it, an *extraneus*, to his daughters or their offspring, one had to conclude he preferred his agnatic grandsons to cognatic grandchildren. As Battista had died with sons, the substitution to the *collegium* was averted. Now that his son had no sons, it was a question of Antonmaria's (cousin) possible rights against the daughters. If the will was taken as favoring men, then Antonmaria stood in good stead. But Sozzini claimed that the bias to men only held in the first substitution of the *collegium* for lack of sons. All subsequent possible substitutions had to be taken in the sense that *sine liberis* meant children of

---

[85] Consilium 1, fol. 221r.

both sexes, although there were many common arguments that *liberis* referred only to males. Sozzini's case was different. The case before him was a substitution in the next generation "de restituendo familie," in which nephews did not seem to be preferred to daughters, who after all were also agnate and "de familia," and closer in degree, and not excluded by statute for a more distant agnate. Although Paolo di Castro had maintained that the testator still preferred sons, and many others, including the guild of jurists in Florence, agreed with him, Sozzini sided with all the Bolognese and Perugian jurists that the testator's intent considered children of both sexes. As a learned man, the testator certainly would have specified sons only if he meant that. So Antonio could not advocate for a share for the daughter, "unless by an immoderate subtlety, by which arise a great many conflicts."[86] Reference to subtlety seems more than ironic from someone who had clearly relished the subtleties of the case before him and had been less than direct in his own treatment. In the end, despite the vital desire for property to remain with the family, it seemed that it would fall to the children of granddaughters and thus out of the family.

There was a highly polemical tone to Sozzini's consilium, as he chided unnamed others for fatuous reading of Bartolus and other absurdities. He was consummately aware of what others had done. And while he had conceded the existence of a fideicommissum, he had in the end drawn limits to it and kept property in the hands of more directly related females and their offspring, in line with the inheritance rules of *ius commune*. It all turned on married daughters' status as *de familia*.

Filippo Decio partnered with Alessandro di messer Antonio Malegonnelli (1491–1555), who came from an old Florentine lineage and had an active political as well as legal career, on a case from the early 1520s, which survives in sealed original in a Florentine manuscript, though it was also later printed in a collection of Decio's consilia.[87] In print it bears a brief descriptive *punctus* lacking in the original, thus seemingly an editorial addition. Tizio had substituted his sons as heirs to each other, if dying without sons. Bernardo, one of them, died leaving Simone as son and heir. Decio was consulted as to whether

---

[86] Consilium 1, fol. 226r: "Ex quo patet quod in prima dicendo de liberis intellexit etiam de feminis, alias expressisset de masculis sicut in sequenti casu, cum esset vir doctissimus prout etiam latius supra in alia q. deduxi. Ex quibus omnibus non video quoniam dictus Antonius possit dicta bona advocare a filiabus et eorum filiis dicti Ghuilielmi nisi nimia subtilitate per quam plerunque contingit querelati."

[87] On these men, see Martines, *Lawyers and Statecraft*, 489–90, 505. ASF, Conventi soppressi sotto il governo francese, Archivio 98, 238, fols. 100r–111v (hereafter Consilium 2), where it is noted that it was *cons.* 636, the number it indeed bore in Decio, *Consilia*, vol. 2, fols. 636rb–37ra.

a grandparental prohibition in a fideicommissum meant that Simone could not freely dispose of the estate. Decio determined that Bernardo's leaving a son ended the substitution and prohibition on alienation.[88] Parallel to the example of Sozzini's case, the character of the prohibition of alienation was at issue. The utility of the consilium for our inquiry lies there, as it did for Decio and Malegonnelli, who had reason to rely on Sozzini's views in formulating their own.

The fideicommissum in this instance was not absolute, as the words of the testament in this example were more precise: "he expressly prohibited alienation of his goods because he wanted them to stay always in his estate among his heirs and descendants."[89] The testator, or his notary, had learned a lesson from Sozzini's arguments, or so it might seem. Still, Simone was not burdened by the fideicommissum because he himself obviated the condition of Bernardo dying without sons. The fideicommissum's condition ended with his succession. In arriving at that conclusion Decio cited seven different consilia by six authors, including Sozzini. There was no obvious language that cascaded such substitutions in perpetuity.

The remaining problem was if the prohibition on alienation kicked in and continued to tie Simone's hands in the handling of the property or its later disposition in a will of his own. Decio thought not, if only because as an "odious" burden it should be restricted to the sons and not extended to the grandsons. Sozzini's consilium figured among his several references showing its authoritative nature. Decio took the prohibition of alienation as consequent to the preceding substitution. The testator had made an explicit prohibition where there already was one tacitly in law (alienation under a fideicommissum was forbidden so that the property could be restored to the substituted heir). Obviation of the substitution removed the onerous prohibition on alienation. Simone was free to bequeath the property to whom he wished. Even the general stated desire to see the property remain among his heirs and descendants did not overrule this reading.

Malegonnelli concurred with Decio, and he did so largely on the strength of Sozzini's opinion. The testator's words concerning alienation outside family did not establish an absolute fideicommissum. They only gave an explanation that he wanted property to remain in the family, "according to what in these same terms seemed to Sozzini in his consilium 227."[90] The

---

[88] Decio, *Consilia*, vol. 2, fol. 636rb.
[89] Consilium 2, fol. 101v: "semper voluit stare in sua hereditate penes eius heredes et descendentes."
[90] Consilium 2, fol. 106r: "sequitur quod illa verba, quia voluit, non possunt importare fideicommissum sed solum inserviunt pro causa prohibitionis inducte iuxta ea que in his propriis terminis videtur Sozi. in consilio suo 227."

fideicommissum expired when the invalidating condition of having a son was met. Decio in another consilium had also approvingly cited Sozzini on this point. In a subtle distinction, Malegonnelli said that many doctors argued that a testamentary prohibition of alienation with an explanation ("quia voluit") was taken as establishing a fideicommissum. But as Decio, Sozzini, and many others held, explanations "quia voluit" could not imply a fideicommissum and especially not a fideicommissum that was conditional and easily resolved.[91] The matter came down to whether it was personal (falling on heirs) or real (falling on the property). Malegonnelli took it here as personal, as it followed on the clauses of substitution. It was an active clause that had to refer to people, not things. It was about the sharers, not what was shared. The prohibition had named Lorenzo and Bernardo. It did not extend explicitly to others; so a prohibition falling on a son did not fall on his son in turn. The grandson also inherited from his father, not his grandfather.

Malegonnelli had to admit that such a conclusion made one wonder about adding the rationale to keep property in the family. That was an active area of jurisprudential debate. In the case in question there was no expressed reason for the prohibition of alienation, but the clause "quia voluit" was added later only to the effect of justifying the prohibition and not to any other effect.[92] One imagines that this conclusion hardly satisfied the relatives who feared their heritage being plundered by whatever alienation Simone was contemplating. But here again, jurists who could have given sweeping durability to a fideicommissum – and found plenty of authoritative legal arguments to that effect – chose not to. But every such decision also illustrated where there was a hole that needed to be plugged. Subsequent wills could contain more and more elaborate clauses. Those reproduced by Calonaci at the end of his book are redolent of that.[93] With regard to issues we have considered, these later testaments made explicit matters like perpetuity, gender of heirs, the extent of the prohibition of alienation, and above all inclusion of all subsequent heirs, so that substitution did not end with the son's son. All also looked to a situation where heirs had been in a sharing situation, from which their heirs in turn came.

6.3   Conclusion

As Zorzoli states, a fideicommissum was an aggregate of clauses constituting an inalienable family patrimony "a program for eternity which the members of a society that does not expect to change will take advantage of

---

[91] Consilium 2, fol. 107v.   [92] Consilium 2, fol. 111r.
[93] Calonaci, *Dietro lo scudo incantato*, 236–72.

habitually."[94] It was a largely aristocratic society that projected itself as based on an unchanging patrimony. It was an aristocracy that was constantly in debt and those debts were often unpaid for long periods. Laurence Fontaine has likened the condition of perpetual or at least long-term debt to the moral economy of the gift, in which debts might ride for a long time and reciprocating was something to manage carefully. Such calculated reciprocity, however, would only arise as the relationship of aristocratic debtor and creditor attenuated and its termination was contemplated. Among aristocratic kin, resolution of debts points to a shift away from the more communal economy of sharing.[95] It was an unchanging patrimony that tied the hands of successive heirs, who could not sell or give away or even lease for a long term.

For jurists like Sozzini and Decio, who understood the impulse to preserve a patrimony in a line of male descent, such restrictions on heirs were hard to swallow. As comfortable as they were with testators' desires to see their lineage and patrimony endure, they nonetheless looked for ways to allow each generation to use and manage property, which would include liquidating assets to redeem debt or at least realistically allowing assets to stand as backing for extensions of credit from others, while also sharing with each other in a more immediate and voluntary manner. In the event, Sozzini allowed Guglielmo to bequeath to his daughters, and Decio and Malegonnelli allowed Simone control of what he inherited. These consilia, despite what seem to be clear expressions of testators' wishes about family and patrimony, allowed property to depart the strict line of male agnatic descent when that arose for lack of sons. They restricted the testators' desires to a single instance of descent, to their own sons, and not on through them and their sons, and theirs in turn, until such time as the direct lines failed, and then collateral lines might step in to the same cascading of heirs across generations. They thus pointed the way for future testaments to devise clauses that were more precise to give enforceable form to desires for perpetual entail of property.

A contemporary of these jurists, Antonio Strozzi, compiled a legal glossary that dealt at some length with the sorts of issues that arose in these cases. He observed that a prohibition of alienation that was "sine causa" was invalid. His example of a valid cause was "because he wanted it always to remain in his family," but also added that such a prohibition, even said to be "perpetuum," did not extend past four degrees from the

---

[94] Zorzoli, "Della famiglia e del suo patrimonio," 177.
[95] Laurence Fontaine, *L'économie morale: Pauvreté, crédit et confiance dans l'Europe préindustrielle*, 78–890, 299.

first person to fall under it.[96] But a certain degree of terminological precision could get one past the limit of four degrees. Strozzi also declared that it was a "communis opinio" that prohibition of alienation "extra familiam absolute" did not imply a fideicommissum (the substitution of the next heir), unless there had been a *contraventio* (that someone had tried to alienate something). That also meant that the property stayed with the current heir and he could choose whatever heir was next in line to him, even an "extraneus ab intestato."[97] But then he also noted that Decio himself had declared in a "beautiful" consilium that an absolute fideicommissum was precisely intended to preclude such heirs:

otherwise it seems when beyond prohibition of alienation words are found that are principally dispositive of the patrimony, or when the reason for the prohibition is precisely alleged, as because he wanted the property to remain always in his family, then among those of the family an absolute fideicommissum arises without contravention and then an extraneous heir cannot be instituted but is prohibited to be successor to him.[98]

Strozzi, like Sozzini and Decio, demanded explicit terms to extend a prohibitive fideicommissum, but given those terms he was quite willing to do so. Those terms directed property to kin only.

These consilia reveal that fideicommissa aroused a number of hotly debated issues. There was no real juristic certainty, though consilia like Sozzini's seem to have gained a stature such that it at least had to be confronted. Acceptance of fideicommissa among aristocratic families was growing. More and more testaments and other legal devices raised the possibilities and forms of fideicommissa, and prohibition of alienation was at the center of them all. But acceptance among the legal fraternity was not easy and simple, and the sorts of constant litigation Muratori later decried had its origins in that difficult acceptance, at least as much as in the thwarted desires of collateral heirs or creditors who sought a share, but not to share. And while it might be objected that the family situations in these lawsuits were not normal, in that there was not a simple transmission from father to son across generations, keeping the patrimony intact, it can also be maintained that, if law was going to be of any real use, it was

[96] ASF, Carte strozziane, 3rd ser., 41/18, fol. 234r: "testator voluit quod perpetuo dicta bona remanerent in heredes et successores suos, quia tunc comprehendentur omnes in infinitum heredes seu saltem descendentes testatoris."
[97] ASF, Carte strozziane, 3rd ser., 41/18, fol. 236r.
[98] ASF, Carte strozziane, 3rd ser., 41/18, fol. 236r–v: "secus videtur quando ultra prohibitionem alienationis etiam verba principaliter dispositiva reperiuntur vel quando ration prohibitionis precise allegatur, ut puta quia semper voluit bona remanere in familia sua, quia tunc inter illos de familia absolute fideicommissum nascitur etiam absque contraventione et tunc non potest institui heres extraneus sibi prohibito ab intestato successurus."

precisely in these nonnormative moments, when transmission and meaning of inheritance were in doubt, that law was of most utility and meaning. That was when a fideicommissum emerged as favorable (to some) or odious (to others).

By the end of the sixteenth century, things were different, thanks in no small measure to the continual flow of lawsuits generated by an institution that imposed a pattern of behavior on heirs, restricted the flow of property, and rendered ownership more or less equivalent to usufruct.[99] By that point the legal literature, oriented to practical forensic problems and disdaining resolutions or new formulations on a doctrinal level, was content to repeat the arguments of men like Sozzini and Decio, among others. Cardinal Domencio Toschi's (1535–1620) eight-volume compendium of forensic conclusions, for example, which devoted about seventy-five pages to issues involving fideicommissum, cites Sozzini and Decio repeatedly, although not, it appears, the particular consilia we have examined.[100] His treatment yields a sense of systematic law on the subject of fideicommissa, to which figures like Sozzini and Decio contributed. Whether such a situation should exist, or was in any way just, equitable, or merely sensible, was not addressed. Those questions were left for Muratori and those like him. Their answers, so opposed to reigning rules of family trusts, are a salutary reminder that the dead may indeed reign over the process of inheritance, but they do not rule it. It is the living who decide the destination of property across generations and the sharing or division of patrimonies.[101] As Widlok further points out, with death comes the end of sharing, and thus the realization that human life is finite, not to be continued in legal, cultural, or institutional ways.[102] But a new sharing arrangement could always arise, if under new terms and with new participants.

[99] Rossi, "Fedecommessi," 184–85, 188.
[100] Toschi, *Practicarum conclusionum iuris*, vol. 3, 778–855.
[101] Friedman, *Dead Hands*, 182–83.
[102] Widlok, *Anthropology and the Economy of Sharing*, 190.

7 Estate Inventories as Legal Instruments in Renaissance Italy

The Oratorio of the Compagnia dei Buonomini di San Martino of Florence, a small chapel, is decorated with a fresco cycle variously ascribed to the workshop of Domenico Ghirlandaio or to a miniaturist with a shop close by, Francesco d'Antonio. Dedicated to acts of charity, especially to relief of the needs of the so-called *poveri vergognosi*, in keeping with their namesake, St. Martin, whose legends contain the story of his sharing half his military cloak with a beggar, the Buonomini were an important source of social charity in fifteenth-century Florence. Impetus for the company's founding in 1441 came from archbishop St. Antonino (Pierozzi, 1389–1459), at that time prior of the Dominican house of San Marco. Among its earliest benefactors was Cosimo de' Medici. Benefactors were "sharply conscious of the rise and fall of families and the precarious nature of their own fortunes."[1] Dale Kent, building on the work of Amletto Spicciani, has established that, at least up to 1470, the chief recipients of the company's largesse were families of young artisans. Thereafter, however, the Buonomini seem to have found deserving objects of charity increasingly among elite families fallen on hard times.

The fresco cycle for the modest chapel has ten images, depicting the gift by St. Martin to the beggar, the revelation of Christ's identity as the beggar in a dream, and the seven corporal acts of mercy (burying the dead, housing the homeless, visiting prisoners, visiting the sick, clothing the naked, and providing for the hungry and the thirsty). But in the Buonomini care for the hungry and the thirsty were merged into a single image, leaving one space for a charitable act peculiar to the late medieval centuries and prevalent in Florence, the dowering of poor women. This was an action that was aimed at (re)covering the shame of the deserving poor.[2] The resulting scene shows a marriage, and while the groom places a ring on the bride's finger and a notary records the event, a buonomo of San Martino hands over the cash dowry (Figure 7.1).

[1] Dale Kent, "The Buonomini di San Martino: Charity for 'the Glory of God, the Honour of the City, and the Commemoration of Myself,'" 62–63; Amletto Spicciani, "The 'Poveri Vergognosi' in Fifteenth-Century Florence."
[2] Cf. Julius Kirshner, *Pursuing Honor while Avoiding Sin: The Monte delle Doti of Florence.*

Figure 7.1 Workshop of Ghirlandaio, *Making an Inventory*, Chapel of the Buonomini of San Martino, Florence.

Next to it there is a final image, generally described as the taking of an inventory. As by law in Florence inventories were conceded only to minor heirs (under the age of eighteen), this image could also be described as caring for orphans/the fatherless. Conversely, as legacies in testaments were also a prominent means by which the company gained funds for its activities, the image might be taken as the front end of the cycle of giving depicted there. In any case, this image is worth direct attention, both for what it shows and for what it does not.[3]

The inventory fresco is closely related to the wedding fresco next to it. Both depict acts of writing/recording. In the wedding the writer is clearly a notary, but in the inventory the same figure is instead poring over the contents of a chest with a buonomo (with the distinctive red cap) and a young boy, while another man is writing, presumably recording what the notary calls out as he finds it. Whereas the center of the wedding fresco

---

[3] Samantha Hughes-Johnson has published a couple of useful studies of the Buonomini and the frescoes: "Early Medici Patronage and the Confraternity of the Buonomini of San Martino" and "Fashioning Family Honour in Renaissance Florence: The Language of Women's Clothing and Gesture in the Frescoes in the Oratory of the Confraternity of the Buonomini of San Martino in Florence."

is taken up by the young spouses, the center of the inventory picture is occupied by a lone female figure, perhaps a servant rather than a widow. There are other women in the doorway behind her. The centrality of the women has been remarked on, as their knowledge of domestic space belied the fact that the property being inventoried was undoubtedly that of a man.[4] The witnesses to the inventory itself, to establish its legality, its public quality, had to be men by law. These women could be witnesses only to help the inventory process and, if needed, to give testimony for a court as to the contents of the inventory.

Generally, knowledge of kin, friends, and neighbors played a vital role in legal matters involving otherwise nonpublic domestic actions and relationships.[5] In that regard too it is worth drawing attention to the fact that the wedding is presented as an outdoors event, highly public by virtue of the many spectators to the action who fill the frame, whereas the inventory is taken indoors. And it may be that the heir was also male – perhaps the chubby toddler partially hidden behind the man recording the inventory before the hearth, or else the youngster by the chest on the right.

Arguably, several things are missing from the inventory painting. Objects, for one thing. The room seems awfully bare. Perhaps a reflection of relatively modest circumstances, but also perhaps an expression of familial reticence to parade all that one owned. The only objects in sight are two stools, a chest, and a spindle in the hand of one of the women in the door (though the writer is clearly sitting on something obscured by his robes). The deceased is naturally not depicted, but neither is his testament (presumably there was one in order for the confraternity to have a claim). Other creditors or legatees of the deceased, except Buonomini, are not in evidence. Nor are there obvious guardians of the young heir, though the man recording might be a *tutor*. The painting, in point of fact, gives us only the beginning of the economic and legal process of inheritance. The entire array of interests around the estate – the sort of interests that could easily come into conflict and involve an estate in protracted lawsuits – was not evident. All in all, the fresco presents a straightforward recording of objects, with the notary, a legal professional, seemingly providing the requisite expertise to draw up the list.

One thrust of this chapter is that an inventory was hardly a simple, straightforward recording of possessions, a list, as the fresco seems to

---

[4] Jill Burke, *Changing Patrons: Social Identity and the Visual Arts in Renaissance Florence*, 50–51.
[5] On this, using French materials, see Hardwick, *Family Business: Litigation*, 107–10.

imply. Inventory was much more a process than a result. The painting is deceptive in that regard. An inventory was not "an objective presentation" of belongings, various domestic and craft items, but "a strategic, biased, and intentional text, a subjective representation of the owner."[6] And that representation could shift as contexts changed for those with an interest in the textual list and the process behind it. Determining what that subjective element might be and how it relates to the management and transfer of patrimony is the problem to be addressed here.

In terms of our approach to patrimony, there is another dimension of inventories to keep in mind. Coming in the aftermath of death, inventory marked an occasion on which sharing generally ended. Portions were allocated on the basis of the contents of an inventory, including what was owed out (bequests and debts) and what was owed to the estate. The inventory kept separate an heir's other property from what he/she was now inheriting, including its debts. But, as we are reminded by what we have seen of arrangements that were possible among brothers, there was also the possibility that inventory became the basis of a renewed sharing. The law demanded some specification of ownership by individuals, but it also allowed the potential for sharing by eliminating those who had no potential or desire to share with others. What typically came into view in legal cases was the division of assets and liabilities, the determination of which was the main function of the estate inventory, even as it listed the items previously shared and now open to division or to loss in order to settle debts.

Although the inventory appears to be a private and domestic act, in contrast to the public nature of the wedding, it was in fact – much like the wedding – a legal act, and in that sense public. The public aspect was embodied in the person of the notary. There were, as we will see, rules and procedures for drawing up postmortem estate inventories, and these met some very specific legal needs. But the legal niceties of inventories are not what has drawn the acute attentions of social historians and art historians to these documents. Scholars have been intent on exploiting these texts to study material culture, artistic consumption, the placement of objects in household space, and patronage. Jill Burke, for example, treats one fulsome inventory as an itinerary through the rooms of an art patron's *palazzo*, realizing that the rooms were in fact "theaters for interaction" and hardly private spaces. In the appendix to her book, *Changing Patrons*, Burke reproduces the long, detailed inventory, omitting the legal apparatus that had to preface the notarial list of belongings, although that was also regularly omitted in the inventories kept by the Florentine Magistrato

---

[6] Allison Levy, *House of Secrets: The Many Lives of a Florentine Palazzo*, 65.

dei Pupilli.[7] We now have as well the important example of the estate inventory of Lorenzo de' Medici in a copy from 1512 made for his grandson and heir, Lorenzo di Piero, intent no doubt on identifying and recovering all that had been lost since the Medici exile in 1494.[8]

It is no accident that many of these examples arise from Florence. The Florentine office that saw to the estates of wards and the conduct of their guardians (the Pupilli) accumulated hundreds of inventories from its founding in 1388 (statutes dating from 1393).[9] But more can be found in the pages of notarial cartularies, because notaries' involvement in inventories was required for them to be valid in law, at least with regard to inheritance.[10] That said, it must be pointed out that there were other occasions and purposes for inventories. Recently, Daniel Lord Smail has utilized lists of objects from court records to determine how creditors used the courts to act against their debtors (in Marseille and Lucca) and what sorts of things they claimed and took to recover their assets.[11] These texts differ from the estate inventories compiled on the occasion of death and inheritance, but they are also closely related, as the settlement of outstanding debts is also a central function of the estate inventory.

Inventories have been exploited in various ways. Alison Smith has used inventories to track the importance of widows and wives on domestic space and material culture in Verona, taking inventories as "internal, family documents, not official, public ones."[12] Philip Mattox and Margaret Morse have used inventories to track domestic sacral spaces in, respectively, Florence and Venice.[13] Giovanna Petti Balbi sees inventories as a feature of Genoese women's control of the estate left by a husband.[14] Likewise, more than thirty years ago, Maria Serena Mazzi and Sergio Raveggi used sixty-five inventories from a variety of occasions to get purchase on the material circumstances of Tuscan peasant households.[15]

---

[7] Burke, *Changing Patrons*, 58–61, appendix 197–220.

[8] Richard Stapleford, ed. and trans., *Lorenzo de' Medici at Home: The Inventory of the Palazzo Medici in 1492.*

[9] Caroline M. Fisher, "Guardianship and the Rise of the Florentine State, 1368–93."

[10] The broad utility of inventories for setting all sorts of debts, including for restitution of dowry, led to their use in a variety of contexts under less formal legal restraints than inheritance. See Maria Serena Mazzi and Sergio Raveggi, *Gli uomini e le cose nelle campagne fiorentine del Quattrocento*, 319–408.

[11] Daniel Lord Smail, *Legal Plunder: Households and Debt Collection in Late Medieval Europe.*

[12] Alison A. Smith, "Gender, Ownership and Domestic Space: Inventories and Family Archives in Renaissance Verona," 380.

[13] Philip Mattox, "Domestic Sacral Space in the Florentine Renaissance Palace"; Margaret A. Morse, "Creating Sacred Space: The Religious Visual Culture of the Renaissance Venetian *Casa*."

[14] Giovanna Petti Balbi, "*Donna et domina*: pratiche testamentarie e condizione femminile a Genova nel secolo xiv," 168.

[15] Mazzi and Raveggi, *Gli uomini e le cose nelle campagne fiorentine del Quattrocento.*

In fact, the inventory had a very peculiar role in inheritance in Roman law. The Roman heir was a successor. He acquired not only the property but also the persona of the deceased (the continuation of that persona in the legitimate son having helped Bartolus come to his definition of family). To him fell all debts and credits, rights and obligations, even if they went beyond the value of the inheritance (*ultra vires haereditariae*). The heir's property could thus fall liable to the debts left to him by the deceased, rendering the inheritance *damnosa* (rather than *lucrosa*). The broadest remedy available to protect such an heir was the legal option to repudiate the inheritance. The heir could simply declare the inheritance left him to be disadvantageous and turn it down, instead of accepting it by an act of *aditio* (not needed for a son inheriting from his father). The estate then passed to the next in line.

Of course, the repudiating heir might thus be losing out on some valuable, or at least treasured, resources; and the deeply indebted deceased's last wishes might never be fulfilled for lack of an heir to see to them. So the further legal option was hit on by the emperor Justinian to allow acceptance of an estate *cum beneficio inventarii*. The heir's liability would be held to the objects and the total value of what was found to be in the estate and duly listed on an inventory, to be undertaken within thirty days and completed no more than sixty days thereafter. A valid inventory also protected the heir's right and expectation to realize something from the estate left to him/her. A quarter (Falcidian or Trebellianic in legal terms) was reserved to the heir against all claims of legatees (but not against the claims of other, prior creditors of the estate, against whom the inventory only established a limit to the heir's liability). Because the inventory affected one's obligations, it took on legal requirements for validity, lest it become an instrument of fraud.[16]

Italian cities, notably so Florence, looked askance at such measures contained in the otherwise prestigious civil law, because they changed the presumed obligations of heirs. Florence carefully hedged repudiation of inheritance with time restrictions and a requirement for public recording in order to prevent fraud in the thwarted expectations of legatees and creditors. She was little more hospitable to inventories. By statute, the benefit of inventory was restricted to minors (and thereby available to their guardians).[17] The law seemed to assume that those under eighteen would have too little awareness of the parameters of an estate, even of the patrimony they grew up on, to make informed decisions about its value and the desirability of accepting or repudiating. Guardians of such

---

[16] Cf. Kuehn, *Heirs, Kin, and Creditors*, 32, 69, and passim.
[17] Kuehn, *Heirs, Kin, and Creditors*, 52–55, 58–59.

youngsters, even if close kin, or their mother, needed knowledge of the estate. The inventory also served as a base against which the conduct of the guardian could be measured when the guardianship ended.

Other communities were similarly restrictive regarding inventories, and some even more so. One Tuscan community, Volterra, however, appears to have left the matter to its civil law form, as did some other communities.[18] Arezzo, in its statutes of 1327, in contrast, set a limit of ten days for an heir to do an inventory if a creditor had gone to court to present his claim on the estate. At the very least, this city determined not to let inventory be a cause of delay.[19]

Siena threw all sorts of limits on inventories. Guardians were required to do an inventory within a month. Failure to do so would result in the guardians' removal from administration of the estate, unless a judge determined that the failure was malicious, in which case the guardian was not removed and instead effectively penalized. Deliberate omission of an item from an inventory was to lead to the *tutor* adding double its value to the estate and being personally liable for that item. In order to avoid protracted lawsuits, however, inadvertent omissions of possessions by guardians acting in good faith were declared of no consequence. The Sienese statute overruled the intent of any testator who in his will had discharged the designated guardians from the obligation to draw up an inventory. This was a rare instance in which the will of the testator was not to be observed. These rubrics arose among a host of others governing the abilities and actions of guardians, so the rules on inventory were seen as protecting the interests of the young, possibly vulnerable heirs.[20] Siena, like Florence, was concerned about those who simply occupied property and conducted themselves as heirs without formal acceptance of the inheritance, or who sought a delay to deliberate on their options. In that regard, inventories were not allowed to keep an heir from having to respond to creditors.[21]

Communities in other areas of Italy adopted similar measures. Bergamo (in 1331) seems effectively to have forbidden inventories.[22] The 1396 and 1498 ducal statutes of Milan forbade *aditio* with benefit of inventory and restricted the time for considering whether to accept or repudiate an estate.[23] An inventory of sorts might be taken to help the

[18] Kuehn, *Heirs, Kin, and Creditors*, 57.   [19] *Statuto di Arezzo (1327)*, 171.

[20] *L'ultimo statuto della Repubblica di Siena*, 94–95, and widely 94–101. On the related matter of repudiation in Sienese law, see Kuehn, *Heirs, Kin, and Creditors*, 56.

[21] *L'ultimo statuto di Siena*, 254–55: "Et quanvis fiat inventarium, nihilominus teneatur in solidum omnibus creitoribus defuncti et etiam legatarii."

[22] *Lo statuto di Bergamo di 1331*, 109.

[23] Biblioteca Trivulziana B 1, fol. 153r: "Nullus de cetero beneficio inventarii esse possit heres nec aliquam hereditatem capere, et siquis dubitaverit adhuc hereditatem alicuius vel se inmiscere detur ei spatium unius mensis ad deliberandum et non plus."

heir's deliberation, but only as an accounting for the heir's information, not as a legal device to limit liability. Juristic commentary on the rubric insisted that the law applied only to Milanese creditors. Benefit of inventory still applied for *forenses* who were not otherwise governed by Milan's law. Estates of minors, however, still had use of inventory. Indeed, Milanese guardians had to do an inventory or lose their position and administration of property.[24]

These statutes were not so interested in the formal requirements of inventories, except with the time limit for completion (which they were intent on shortening). It was the period of indeterminacy during the confection of an inventory that was most bothersome. Baldo, for example, faced a case in which one litigant alleged an inventory to reduce his exposure to creditors, but Baldo had found that it was absurd that the debtor continued endlessly to litigate on the basis of the inventory, thus dissipating the estate.[25] Statutes were framed to protect both the rights of creditors, especially against fraud, and the rights of defenseless minors. Inventories hurt the first, potentially, but helped the second.

Of course, what statutes purported to say was not necessarily how they were read, notably so by legal professionals. There is evidence from Florence, for example, in the statute commentaries of local practicing jurists that provides insight into such readings. Alessandro Bencivenni (1385–1423) noted that the statute did not allow benefit of inventory to one in possession of an estate but claimed that if one abstained from it, benefit of inventory remained possible for the next in line. It could be useful in the face of legatees, for there was no hard deadline for paying off bequests, some of which could languish for years.[26] Another Florentine commentator, Tommaso Salvetti (1390–1472), agreed with him.[27] But the reality of abstaining from an estate for fifteen days and more (as the law required), especially for children, was difficult, to say the least. Fear of fraud hurting creditors in the transmission of an estate was, nonetheless, quite real in a city such as Florence.

Certainly, there were acts of fraud and deception involving these legal actions – repudiation and inventory. By the end of the fifteenth century, some Florentines were forthright about their strategy of repudiating estates so that they devolved to heirs next in line who were minors. Their nominal ownership then allowed for recourse to benefit of inventory.[28] Such clever maneuvers were completely legal, if a bit duplicitous. But inventories themselves could be acts of deceit, at least disguising or withholding

[24] *Leges et statuta ducatus mediolanensis*, 398–401, 480.
[25] Kuehn, *Family and Gender*, 179–80.   [26] BNF, Fondo principale 435, fol. 18r–v.
[27] BNF, Fondo principale 434, fol. 70r.
[28] Kuehn, *Heirs, Kin, and Creditors*, 102, 165–67.

assets.[29] And not only contemporaries of the heirs had to be wary of these lists. Historians of whatever stripe who make use of these documents have to be on their guard. As Giorgio Riello says, inventories "are neither uncontaminated records of objective reality, nor simple literary manifestations divorced from materiality. They are instead forms of representation that are influenced by social and legal conventions and by the specific economic and financial values attributed to artifacts and commodities."[30] He goes on to advocate treating inventories as "fictions," less about what they include or exclude than about who is affected by them. Lena Cowen Orlin likewise cautions against taking inventories as "transparent texts," as they were made with awareness of an estate's outstanding debts.[31] Revisions and omissions made sure inventories were not impartial "snap-shots" of an estate but were replete with difficult-to-hear silences.[32] Adrian Evans likewise warns that inventories are not simple representations "but forensic evidence of history in the making."[33] In his view, then, inventories were hardly pro forma documents, while certainly not uninformative.[34] All of this is also missing from the Buonomini frescoes.

One limitation of most inventories, as Renata Ago has noted, is that "inventories recorded and organized objects: only that which was property, in the strict sense of the term, came to be included in these documents. A spouse's goods were not included in this tally." The wife's goods were identifiable, at least in part and in certain forms (e.g., clothing and household linens) in the contents of chests (*cassoni*) that housed them.[35] Restitution of dowries was a primary debt on an estate and drove the presence of estimators, renowned for their sagacity in denominating a value to household goods. At times their estimates were fraudulent, to set a value other than that set out in a notarial dowry settlement, which was often different from what was actually delivered from a woman's family to her spouse.[36] Children too might have

[29] Julie Hardwick, *The Practice of Patriarchy: Gender and the Politics of Household Authority in Early Modern France*, 180, notes the example of a woman who asked other women to help in hiding household goods before an inventory was made.

[30] Giorgio Riello, "'Things Seen and Unseen': The Material Culture of Early Modern Inventories and Their Representation of Domestic Interiors," 125–27.

[31] Lena Cowen Orlin, "Fictions of the Early Modern English Probate Inventory."

[32] In contrast, note the posing of the dynamic nature of wills against the "static" inventories by Samuel Cohn, Jr., "Renaissance Attachment to Things: Material Culture in Last Wills and Testaments," 997.

[33] Adrian B. Evans, "Enlightening the Archive: Glimpsing Embodied Consumption Practices in Probate Inventories of Household Possessions."

[34] Steven Epstein, *Wills and Wealth in Medieval Genoa, 1150–1250*, 36.

[35] Cf. Cristelle Baskins, *Cassone Painting: Humanism and Gender in Early Modern Italy*; Brucia Witthoft, "Marriage Rituals and Marriage Chests in Quattrocento Florence."

[36] Lanaro, "La restituzione della dote."

separate holdings that were therefore not the property of the deceased and should not have appeared on an inventory of his property.

Along the same lines, Roisin Cossar cautions that inventories should not be read as "transparent records of lived experience" but as a depiction of what the compiler of an inventory thought about how the household should be seen.[37] Inventories were "never a complete catalogue" of a household's contents. Inventories met the needs of heirs, legatees, and creditors, and in that regard also obscured ownership of items, "presenting them as common household property,"[38] as shared, and attending mainly to what was fungible, not what had little resale value. Another scholar who has utilized numerous inventories in a study of family palazzi, James Lindow, has noted that there was opportunity to hide goods or remove them from the premises before an inventory could be done, and even honest assessors might at least move goods around to facilitate assessing their worth.[39] Inventories, in short, although they appear easily to play to presumptions of a single property unit, were not, in fact, intended to be faithful accounts of every household object, a record of a singular, undivided, shared patrimony. They were not some sort of warehouse list of contents; they were assertions of liability, which could include intangibles as well as tangible objects. Everyday practice might very differently commingle these belongings and make access equally available, and people were aware of the difference between the experience of their property and the legal definitions.[40] Inventories have been rich sources for many scholars, giving a documentary dimension to our desire to determine material histories, patterns of consumption, and a nonverbal symbolic nexus. But they were not simple, naive lists. They were caught up in interests, practices, and meanings.

As one element to keep in mind, the language of inventories, as taken down by notaries for the purpose of limiting liability on estates, was in fact plural. There was the language of law, to be found mainly in the beginning and end of an inventory, and highly distinguishable for being in scholastic Latin rather than the vernacular (or a Latinized version of it), which was employed in the description and listing of properties. The legal language was also the one deployed in any legal disputes that might arise over an inventory. It was a language cultivated first and foremost in the lectures and disputations of the law schools. It was the language, as well, employed by the notaries (like that in the San Martino frescoes) who drew up

---

[37] Roisin Cossar, *Clerical Households in Late Medieval Italy*, 50.
[38] Cossar, *Clerical Households in Late Medieval Italy*, 53.
[39] James R. Lindow, *The Renaissance Palace in Florence: Magnificence and Splendour in Fifteenth-Century Italy*, 136–37.
[40] Renata Ago, *Gusto for Things: A History of Objects in Seventeenth-Century Rome*, 217.

inventories. This dimension of inventories distinguishes them from the largely vernacular lists that a magistracy such as the Magistrato dei Pupilli in Florence utilized to keep track of income and outgo from an estate during the minority of its owner.

One assurance regarding inventories lay in the presence and oversight of a notary as the source of *publica fides* and compiler of a public instrument. As we will see, the notary's presence was a legal requirement, though his close monitoring of the list of objects may not have happened. He might only have accepted what someone else had already done. He still gave that list probative weight and provided the legal clauses of execution.[41] He was more than a mere clerk.[42] We will also see that in some situations a judge was required, in addition to a notary, to guarantee more fully that the interests of heirs and creditors were being protected. In order to come to grips with these texts, it is necessary then to come to grips with the legal rules and definitions. There is no better place to begin that process than the legal treatises concerning inventory attributed to the foremost jurists of the end of the fourteenth century, the brothers Angelo and Baldo degli Ubaldi, both active in Florence for parts of their lives.

7.1   Inventories in *Ius Commune*

There were different types of inventories, even in the eyes of the various laws, and each therefore had different features and potential reasons to disclose or disclaim objects and assets. There were also inventories made by guardians to record what their wards had fallen heir to. These two types of inventories were closely related, but in the latter it was the guardian's potential liability that was of concern, and that liability extended to a summation and accounting of the guardianship that ended when minor heirs came of age (or died). There were also inventories that served to tell an owner what he owned and to track the movement of objects especially, such as those utilized by Barbara Furlotti in her study of a sixteenth-century noble and his property.[43] In terms of law, however, it was the estate inventory for benefit of the heir and his liability that was the standard and the focus of interest.

---

[41] On the notary's role in inventories, see Elisa Mongiano, "Attività notarile in funzione anti-processuale."

[42] Stapleford, *Lorenzo de' Medici at Home*, 24, refers to the compiler of the original Medici inventory as a professional "clerk."

[43] Barbara Furlotti, *A Renaissance Baron and His Possessions: Paolo Giordano I Orsini, Duke of Bracciano (1541–1585)*.

Angelo's *Tractatus de inventario* is a short but nicely systematic text. It began with the basic legal departure that an heir who did not make an inventory was bound to meet all *legata*, even beyond the value of the estate, and could not subtract the Falcidian quarter that was otherwise the minimum share that had to remain to the heir (*quarta debita iure naturae*) after satisfaction of all bequests and debts.[44] So the utility of the inventory in general terms was clear from the start. Angelo asserted that the inventory had to be drawn up where the estate (or its *maior pars*) was. The heir had to be personally present, as a proper inventory required his signature and a sign of the cross in his hand. A notary was required. Presence of a judge was not necessary, but useful, as a judge functioned "so that all suspicion of such process may cease."[45] A minimum of two witnesses was required, if the creditors and legatees otherwise declined to appear.

The temporal window of opportunity to draw up an inventory began to run immediately on the death of the *de cuius*, as soon as the heir learned of his possible windfall. The heir had thirty days to commence inventorying. Further, "the inventory must be made of the goods found in the estate at the time of the deceased's death … and you add also names of debtors and creditors."[46] Innocent omissions could be excused, but any such omitted property was liable for the estate's debts also. Customarily a *protestatio* was offered by the heir or guardian to the effect that any such omissions were inadvertent. Then again, any gain to the estate that arose after the death did not have to be listed, as the heir (and the deceased) was only liable for what was there at the time of death. But if the heir entered the property (*se immiscuit*) without making an inventory, he was fully liable. Allowing a protest that the heir was unable to make an inventory only kept the status of the property and its obligations in doubt. So such protests were not to be entertained.

Angelo's treatment of the general legal parameters of inventory was consistent with his treatment in specific cases, at least in one we can find in his surviving published consilia. Angelo was asked if an heir who had made an inventory was free, beyond the *vires haereditariae*, from an obligation of the testator that was pledged, under a certain penalty, to touch the testator and his heirs. Angelo noted that there were two benefits to inventories, one regarding the Falcidian quarter and the other

---

[44] On Falcidia, see Borowski and du Plessis, *Textbook on Roman Law*, 233–34.

[45] Judges were regularly inserted in processes of evaluation to preclude at least more obvious forms of fraud. See, for example, Andrea Marchisello, "Il giudice, il diritto, la forza: note sull'esecuzione della sentenza civile in epoca moderna," 76.

[46] Angelo degli Ubaldi, *Tractatus de inventario* in *Tractatus universi iuris*, vol. 8, part 2, fols. 155va–56rb: "inventarium debet fieri de bonis tempore mortis defuncti in hereditate inventis … et tu adde et nominibus debitorum et creditorum."

regarding the creditors.[47] These made sure the heir got something and could not be held beyond the value of the estate. Conditional debts falling on the heir, however, were his fault and responsibility. So the heir in this case did not enjoy the benefit of inventory to escape debts he had willingly embraced and that made an estate *pauperior*.[48]

Baldo's *Tractatus de aditione cum inventario* was more concerned with the formal requirements of the inventory document, offering a hypothetical example drawn up before a Perugian notary and judge. Witnesses, creditors, and legatees were all duly summoned. Witnesses testified to their knowledge of the deceased's property and of the heir, and they asserted their own good reputation (*esse bonae conditionis et famae*). The heir did the recording and placed the sign of the cross on his work. Creditors and legatees stated their claims. The heir had one month to begin the inventory process and two months more in which to complete it, at which point (generating a second legal document) the interested parties were again gathered. Then the heir entered his *protestatio* regarding inadvertent omissions and signed the inventory before those witnesses. Witnesses signed in a particular form, as did the notary.[49]

These brief treatises, as we have seen, were concerned with formal requirements for inventories. Only Angelo ventured into the broader area of applicable law to clarify the heirs' obligations in the face of failure to complete an inventory. But it is also apparent from their few pages that inventories raised legal difficulties, and they continued to do so. In contrast to the brief treatises of the brothers Ubaldi, fed by the continuing flow of cases and judgments in the interim, was the much lengthier treatment accorded inventories by Francesco Porcellini (d. 1453), a – Paduan.[50] He treated seven questions across six chapters, by far the briefest being the first, which declared that the purpose of inventory was that the will of the deceased be faithfully fulfilled while legatees and creditors were not defrauded.[51] The second issue concerned the persons required to make an inventory (e.g., guardians). Mainly he discussed the constraints on guardians, who had to make an inventory and could find themselves liable for omissions, especially deliberate ones.

---

[47] Angelo degli Ubaldi, *Consilia, cons.* 329, fols. 232va–33ra: "Beneficium inventarii solenniter confecti, duo inducit. Unum, circa falcidiam, ut eam detrahere possit de legatis singularibus: aliud, in creditoribus, ut haeres non teneatur ultra vires haereditarias" (232va–b).

[48] Ubaldi, *Consilia, cons.* 329, fol. 232vb.

[49] Baldo, *Tractatus de aditione cum inventario*, in *Tractatus universi iuris*, vol. 8, part 2, fol. 323ra–vb.

[50] Francesco Porcellini, *Tractatus de confectione inventarii*, in *Tractatus universi iuris*, vol. 8, part 2, fols. 156rb–65ra.

[51] Porcellini, *Tractatus de confectione inventarii*, fol. 156va.

Porcellini's second chapter set out eight requirements for a valid inventory, which were in line with what Baldo had already specified.[52] Items not included that emerged later had to be inscribed by a notary before at least two witnesses. A substituted heir, who succeeded to a minor, still had to draw up his own inventory, even if the now defunct heir had had one, to cover all property at the time of the first heir's death. The third chapter then broached the issue of what was to appear in the inventory. The easy answer was all *mobilia* and *immobilia*, corporal and incorporal, including debts owed by or to the heir that were substantiated by written evidence. Failure to make a *protestatio* of good faith against any omitted assets meant the inventory failed (no Falcidian quarter was guaranteed to the heir).[53] Porcellini gave examples in both first- and third-person form.

Chapter four addressed the effect of inventory. The heir with inventory was bound to creditors within the limits of the estate assets, gaining the Falcidian quarter at a minimum, dispensing bequests and debts in a form he saw fit, deducting expenses for funeral and related matters, and for notaries and other legal costs.[54] Failure to inventory put an heir in liability *insolidum* and *ultra vires haereditariae* and also lost him the Falcidian quarter. The fifth chapter then launched into the much-disputed question whether a son, in not making an inventory, lost the *quarta debita iure naturae*; that is, the legitimate portion due him, which was a stronger right than the Falcidian quarter available to other, less immediate heirs. It could be maintained that the quarter arose in nature, not in an inventory, as it was to provide for the child's well-being. One had to respect Bartolus's formulation that the *filius* could be said to be "quasi dominus" of property with his father and was at the least entitled to something as his support, no matter the number of debts. The inventory then seemed suited to other sorts of heirs, the *haeredes extranei*, who were not due a guaranteed portion unless they made an inventory.[55] The *extranei* were, in contrast, admitted "ad lucrum, et filius ad debitum." Again in contrast, even the disobedient son, according to Porcellini, was able to keep his quarter in some circumstances. His reasoning was that the legitimate portion was due to the heir even on intestacy, such that an inventory "makes it about impossible that the estate take a great loss or [bad] business and in consequence that the heir should

[52] Porcellini, *Tractatus de confectione inventarii*, fols. 157vb–58rb.
[53] Porcellini, *Tractatus de confectione inventarii*, fol. 159ra–vb.
[54] Porcellini, *Tractatus de confectione inventarii*, fols. 159vb–60rb.
[55] Porcellini, *Tractatus de confectione inventarii*, fol. 161ra, which offers a numerical example.

defraud creditors and legatees."[56] So there was finally a point at which even a son could lose his natural right, but by and large the legal protection of that legitimate share, to Porcellini, did not even require an inventory.

The sixth and final chapter discussed the problem of the Trebellianic share in the absence of inventory. Whereas the Falcidian quarter was a guarantee of a net share to an *extraneus*, the Trebellianic applied to trusts (fideicommissa), providing a quarter from the heir to the next in line.[57] Porcellini distinguished between particular and universal trusts (absolute, in Sozzini's terms), as in the latter the heir had to pass along all property and not just three-fourths. Was an inventory needed? It could be argued that failure to inventory led to a presumption of malign intent on the part of the heir, and so justified loss of the Trebellianic portion. But Porcellini insisted that no such presumption could hold against one who took an estate under trust with the burden to pass it along to the next in line.[58] So the fideicommissary heir who did not have an inventory did not lose his Trebellianica.[59] This was, to be sure, a contentious area of law, and Porcellini showed off his knowledge of all positions in a succession of arguments and responses. His references to practice and questions that arose therefrom are eloquent testimony to the viability of inventory as a legal device.

Increasing use of the fideicommissary trust raised peculiar problems about the use of inventory. The legal glossary of the Florentine jurist Antonio Strozzi (1454–1523) reports that an heir by terms of a fideicommissum was required by law to make an inventory, in view of the charge on him to restore the estate to the next in line, and that the testator ordinarily could not release him from that duty. However, insofar as the rights of legatees or fideicommissary heirs were concerned, as those two categories of people were only created and identified precisely in the pages of the testament, the testator could prejudice their rights by remitting the need for inventory. The rights of other creditors still had to be honored and could not be prejudiced by failure to inventory.[60]

---

[56] Porcellini, *Tractatus de confectione inventarii*, fol. 162rb: "et reddit se certam lex quod haeres si solemniter conficit invent. quod quasi impossibile esset quod haereditati dero-getur saltem in magno damno vel negocio, et per consequens creditores et legatarios defraudaret."

[57] Borowski and du Plessis, *Textbook on Roman Law*, 247–48.

[58] Baldo, *Tractatus*, fol. 163rb–va.

[59] His conclusion: "quia ista stant simul, quod isti non conficientes detrahant quartam et tamen teneantur ultra vires haereditatis" (fol. 164vb).

[60] ASF, Carte strozziane, 3rd ser., 41/17, fol. 499r: "Heres gravatus restituere hereditatem per fideicommissum tenetur conficere inventarium rerum hereditariarum, nisi sit a testatore exoneratus a confectione inventarii."

7.2   Some Florentine Inventories

In July 1419 a Florentine woman, Telda, daughter of Uberto Albizzi, widow of Ardingo di Corso de' Ricci, came before a notary to repudiate the estate left her by her brother Gianni, which came to her by way of her other brother, Giovanni, who had died just eight days earlier. Later that day her third brother, Piero, and her nephews, Tommaso and Alamanno d'Albizzo, with their paternal grandfather, Baldassare, as their guardian accepted the same estate, which was in keeping with the testator's wishes that after Telda the estate go to the grandsons of Baldassare (half share) and to those of Piero di Vanni Albizzi, who immediately followed with their acceptance of Gianni's patrimony (that is, Bartolomeo and Maso di Niccolò di Piero). Some of these heirs, obviously, were minors, but only Alamanno was explicitly said to be young. These heirs and their guardians then asked that two notaries be appointed as their legal agents (*procuratores*) with instructions to take possession of whatever debts were owed to the estate. Yet it was almost a year later that Baldassare Albizzi, acting as guardian to Tommaso (who had been termed over eighteen in the first document), finally had an inventory drawn up, repeating acceptance of the estate, this time explicitly with benefit of inventory. In the meantime, as the text discloses, a number of debts and debtors had been tracked down.[61] At least for a while, until division, these various heirs were sharing with each other to some degree. Because one was a minor, all effectively gained a benefit from his inventory of the shared assets.

   Years earlier, a mother as guardian to her son, namely Bartolomea, daughter of Amelio Avolte, widow of Manno Donati, sought out funds owed the boy on several occasions, each time asserting that the debt emerged in the process of inventory and she needed to add it to what had previously been uncovered. This process began in May 1406 when Bartolomea became her son's *tutrix* (there were also two sisters but the inventoried bits were all ascribed to young Manno) and accepted the intestate *haereditas* for him. The immediately composed inventory listed a house in Florence, a farm at Quintole, two farms in San Cervasso, monte credits of 1,198 florins, and 45 florins for *paghe*. She returned a few days later to report having found, to add to the inventory, a chest with seven grammar books and a host of domestic implements and clothing, culminating in four pairs of *lentiaminum veteres [sic] pro familia*. She also had designated a man named Maso di Zanobi as her agent for a year, "because of the weakness of her sex and person and because of

---

[61] ASF, Notarile antecosimiano 679, fols. 28r–30v (29 July 1419), fols. 181v–83v (5 July 1420).

emerging impediments personally she cannot interest herself in business for her ward," precisely to wrest monte credits from civic officials.[62]

This hardly ended Bartolomea's efforts as guardian, though there was a gap of seven years before she again appeared before the same notary to adjust the inventory. First there were 10 florins owed by the Florentine monte. Four months later there was the more substantial sum of 232 florins in the public debt. Two years later she added to the inventory another *monte* charge of 42 florins, and four months after that *monte* debts of 13, 285, and 12 florins in different funds. On each occasion at the end of the notarial act came the *protestatio*: "that for now she finds no other goods in the estate or the goods of said minor and if she might find some she will add to the inventory or otherwise compile a new inventory."[63] Another widow of a notary, acting with her fellow guardians, revised her previous inventory by adding a list of textile items and other things, as well as a brief list of people who owed the deceased substantial sums, the largest being 230 lire. Similarly Margherita, widow of Giovanni di Luigi Castiglionchio, as guardian for their seven children, produced an addition to their inventory of a further claim to six florins arising from an assessment of 1397.[64] Despite the time limits posed in the law for completing an inventory, these examples show that, in the presence of notarial authority and deploying the proper language, it was possible to delay or at least amend inventories, notably where fixing debts owed to the estate were an issue. Nor were credits the only financial investments or forms in question. In 1409 Zanobi di messer Andrea de' Bardi, as guardian for the estate of Stagio Cionellini, added to the inventory the monetary claims he had against Giovanni di Sandro (3 florins and 37 lire and 11 soldi), who had been ordered by the court of the podestà to pay Zanobi for expenses incurred for a lawsuit.[65]

A long and very formal inventory from 1415 offers a view of the legal process disclosed in the notarial record.[66] On 13 May 1415 Caterina, wife of Giovanni di Donato Barbadori, daughter of Filippo di Neri Ardinghelli, and her sister, Giovanna, wife of Bernardo di Vieri Guadagni, were given the judgment of an arbitrator. Antonio di Vieri Rinaldini had been chosen by these two women to determine matters

---

[62] ASF, NA 9036, fols. 50r–54v (26 May 1406): "quia propter debilitatem sexus et personae et propter imminentia impedimenta personaliter omnibus interesse non potest negotiis dicti pupilli."

[63] NA 9038, fol. 91r (10 July 1413), 121r–v (9 November 1413), 300v–301r (29 November 1415), 325v (19 March 1416): "Protestans quod per nunc nulla alia bona invenit in hereditate vel bonis dicti pupilli et si una inveniet inventario addet et seu alias de novo conficiet inventarium."

[64] ASF, NA 9035, fols. 26v–27r (27 April 1401) and fol. 30v (11 August 1401).

[65] ASF, NA 9037, fol. 165v.   [66] ASF, NA 9038, fols. 244r–52r.

between them and their sister Lisa, who used her brother-in-law, Bernardo Guadagni, as her agent. Clearly this was all worked out within the narrow range of affinal kin to deal with the inheritance from the women's mother, Lapaccia. There was, in fact, a fourth sister, Andrea, who was a nun in the convent of Santa Lucia, but she was not heir to a share of her mother's property. Rather she was left a singular bequest: an outstanding charge on the estate.

Lapaccia's testament had contained a number of bequests, in fact for over half its value, while leaving the rest to the three who were now parties to the arbitration. The arbitration revolved around the fact (uncontested by the parties) that Lisa had appropriated more than a third of the estate to herself and thus was in debt to her two sisters. The arbitrator declared that all else in the estate belonged to Caterina and Giovanna; Lisa had no further claims, but he also did not diminish her share. Sharing among these sisters had not been evenhanded, but it was true sharing while it lasted (no keeping of exact accounts or equalizing shares when it was over).

The arbitration provoked a subsequent flurry of legal activity. Immediately Caterina and Giovanna accepted their mother's estate with the benefit of inventory and appointed Giovanna's husband, along with two notaries, to draw up the inventory. On 12 June, with Bernardo Guadagni as their *mundualdus*, the women reported the lengthy inventory to the podestà of Florence and one of his collateral judges (both men doctors of law). They took no chances about the necessity of a judge for the inventory's validity.

Briefly, the contents of the inventory were three farms (*poderi*) located in San Martino a Sampergnano (Calcina) with other pieces of land, which had all been sold in May to pay out the testamentary bequests, and for which they had realized 812 florins. Otherwise there was a long list of "masseritias et res": such things as candle holders, knives, various linens, bedclothes, clothing, and many items of which were said to be in "sad" (*tristis*) condition. These had already been sold and fetched various sums, as had a black mantle. Another list of belongings had brought almost 95 lire when sold off two years before by Arrigo Davanzati as executor. While a short list (a bed, barrels, containers) of things remained, Davanzati had also sold 38 pounds of salted pork and 10 staia of spelt. Sums had been collected from debtors and also sold were oil, half a goat, spelt, and a large quantity of grain worth over 123 lire. After these assets came a list of debts, including the testamentary *legata*, funeral expenses amounting to 194 lire, and mourning wear for 109 florins; and 4 florins and 30 soldi for expenses of the executors. Bequests went to the cathedral and city walls (20 soldi each, as customary), the society of San Pietro Martire (200 florins), Santa Maria delle Campora (50 florins), Santa Maria dei Servi (25 florins), the Bigallo (25 florins), Or San Michele (25 florins), *fratres angelorum* (12 florins), and San Benedetto (12 florins). Seven Dominicans at Santa Maria Novella received 1 florin each. The daughter in convent, Andrea, was to receive 4 florins annually to the total of 50. The executors were owed 182 florins for having discharged various debts, including 34 florins Lapaccia had owed her servant, Margarita, as well as *prestanza* assessments owed to the gonfalone. Another list of goods followed. These were said to have come to Lapaccia from Piero di Giovanni Lippi or his wife, and had to be returned to him. Other items were due to the servant Margarita and to Caterina's husband.

The entire process was then completed in almost strict accord with Baldo's requirement for a valid inventory. The women offered their protestation on Scripture that there was nothing else and that they had acted in good faith. They were described as unlettered, so the subscription was made by the notary Domenico d'Arrigo Mucini. The proceedings went on in the Badia because women could not enter the palace of the podestà across the street. Worthy witnesses were named, who testified that they knew Lapaccia and her daughters. Creditors were absent but had been summoned, and notaries were named as their surrogates. Caterina and Giovanna drew a sign of the cross with their own hands. Witnessing notaries then added their own signatures and attestations: Domenico Mucini first and at more length, then ten others. Ser Antonio di Stefano's attestation was rendered in vernacular rather than Latin, though it was effectively a spot-on translation of the others. All the formalities were performed in due fashion. It would have had more heft, including against the estate's creditors, if a judge had been present; but being just across the street from the podestà and engaging other notaries as witnesses raised the level of trust appreciably.[67]

This inventory, because of all the sales, also offers a unique possibility of figuring out the estate's worth. Effectively, equating florins and lire at 81 soldi per florin,[68] assets came to 895 florins, liabilities and bequests to 793. There were a few belongings not otherwise sold or evaluated. Over 400 florins of liabilities came from the testamentary bequests. The accounting is slippery, however, as some of what was owed to the executors was for meeting some of the bequests, so there is some double counting.

---

[67] Cf. Mongiano, "Attività notarile in funzione anti-processuale."
[68] The figure comes from Richard A. Goldthwaite, *The Building of Renaissance Florence: An Economic and Social History*, 430.

The success of sales in this instance – of land, household objects, and foodstuffs – also seems to reinforce a point made by Ann Matchette that, despite the arguments of normative texts on family management and books of *ricordanze* regarding preservation and perpetuation of family wealth, in fact "the frequency of these proscriptions suggests that subsequent sales by heirs were perhaps more the norm than the exception."[69] Admittedly, the inventory we have just examined involved women inheriting from their mother. Normal processes of lineage perpetuation were not in play. The liquidation of the mother's assets seems calculated to foreclose any memory of her position in the ancestry of the Barbadori or Guadagni. Disposal by sale (in fact conducted by male agents) "had much more to do with concepts of agency and wealth than with family memory."[70] The resulting funds went to the constitution and lifestyle of the lineages into which the daughters had married.

Notarial inventories were sometimes quite forthcoming and at others enormously laconic. In one example, in May 1406, the youngster Filippo d'Arrigo di Filippo Rucellai was emancipated and given a house near Santa Maria Novella in Florence. The next day his mother gave him two-fifths of each property listed (a farm and nine pieces of land) with the condition that for three years her son could not be forced to divide the properties by Francesco di Ricco Bonaparte, her brother. Then the boy's father stepped forward acting as tutor for his emancipated son (said to be older than an infant, seven at least) to make an inventory, which listed his emancipation gift and his mother's gift.[71] This was an inventory that was not strictly a matter of inheritance, though the son had suddenly come into property in his name more or less as an heir did. In any case, exactly one year later, mother and father entered into binding arbitration concerning her gift to Filippo, its terms regarding her brother Francesco, and an earlier arbitration she had had with Francesco in 1403. Now it turned out that the emancipation, gift, and conditions placed on it, were all a ploy:

in truth said goods and rights were transferred to said Filippo for defense of said wife because she was oppressed by Francesco di Ricco Bonaparte, her brother, and as a precaution, lest Francesco by his pride or power or terror should deprive said woman of her rights and molest her in said goods.[72]

---

[69] Ann Matchette, "'To Have and Have Not': The Disposal of Household Furnishings in Florence," 705.
[70] Matchette, 708.   [71] ASF, NA 9036, fols. 42r, 42v–44r, 44r–45v.
[72] ASF, NA 9036, fols. 123v–25v (11 May 1407): "in rei veritate dicta bona et iura fuerunt translata in dictum Filippum pro defensione dicte domine ex eo quia opprimebatur a Francisco Ricchi Bonapartis eius fratre predicto et ad cautelam ne ipse franciscus per

The arbiters adjudged all those goods to be hers and the gift to the son to be fictitious and of no validity. But things were not yet quite right for the Rucellai couple, as two months later Arrigo, Filippo's father, now acting on behalf of Francesco Bonaparte's widow, who was guardian for her son, established that the boy, as his father's heir, owed Arrigo's wife 200 florins.[73] Here we are confronted with creative use of law, including inventory, to protect shared property that came into the household by way of the wife. What drove the maternal uncle to pose such a threat to his sister is impossible to say. His actions, unlike his sister's, appear to have been outside the law; certainly they were indicative that they were in separate households.

The widow Ginevra, wife to Tommaso di Gualtiere dei Biliotti and daughter of Lorenzo di Totto de' Bardi, had herself named *tutrix* for her posthumous son, Tommaso, and accepted the estate for him. The inventory revealed a house in Santa Felicita, and half a farm at Quarantola. Two days later Ginevra returned to remake the inventory, adding various household linens and implements, jewelry, furniture, books, grain, and other foodstuffs.[74] The first inventory seems to have been the result of a somewhat hasty move to secure the estate, regarding its major immobile assets, including satisfying the requirement to make an inventory, followed by a more protective, and correct, version. A similar occurrence involved Dea, wife of Michele Bonichi, daughter of Piero di Giovanni da Statanea, and his heir by testament for half. She took her husband as *mundualdus* and took possession of the estate with the benefit of inventory. It revealed assets consisting of two houses and another half of one in the popolo of Santa Maria Maggiore, three pieces of land near Impruneta, and various monte credits (totaling 738 florins), along with furnishings, shop tools, and supplies to be shared with her stepmother. There were also liabilities, including bequests in the will, use of a house for a cousin, and return of dowry to Piero's two wives. A succession of attestations with signatures completed the legalities. Nonetheless, that was not good enough. On 29 June 1411 Dea was back before the notary to put together a much more detailed inventory, with a four-page list of small debtors and the amounts they owed, and a longer list of obligations owed her by others. The same roster of signatures again attested to the accuracy and lack of intent to defraud.[75] These two inventories are reminders that it was clearly not enough to eyeball objects; especially with monetary obligations, it took some time and effort to ascertain the

    superbiam vel potentiam suam et terrorem privaret ipsam dominam suis iuribus et eam in dictis bonis molestaret (fol. 25r)."

[73] ASF, NA 9036, fols. 191r–93v (17 December 1407).

[74] ASF, NA 9037, fols. 346v–47r (2 November 1411) and 347v–49v (4 November).

[75] ASF, NA 9037, fols. 289v–90r, 290r–96v (28 April 1411), and 329r–38r (29 June 1411).

inheritance. For a married woman compiling the inventory of her father's estate, in which she had not been an inhabitant on site sharing part of it for some time, there were many things that would have been unfamiliar. Again, such texts, beyond their undoubted interest in obfuscating and concealing, were designed to bring into the open the very shared essence of a patrimony in the listing of household furnishings and implements, numerous debts and credits, and even in the omission of things like sums of cash.

Inventories were also kept by the Magistrato dei Pupilli. As James Lindow observes, these inventories were rather cursory about *immobili*, generally content with describing the *confini* of a building or plot of land, while going into detail on the *mobili*.[76] While the sharing community of a resident family could well go on after the *capo di famiglia*'s death,[77] it was also the case that the possible press of debts to outsiders led effectively to a detailed listing of the very implements and artifacts of a shared household economy. That is what Pupilli inventories amount to. It was perhaps possible to be brief with lands because they were too evident to slip past and with monte shares because the city had its extensive records on those holdings. Utensils and linens were another matter. Pupilli inventories were the beginning of a running record of transactions by or for the guardians of the minors left in the officials' charge. Such records were vital for legally discharging the guardian when the responsibility ended. For the heir of Neri Covoni that process was from 16 December 1424 until 5 October 1425. An inventory of "possessioni" covered a city house and several farms, including who was renting each and what the rent was. Then came an inventory of "masserizie," in fact several separate lists of furnishings, clothing, and implements, followed by a list of obligations of the city to the estate, and then individuals who owed various amounts that went on for pages. A roster of "creditori" completed the inventory, signed off by two officials – the same two as at the start of the inventory – on 4 October 1426 (and yet followed by an entry for another creditor).[78] The insertion of dates creates some confusion as to what was in fact equivalent to an inventory at the time of death. Expenses of the guardian are, for example, included.[79]

The compiling of an inventory constructed the very objects it recorded. It made things property, as Ago noted. It made them of value (not necessarily precise).[80] The fairly detailed inventories we have just seen

---

[76] Lindow, *The Renaissance Palace in Florence*, 120.
[77] Lindow, *The Renaissance Palace in Florence*, 137–38.
[78] ASF, Magistrato dei Pupilli avanti il Principato 158, fols. 18r–23r.
[79] ASF, Magistrato dei Pupilli avanti il Principato 158, fol. 23r.
[80] In similar fashion, there is Tom Johnson's discussion of the listing of salvaged objects from shipwrecks: "Medieval Law and Materiality: Shipwrecks, Finders, and Property on the Suffolk Coast, ca. 1380–1410."

are also reminders that the items recorded in these documents were receptacles of value. They were liquidated to cover debts. Daniel Smail and others who have studied markets and mechanisms of debt and credit have pointed to this function of objects, whose existence was substantiated by judicially driven lists.[81] So while the inventory reassured the heir that he/she would not be further exposed to the claims of creditors, the inventory also furnished assurance to the creditors that there was something of value in the estate. In thus providing something to both sides, inventories could also be the center of conflict. They raised legal problems that needed resolution from experts.

7.3   Cases and Consilia

A Vatican manuscript carries a copy of a consilium of Bartolus of Sassoferrato concerning an inventory. The case is preceded by an exemplary copy of a notarially composed inventory labeled "Forma inventarii" and itself labeled "De confectione inventarii."[82] It was transmitted to Francesco Damiani da Pisa, Jacopo Bottrigari (ca. 1274–1347), and Bartolus. The estate in question fell to the deceased's wife, minus a number of bequests, but the inventory was not completed in the presence of the legatees, who had not been summoned specifically but by a "generale proclama" made to anyone with a possible interest in the estate. The wife in fact was unaware of the inventory ("ignara literarum notarium"), which the notary had signed for her. Also there had not been present three witnesses acting in place of the legatees, although there had been present six witnesses "bone fame et opinionis." So there was doubt that the inventory was valid, such as to give her the right to seek her Falcidian quarter and such as to allow her to allege ignorance in her defense against the claims of legatees and creditors.

The case against the wife seemed strong as Bartolus first presented it. Interested parties had to be cited to appear, and while a general call might suffice for the creditors, it did not suffice for legatees whose very identity was only disclosed in the will. Nor did the wife have a claim to seek recovery. That belonged to a minor but not to a female (an interesting distinction of two relative states of legal incapacity).[83] Bartolus, however, thought that a public summons was enough. Legatees and creditors did not have to be present if a judge was, as he was considered to be protecting their interests in the accuracy of what was recorded. In fact, there had

---

[81] Smail, *Legal Plunder*.
[82] Biblioteca Apostolica Vaticana, Vat. Lat. 8069, fols. 206r–v (inventory), 207r–9r. It offers no list of objects, merely referring to "praedicta bona."
[83] Biblioteca Apostolica Vaticana, Vat. Lat. 8069, fol. 207v.

been six good witnesses in this case, even if none of them had been designated as watchdog for legatees' interests. Bartolus ended up defending the notary's signing for the wife, if only because the document was immediately placed in public record.

Issues of the proper form of an inventory and of its consequent invalidity were real. It was one way for an interested party to challenge an attempt to hide behind an inventory to limit or eliminate a debt. Beginning one opinion with the declaration that "inventory of an heir is a precise thing [scrupulosa res] and often even diligent ones fail," Baldo listed the principal elements of a valid inventory (*solemnitates*): time (one month to begin and more time to finish), *materia* (items to be listed), and a notary (*auctoritas*). Then there were creditors and witnesses (two if creditors were present, three if not), and the necessity for the sign of the cross (a regular feature of notarial inventories). Summons of legatees had to be made to them personally or at least at their residence. In the case before him, the presence of a judge, Baldo argued, vitiated any shortcoming in the number of witnesses or the subscription. He declared the inventory in this case valid, although he moved on to void an arbitration agreement – the act of someone not formally a judge – for not hearing both parties.[84] That damage was minimal, as the parties could always proceed to another arbitration.

In other cases Baldo argued that the mere fact that goods were found in the deceased's home did not mean that they were in fact his and therefore to be included in an inventory. In this case one witness claimed that a "pelandria coloris azurini" was the deceased's, but not included in the inventory, while a second witness mentioned a different omitted object. The seeming agreement that the inventory was imperfect did not, however, mean there had been theft or deliberate fraud or that the omissions provided sufficient basis to overturn the inventory. A judge had been present when the inventory was drawn up, and the judge's authority rendered it "perfect and valid." Obviously, the presence of witnesses had not prevented these omissions; but there could be no presumption that witnesses knew the dealings of another. That knowledge had to be proven, though it was easy to do so with witnesses who were part of the household.[85]

In yet another instance, Baldo noted that the sign of the cross was a strict requirement for an inventory according to one line of thinking – to the effect that "he who makes the sign of the cross, beholding this terrible sign, has it in mind, lest he commit deceit or fraud, as now one has the gospel placed before his eyes, as he is sworn, touching the sacred

---

[84] Baldo, *Consilia*, 4 *cons.* 147, fols. 36vb–37ra. [85] Baldo, 5 *cons.* 414, fol. 138ra–b.

scriptures."[86] But there was an opposed line of thought, which Baldo elaborated and followed, to the effect that a lack of the sign of the cross did not vitiate an inventory. It was a mere trapping that was not of the substance of the act. Tellingly, inventories of Jews and Saracens were valid without the sign of the cross, so those of Christians should be too. In a similar vein, there were arguments that an inventory failed when interested parties were not summoned and thus absent, lest they be defrauded. But as their failure to appear, once they had been summoned, did not void the inventory, failure to summon them did not seem substantive either, as long as there were creditable witnesses otherwise.

The collective import of these positions was that inventories rested on the good faith of the heirs and the public authority of the judge. The various "solemnities" as to form were secondary, including uncorroborated witness testimony. Baldo was willing to turn the benefit of inventory into a flexible instrument to lessen the debts and obligations an heir faced and to assure the minimal quarter share. The fact of a patrimony in passage to be shared by a new generation was more important than the formalities of the law, at least past a minimum level.

The increasingly perplexing issue was what, if anything, an heir might retain as his own, distinct from the mass of the estate held in trust (fideicommissum) to be preserved and handed along to the next heir. The more estates devolved in fideicommissum, the more this issue popped up for later jurists in the fifteenth century. This was the question that came before Paolo di Castro. He distinguished that the heir had protection against legatees and fideicommissarii, versus estate creditors. However, provision of inventory did not leave an heir liable *ultra vires* to such beneficiaries of a testament.[87] The vital distinction was that the sort of general trust being applied in testaments throughout Italy was a universal trust, not in a particular object but in the entire estate. In Paolo di Castro's eyes it was not possible for a universal fideicommissum to exceed the value of the estate. Even provision for debts owed to others (*aere alieno*) did not reduce a fideicommissum, because it was *in iure* and not *in corporibus*. His conclusion was that "the penalty for not making an inventory is today that nothing can diminish what is owed or left to another, but he is liable to fulfill that all the way to a quarter, even of his own resources."[88]

---

[86] Baldo, 1 *cons.* 383, fol. 123rb–vb: "qui facit signum crucis, aspiciendo hoc terribile signum in mentem habet, ne committat dolum, vel fraudem: sicut interdum evangelium ante oculos positum facit, quod videtur iuratum sacrosanctis tactis scripturis."

[87] Paolo di Castro, *Consilia*, 3 *cons.* 11, fols. 13va–14rb.

[88] Di Castro, *Consilia*, 3 *cons.* 11, fols. 13va–14rb: "Poena vero non conficientis inventarium est hodie ut nihil possit deminuere de eo quod debetur vel relictum est alteri, sed teneatur adimplere usque ad unum quadrantem etiam de propriis facultatibus" (14ra).

In another case, Paolo di Castro had to determine if an heir who had simply accepted an estate without benefit of inventory could later, within the allotted time, have an inventory made and enjoy its protection. The attorney arguing against this heir had, properly in Di Castro's eyes, raised the doubt that anyone who accepted an estate (*aditio*), or simply entered into it (*se inmiscere*), or acted like an heir in some legal act affecting the estate (*pro haerede gestio*) could not later enjoy benefit of inventory. But Di Castro defended the heir, because nothing he had done or said indicated that he was certain of the estate's positive value. One could accept an inheritance with the assertion that it was useful and valuable (*utile et lucrosa*), just as one would assert the opposite in repudiating an estate.[89] In this instance the heir had simply taken it, without a *protestatio* about having an inventory. In fact, the heir had acted to obligate some revenue for debts owed to the estate. At best this was an indirect acceptance by an heir who moved well within the timeframe for an inventory (two days, in fact) with formal acceptance.[90]

Di Castro began his examination of another case with the observation that there was disagreement among jurists whether failure to inventory cost the heir his Trebellianic share. Jacopo de Belviso (1270–1335) had said no, but others, including Cino da Pistoia (1270–1336), had said failure to inventory cost the heir, not if he had immediately to pass the property to a fideicommissary substitute, but if he got to hold onto it for a while, which seemed to be the case before him, where restitution to the next in line happened.[91] The tipping point was that with a fideicommissum universale all interested parties had to be summoned to the inventory. As he put it, "an inventory is made lest the heir subtract and hide estate assets . . . and thus it concerns universal fideicommissary heirs that one be made."[92] In the case before him there had been opportunity to conceal estate assets and thus there should now be no room for subtraction of a Trebellianic portion. Indeed, the case facts as transmitted to Di Castro indicated that the heir "had alienated and dissipated a great deal in harm to the fideicommissum and so he could both subtract and hide things, and as good faith was not served, there was no place for subtracting" any more.[93] The other point he had to consider was that there was a difference between an heir's inventory and

[89] On this, Kuehn, *Heirs, Kin, and Creditors*, 31–32.
[90] Di Castro, 1 *cons.* 274, fols. 132va–33ra.   [91] Di Castro, 2 *cons.* 36, fol. 19rb–va.
[92] Di Castro, 2 *cons.* 36, fol. 19rb: "quod hoc facere debet haeres, non solum quando timet ne patiatur damnum sed etiam si vult lucrum consequi, scilicet detractionis quartae. . . . Praeterea inventarium fit ne haeres subtrahat et occultet res hereditarias."
[93] Di Castro, 2 *cons.* 36, fol. 19rb: "quod multa alienavit et dissipavit in derogationem fideicommissi sic et subtrahere et occultare potuit, et propter bonam fidem non servatam, non sit locus detractione" (fol. 19va).

a guardian's.[94] But there was also a difference in audience, as the testator had demanded that the guardian draw up the inventory for managing the heir's minority, but that did not excuse the heir from that chore as far as creditors and legatees and trustees. So his failure to draw up an inventory cost him the Trebellianic quarter.[95] Paolo di Castro emphasized the difference between notarial and tutorial inventories, such that, in his eyes, the guardian's inventory did not obviate the heir's (even if, as in notarial registers, the guardian compiled and submitted the inventory).

Finally, ending our journey through Di Castro's consilia, there was a case from Siena with a long and complicated set of facts. A man named Niccolò had made a testament in November 1437 that contained some pious donations, and by which he gave his widow Bartolomea usufruct on all his property in widowhood, on condition she not seek return of more than 50 *aurea* from her dowry of 1,000 florins. His heir was Galgano di Jacobo, his nephew. According to the vernacular text reproduced from the will, Niccolò also left his household items to Bartolomea. Galgano was to honor those wishes on penalty of losing the estate. Niccolò pointedly wanted him to treat Bartolomea like his mother, including covering her debts.[96] Further, Galgano was directed to make an inventory within three months and make copies, including for the friars of Sant'Agostino, while he was also forbidden to alienate any property in perpetuity. The inventory was to be entered in a book of at least 300 sheets, which would also be used to record revenues and their use to increase the estate (one third), to be distributed "for God" (another third), and the rest for Galgano. Were Galgano to fail in this, Niccolò deprived him of the estate and substituted another nephew, Giovanni di Guccio. Similar failure on Giovanni's part would put it in possession of Sant' Agostino.

A codicil added to the will on 24 April 1438 provided Paolo d'Antonio a quantity each of grain and wine; a man named Niccolò received a measure of grain, as did monna Giovanna. Niccolò the testator died shortly thereafter. In June Bartolomea declared her willingness to accept the lifelong usufruct in her husband's estate. Galgano, for his part, satisfied the bequests in the codicil in May, and the recipients gave him a legal release. He also fulfilled the bequest to the bishop of Siena. But the substitute heir, Giovanni di Guccio, called attention on 14 October to the fact Galgano had not made an inventory or the required copies. Ninety days had elapsed since the testator's death and since acceptance

---

[94] Gigliola di Renzo Villata, *La tutela: Indagini sulla scuola dei glossatori.*
[95] Di Castro, 2 *cons*. 36, fol. 19va.
[96] Di Castro, 2 *cons*. 292, fols. 141ra–43ra, at 141rb.

of the estate in the form of paying off the bequests. So Giovanni on his own authority took possession and had a public instrument drawn up to cover his action. Galgano went to court three days later and Giovanni answered summons to contest his claim, alleging of course the failure to inventory.

Nine legal issues were raised by this set of facts, three of which related to inventory. However, the first and crucial problem was to decide if Galgano's status as heir was conditional (hinging on certain performances or conditions prior to *aditio*) or not (that is, occurring under certain restrictions once he was heir). The stipulations not to molest Bartolomea and to draw up an inventory and keep accounts made no sense prior to *aditio*. And Galgano's actions were indicative of *aditio*. So then the problem of the inventory arose. First Di Castro stated, following the common opinion among doctors, that this inventory did not require the full formalities (*solemnitates*) of a notarial document. It was only a means of memory for the testator and of the burden falling on the heir, simply a *descriptio*.[97] The problem otherwise was to determine when the three months demanded by the testator began to run. Di Castro said the period began not with the testator's death but only when his widow took her share, which set in motion other testamentary matters. He went further, saying that it began not with *aditio*, which was only a matter of intent (*animo*), but with fulfillment of the steps set out in the will (by actions, as paying out the *legata*). So the fact that Galgano had delayed for three months his own *aditio* was not a result of negligence on his part. Still, by that failure to inventory, he lost the inheritance to Giovanni. If one wanted to argue that the lapse of time was not a serious defect and should not deprive the heir, the response was that such was the express wish of the testator, "which cannot be resisted."[98] It was both by will of the testator and by law, "which is made to protect the will of the testator," that Galgano was deprived of the estate in favor of Giovanni.[99] The courts should not back his claims because of his negligence and the testator's clear desire to keep all the inheritance together for the next heir by the prohibition of sale, lease, pawn, and so forth. Indeed, as the inventory he failed to make did not have to be formal, it was not a particularly onerous task he had dodged.

---

[97] Di Castro, 2 *cons.* 292, fol. 142rb: "illud inventarium ... est quaedam descriptio bonorum hereditariorum, quam testator voluit fieri ad commodum haeredis, unde dico quod in isto nulla requirebatur solennitas, vel citatio creditorum haereditariorum vel legatorum, et poterat fieri manu privata."

[98] Di Castro, 2 *cons.* 292, fol. 142va.

[99] Di Castro, 2 *cons.* 292, fol. 142vb: "quae fit pro conservanda voluntate testatoris."

This case shows us an important distinction between formal, notarized inventories and other, informal, undoubtedly vernacular descriptions of property. In this case correlative demand for copies and for careful keeping of accounts shows a mode of mercantile and legal thinking – a vision of inventory and other texts as protective and probative. This was neither the typical heir's inventory nor that of a guardian. It came closer to the latter in that it contained the direction to have available a book containing 300 sheets, seemingly intended for entering continuous accounts. But it was also a device to perpetuate some form of sharing in the deceased's household.

Benedetto da Capra (1390?–1470), a Perugian, took up a case with different complications. An old man named Angelo Nardi da Borgo had a natural son, Giovanni, over twenty-five, and four legitimate sons. Giovanni had a text, in his own hand, in vernacular, claiming to be an inventory of some "mobili et danari" of Angelo's, of which a notary had been asked to corroborate and confirm the truth. About three months after that Angelo made a will, naming Giovanni and the four legitimate brothers (Nardo, Meo, Cristoforo, and Jacobo) as heirs equally, with Giovanni as guardian for the others as minors. Giovanni was enjoined to make an inventory and, for any business he envisioned, to take counsel with a friend, Antonio di Pietro. Angelo died five years later, and Giovanni took on the burdens of guardianship of the three surviving brothers (minus Jacobo), and drew up the inventory, which revealed that the estate was owed by several persons, and there was a credit on the books of Cristoforo and Giovanni di ser Santi in Florence, as well as various household items. But some things were also missing, such as simple exact quantities of money detailed by Giovanni in writing in his hand, quantities described in the inventory made by Angelo, or quantities of money that were deposited in the bank of Isaiah of Mutilo, and a thousand florins described in the inventory by Giovanni's hand, plus 600 florins or so taken from the bank of Giovanni di ser Santi, also described by Giovanni.[100] This incident reminds us, if nothing else, that monetary instruments were more easily neglected or forgotten (or hidden?) than tangible objects. The brothers, once grown and the guardianship at an end, sought an accounting of those sums taken by Giovanni. That these sums were not contained in any of the inventories was a problem. Capra hinged his consilium around the distinction between ownership and possession. It was well known that possession was more easily lost, even more so with *mobilia*, which were *vilis et abiecta*. So it might well be that items held by Angelo at one point would be lacking at

---

[100] Benedetto da Capra, *Consilia*, cons. 161, fols. 195va–97ra, at 195vb–96ra.

another. But Angelo had ownership (*dominium*), not mere possession, and ownership was presumed continuous, unless its loss/transfer was demonstrated. In fact, even objects merely in possession had to be presumed to be part of what a testator had, unless the opposite were proven. As the goods in question were figured into the deceased's estate, it was incumbent on Giovanni to render account of them, to account for the results of his deceit or neglect, "as on the belongings of these wards or adults he must display that diligence that a father must perform in good faith on his belongings."[101] It was more than a bit unusual to trust an illegitimate son with guardianship over legitimate half-brothers, let alone make him an equal heir, and that without legitimating him. Giovanni was in a position to make up against his younger brothers any slights, real or imagined. Certainly there was no assumption made (except by his father) of good will on his part. Making an incomplete inventory was as actionable as not making one at all. Giovanni could not deny the fact he had hidden assets, or at least he could not yet be excused from his guardianship.[102] Perhaps there was less trust for the illegitimately born Giovanni,[103] or merely no love lost when the half-brothers reached adult age. Yet it may also have been that some of what did not appear on the estate inventory had in fact been lost by perfectly legal means. It seems an accounting battle was ahead. But this case again alerts us to the possible abuse of inventory, to the hiding of assets and avoidance of duties.

In the case of a man named Niccolò, who had taken an estate with the benefit of inventory, Pierfilippo da Corgna (1420–92) argued that he could not be personally constrained or jailed, though he was liable for debts on the estate, but not *ultra vires haereditarias*.[104] Even though by statutory law a guaranteed (*guarantigiata*) act was subject to immediate execution, and even though a person with means to repay a debt could be incarcerated, that was contrary to *ius commune* and subject to strict construction. Niccolò with the benefit of inventory was not bound in his person. The harsher statute could not be allowed to inhibit his rights in *ius commune*. He had a real, not a personal, obligation to respond to the estate's debts. The problem for Niccolò was that he was being prosecuted not as heir but as a result of his own promises in contracts. Inventory did not protect him from himself; he was expressly and specifically obligated.[105]

---

[101] Da Capra, *Consilia, cons.* 161, fol. 196vb: "circa res ipsorum pupillorum vel adultorum illam diligentiam adhibere debeat, quam paterfamilias rebus suis ex bona fide praestare debet."

[102] Da Capra, *Consilia, cons.* 161, fol. 197ra.

[103] See Kuehn, *Illegitimacy in Renaissance Florence*, 87–102.

[104] Pierfilippo da Corgna, *Consilia*, 3 *cons.* 31, fols. 48vb–50rb.

[105] Corgna, *Consilia*, 3 *cons.* 31, fol. 49va.

Whereas Niccolò had made an inventory but foolishly exposed himself, the next case was about someone who did not make an inventory. In that case it would seem things should have been simple: "one not making an inventory is held to satisfy the legatees in total and thus also beyond the value of the estate and even of his own [property]."[106] Further, according to a jurist named Niccolò di Materasso, "the presumption is that one not making an inventory might steal hereditary property" ("praesumptio est quod non conficiens inventarium subripuerit bona hereditaria"). Bequests (as opposed to outstanding prior debts) had to be reduced to provide the legitimate portion, but without inventory the heir was bound *ultra vires* even on the bequests, beyond the legitimate quarter, if necessary.[107]

By the early sixteenth century we find Filippo Decio arguing in one case that the heir had made an inventory to protect his rights to at least a quarter against the bequests lying on the estate. What was left to him after subtraction of the bequests was not sufficient to constitute a quarter of the estate, so the legatees had to answer on a pro rata basis for the supplement, and by implication for the sister's dowry. One of them was the wife of the deceased (not said to be mother of the heir), to whom some supplement in addition to return of her dowry was left to ease the conditions of her widowhood. The question was the validity of the inventory. Decio rehearsed matters, such as when the thirty-day limit began (there had been a delay between the death and the *aditio* of the estate, occasioned by absence and the current difficulties of travel, the need for a *protestatio* in case of later corrections to the inventory, the sign of the cross, summoning of creditors and legatees, sixty days to complete the inventory, the good faith exclusion against any inadvertent omissions, the presence of a notary, the signature of the heir, and witnesses). In the end, the wife need not receive the bequest if the assets of the estate were not sufficient. This was in keeping with the principle

that with inventory heirs may have the estate without risk and may use the law of Falcidia against legatees, and they are held to hereditary creditors only insofar as the things and substances that come to them are worth and satisfy them who first come as creditors, and if nothing is left, later emerging creditors are rebuffed, and heirs lose nothing more of the estate's substance.[108]

---

[106] Corgna, 3 *cons.* 148, fols. 184va–86ra, at 84vb: "non faciens inventarium tenetur satisfacere legatariis insolidum et sic etiam ultra vires hereditarias et sic etiam de suo."

[107] The consilium, fols. 749va–50ra, goes on to discuss the consequences when a widow chose not to stay in her husband's house by the terms of the will – one of those *legata* to be held to or diminished.

[108] Filippo Decio, *Consilia* (Lyon 1522), *cons.* 633, fols. 20va–21rb, at 21rb: "quod facto inventario hereditatem sine periculo heredes habeant et legis falcidie adversus legatarios utantur beneficio et in tantum hereditariis creditoribus teneantur in quantum res et

There was a valid inventory that protected the heir and even spread a bit of his liability, in the absence of a true quarter, to the particular legatees, who held more than three-fourths of the estate. The daughter's claim to return of her dowry, however, was ironclad.

Bartolomeo Sozzini confronted issues of inventory in the changing context of inheritance at the end of the fifteenth century, when increasing use of the testamentary fideicommissum seemed to tie property in perpetuity to a line of descent. The needs/desires of the inheriting generation might fall afoul of those of the bequeathing generation, as arose in a case, requiring two distinct consilia, that came to him from Bergamo.[109] The legal problems were initiated in the testament of Giovanni da Trinitate, which established a fideicommissum by setting down an order of succession and prohibiting alienation of property *extra familiam*. It could be argued that the prohibition fell only on the sons, not on further heirs, because a restriction of their ownership and agency was "odiosa." But Sozzini held that the prohibition fell on all members of a *familia*, including unborn generations, "so they might live from the aforesaid [property] and maintain their honor."[110] It fell on successive generations even beyond the fourth degree for the same reason – maintaining the *honorem domus*. It was not *odiosa* if seen from a different vantage point: "for although to the extent it prohibits alienation the matter is harmful and [to be] restricted, to the extent however it provides for sons and those to be born of them, the matter is favorable and can be expanded."[111] Now in the case at hand, the great-grandson of the testator, Pierfrancesco, had directed property to his mother, Caterina, as his heir. But in making his mother his heir, a person not eligible to be his (intestate) heir according to local statute, he had arguably broken that prohibition of alienation. Those who were not of the family were excluded by the language of Giovanni's will, and the mother (however strange this may seem to us) was not of the family (in the sense of the agnatic lineage).

So no matter what Pierfrancesco had done, agnates could step forward to claim the property, and that is what Count Bartolomeo's son, David, a fifth-degree agnate, had done. He could quash the effective "alienation" to the mother. But a second issue regarding the use of inventory weighed

substantie ad eos devolute valeant et eis satisfaciant, qui primi veniant creditores, et si nihil reliquum est posteriores venientes repellantur et nihil ex sua substantia penitur heredes amittant."
[109] Sozzini, *Consilia*, 3 *cons* 43 and 44, fols. 46ra–49ra.
[110] Sozzini, *Consilia*, 3 *cons* 43 and 44, fol. 46va: "ut possint vivere de predictis et honorem suum manutenere."
[111] Sozzini, *Consilia*, 3 *cons* 43 and 44, fol. 46va: "Nam licet quatenus prohibet alienationem materia sit odiosa restringibilis, quatenus tamen providet filiis et mascituris ex eis, materia est favorabilis et ampliabilis."

on the case, and it "is not a small difficulty." Pierfrancesco, in addition to naming his mother his heir, had alienated property to her. It then passed to Ursula, a sister. David wanted to revoke that alienation, so the property remained part of the estate he was claiming, but two arguments seemed to be in his way. One was that as Pierfrancesco's heir, by standard clauses inserted in contracts of property alienation (sales or gifts), he was bound to respect obligations on the estate, including protecting alienees from "eviction." The other was that as an heir who thus "lucrum sentit," David could not impugn the estate's value. These seem weak arguments, however, and they certainly seemed that way to Sozzini, who brushed them off with (for him) amazing brevity. If the fideicommissum fell to Ursula, as Caterina's heir, she could take the trust owed her even without making an inventory. The fideicommissum provided the heir with a different claim that did not need the protection of an inventory. Paolo di Castro had been consistent to this line of thought, said Sozzini, and so he followed his lead. Thus Ursula could deduct her basic share from the estate. David could demand the entire extent of the fideicommissum (or at least two-thirds), even though there was no inventory to protect him otherwise against the claims of creditors and legatees.

Another case involved the estate of Vinceslao da Brescia, whose grandson Agostino petitioned against Vinceslao's brother Giovanantonio, the heir.[112] The expectant heirs wanted the current heir to make an inventory. At first blush the weight of legal scholarly opinion was that the heir in fideicommissum was bound to make an inventory, "but in our case it seems the testator wanted to exonerate the heir by himself making an inventory." The testator had included an inventory of what fell under the fideicommissum, so there was no need for another. But a notary had been brought in to draw up one and there were discrepancies. Sozzini went with the witnesses to the testator's will, declaring that the notary (*tabellio*), though expert, was more liable to err as not directly knowledgeable on the facts of the estate. One could imagine no reason for the testator to make an inventory but that he intended its contents to be subject to the trust, and what he left out of inventory not to be subject to it. If he wanted money and other mobilia to be subject to the trust, so much more should he have made an inventory of them, especially if he wanted the heir not to be held to make an inventory.[113]

---

[112] Sozzini, *Consilia*, 3 *cons*. 51, fols. 53vb–54va, at 53vb: "contra quos replicatur quod ex quo testator inventarium fecit, non est obligatus aliud facere, praesertim cum alia bona quam in inventario apposita, non venient restituenda, unde queritur quid iuris."

[113] Sozzini, *Consilia*, 3 *cons*. 51, fol. 54ra: "si ergo voluisset pecuniam et alia bona mobilia subiacere fideicommisso, fortius de his fecisset inventarium, igitur apparet quod dicta bona mobilia et pecuniam noluit fideicommisso esse subiecta" (fol. 54va).

The whole issue of the inventory became a lace work of presumed intent. The testator placed certain immobilia in inventory, which were subject to repurchase, according to the trust, and he wanted money set aside and deposited, from which other immobilia might be bought as relatively safe investments, and so he provided for indemnity of the trustees. Because he did not mention the money in the chest, it appeared that he did not want that property subject to the trust.[114] Agostino had twice asked the testator if he were placing a condition on the use of the cash he was leaving, and both times the reply had been negative. As witnesses confirmed, Giovanantonio was a creditor to Agostino and Vinceslao for a large sum. He was just relieving their debts. There was seemingly no need to make another inventory.

In this instance the inventory was not quite the same as others we have seen, if only because it was made by the testator, not the heir. The heirs next in line, the grandsons, voiced their concerns about what they might share when Giovantonio passed the trust to them. There was no question of accepting an estate with limited liability, as the liability was already limited by the trust. But the same basic issue was still in play – the inventory was about debts and credits, and trust. The inventory figured in bankruptcy proceedings, alongside the sequestration of a debtor's belongings, in order to enumerate what was available to satisfy outstanding obligations.[115] Testimony of the owner, especially in the form of business records or other "scritture contabili," was a vital piece of the process. Here it was noted that certain elements of the estate (cash) were omitted from the inventory and so not protected under the terms of the fideicommissum prohibiting alienation. And this testator even left cash with instructions to purchase and thus refashion the patrimony from what it was in detail in the inventory.

7.4   Conclusions

We cannot say with certainty that the opinions of these various jurists carried the day in court. Most of these opinions were partisan – not necessarily openly so, but some did mention the arguments of the "other side" (pars). Yet however partisan some of these judgments may have been, they show us quite well the types of legal issues that arose repeatedly (evident even from our small sample) regarding inventories. These included the consequences of failure to make an inventory, hiding/

---

[114] Sozzini, *Consilia*, 3 *cons.* 51, fol. 54va.
[115] Umberto Santarelli, *Per la storia del fallimento nelle legislazioni italiane dell'età intermedia*, 101–6.

omitting assets from it, and the necessity or not of the presence of interested parties (creditors, legatees, substituted heirs), not to mention of disinterested witnesses and a judge; that is, the formalities (*solemnitates*) required for validity of an inventory, rights to a Trebellianic or Falcidian quarter. Though the issue of fraud in concocting an inventory was rare, it was clearly a concern both in the *ius commune* and the *ius proprium*. The rarity of cases may be testament to how hard it could be to smoke out such fraud. It is hard to dismiss the statutory terrain on this problem. But it also may be that there were relatively few frauds perpetrated by means of inventories. On the other hand, money or its equivalent was clearly a slippery commodity and occasioned some possible frauds. It is worth noting that the examples of inventories we have seen, with the exception of fiscal receipts in the public debt, rarely disclose any quantities of cash. It is hard to imagine that there were not a few coins on hand when an owner died, but it is easy to imagine them being pocketed without notice.

The litigants behind these cases, even when failing to make an inventory, had a directed awareness of it as a legal protection, a device to be exploited, if not always legally. They were aware of its effect as a form of control on guardians, who were in a position to perpetrate frauds of their own with someone else's property. But inventories were also a form of protection for guardians, limiting their responsibility to the sums, objects, instruments, and properties listed. Waiving inventory by a testator for a guardian or heir he had named was a measure of trust and a lessening of burdens, but it also jeopardized the sort of protection an inventory was legally intended to provide.

In terms of a sharing domestic economy, inventories emerge as an ambivalent source. They ostensibly display the property of one person (the deceased), although that may also now be the shared property of more than one equal owner. As a list of assets, the inventory sets a limit of liability, while every item on it is equally subject to covering debts and bequests. The inventory quite nicely papers over the transition of holdings, obscuring what is not included in it, highlighting what is, and making possible the sharing of something following the deceased's death. Above all, the fairly long lists typical of so many inventories (utensils, tools, furniture, decorations, linens, pottery, kitchen vessels, candlesticks, clothing, and so much more), while absolutely intriguing as historical sources into material history, concentrated on what was least knowable and certain about a shared estate (especially for those outside the house). Witness testimony was important corroboration of those items and for a sense of their monetary value. Real property, taxes, and other forms of debt, on the other hand, were open to establishment by other means (documentary mainly). Above all, in a world so dependent on credit in various forms, it was indeed, as Andrée Courtmanche says, a rare estate that was not burdened with debts, and so in need of the legal and managerial advantages of inventory.[116]

If we return then to where we started, in the chapel of the Buonomini of San Martino, we can now appreciate even more what was left out or elided by the deceptively simple image of people finding and recording objects in a house. There might have been disputes arising in the aftermath of the effort to record belongings. There may be a good reason so little in the way of household utensils and objects clutter the pictorial space. Certainly, plenty of inventories are no more cluttered than the pictorial space. The creditors and legatees are not present in the painting, unless they are represented by one or more of the men in the room. The interests and claims of others (than the Buonomini) are not represented. We do not know if this was an inventory for the guardian or the heir, but the Florentine restriction of benefit of inventory to minors effectively elided any such difference in practical terms. We have no more clue now as to the contents of the deceased's will. We can assume there was a testament only because of the social space in which we find the painting. The image was simply familiar to the Buonomini, represented in the fresco, who lived off bequests and needed inventories to delineate and secure their share.

Certainly the documents give us a deeper sense of inventories and the process behind them, even as we have seen some jurists dismiss some requirements, and others who have asserted that inventories were unnecessary to protect heirs' rights to a portion. Inventories served as a device of credit/trust when the person who had some level of trust (hence had been able to incur the debts) was gone.[117] All inventories raise questions. Whose objects were they? What assurances were given about the accuracy of the list and the estimates of value? Were those assurances sufficient? Were the creditors and legatees (possibly even the Buonomini) present? How public was this event otherwise taking place in a domestic interior? Inventories are complex and undeniably rich sources, windows onto aspects of life that turn up rarely, if at all, in other sources. But inventories too were legal sources, and we risk missing the nuances of these texts if we fail to take account of that dimension of them.

---

[116] Courtmanche, *La richesse des femmes*, 281.

[117] In this regard too, estate inventories had parallels to inventories of business assets, usually preparatory to liquidating the partnership. See Padgett and McLean, "Organizational Invention and Elite Transformation." See also Padgett's unpublished study "Economic Credit in Renaissance Florence," 9–10, in which he points out that old accounting methods privileged the transaction, while the new double-entry records focused on the ongoing credit relationship.

8 Prudence, Personhood, and Law in Renaissance Italy

A shared family patrimony need not be under the nominal and formal control of all. One person, most often a *paterfamilias*, would legally have control, while others, like sons and wife (or brothers in a *fraterna*), were dependent on his good management, knowing how and what to do, and when, with market transactions, legal devices, and other tools of patrimonial management. While the conduct of family affairs might be in one pair of hands, the results of managerial failures – no less than the results of managerial successes – were shared by all.

This consideration brings me now to Elizabeth Mellyn's study of insanity, *Mad Tuscans and Their Families*. In point of fact, in studying legal and judicial records touching those accused of mental impairment, Mellyn finds that definitions of madness in courts (*mentecaptus, furiosus*) increasingly focused on economic behavior, linking prodigality to madness, so that by the sixteenth century an ethical standard of "patrimonial rationality" was in place. The merely sinful spendthrift of the fourteenth century had by the sixteenth become "a patrimonial saboteur." In consequence, concerned family members faced with the problematic behavior of a relative had more institutional options in the sixteenth century than earlier. This development coincided with the increasing use of the fideicommissum, generally the product of the testament of one provident ancestor.[1] As Mellyn remarks, such inheritance schemes were "counterproductive in the extreme" if the patrimony was in the hands of a less than competent manager.[2]

But who was a competent manager? Or who was so *furiosus* as to be obviously incompetent? There had to be legal standards and procedures in place to determine for judicial purposes if one were *mentecaptus* or *furiosus*. Crucial in making the legal case to place someone under guardianship and to invalidate legal contracts was the evidence provided by witnesses, even more than testimony from someone in the learned medical community. Anyone sufficiently close and well informed about

---

[1] Cf. Kuehn, *Family and Gender*, 266–95; Calonaci, *Dietro lo scudo incantato*.
[2] Mellyn, *Mad Tuscans and Their Families*, 22.

another's affairs could usefully contribute to a judgment as to that other's patrimonial rationality. Patrimonial rationality was something potentially in possession of all people, not just the fascinatingly productive merchant, courtier, or artist. As Mellyn notes, Bartolus laid this out in his late treatise on witnesses, where he also concentrated on the substance of *res corporales* – the things witnesses might know of. More particularly, to Bartolus it appeared that "without any specialized training, the average head of household should have the capacity to manage and transmit a patrimony."[3] This was what he labeled economic prudence (*oeconomica prudentia*). But this prudence remained difficult to pin down, even if people seemingly trusted that they knew it when they saw it.

Prudence had the quality of those attributes of the individual that Douglas Biow has termed a *nescio quid* ("I don't know what").[4] Biow invokes the term in order to argue for an important form of individualism, wherein an individual is "understood as someone with a mysterious, inimitable quality, a signature style, and/or a particular identifying mode of addressing the world."[5] What Biow stresses is that there was something about Renaissance individuals, or at least those who aspired and rose to a level of distinction that might lead us to term them individuals.[6] Figures such as Machiavelli, Castiglione, and Cellini operated with and gave expression to such mysterious qualities: Machiavelli's famous notion of *virtù*, Castiglione's equally well-known *sprezzatura*, Cellini's sense of artistic taste.[7] Prudence was also a type of *nescio quid*, somehow knowable but hard to pin down. It was something also, at least in terms of law, that was widely available and shared, or at least identifiable to many, if not all. In that regard it was dissimilar from the far rarer qualities of *virtù* or *sprezzatura*. It was just that as something much more common, prudence could not only be described, it could be cultivated.

Qualities such as *virtù* are all linked by Biow to the Greek notion of *techne*, "productive or practical, rather than theoretical or speculative, knowledge."[8] Prudence too was a form of practical reason. Those who had mastered such skills could explain and teach them, either through

[3] Mellyn, *Mad Tuscans and Their Families*, 111.
[4] Biow, *On the Importance of Being an Individual in Renaissance Italy*.
[5] He puts his position in contrast to that of Stephen Greenblatt (the person as culturally constructed and performed) and, to a lesser extent, that of John Jeffries Martin (self as product of cultural factors, such as sincerity, interiority, inner character): Stephen Greenblatt, *Renaissance Self-Fashioning: From More to Shakespeare*; John Jeffries Martin, *Myths of Renaissance Individualism*.
[6] Biow, *The Importance of Being an Individual*, 3.
[7] What Biow terms "his delightful version of Renaissance chutzpah" (*The Importance of Being an Individual*, 59–67, 72–81, 101–3).
[8] Biow, *The Importance of Being an Individual*, 23.

rules or through demonstration and experience. But there was no guarantee to simply applying a set of rules.

Francesco Guicciardini, a university-trained and practicing lawyer, offers us yet another term, discretion, which one either had or had not, another mysterious talent or *nescio quid*. It got one past books and rules, past unanticipated circumstances. But unlike even Guicciardini's discretion, patrimonial prudence then was not individualizing but in line with a normative standard (if vague, in fact) applicable to most people (much like the later legal standard of the reasonable man). A stream of advice literature tried to suggest how to achieve it.[9]

One such was Torquato Tasso's dialogue, *Il padre di famiglia*. Therein he allocated prudence (along with fortitude and liberality) to the *padre*, while the *madre* possessed modesty, *pudicizia*, and shame.[10] In their partnership for running the household, there was a division of labor. "With merchandise, with food, with work and with advice the father of the family will govern in such a way that they will be content with him and he will remain satisfied with their efforts."[11] The very stuff of sharing is what held relations together. While Tasso drew another distinction – namely, that to a father fell the increasing of family resources and to a mother fell preserving them – he conceded that preservation was appropriately common to both. If the wife and mother had a role in preservation, it was because parsimony was more properly of women, in contrast to men's liberality, which all smacks of the legal adage that women were the *genus avarissimum*.[12] Fathers were just better cut out for activities outside the home and thus for acquisition, although, Tasso cautioned, they should operate as *padri*, not as *mercanti* who stayed away from home too long in distant places. He had to remember that "wealth is nothing other than a multitude of instruments belonging to family and of public concern."[13] A father had to have enough to meet the needs of the family, without Tasso in any way being able to say what that might be in any absolute terms.

Men as heads of household were expected to be good managers, hard workers, keepers of good company, and simply astute, as Julie Hardwick found for Nantes in the sixteenth and seventeenth centuries.[14] Conflicts about their management were common, as members of households had their own interests and needs. And disagreements about matters of household economy were not necessarily privately held within the circle of those sharing a patrimony and its ups and downs. Spendthrift patterns

---

[9] Cf. Frigo, *Il padre di famiglia*.   [10] Tasso, *Dialoghi*, 105–58, at 129.
[11] Tasso, *Dialoghi*, 135.   [12] Tasso, *Dialoghi*, 146; Kuehn, *Family and Gender*, 54.
[13] Tasso, *Dialoghi*, 152.   [14] Hardwick, *The Practice of Patriarchy*, 91.

or plain laziness were discernible to others too. The "boundaries of households were quite permeable," so it was easy for others to know what was going on even in other households.[15] Kin and neighbors could react to what they saw as flawed management, and even testify to such in court. Lawsuits remind us that at some point a pattern of (mis)management rose to a level that impelled open and public conflict. Accusations of insanity were extreme forms for kin to contest what they took as bad or at least dubious management. Bad management and prodigality, but especially donations of property to outsiders (amounting to alienation of shared property), frequently provoked hostile reactions, including accusations of insanity.

The thing is that, while discussions of prudence in ethical and legal writings might lead to the impression that there was only prudence or its lack – that one acted prudently or did not – there was a gap between simple imprudent management and insanity. Sometimes people just failed, or things turned out in unforeseen ways (and herein lies the obsession of Machiavelli, Guicciardini, and their contemporaries with fortune). There had to be a range of improvident behavior that yet was not beyond the edges of sanity, that was explicable and rational on its terms. Property management was not easy. Prudence was not simple to pin down at the point of calculation, decision, and action, even if it was clear in the successful or unsuccessful aftermath.

And here is where there is an evident contrast between Mellyn's prudence and Biow's *nescio quid*. While Biow sees ways in which men could express an approved individualism, Mellyn's insane were evidently individuals in a negative sense. Anthropologically, an individual is eccentric, an outlier, a bad fit, one who does not share when he should.[16] In those terms the *nescio quid* of prudence was what marked (at least potentially) everyone else, the socially normal persons, not the eccentric individuals. These then were also the legal persons of the era, increasingly identifiable with their will and freedom: "freedom was the faculty of dominating others, a capacity to express oneself plainly through forms of possession and which resolved into a 'dominating tendency toward external reality'."[17] It was the failure to exercise that dominating *voluntas* that provoked charges of insanity. Prudence, then, at least on some elementary level, was common and presumed among adult male property owners, and thus quite other than the rare and astounding, if also hard to pin down, qualities like *sprezzatura*, *virtù*, or discretion. That is not to

---

[15] Hardwick, *The Practice of Patriarchy*, 101.
[16] Cf. Widlok, *Anthropology and the Economy of Sharing*.
[17] Gigliola di Renzo Villata, "Persone e famiglia nel diritto medioevale e moderno," 471.

say that certain people were not more prudent than others; there were evident inequalities. It is how these then affected the purportedly shared economy of the patrimony that is where people looked for prudence.

8.1   Prudence

In one sense, prudence was the mother of all virtues. In Aristotle's terms, picked up by Cicero and elaborated in the thirteenth century by Aquinas, prudence was a form of skill and knowledge applied to particulars. The person with the ability to recognize what contributed to a genuinely human life and what did not, who understood things without necessarily knowing how to demonstrate them, had prudence.[18] It figured among the cardinal virtues of Christianity and was often linked with one of them: justice. By prudence one would decide what was good and desirable, and what was bad and to be avoided. On one level it was about self-interest and self-management. But people also lived in communities, each having its own form of *bonum commune*. Family is one such and to Aquinas it was a basic good.[19]

There was a wider, less technical discourse about prudence that circulated in learned and wealthy social circles. This was the literate audience where vernacular culture and humanism crossed and interweaved – nowhere more so than in Leon Battista Alberti's dialogues on family life, *I libri della famiglia*.[20] Much of the third book is dedicated to discussion of the proper family manager and father, *massaio*. Noting the necessity for a family to have wealth, the discussants (the elder Giannozzo Alberti and the younger Lionardo) come to the contrast between avarice and prodigality, and conclude that lavish spending is "not admired by prudent men."[21] At that point in the dialogue Lionardo invites Giannozzo, if only for the benefit of the younger Alberti present, to give his thoughts on good management. Giannozzo begins by slyly disparaging books on the subject, and Lionardo admits that "they say nothing different from what any diligent father of a family observes for himself."[22] Again, this is not esoteric matter but somehow comprehensible to anyone with a little reflection. Giannozzo reaffirms that, as he cannot read Latin, his wisdom comes from everyday experience and not books. Difficult as it was to be *massaio*, it did not take special education to know, for one thing,

---

[18] James Gordley, *Foundations of Private Law: Property, Tort, Contract, Unjust Enrichment*, 7, 196–97.

[19] See the entry in the *Stanford Encyclopedia of Philosophy*, s.v. "Aquinas's Moral, Political, and Legal Philosophy."

[20] Alberti, *Family*, 158–63, 195–97, 204–5, 210–18, 230, 239.   [21] Alberti, *Family*, 159.

[22] Alberti, *Family*, 163.

that "the world is full of deceit." The young, in their ignorance and inexperience, should revere their elders, especially those who made their fortune and took advantage of opportunities and resources without recourse to fraudulent or dishonest means. Fathers were to give their sons a good example so they became neither avaricious nor prodigal.[23]

One element of prudent management was to anticipate "certain major expenses," such as clothing, weddings, and dowries, to meet which some sort of "civic occupation" was a good idea. Kin and trusted friends too were necessary and had to be cultivated. The "fool" was one who thought he could "maintain his dignity and preserve his fortunate position without the favor and aid of his family."[24] The fool was thus the detached individual. Lionardo is finally compelled to remark,

> It is my impression, Giannozzo, that to undertake to be the father of a family as you have defined him to us would be a heavy task: managing one's own possessions, ruling and moderating the affections of the spirit, curbing and restraining the appetites of the body, adapting oneself and making good use of time, watching over and governing the family, preserving one's property, maintaining the house, cultivating the farm, managing the shop.[25]

And Giannozzo conceded that the father had to sit in the midst of all and be ever alert. But it was also necessary to be out of the house engaged in affairs and to not get lost in every little trifle. So a diligent wife as domestic partner was also essential, thus Giannozzo explains how he schooled his young wife in those of his affairs he figured suited her female limitations, arriving at a point where he could count on her "reliable loyalty and hard work."[26]

Alberti's work was taken to heart by Florentine merchants and householders such as Giovanni Rucellai (1403–81), who left a book of advice for his sons in hopes that they would prove *massai*, preserve their family *sustanze*, and not get overly involved in public affairs to the detriment of domestic concerns.[27] He counseled his sons to "take great care and good attention to preserving the wealth and your other domestic things, as much as your needs require."[28] To that end he instructed them to exercise care in the selection of business partners, employees, and customers, and to keep meticulous records (resulting in hands stained with ink). The usual admonishments about prudence (*masserizia*) adorn his pages:

> Yet good management lies not only in preserving things as much as using them in needs: not using things for needs is greedy and blameworthy. It is proven that

---

[23] Palmieri, *Della vita civile*, 136, discusses prudence on a civic level.
[24] Alberti, *Family*, 199.   [25] Alberti, *Family*, 204–5.   [26] Alberti, *Famiy*, 210–18.
[27] *Giovanni Rucellai ed il suo Zibaldone*, vol. 1: *"Il Zibaldone Quaresimale"*, 42–43.
[28] *"Il Zibaldone Quaresimale"*, 43.

preserving and spending wealth with prudence is worth more than prosperity, industry, and gain. Those who use things as, when, and as much as is needed, and not more, serve the rest, them I call good stewards those who wisely keep the median between too little and too much.[29]

With such proper and controlled spending the father would conserve both his wealth and the unity of his family. Avarice was "odiosissima" but one had to measure one's spending as well: "I consider careful management to be most useful and he who throws away his wealth to be mad (matto)."[30] It was better to die than live in miserable poverty, but one had to spend: "I have schemed to be regarded not for spending what I don't have by honest management, nor so careful that I am not considered liberal, and so I advise you must act." Still, his sons would find "that to keep and spend wealth with prudence is worth more than prosperity, industry, or gain."

Other Florentines like Giovanni di Matteo Corsini have left accounts of their prudential management in economic and legal dealings. At one point Corsini's *ricordanze* reveal deals in which his brother Niccolò's involvement was covered by legal clauses, including one that nominally lodged ownership with Giovanni, although the property was bought for Niccolò.[31] Prudence did not necessarily come without a certain level of deception or, more directly, without taking advantage of law's instruments or loopholes. Legal actions too were part of the toolkit of the *massaio*. In its way every family account book was a set of instructions on how to manage the patrimony, as well as a history of its management. The homes and markets were replete with advice. So much advice speaks to a sense that prudence could be acquired and practiced and had to be for the sake of all who shared a common *substantia*.

In a more philosophical manner, Latinate humanists turned their attention to *prudentia* in an erudite, but no more precise way. They found prudence within the Aristotelian rhetorical tradition and were struck by its role as an act of interpretation preliminary to action.[32] The orator was equipped not only with eloquence but also with prudence. He could provide past examples of prudent acts and the very act of composition required skills of judgment and discernment similar to practical needs for action, as Giovanni Pontano (1429–1503) claimed.[33] Pontano, starting from an Aristotelian ethics, turned the discourse from contemplation of virtue to the difficulties humans faced in making ethical

[29] "Il Zibaldone Quaresimale", 16.   [30] "Il Zibaldone Quaresimale", 16.
[31] Il libro di ricordanze dei Corsini, 111–12, 118.
[32] See Victoria Kahn, Rhetoric, Prudence, and Skepticism in the Renaissance.
[33] Kahn, Rhetoric, Prudence, and Skepticism in the Renaissance, 40.

choices,[34] notably on the questions of justice that arise in his *De prudentia* (written 1496, or 1498–9). Interestingly, in another treatise, *De magnificentia*, Pontano mentions prudence in connection with marriage, where humans seek out a partner for procreation in a manner so different from that of beasts.[35] He thus placed prudence at the origin of that very institution, the family, that was the realm of prudential activity in the law.

Domestic matters were where prudent advice was most needed and rewarded.[36] But *prudentia* was neither science nor art but energized in actions.[37] *Prudentia* was distinct from *sapientia* because it did not contemplate matters of the heavens and the gods; it dealt with human affairs (again, including domestic) – "what constitutes family wealth or acquisitions, what seems good and appears useful and pleasant or contrary to misfortunes, which are considered bad and harmful."[38] *Patresfamilias* and rulers alike were to contemplate what was useful and what harmful, what was to be avoided or approached with caution. This required experience of particular things. The prudent man, who in reality had to be an older man who had had time to learn, could then give good advice to others.[39] Obviously there was not yet prudence among the young, with their *imbecillitas* and *temeritudo*, and prudence was something more than mere forms of mental agility, such as *solertia*, *sagacitas*, or *astutia*, as all those could lead to fraud. Pontano found three types of prudence: domestic, civic, and legal, which were exhibited in "many who today are popularly called wise and whose responses and judgments are said to be of the wise."[40] Here then law rose to its own category, its own range of particulars and experiences, as jurisprudence.

Interesting are Pontano's disquisitions on things like simulation, "which are thoroughly unworthy of the habits of good men, for in virtue must be nothing fake, nothing simulated."[41] But fortune was such that *simulare*, *dissimulare*, and *fictio* were necessary and at times worthy of high praise. Dissimulation and simulation (keeping a secret, telling a lie) were forms of behavior much discussed in the Renaissance. Instrumental rationality in public life was what Castiglione, Machiavelli, and Guicciardini grappled with, and they demanded a bit

---

[34] Giovanni Pontano, *I libri delle virtù sociali*, 11.
[35] Pontano, *I libri delle virtù sociali*, 204–6.   [36] Pontano, *De prudentia*, fol. 36r.
[37] Pontano, *De prudentia*, fol. 40r.
[38] Pontano, *De prudentia*, fol. 42r. And see Matthias Roick, *Pontano's Virtues: Aristotelian Moral and Political Thought in the Renaissance*, 65.
[39] Roick, 136–37.
[40] Pontano, *De prudentia*, fol. 53r–v: "plures quos hodie pervulgate quidem sapientes vocant et quorum responsa ac sententias sapientium esse dicant."
[41] Pontano, *De prudentia*, fol. 53r–v: "qui mores bonis viris omnino habendi sunt indigni, namque in virtute nihil fictum inesse debet, nihil simulatum."

more than self-honesty in domestic affairs.[42] Recognition of the utility of dissimulation is what John Martin has characterized as a "refashioning" of prudence, paired with the invention of its counterpart, sincerity, as the cultivation of a sense of interiority of the self and the expression of emotions.[43] This is a prudence more in line with Pontano's second type, civic prudence, at least in that Martin develops his ideas on Machiavelli and Castiglione. Insofar as prudence was known by its results above all, there was some willingness to concede the utility of disingenuous activity.

There was an expectation that some modicum of prudence resided in every responsible householder and citizen, even while transparently prudence was not evenly distributed through society. The resources pooled in a family included the varied increments of prudence contained in its members. The best a family could do in some sense was to make sure that those with the most prudence had the largest roles in the domestic economy.

8.2   Prudence in Law

Law had little to say, on the whole, about prudence, for all that jurisprudence was its own peculiar contribution to the broader genus of prudence. Those who had juristic prudence were called on by communal judges and litigants to put that prudence at their service in consilia, by which they demonstrated their prudence.[44] In the most comprehensive recent treatment of the subject, Orazio Condorelli found little concern among the entire range of the glossators to comment on civil law texts that broached the issue of prudence.[45] Condorelli found the most interest in *prudentia* on the part of canonists; and even Baldo degli Ubaldi was not concerned with addressing the issue of prudence in crucial texts (e.g., D. 1.1.1).

Application of a practical virtue was seemingly to be left to practice and not to the exposition of a *scientia* like the law. The legal dictionary of Alberico da Rosciate, who did concern himself systematically with the interpretation of local statutes in relation to the universal *ius commune*, put little effort into an entry on *prudentia* (only listing its seven parts: *memoria, providentia, intellectus, ratio, docilitas, experientia, cautio*). What attention

---

[42] Cf. Jon R. Snyder, *Dissimulation and the Culture of Secrecy in Early Modern Europe*, 25.

[43] John Jeffries Martin, "Inventing Sincerity, Refashioning Prudence: The Discourse of the Individual in Renaissance Europe."

[44] Cf. Massimo Vallerani, "*Consilia iudicialia*, sapienza giuridica e processo nelle città comunali italiane"; Kirshner, "*Consilia* as Authority."

[45] Orazio Condorelli, "*Prudentiae in iure*: la tradizione dei giuristi medievali (prime ricerche)," 141.

he gave to the topic, in which he enlisted the works of Aristotle, Aquinas, and Egidio Romano (d. 1316), was mainly on the prudence appropriate to a political community.[46]

The one place Bartolus touched on *prudentia* is in his unfinished treatise on witnesses, *Liber testimoniorum*.[47] His concern was to delineate how rational and trustworthy witnesses might be. He posited that *prudentia* (first among the four cardinal virtues) emerged as a *habitus activus* operating on particulars, itself further distinguished into eight operations (*cognitio, docilitas, experientia, deliberatio, solertia, providentia, circumspectio, cautio*). Bartolus also listed four different types of prudence by their realm of activity: *prudentia singularis* was about governing one's self; *prudentia economica* was that of the diligent head of household; and there were also *prudentia regnativa* (proper to a prince), a related *prudentia civilis* of those subject to a civic government, and *prudentia militaris*.[48] The opposite qualities were the imprudence of minors or the insane, whose *dolus* or *culpa* resulted in mismanagement.[49]

Patrimonial management involved the family's *substantia*. In Bartolus's mind, for his purposes, that *substantia* was corporeal.[50] But knowledge of different sorts of things called for different sorts of witnesses. There were those things that all persons alike knew (stone, wood, etc.), to which one could give testimony and be cross-examined as to texture, color, and so forth. Proximity was all that was needed to qualify such a witness. Some things were known only to certain persons equipped with an expertise or experience (precious stones, etc.), such as jurists, merchants, and artisans. But there was also a third category of knowledge that required yet greater expertise, that more properly called for judgment rather than mere testimony. This was where the prudence of the judge/jurist came into play.

Bartolus further distinguished *prudentia* from *sapientia* and *scientia* and *ars*.[51] Here he could offer the idea that where one might be said to be a "great" jurist or doctor, that did not mean he was prudent. Not everyone had that capacity, which was active and not speculative, at least not perfectly. In Biow's terms it was *nescio quid*. In all, Bartolus found that

---

[46] Condorelli, *"Prudentiae in iure,"* 138–40.
[47] This treatise survives in a number of manuscript and printed editions, as Bartolus, *Tractatus de testibus*, in *Tractatus universi iuris*, vol. 4, fols. 63rb–71ra. We will rely on the unsurpassable recent edition of Lepsius, *Der Richter und die Zeugen*. See Diego Quaglioni, *"Civilis sapientia": dottrine giuridiche e dottrine politiche fra medioevo ed età moderna*, 111–19.
[48] Condorelli, *"Prudentiae in iure,"* 157–58.
[49] In general, Lepsius, *Der Richter und die Zeugen*, 148–56.
[50] Lepsius, *Der Richter und die Zeugen*, 245–46.
[51] Lepsius, *Der Richter und die Zeugen*, 280.

true *prudentia* consisted of nine qualities, versus Alberico's seven (*memoria, intelligentia, experientia, docilitas, deliberatio, sollertia, providentia, circumspectio, cautio*), and surely there was no one who had the entirety in perfection. At best, there were some who might have a perfect combination of some of these for some specific actions.[52] And yet Bartolus went on immediately to proclaim "any adult is presumed to be prudent by an imperfect prudence, unless the contrary is proven. Everyone seeks the good naturally, everyone has reason from the fact he is human. There are in us also certain principles of things knowable and to be done, although not perfectly. From this it is in us naturally to consult experts and to believe in them humbly, as it is written, as a support for your prudence."[53]

The most Bartolus has to say about *prudentia oeconomica* is that it was evident when one was entrusted with making someone a guardian or with the arrival of full maturity to one's child. It was demonstrated by suitable witnesses to honorable conduct, uprightness, and proof of "creditable life." One presumed prudence from honest "conversation." One might rule his family, feed his animals, and farm his estate as he wished. And generally one was moderator and arbiter of his own affairs. The customs that were observed by the majority could be called the customs of the city, which, for the jurist, meant it was one thing to dispose about the family of nobles and the rich, and another to determine a proper standard for middling and humble folk.[54]

The father was presumed, though not guaranteed, to be prudent in household management. Such a man operated by the local wisdom, plowed his land, fed his livestock, and even behaved in accord with his station in life. Were there doubts about his prudence, testimony could be taken. A witness could attest to having observed someone being a diligent householder for years, and leading an honest life. Economic prudence was substantiated, in other words, by "vulgi opinio."[55] Anyone and everyone had some sense of what prudence was and who had it. As prudence was a habit of mind and not limited to any singular act, failure of any one enterprise was not a sign of insanity, just a result of some type of negligence or bad luck. A treasured legal precept was to live honestly (*honeste vivere*). What was not honest was for a man of middling social status to act like a magnate, to dress and eat beyond his means and station in life. Here was where witnesses could corroborate or deny whether one lived honestly and was a prudent manager:

[52] Lepsius, *Der Richter und die Zeugen*, 156–57, 284.
[53] Lepsius, *Der Richter und die Zeugen*, 285.
[54] Lepsius, *Der Richter und die Zeugen*, 286–88.
[55] Lepsius, *Der Richter und die Zeugen*, 291.

If witnesses are asked particularly what acts they saw him do, they must respond, for example, that he saw him govern his family in the manner of a diligent father, rent his land, frequently sell [produce] at appropriate times, and so on. And if they did not speak about all the acts emerging in the [allegations], their testimony is not vitiated, and if different witnesses say they saw different acts pertaining to this, they were not alone, as in similar cases.[56]

Partial testimonies mounted up because the presumption was in favor of prudence as something at least partially available to all. It is true that there were different occupations and tasks, so while everyone might be familiar with the local way of cultivating vines or processing oil, there were others, like horse trading, that were not so transparent. In these maybe only one member of a domestic group had sufficient expertise and had to transact on behalf of all.

Imprudentia arose from the incapacities of the insane or the young, but also from negligence (*dolus*) or fraud (*culpa*). The insane, Bartolus conceded, might have lucid intervals, just as they might fake their disability to escape some consequence.[57] Bartolus relayed the tale of a Perugian who feigned insanity for two years, biding his time to exact revenge on his brother's killer. Awareness of present circumstances and memory of the past were evidence of sanity; so too their lack was an important index of insanity. Not all "bad and dishonest" (mali et inhonesti) acts came to the attention of the law, but all stood in contrast to the prudent domestic manager as the standard to follow.[58]

8.3 Consilia and Jurisprudence

While civilian jurists appear not to have spent time theorizing about prudence, they did encounter plenty of cases in which the results of prudence, or its lack, were in play. They faced the matter most squarely perhaps in cases in which someone's mental competence was called into question. Mellyn has examined a couple of these, and we can begin there. These cases were a matter of witnesses, and they were also about the very standards of behavior, insanity or diligence, that they were called upon to assess. It was not just that witness testimony could be shot full of holes; there were positive arguments in favor of prudential management by the one accused of insanity.[59]

The Sienese jurist Mariano Sozzini the elder invoked the legal presumption of sanity when he argued on behalf of Niccolò Meliorni against

[56] Lepsius, *Der Richter und die Zeugen*, 290–91.
[57] Lepsius, *Der Richter und die Zeugen*, 301.
[58] Lepsius, *Der Richter und die Zeugen*, 171.
[59] Mellyn, *Mad Tuscans and Their Families*, 168–70.

the guardian of Giovanni Vernelli on appeal of an earlier sentence in favor of Vernelli. The guardian for the supposedly insane Vernelli had successfully argued that Vernelli was not sane at the time a public instrument was redacted stating that property had been returned to him in accord with an inventory – thus voiding any claims Vernelli had against Meliorni.[60] Sozzini pointed to the presumption of sanity and the presumption in favor of an act duly recorded by a notary as placing the burden of proof fully on the guardian. Had he met that? It seems he had produced witnesses testifying that they had seen "signa dementium," such as "saying things that were derisive and unknowing and not suited to a sane mind" (loquendo derisoria et insipientia et non convenientia sane menti). Indeed, three people testified that Giovanni had wanted to be called *mentecaptus* (something Mellyn sees as shrewd in fact). Two others spoke "about an ox that he returned because it had no teeth in the upper jaw" (de quodam bove, quem reddit, quia non habebat dentes in superiore mandibula). And witnesses affirmed that this had been his state of being continuously for twenty years. He was insane before the instrument was drawn up, and at that time, and after. So there was evidence of mental deficiency, which would seem to have been the reason for the guardian's suit and for a favorable judgment in the court of first instance.

Sozzini countered the witness testimony first on technical grounds. They had not provided a basis for their knowledge of Vernelli, and they appeared to be making judgments about his actions and not just describing them. One could not just declare that another person was inebriated, for example; there had to be testimony to the effect that he was seen drinking, staggering about, and so forth.[61] Even if such judgment were accepted, it only held good for the particular moment of inebriation and not for twenty continuous years. It was not an appropriate argument in this case. And there were witnesses to the opposite effect, and they had some good points: "namely that just about continuously he exercised the craft of wool working and that he had a wife of good parents and citizens, which is not usually done or had except by men of sound mind."[62] Giovanni was thus in a socially recognized position to be a prudent householder. There was a clear contradiction in the testimonies.

Here, then, is where Sozzini introduced a vital notion that actually served to account for all the testimony and still allowed him to make his client's case. Giovanni enjoyed lucid intervals (*delucida intervalla*). At

---

[60] Sozzini, *Consilia*, 1 *cons.* 42, fols. 88rb–89rb.
[61] Sozzini, *Consilia*, 1 *cons.* 42, fol. 88vb.
[62] Sozzini, *Consilia*, 1 *cons.* 42: "bonas rationes, scilicet quod quasi continue exercuit artem lane, et quod habuit uxorem ex bonis parentibus et civibus, quae non solent fieri nec haberi nisi ab hominibus sane mentis" (fol. 89ra).

times he was *sane mentis*; at others he was *fatuus*. The fact that he did things that were *signa fatuitatis* did not mean that at another moment he was not coldly rational. He did not act insane all the time. The idea of lucid intervals, it has to be said, was not unique to Sozzini. It was found among medical writers, who were at times summoned to court to give their learned opinions (also called consilia) on a variety of issues, including sanity. Sozzini did not have medical testimony before him to insinuate into the legal context, so far as we can tell, but the law was able to contemplate lucid intervals.[63]

What then of the instrument of quitclaim from the inventory in question? Was it the product of a raving moment or a more sedate lucid interval? If the latter, then the presumption of sanity was valid. But even if it had happened close on an instance of insanity, it still could not be presumed he was *fatuus*.[64] The fact that he recognized property as his and acted to get it argued for sanity, as Bartolus had said in his treatise. How could one tell if an act arose *in quiete* or *in furore*? According to Bartolus, said Sozzini, "if he does what any diligent person would do, then it shows the act is done in calm: Whence in our case if Giovanni receives his things, and for what was received had an instrument drawn up, he did that which any very diligent person would do and so it shows it was done calmly."[65] As proof of the opposite was simply not conclusive in this case, the public instrument should stand. It is not hard to see a legal professional moving to uphold as valid a correctly performed and recorded legal action. The opposite would produce chaos, potentially calling into question any number of legitimate acts on an easy assertion of insanity riding on a thin veil of witness testimony to unusual behavior. Those who had stood in line for Vernelli's assets, who were advantaged in sharing with him, tried a legal ploy to retrieve what had been an obligation on Meliorni. There seems to have been enough evidence to raise suspicions about Vernelli's sanity, but also enough to launch a cogent counterargument.

In another case the prospective heirs of Giovanni di Enrico da Zuchano contested a gift he had made, a gift that greatly diminished otherwise the value of the potential *haereditas*, on the grounds that he was *mentecaptus* and had been since youth. Did the evidence presented rise to the level of substantiating that allegation? Filippo Decio posited that the way to prove

[63] Monica Calabritto, "A Case of Melancholic Humors and *Dilucida Intervalla*"; "'Furor' melanconico tra teoria e pratica legale."

[64] Sozzini, *Consilia*, 1 *cons.* 42, fol. 89rb.

[65] Sozzini, *Consilia*, 1 *cons.* 42, fol. 89rb: "si autem facit quod quilibet diligens fecisset tunc ostenditur actum esse gestum in quiete. Unde in casu nostro si Ioannnes recepit res suas, et de receptis fuit conceptum instrumentum facit illud quod quilibet diligentissimus fecisset et sic ostenditur factum fuisse in quiete."

insanity was from testimony of neighbors – that such a person was non-responsive or said things that showed, among other things, "he did not have an organized memory" (memoriam non habebat ordinatam).[66] Incomprehensible speech was also an indicator. In the case of Giovanni, all his relatives, including his father, supposedly considered him insane.[67] So Decio went through the testimony of witnesses one by one, while also noting that there were witnesses for the other side maintaining Giovanni was sane.

Decio, in fact, sided with them, at least in that he did not find sufficient proof of Giovanni's alleged insanity. In doubt, one presumed sanity. In this case there was also a valid public instrument of the donation, with its witnesses and a notary, authorized by messer Marchione, a judge. That document could not lightly be ignored. The donation itself was deemed also to be the sort of act a prudent manager would undertake. In Decio's words, "because it was done maturely, just as any prudent person would do it, for as he did not have sons he made a gift to his nephew by his brother, and this is intuited about the same brother who was rewarded by the gift from his brother and he kept usufruct for himself all his life."[68] Giovanni had lodged ownership with his nephew but effective use (day-to-day control) with his brother. Furthermore, the donation had been observed for several years, which meant it was harder to revise it now. Witnesses for the defendant (three of whom were priests who had served as his confessors) had admitted that Giovanni had been grossolanus (coarse), but grossolanus did not rise to the level of mentecaptus. He could understand what he was doing.

Decio also raised suspicions about the bill of questions to be put to the witnesses for its "magna et exquisita insolitaque diligentia," which he took to be the product of experts knowledgeable in crafting arguments ("peritissimis viris"). The three key witnesses for the plaintiff seemed to parrot the same carefully rehearsed lines. It was hard to believe, moreover, that Giovanni had been insane all his life, and he had lived to be seventy, while the witnesses were young and thus could not have known him that long. The three were also related to each other – another point of suspicion. Beyond that, the witnesses had spoken only in general terms and not about particular actions. Throwing stones in the street, for

[66] Decio, 3 cons. 448, fols. 93vb–95ra, at 94ra.

[67] Decio, 3 cons. 448, fol. 94ra: "plenius dicitur quod parentes sui et omnes consanguinei et omnes qui ipsum congnoscebat semper et continue reputaverunt et tenuerunt ipsum Johannem pro mente capto stulto et fatuo."

[68] Decio, 3 cons. 448, fol. 94va: "quia fuit facta mature et prout quilibet prudens illam fecisset, nam cum ipse non haberet filios fecit donationem nepoti sui ex fratre et hoc intuitur ipsius fratris qui erat de ipso donatore fratre suo benemeritus et reservavit sibi usumfructum toto tempore vite eius."

example, was not necessarily an act of insanity, for even quite learned and sane people might have a good reason to do that. Nor was it the case that all Giovanni's kin thought him insane, and certainly not his father, who had seen fit to name him heir along with his brother.[69] It helped too that priests were among those testifying to Giovanni's normality.

In another case concerning inheritance, Decio had claimed that a man had every right to throw his belongings into the sea (thus depriving his nominal heirs).[70] He offered this image in a consilium in support of arguments by two Florentine jurists, Ormanozzo Deti (b. 1464) and Giovan Vettorio Soderini (1460–1528). The question was whether a legitimated son excluded someone substituted in a testament on condition there were no legitimate sons.[71] The son had not been born legitimate, but his legitimation might have given him sufficient fictive weight to qualify as a legitimate son and exclude the agnate substituted in the absence of a legitimate son. The argument was that if the legitimating authority had expressly allowed the legitimatus to exclude a substitute, then the substitution failed. But Decio argued that even the emperor had no right to abrogate a will.[72] At least the substitute whose prerogative might suffer from a legitimation should be summoned to be present for that event.

It was around the second legal problem, the estate of Bernardo *patris legitimati*, that Decio invoked the maritime image: "because it is a question of the goods of the same Bernardo in which he had free power and in which legitimation the will of the father mattered ... because in such a case it is not a question of prejudice to the agnates, as a father can throw his goods into the sea if he wants."[73] Supporting citation was to the commentary of Baldo degli Ubaldi, who indeed made the same observation.[74] A father could share his patrimony with his legitimated son, just as he had, we presume, shared food and shelter with him from the moment he had accepted the obligations of paternity over the bastard child, let alone legitimate him. The legal fiction of legitimation gave the

---

[69] Decio, 3 *cons.* 448, fols. 94vb–95ra: "quia pater illum simpliciter et equaliter cum fratre heredem instituit nec aliam circa eum fecit dispositionem, nam si illum mente captum reputasset verisimiliter aliam provisionem quo ad eum fecisset."

[70] Decio, 2 *cons.* 557, fols. 171rb–72ra, at 171vb.

[71] See Kuehn, *Illegitimacy in Renaissance Florence*.   [72] Decio, 2 *cons.* 557, fol. 172va.

[73] Decio, 2 *cons.* 557, fol. 172va: "quia agitur de bonis ipsius Bernardi in quibus ipse habebat liberam potestatem et in tali legitimatione voluntas patris multum facit ... tali casu non agitur de preiudicio agnatorum, cum pater possit bona sua proiicere in mari si velit" (fol. 171vb).

[74] Baldo degli Ubaldi to pr. C, *Opera omnia*, vol. 1, fol. 3ra: "Et si dicas preiudicantur venientibus ab intestato, hoc nego, quia non habebant aliquod ius tempore legitimationis, nam cum pater possit bona sua proiicere in mare ut in l. prima de inoffic. donatio et de condi. et demonst. l. Maevius multo magis potest per actum civilem et permissum."

son a more powerful claim than the more distant agnates who could, asserted the jurists, have suffered the sight of their inheritance (which they had never shared with the testator, unlike a son or even an illegitimate one) sinking beneath the waves.

In both these cases insanity was alleged by those who were effectively penalized by a legal act (donation in the first, legitimation in the second) that diverted property from them to someone else (a brother's son, an illegitimate son). They were, however, contesting perfectly valid legal acts. Property was not, in fact, being cast into the sea. That would have been deemed insane, though it may well not have been reversible.

While no one's sanity was at issue, and the point was raised to evoke the sense of gratitude sons should have for their father's provident management, it is nonetheless indicative of the distance to be traversed between mere mismanagement and judicial finding of insanity. The legitimation was not voided; the beneficiary of paternal largesse there simply could not preclude a substituted son from also inheriting. The right of the owner to throw away his property was not denied or contested. How that might be prudent or diligent, however, is hard to see. Decio seemed quite willing to let persons pursue a wide range of behaviors.

In another example, Decio handled a Sienese case that he claimed was straightforward and not in need of a lengthy treatment.[75] Silvio Piccolomini had gone to the Balia to have his brother Aeneas declared incompetent as a prodigal and given a guardian (Silvio). That request had been granted, but now Silvio had returned to court and wanted his brother again declared competent. Decio went over various reasons that in the eyes of the law proved prodigality and thus insanity. Silvio had claimed "that Aeneas dissipated and consumed nearly all his mobile goods of no little value and to a great degree had obligated his immobile goods, and their fruits and returns by his bad governance and his defect without any legitimate cause or excuse."[76] That certainly seemed to meet the description of a *prodigus*. Decio, however, said that witnesses were needed "because they see him every day run down and greatly overspend what his resources can bear" (quia vident quotidie illum dilapidare et valde ultra expendere quam portent facultates). It was further assumed that close relations such as a brother were in a position to identify and substantiate prodigal behavior, to be reliable testimony from within the sharing household.

[75] Decio, 1575, 1 *cons.* 274, fols. 298ra–99ra.
[76] Decio, 1575, 1 *cons.* 274, fol. 298rb: "quod Aeneas dissipavit et consumpsit quasi omnia bona mobilia non mediocris valoris et pro magna parti obligavit bona immobilia et fructus et proventus ex malo eius regimine et eius defectu sine aliqua causa vel excusatione legitima."

But Silvio had clearly had second thoughts. As *curator*, Silvio had obligated himself to administer his brother's property responsibly and see to his debts, and to render an account of his stewardship. But Silvio had not had drawn up an inventory of his brother's holdings, something otherwise incumbent on a guardian on entering into his responsibilities.[77] It also fell to Silvio's fault (*culpa*) that no *fructus* had been received or recorded in any sort of account, as required by law. Finally, no payment had been demanded from Aeneas's debtors, which also fell to Silvio's *culpa* and *negligentia*. So Silvio tried to argue against his guardianship on procedural grounds – effectively that he had not been a diligent guardian.

The technicality that Aeneas had not been summoned to be present at the establishment of the guardianship was determined not to invalidate it. For one thing, the Balia was assumed to have operated *rite et recte* in establishing the guardianship; for another, Aeneas had later ratified it; for a third, the legal equation of *prodigus* and *furiosus* meant that his presence was not required in any case.

The finding against Silvio was clear. He was to be compelled to undertake administration of the guardianship decreed to him, because Aeneas suffered from the fact Silvio did not take up care and administration as he was supposed to.[78] Silvio seems to have asserted a sharing relationship with Aeneas, to be folded into a guardianship in his control. He either found that an onerous burden, or he had succeeded in siphoning off revenues and whatever else had disappeared for lack of inventory. In any case, he tried to get out of it but was held to the original judgment.

If things were as bad as Silvio claimed in first getting guardianship, he might have faced a sticky situation in which he stood to lose his own property in covering his brother's debts. If he thought he could get his brother's legal acts annulled, he seems to have failed. In a real sense it was thus Silvio who emerged as imprudent. He had claimed only procedural improprieties in setting up guardianship, though he had probably himself been most negligent with regard to the inventory and accounts.

In a different example, the Milanese Giason del Maino had to consider whether one old man had lost his mind when he gave all his property to a charity. This act seemed all the stranger for the fact that the man in question, Tommaso de Sanignone, a Genoese citizen, had gone to the rare step of formally adopting (technically, adrogating, as he was *sui iuris*) Agostino Picamilo, his nephew (cognate).[79] Tommaso was eighty-one; Agostino thirty-seven. Tommaso had drawn up a testament naming

---

[77] Decio, 1575, 1 *cons.* 274, fol. 298vb.   [78] Decio, 1575, 1 *cons.* 274, fol. 299ra.
[79] Maino, *Consilia*, 4 *cons.* 141, 513–20. On adoption, see Kuehn, "Adoption à Florence à la fin du Moyen Age."

Agostino his *haeres universalis*, but he had also *inter vivos* given away all he owned to the Misericordia of Genoa, for the *pauperes Christi*. The legal questions regarded what sorts of rights Agostino had in view of the adoption, the testament, and the charitable gift.

Maino was following on the prior consilium of another jurist, though he seems to have operated independently. First he considered whether the testament naming Agostino as heir could be simply revoked by declaration to that effect in the later act of donation. There were legal reasons, which tended to gravitate around the larger number of witnesses needed for a valid will as opposed to a gift, but more pointedly there was the accusation that at the time Tommaso "was not in good sense and sound intellect but insane and mindless or seized" (non erat in bono sensu et in sano intellectu sed insanis et amens seu mentecaptus) and thus "deceitfully and fraudulently he was led to revoke his testament" (dolose et fraudulenter fuerit inductus ad revocandum illud testamentum) by the priest Ilario and Tommaso's own slave girl, as well as the *sapiens* of the Misericordia.[80] There were witnesses to these allegations, but it was also the case that they were so difficult of proof that it was allowable to proceed by conjecture and circumstances. It seems there had been a conspiracy to deprive Tommaso that had taken advantage of the elderly man.

Agostino had a double claim on Tommaso's estate. As nearest relative he would have claimed on intestacy anyway, without the added assurance of adrogation and the testament. The instrument of adrogation contained Tommaso's promise to love Agostino (*diligere*) and treat him as a legitimate and natural son. So the true substance of the suit was whether Tommaso had effectively disinherited him as a result of the pious donation, and whether he could do so. His insanity at that moment was established by several witnesses, but especially Giovanello Doria, a barber, who reported that "after pleas and suggestions made to him by the priest Ilario, said lord Tommaso acted as demented and insane and threw his arms here and there and he made many noises in the piazzas and in church and at home, just as foolish men do."[81] That a *furiosus* made a legal act in proper form did not make it valid; it was not made *in bono sensu*. If he did not have lucid intervals, even if he nonetheless followed the proper form, even given that the notary said he acted with a sane mind, still the testament was not valid.[82] Tommaso could not have been in his

---

[80] Maino, *Consilia*, 4 *cons.* 141, 515a.

[81] Maino, *Consilia*, 4 *cons.* 141, 516b: "post subornationes et suggestiones ei facta per presbyterum Hilarium, dictus Dominus Thomas factus est ut demens et mentecaptus et iactabat brachia hinc inde et faciebat multos clamores in plateis et in ecclesia et in domo, prout faciunt homines insipientes."

[82] Maino, *Consilia*, 4 *cons.* 141, 517b.

right mind to make such a donation and deprive his nephew and adopted son. Furthermore, the *sapiens salariatus* of the Misericordia had colluded with other officials of that body to split the proceeds of Tommaso's gift, with a fifth for himself and his wife and heirs. The *sapiens* had responded to the charge to that effect by claiming that he had been joking when he talked to the officials ("quodammodo iocose dixisse"). The donation had also occurred in secret, and there were immediate suspicions on that score. In fact, the Misericordia officials had locked the door of Tommaso's house to keep Agostino out.[83] Agostino had the right to contest an unduteous testament, and through that an unduteous donation, especially when given to *extranei*, not part of the family, the same family of which the adoptive father had promised to treat Agostino as a true member. To uphold the donation would lead to the "absurd" result of rendering the *adrogatio elusoria* and *inanis*. In a final flourish Maino maintained that the integrity and prudence of the officials of the Misericordia surely would not want them to perpetrate a "great impiety and inequity" that would arise if they insisted on retaining the gift to the harm of the testamentary heir, a duly adrogated son.

There is a certain irony here in the final appeal to prudence, as argued ably by officials of a charity, who would do all they could to increase its resources, which they did in enlisting Tommaso's generosity in the first place. And Decio had allowed, as we have seen, that a father could throw away all his goods into the sea if he wanted, thus depriving his heirs. But the sea could not be importuned to return it, as the officials of the Misercordia undoubtedly could.

8.4   Conclusions

Prudence was not necessarily a shared virtue, but its positive results could be and were shared. When prudence was sorely lacking, with insanity, those otherwise sharing (or hoping to) a patrimony tried to use law to escape or minimize its effects. The insane did not share, except by default and negatively or with the wrong people. In fact, the accusation of insanity was more context-dependent and not a simple standard to be imposed. Those hurt by a legal act of property management had reason to contest the act on grounds of insanity. The alleged insane person was being pushed beyond the pale – positioned as outside the household, no longer sharing with the family.

To insert, as we have in some sense, the perspective of jurists into the mix has been to lodge yet another ambiguity into it all. Jurisconsults

---

[83] Maino, *Consilia*, 4 *cons.* 141, 518a.

worked to normalize most practices and minimize the amorphous and imprecise *nescio quid*. So when there was a notarial instrument, the intervention of a judge, an established type of guardianship, there was a good basis to argue that the persons and acts in question had been subsumed in ongoing known legal categories. Jurists also faced or proposed notions such as that of a lucid interval – the fact that something like insanity or even prudence was not an unchanging condition but a temporary affect.

Mellyn goes over instances of restraints on the insane being lifted, of families' estimation of members changing or being challenged.[84] It is this temporal dimension that further distinguishes prudence from the *nescio quid* that might become the core of the individual personality of the courtier or secretary. True, Machiavelli could and did show any number of examples of failure of *virtù* by even the most admirable princes; but there was still some sort of quality there that he believed could be captured and even institutionalized by a capable founding figure. The prudent father could only hope to impart lessons to his sons and hope they would heed them and realize that he at least had not thrown all his belongings into the sea.

If we accept Biow's perspective that people in the Renaissance experienced their world "as a collectivity and implicitly thought in the first person plural" but nonetheless were able "to forge individual identities and address the world in a particular manner," we also have to accept that part of the possibility lay in the fact that law did see the world in terms of distinct legal persons and their particular rights, claims, and obligations.[85] Those rights and claims operated in a context of collectivity, of first-person plural, and were mapped out in terms of those within that collectivity; but they were, nonetheless, at some point singular. A patrimony for all was established as a family trust in the will of one person, nominal owner of it all, as testator. That testator shared a capacity for prudence and his property (at least nominally) with his heirs, and they, in turn, held their singular title to (at least a share of) the property. That title included, as Decio noted, the right to throw away all one had and thus frustrate the collectivity. That same right of a person provoked kin to lodge accusations that someone was *furiosus* or *mentecaptus*; to strip that kinsman of legal personhood.

A culture and practice of sharing was clearly violated in these cases. Someone demanded to stop sharing. Someone ceased to share, or began to share with the wrong others. That made him seem insane. While such demands to cease sharing had also been made between brothers in their

---

[84] Mellyn, *Mad Tuscans and Their Families*, 111–26.
[85] Biow, *On the Importance of Being an Individual in Renaissance Italy*, 226.

various *fraternae* and *societates*, here they seemed to be unilateral and incomprehensible, not to mention absolute. The law and its practitioners were caught in the middle, between the demands of singular persons and the refusals of others. The best of these jurists employed their *prudentia*, and displayed their grasp of a craft, a *scientia*, but in the realm of practice. They most often did so, it is true, at the behest of one interested party, the paying client, but that made their expertise no less formidable. But the law also reminds us that there was a range of play for a legal individual, and differing degrees of prudential behavior, down, if not to *furiositas*, then to *imbecillitas* or other terms law applied to minors, women, or other vulnerable and incomplete legal persons. In that range there was then room for distinguishing oneself – for being compellingly different, even a maverick, without being labeled insane. Law allowed, when needed, a certainty, a set of labels to determine a situation at any one time (a lucid interval, or not), to define and categorize, to – if you will – take the *ne* out of the *scio* (*quid*).

9   Addendum
A Final Case

Many legal rights and actions overlapped and combined in any particular situation. Wives and sons, for example, had differing rights to assets of the same household. So many cases centered on the problems of inheritance, as we have seen countless times. But there were other issues at play, even in one and the same case. The drive to limit liabilities in adverse circumstances understandably drew attention to individual versus shared rights, to disabilities of age or sex, or simply to legal technicalities that might be cited to advantage. To give some idea of the conjunction of several areas of patrimonial law potential in any one case, I offer a final, quite illustrative example. It is a case that comes from the consilia of a less prominent but respected jurist of the first half of the fifteenth century, Floriano da San Pietro (13 ...–1444), who taught at Bologna but contributed his thoughts to cases from Florence and elsewhere. In this instance we have a consilium among several that were included at the end of a print edition of his commentary on some texts of the Digest.[1]

    Floriano there confronted a dense set of facts and claims, culminating in four legal questions. It is an unusually thorough set of facts, so we can say a bit more about this case than of so many others. Reghina of Montefiore had been married for forty-six years to Antonio di Cecchino. She had come to the marriage with a very modest dowry of only 40 lire. That in itself is an interesting feature of this case, as Antonio certainly could have found a wife with a larger dowry, more appropriate to his social status, given the amount of money he left after his death. Of course, a smaller dowry would have rendered his wife less influential in the household's financial affairs, with a smaller "debt" to repay in the return of the dowry after marriage. But the small dowry may also indicate an attraction between the couple that rested on something more and other than material considerations. In any case, in his testament Antonio left her only that small dowry and all her clothing, as well as the right to stay in their house during her widowhood, along with food and clothing for her

---

[1] Floriano da San Pietro, *In primam et secundam ff Vet. partem, tum in tres etiam secundae Infortiati insigniores titulos de Leg. commentaria, cons.* 21, 283a–89a.

needs. He named his brother Cecchino as his heir and left a sum to his daughter, Nobile.

But this left his widow, nonetheless, poor and needy, with all told less than 100 lire to her name, whereas Antonio was said to have died wealthy (*dives*). So it is no surprise that Reghina remained in the marital abode and took her nourishment there in accord with her husband's will. It was Reghina's right to share in the patrimony as widow that was more valuable, by far, than the paltry possessions in her name. The terms of Antonio's testament nonetheless left her to realize much less than her brother-in-law Cecchino stood to gain.

The brothers Antonio and Cecchino in fact lived together for a long time, contributing to a common patrimony, which implies that Antonio's will was aimed at keeping the shared household with his wife and brother functioning as such after his death. It was a household with a distinct division of labor. Antonio in fact had been a merchant and craftsman, having a tailoring business and an apothecary shop. He was frequently away from home on business, buying wool and silk cloth, but also trading livestock from time to time. When he was thus operating "de suis laboribus," he kept distinct accounts in his name without mention of Cecchino. He kept that particular source of income and potential liabilities to himself, and in that regard may have been protecting the household from any problems that might arise in the business. Other transactions, unrelated to Antonio's business ventures, were entered with Cecchino's name included, notably in purchases of land or other immobilia. In fact, Cecchino was at no time involved in anything non-agricultural, in contrast to Antonio (who was termed *industriosus*), being content to see to the fields "bringing produce to the house, and wood and other things as he was able" (portando fructum ad domum, et ligna et alia secundum possibilitatem suam). The evident distinction in occupations probably accounts for the fact that, following Antonio's death, Cecchino took 1,000 florins for himself from a chest, admitting to the "theft" repeatedly. In the face of the loss of the income Antonio had brought in, as heir Cecchino moved to secure the more liquid assets his brother had accumulated. But he was also taking the cash for himself, depriving Reghina of any benefit of the stash.

So Antonio, Cecchino, and Reghina had formed a sharing household with a separation of tasks. Reghina, we assume, filled the role of typical wife, while Cecchino saw to the land and Antonio carried on as a merchant. Their efforts and resources were pooled, and that arrangement's perpetuation was the aim of Antonio's testament. It is intriguing to speculate on what sort of arrangement this household was for the brothers and Antonio's bride. Antonio was probably gone from the house for periods, but there were also moments when bringing in crops or other tasks had to tax Cecchino's efforts. In any case, for Reghina things had decidedly changed with Antonio's death. Her provision now rested on some clauses in Antonio's will and the benevolence of Cecchino, an admitted thief of a considerable amount of money, looking out for his own interests. There was no longer a full sharing of resources.

Against this situation, Reghina, with Floriano da San Pietro as a consultant attorney appointed by the presiding judge, moved a suit seeking more from her husband's estate, alleging the authentica *Praeterea* of the Codex title *Unde vir et uxor* (*C. 6.18.1). This text provided that where there was a marriage without dowry, such that a widow faced penury, she could succeed along with the children to a fourth of her husband's estate. This was seemingly a more generous treatment than Antonio's testament had provided. But Reghina also faced allegations in response that she had been adequately compensated by her rights to dwelling and alimentation. Also alleged on Reghina's behalf were doubts about whether the brothers had had a *societas omnium bonorum* and whether that gave her entree to more of her husband's property, and whether Cecchino's assertion about taking the money constituted proof that the sum was part of the estate available to her. The case thus involved spousal claims and the potential *societas* of the brothers. Inventory too, as well as prudent management, came to figure in the case.

Praeterea was a brief addendum to the basic rule of civil law that established a spousal right to inherit as a last resort, only coming into play in the face of the fisc.[2] Initially it could be claimed that Reghina had no recourse. Modest as it had been, she had a dowry that had been returned to her by testament. Nor could she be termed a *pauper*, it was said, when she had the wherewithal to survive, as also left her in that will. Floriano da San Pietro laid out those arguments, but then pivoted to the contrary on the observation that the husband knew his wife's dowry did not amount to the quarter that *Praeterea* demanded. He was being less than tightfisted, it seems, in order to keep her in the household with his brother. Against such behavior Floriano argued that both Baldo degli Ubaldi and Niccolò dei Mattarelli (1240–1314?) accorded a wife a full quarter even in testate succession. In essence, if a husband accepted a wife without dowry, "it seems still there is a contract between them that the wife should have this fourth part" at the dissolution of the marriage. This was a debt "rooted in the person of the wife" (*radicatum in persona mulieris*). Even in Lombard law a wife gained a fourth from her husband. So Floriano determined that *Praeterea* applied, even when there was

---

[2] Codex (Lyon, 1558–60), to *C. 6.18.1.

a testament and when the *haereditas* fell not to children but to an *extraneus* (as a brother was). The same principle held for a small dowry as for no dowry. That hers was a small dowry was clear to anyone, as "no one can live on twenty ducats for all his life, but maybe a year or so."[3] Twenty ducats was a nice round figure, not even approximating a modest unskilled worker's annual wage, an amount certainly less than Reghina was accustomed to while Antonio was alive.[4] There was no doubt in Floriano's mind that Reghina could be termed *pauper*, and any judge looking at such a case had to take into consideration the quality of the person before him, who was someone who must have lived well while her husband was alive ("in magna quasi delicantia"), but then fell on relative penury after his death, especially in the face of an *extraneus* as heir. Her share had been more than what was compensated in Antonio's testament.

Floriano proceeded to argue that the terms of Antonio's testament, its bequest of domicile and sustenance to Reghina, did not obstruct her rights to a quarter. As a woman she was presumed to be ignorant of the terms of her husband's will and thus also presumably stayed in the house not *ex causa legati* but as a way to maintain her privileged claim on household assets for her dowry.[5] That could all be proven by written instruments or witness testimony. But Floriano acknowledged that her hypothecary rights as *creditrix* for her dowry presented a stronger and more useful title, prior in time to any testamentary bequest, and to be acted on from her husband's *substantia* before any bequests. Her sustenance in the meantime was to be computed as part of the quarter she was seeking. However, it was also the case that "it would not be suitable that she have alimenta, the quarter, and the fruits of the quarter."[6] There were limits to her claims. Here then was where he turned to addressing what fell to Cecchino.

There was no written contract of partnership between the brothers expressing their consent to a particular state of affairs, but from their patterns of interaction over many years, a tacit contract could be construed. Various doctors had addressed ways to establish a tacit *societas*. Riccardo da Malombra (d. 1334), Oldrado da Ponte (d. 1343), and Raniero da Forlì (d. 1358) required "living together, pooling in common their gains" (insimul habitatio, lucrorum in communem collatio) and

---

[3] Floriano da San Pietro, *In primam et secundam*, cons. 21, 286a: "ex viginti ducatis nemo possit ali toto tempore vitae suae, sed uno anno quasi, patet unicuique."

[4] Goldthwaite, *The Economy of Renaissance Florence*, 574–77.

[5] Floriano da San Pietro, *In primam et secundam*, cons. 21, 287a: "ex causa conservandorum iurium hypothecariorum pro dotibus suis."

[6] Floriano da San Pietro, *In primam et secundam*, cons. 21, 288a: "non autem conveniens esset, quod haberet alimenta, quartam, et fructus quartae."

"not keeping accounts" (non reddita ratio). In the case of Antonio and Cecchino it certainly seemed "they lived together, shared their property, did not render accounts, and had instruments made in the name of their common interest."[7] They shared. They did not act as givers of gifts to each other, carefully calculating reciprocities, or as heirs intent on dividing the estate. Floriano, however, pointed to elements that sullied this neat image of a shared patrimony. As he saw it, the brothers held in common their *haereditas* and all *immobilia*, and whatever Cecchino brought in from his agricultural work.[8] Otherwise Antonio operated on his own and in his own name, and to his own account when he traded livestock, apothecary items, and other things – not that he did not contribute funds for the purchase of lands, animals, tools, and such. His money after his death was computed as his own (*in massaria propria*). He kept separate account books on his market activities. This household, in other words, worked around a sort of rural/urban economic dichotomy. So there was an accounting to do, to see what in fact had been inherited and ascribed to common ownership, and to see if Antonio had appropriated common funds into his business transactions. From anything Antonio had taken, half should be returned to Cecchino as his beforehand, and Reghina should get what added up to a quarter, after taking into consideration her prior consumption in widowhood. The rest fell to Cecchino as his brother's heir. Now there were going to be clear limits to any sharing between Reghina and Cecchino.

What Floriano gave form to, and it seems to make sense in this perspective, is the idea that Cecchino's "theft" of 1,000 ducats may have been his peremptory way of claiming his inheritance from his brother's otherwise separate activities. As heir, if not previously as brother, he was due a full sharing of the *substantia*. Cecchino's theft was termed a *culpa levissima*, on the idea that half of it was his already, and because it was intended to cover for Antonio's imprudent management in leaving the money sitting in a chest, not invested toward some profit. This foolishness and Cecchino's actions to protect the money should not hurt Reghina's rights, especially as Cecchino accepted the estate without consulting her, did not make an inventory, and did not divide his own property from the

---

[7] Floriano da San Pietro, *In primam et secundam*, cons. 21, 288a: "istos simul habitasse, bona contulisse, rationem redditam non esse, et instrumenta communi nomine cantare fecisse tam de magistro Antonio quam de Cecchino, ne dum tacuisse."

[8] Floriano da San Pietro, *In primam et secundam*, cons. 21, 288b: "dictus magister Antonius circa gubernationem et manutentioneem dictorum bonorum et fructuum (ut magis industriosus) operam dabat, dictos fructus venales vendendo, et dum opus erat conservando expresse deprehenditur societatem initam fore solum et dumtaxat circa bona haereditaria et bona immobilium et alia quae communi nomine per dictum Cecchinum ostenderentur empta et acquisita."

hereditary property. No matter how his dead brother had seen things, Cecchino as heir was establishing the shared economy of all belongings after Antonio's death. Had he made an inventory, he would have been conceding something separate about Antonio's share, though he would have been deflecting any outstanding liabilities from Antonio's business dealings. The only part that was not his was what fell to Reghina as dowry or by the testamentary provision for her residence and upkeep, and now by the addition of Floriano's support for her claims by means of *Praeterea*. In other words, Reghina got what had been given her by father and husband. Floriano's conclusion was that Reghina could claim her quarter of her husband's *substantia* and of his separate holdings and a quarter of the 1,000 florins. That, of course, might resolve the financial matters, but one wonders where Reghina, no longer *pauper* one assumes, would live and how she would manage her holdings. From part of a sharing house-hold economy, she was nominally reduced to a family of one (as was Cecchino, it seems). Perhaps they continued to get along after the legal issues were resolved. Nothing was said about the daughter Nobile, whose dowry had been left her by her father. Her residence and upkeep were never mentioned. We have no way of knowing at the moment. But the bases of further relationships among the three had been thoroughly altered.

Here, as in all the cases, we see actions of people using and at times abusing the law in troublesome situations that called for some sort of learned intervention to make sense of it all. These troublesome situations resided in the many ambiguities within the law and in the overlapping portions of it brought into contact by social actors. We have seen two brothers and the wife of one, having successfully lived together for forty-six years, come face to face with the need to resolve a sharing community into individual rights, precipitated by the death of one. Death was often the great confounder (the point where sharing most evidently ended, according to Widlok),[9] but marriage and bankruptcy (or the immediate threat of it), to name just two, were also frequent catalysts of change in relationships and legal rights. The *substantia* that Bartolus attempted to see as the enduring and defining element of *familia* was in fact, as was the *familia*, fragile and tenuous, pushed and pulled between the sharing and common fellowship of kin and household, on the one hand, and the individualistic claims and assertions, even as embodied in law, which were freer to emerge when death or financial disaster threatened, on the other.

---

[9] Widlok, *Anthropology and the Economy of Sharing*, 187.

10   Conclusion

> The problem ultimately for the student of the family is that of remembering that he is dealing with a concept, a creation of men's minds and of their culture, rather than with a material thing. As a way of understanding social structure, it can be as helpful or as problematical as its sometime rival, class. To pretend that the family is something else, a biological relationship or a household, is to risk impoverishing the investigation.
>
> Casey, The History of the Family, 166

We began this book with Bartolus's conceptualization of family. That concept rested on the idea of a patrimony and its transmission from father to son, based on sharing of rights and material resources. That patrimony, as Casey says, should be seen as a "network of obligations, to neighbours, family members and the seigneur, rather than as property in the modern sense."[1] The eighteenth-century attack on entails and trusts ushered in a revolution in the concept of property and family, and in the concept of the legal person, as ownership came to be seen in absolute terms, the holding of one person as owner, no longer simply a node through which ran a web of social obligations and expectations.[2] There could be no blurring of distinctions between father as owner and son as owner. There was only one owner of modern property.[3] That was because property was conceptualized in terms of markets and their transactions, valued in terms of currency in the present rather than in terms of continuity with past and future. It was about public use and activities; it was not about the sharing of domestic space and consumption, however vital that was for those involved.

Within that more malleable older sense of property, the substance behind family, lay the important fact and right of shared existence.

[1] Casey, *The History of the Family*, 144.
[2] Casey, *The History of the Family*, 136, 139–42, 154.
[3] For a comprehensive account of property in law, see Grossi, *Il dominio e le cose*, esp. 86–93.

228

Husbands, wives, children, and siblings (especially brothers) shared. These sharing relationships were shifting. The needs of those sharing changed over time. Households were ever changing, but they could also endure through changes. Part of the way they did so was by operating on a sense that the heir was a steward to see to the perpetuation of patrimony to the next and subsequent generations.[4] That stewardship was backed up by the interest of all others in a community in keeping every family contributing to the common good. Neighbors knew what neighbors were up to, hence they could testify as to others' sanity, to the value of their goods, and to the legitimacy of their children (if need be). The fish-bowl existence of the early modern family, open to its neighbors and kin, became the private and separate sphere of the modern family.

The families of Italian communities, especially of the city-states that Bartolus had in mind as he equated *familia* with its *substantia*, faced the claims of ancestors, living kin, and generations to come. They moved as necessary, vacillating between shared and collective existence and the assertion of singular ownership and liability. Communities assembled statutes that placed shared existence and liabilities at the center of so much of social and legal relations, but they also harbored individual claims and legal actions. They understood the need to split and divide responsibilities, and they feared them at the same time. Repudiation of inheritance and the limits on the use of inventory in some communities are just a couple of examples that we have seen.

By the seventeenth century, after decades of the elaboration of legal devices, notably the testamentary *fideicommissum*, and equally after decades of judicial intervention and the formulation of rules disguised as the *communis opinio doctorum*, it had become difficult to maintain the fictive equation of property and family. Property was a marketable commodity and not just a familial (often inalienable) possession. The state of legal and social discourse can be judged from the pages of one of the more illustrious jurists of the seventeenth century. In 1606 the eminent cleric, archbishop, and cardinal Domenico Toschi (1535–1620) published an encyclopedic eight-volume compendium of legal opinions, rules, and definitions. Several pages were devoted to matters of *familia* and *familiaris*. Toschi began by positing three types of family: perpetual (an institutional family, such as a monastery); one set on terms of *familiaritas*, such as the household of the pope or of cardinals (a focus of his professional interests); and the *familia prophana et mercenaria*. This form was described as domestic and "they are family members (*familiares*) who live in the

[4] Cf. Gottlieb, *The Family in the Western World*, 204.

same house and under the power of another."[5] *Familiares* were long-standing *commensales*, living with and off the property of another. The family consisted usually of parents, children, wife, daughter-in-law, slaves, and laborers.[6] Otherwise it was conceded that typical testaments called to a fideicommissum those of the family of the testator, mainly only the males. The word that Toschi interestingly did not employ was *substantia*. The issue of inheritance that had animated Bartolus had faded into the background (or, rather, it would be dealt with extensively under other headings). It was coresidence and commensality that *familiares* shared and consumed, in relation to the singular directing head of household, for whom the house was a metaphorical term for all "de agnatione et de familia sua."[7] Toschi's concern was the hierarchical relationships of the people in the family as an ongoing unit. *Familiares* might be kin, but they need not be. They were in a relationship of dependence, however, as the first form of *familiaritas*, the first form of jurisdiction, was that of father over child, to be followed by that of master over slave, husband over wife, and head of household over free-born servants.[8]

Even in his later appendix to the eight volumes, Toschi continued to emphasize coresidence, if not with wife or children, then still with those gathered under one roof ("retinet in domo familiam suam").[9] His treatment of *habitatio* declared that habitation "is about him who receives there persons belonging to him and promiscuously lives with them" (qui recipit ibi personas ad se pertinentes et promiscue cum eis habitat), which, he went on, was where one slept, ate, and drank.[10] Likewise he did not entertain the idea of a shared ownership, however *improprie*, of father and son. Rather than follow Bartolus's lead, he insisted that patrimony was *haereditas* of the father, but once the son accepted it, it became *haereditas* of the son.[11] Toschi had to concede, however, that there were still ways, including restitution of property according to the dictates of fideicommissa or of the legitimate portion in intestacy, that

---

[5] Toschi, *Practicarum conclusionum iuris*, vol. 3, 592.
[6] Toschi, *Practicarum*, vol. 3, 595: "parentes, liberi, uxor, nurus, servi, coloni seu adscriptitii."
[7] Toschi, *Practicarum*, vol. 3, 595.
[8] Toschi, *Practicarum*, vol. 3, 592: "Quadruplex est familiaritas; potestativa una, quam habet pater in filium et haec fuit prima iurisdictio quae fit in mundo; secunda est quam habet dominus in servum; tertia est quam habet maritus in uxorem circa correctionem morum; quarta est quam habet dominus in servitorem personam liberam, quae est modica."
[9] Toschi, *Additiones locupletissimae ad caetera octo volumina*, 291.
[10] Toschi, *Practicarum*, vol. 4, 196.
[11] Toschi, *Practicarum*, vol. 4, 201: "Et propterea haereditas patris mei mihi delata postquam est agnita, non est amplius haereditas paterna, sed mea." And see p. 205.

meant that *haereditas* continued to be thought of as that of the deceased.[12]

For Bartolus, in contrast, patrimony was shared in the present and over time. The equation of family and substance took off from the intuition that patrimony was both individually owned and yet shared and transmitted – thus leading to the legally tenuous notion that the son was "quoddammodo dominus" of the property with his father. Sharing emerged as well in the notion of a *ius familiaritatis*, a right conceded to spouses and children in certain situations. What a wife brought to a household, her dowry, was shared with husband and children – so much so that her control over it was limited during marriage, unless her husband's management threatened to cost her dowry. But the sense of sharing was most complete and obvious in the depiction of the *societas omnium bonorum* between brothers, a subject for which Bartolus conceived and began a monographic treatment, for all that it was always anticipated that such a *societas* would most likely come apart at some point.

The law ascribed ownership and its attendant rights and actions to single persons. There certainly could be and were multiple owners of a single item, or patrimony, but each was attributed a proportional share in law, even if the ability to dispose of that portion was hardly possible without the participation or acquiescence of the other co-owners. True, at times law admitted to overlaps and even provided instruments by which claims could be combined and merge into one, most notably so in the *societas omnium bonorum* among brothers. But even in that instance, things could quickly dissolve into separate portions and detailed accounting. The recourse to multigenerational trusts and substitutions of agnates that formed the core of *fideicommissa* presumed precise ownership rights attached to relationships over time.

Still, the law as used and interpreted in fifteenth- and sixteenth-century Italy made things like sharing among brothers, parents and children, even between spouses, possible. In most households the sharing of the patrimony was hidden behind a father's supposedly undivided control over it, and in his sons' legal incapacity when subject to *patria potestas*. Within that nexus, however, there was provision for the contributions to and from children, mainly sons, generally in some form of *peculium* and taking stock of sons' *industria* as a contribution more uniquely their own. *Industria*, like prudence, could not be expected in all instances. Sometimes division went further, as in emancipation, which at least severed mutual liabilities between father and son. Sharing also hid behind the fact that ordinarily wives brought property of their own, a dowry, to

[12] Toschi, *Practicarum*, vol. 4, 202.

the marital household. The dowry was intended to help sustain the burdens of matrimony otherwise shared with husbands. But wives also had little active control (except in cases of blatant incompetence in its management on the part of husbands). The main restriction lay on the powerful conventional guarantees that wives could retrieve their dowries on the end of their marriage.

Brothers, in contrast, generally freed from *potestas* by their father's death, began with nominally separate (if equal) rights; but they could choose to merge those rights and their fortunes in a continuity of brotherhood as a coresidential and business partnership. There were even those, like Baldo degli Ubaldi, who were willing to entertain the notion of a full sharing brotherhood where business ventures or even type of lucrative occupation were dissimilar. What mattered was the effective pooling of all income, whatever the source, and meeting needs without accounting the costs.

The wife's property brought to the marriage was never fully assimilated into the husband's patrimony, unless and until sons or children inherited it from her. It remained at least, to use Chabot's insightful term, a debt that had to be met. But as she also shows, it was a debt whose payment was resisted or delayed, and there were hopes that in the next generation, when the children inherited their mother's dowry, it would be finally and fully merged into the agnatically transmitted inheritance.[13] Still, as with the *consignatio dotis*, the wife's property as legally separate became an important device to perpetuate some form of sharing household against debts that threatened to leave it in penury. The distinction concerning spousal property could prove useful.

The moment (in fact a process unfolding over time) of inheritance demanded care and vigilance. The legal device of the familial trust, fideicommissum, was one important measure limiting, as it did, any individualistic departure by one who inherited under its terms. As we have seen, such restrictions on freedom of disposition met with a great deal of legal skepticism and resistance. It was only when the trust became most expansive – and only when undeniably so, in demanding the retention of property within the *familia* in perpetuity – that jurists came to accept the imperative of sharing the estate over time. Also effective in identifying and tying property to the next generation was the estate inventory, especially when the heir was legally underage. By law, the heirs' liability for debts outstanding on the estate was limited to the contents and value of the inventoried items. Without inventory the heir was liable *ultra vires haereditatis*. So the inventory, in its listing of assets,

---

[13] Chabot, *La dette des familles*, 135–86.

corporeal and incorporeal, worked a separation of other property from the estate and a protected right to come away with at least a quarter of the wealth. Above all, the typical inventory ferreted out the implements and other possessions that were shared and whose condition and value were unknown to those outside the circle of sharing. As easily fungible assets or as treasured heirlooms, something would be there to carry over for the next generation, thanks in part to diligently constructed inventories. Surviving inventories are an unrivaled source of useful historical insight, but they are also sources that need to be treated with care.

The patrimony itself was to be treated with care, because failure to do so could be catastrophic for a family – as sharing unit and as line of descent. The prudent manager was a nebulous ideal figure, somehow to be defined from witness testimony, if there was doubt, with the assumption of what a prudent manager would do or not do in a particular situation. Severe failure to meet that vague standard left one open to charges of madness (*furiosus*) or mental deficiency (*mentecaptus*). Here the law provided remedies and operated with a sense that those unfortunate enough to share their patrimony with a mad spendthrift should not have to suffer without some recourse. The law's experts had to proceed on the basis of testimony as to particulars of behavior for the most part. In any case, the law could not provide guarantees of prudence. A man like the Florentine Giovanni Rucellai could enjoy his success in accumulating a handsome patrimony, but by the end of his life he also had to lament the loss of most of his fortune and important assets, such as the villa at Poggio a Caiano. He was undoubtedly no less prudent across his life, but economic situations and political actions with undeniable economic consequences were not consistent by any means.[14] His actions were not prudent necessarily, but they did not rise to the level of insanity. He did not willfully destroy his belongings; he did not give them all away to the disregard and detriment of his sons, his presumptive heirs. Indeed, Rucellai left his sons, if not as much wealth as he would have liked, a book full of advice culled from his active life.[15]

In fact, many of these legal rights and actions overlapped and combined in any particular situation. Wives and sons, for example, had differing rights to assets of the same household. The drive to limit liabilities in adverse circumstances understandably drew attention to individual versus shared rights, to disabilities of age or sex, or simply to legal technicalities that might be cited to advantage. Aside from such moments, however, the so-called patriarchal family of the early modern era has

---

[14] Cf. Molho, Barducci, Battista, and Donnini, "Genealogy and Marriage Alliance."
[15] Rucellai, *Zibaldone quaresimale*.

usually been seen as a stifling arrangement, squelching individual initiative and emotion, be it in choice of career, of spouse, or of free use of property. No longer are large patriarchal households seen as remnants of a more primitive household form, perhaps, but they are still not the nuclear family on which capitalist markets would come to depend.[16]

There were limits to patriarchy, no matter how much it was bolstered by law. Heirs faced restrictions. Spouses had separate holdings. What was shared could also be claimed by someone. It took energy and effort to maintain sharing and household authority, to match the changing needs and expectations of family members.[17] Failure to be an effective manager of family resources could certainly erode otherwise expected lines of household authority.[18] Gifts could occasion conflict, as the ties they cultivated did not necessarily serve the entire family and had to be accounted for when it came time to divide a shared patrimony.[19] Disproportionate gifts, as we have seen, were sometimes contested as the acts of a mentally deficient manager. Division of patrimony itself could generate strategies of cooperation as well as conflict, but they were "pursued to further the interests of each heir's household, rather than secure the integrity of the patrimony and the future of the lineage."[20] *Familia* was *substantia* because it was hard to conceptualize one without the other.

---

[16] A summation of such views of the family, contested in part, is offered by Jack Goody, *The European Family*, esp. 170–72.
[17] Hardwick, *The Practice of Patriarchy*, 52.
[18] Hardwick, *The Practice of Patriarchy*, 91.
[19] Hardwick, *The Practice of Patriarchy*, 118–19.
[20] Hardwick, *The Practice of Patriarchy*, 156.

Bibliography

Primary Sources

Archival

Archivio di Stato, Florence (ASF)

    Carte strozziane
    Catasto
    Consiglio del Cento
    Conventi soppressi sotto il governo francese, Archivio 98
    Magistrato dei Pupilli avanti il Principato 158
    Notarile Antecosimiano
    Provvisioni registri
    Biblioteca Apostolica Vaticana

    Vat. Lat. 8069
    Biblioteca Nazionale, Florence (BNF)

    Landau Finaly 98
    Principale, II, iv, 434, 435
    Biblioteca Trivulziana, Milan

    B 1

Printed

Alberti, Leon Battista. *The Family in Renaissance Florence.* Translated by Renée Neu Watkins. Columbia: University of South Carolina Press, 1969.

Alberti, Leon Battista. *Opere volgari.* 2 vols. Edited by Cecil Grayson. Bari: Laterza, 1960.

Balduini, Jacopo. "La summula de fratribus simul habitantibus di Jacopo Balduini." Edited by Andrea Romano. *Rivista di storia del diritto italiano* 48 (1975): 123–70.

Barbaro, Francesco. "On Wifely Duties," in *The Earthly Republic: Italian Humanists on Government and Society*, 179–228. Edited by Benjamin G. Kohl and Ronald G. Witt. Philadelphia: University of Pennsylvania Press, 1978.

Bartolus of Sassoferrato. *Consilia, Quaestiones et Tractatus*. Venice, 1585.

Bartolus of Sassoferrato. *Opera omnia*. 10 vols. Venice, 1615.

Bartolus of Sassoferrato. *Opera omnia*. 11 vols. Venice, 1570–1.

Bartolus of Sassoferrato. Tractatus de testibus. In *Tractatus universi iuris*, 29 vols., vol. 4, fols. 63rb–71ra. Venice, 1584.

Benedetto da Capra. *Consilia*. Venice, 1576.

"Brighe, affanni, volgimenti di stato": le ricordanze quattrocentesche di Luca di Matteo di messer Luca dei Firidolfi da Panzano. Edited by Anthony Molho and Franek Sznura. Florence: SISMEL-Edizioni del Galluzzo, 2010.

Carpano, Orazio. *Statuta ducatus mediolanensis collecta et commentarius illustrata*. Frankfurt, 1600. [Quoted in Max Weber, *The History of Commercial Partnerships in the Middle Ages*, trans. and intro. Lutz Kaelber (Lanham, MD: Rowman and Littlefield, 2003), 176.]

Castro, Paolo di. *Commentaria in digesti novi partem secundam*. Lyons, 1553.

Castro, Paolo di. *Commentaria in Digestum infortiatum*. Venice, 1575.

Castro, Paolo di. *Consilia*. 3 vols. Venice, 1571.

Codex. Lyon, 1558–60.

Corgna, Pierfilippo da. *Consilia*, 5 vols. Venice, 1534/5.

Corpus iuris civilis. Edited by T. H. Mommsen, W. Kroll, P. Krueger, and R. Schoell. 3 vols. Berlin: Weidmann, 1928–9.

Decio, Filippo. *Consilia*. Lyon, 1522.

Decio, Filippo. *Consilia*. 2 vols. Venice, 1570.

Dominici, Giovanni. *On the Education of Children*. Translated by Arthur Basil Coté. Washington, DC: Catholic University of America Press, 1927.

Ficino, Marsilio. "Epistola ad fratres vulgaris," in *Supplementum ficinianum*, 115–19. Edited by Paul Oskar Kristeller. Florence: Olschki, 1945.

Floriano da San Pietro. *In primam et secundam ff Vet. partem*. Bologna, 1576.

Gli statuti veneziani di Jacopo Tiepolo del 1242 e le loro glosse. Edited by Roberto Cessi. Venice: Reale Istituto Veneto, 1938.

Guicciardini, Francesco. *Ricordi, diari, memorie*. Edited by Marco Spinella. Rome: Riuniti, 1981.

Il libro di ricordanze dei Corsini. Edited by Armando Petrucci. Rome: Istituto Storico Italiano per il Medio Evo, 1965.

Leges et statuta ducatus mediolanensis. Milan, 1616.

Lodovico a Sardis Ferrariensis. *Tractatus de naturalibus liberis*, in *Tractatus universi iuris*, 28 vols., vol. 8, part 2, fols. 29vb–45va. Venice, 1584.

Lo statuto del Comune di Bologna dell'anno 1335. 2 vols. Edited by Anna Laura Trombetti Budinesi. Rome: Istituto Storico Italiano per il Medio Evo, 2008.

Lo statuto di Bergamo di 1331. Edited by Claudia Storti Storchi. Milan: Giuffrè, 1986.

Machiavelli, Niccolò. *The Essential Writings of Machiavelli*. Edited and translated by Peter Constantine. New York: Modern Library, 2007.

Maino, Jason da. *Consilia*. 5 vols. Frankfurt, 1609.

Maino, Jason da. *In secundam codicis partem commentaria*. 1573.

Masi, Bartolomeo. *Ricordanze di Bartolomeo Masi calderaio fiorentino dal 1478 al 1526.* Edited by Giusseppe Odoardo Corazzini. Florence: Sansoni, 1906.

Morelli, Giovanni. *Ricordi,* in *Mercanti scrittori,* 101–339. Edited by Vittore Branca. Milan: Rusconi, 1986.

Muratori, Ludovico Antonio. *Dei difetti della giurisprudenza.* Edited by Arrigo Solmi. Rome: Formiggini, 1933.

Niccolini, Lapo. *Il libro degli affari proprii di casa di Lapo di Giovanni Niccolini de' Sirigatti.* Edited by Christian Bec. Paris: SEVPEN, 1969.

Palmieri, Matteo. *Della vita civile.* Edited by Felice Battaglia. Bologna: Zanichelli, 1944.

Pellegrini, Marcantonio. *Consilia.* Venice, 1600.

Pontano, Giovanni. *De prudentia.* Florence, 1520.

Pontano, Giovanni. *I libri delle virtù sociali.* Edited by Francesco Tateo. Rome: Bulzoni, 1999.

Porcellini, Francesco. *Tractatus de confectione inventarii,* in *Tractatus universi iuris,* 28 vols., vol. 8, part 2, fols. 156rb–65ra. Venice, 1584.

Ricostruzione di una famiglia: i Ciurianni di Firenze tra xii e xv secolo, con l'edizione critica del "Libro proprio" di Lapo di Valore Ciurianni e successori (1326–1429). Edited by Isabelle Chabot. Florence: Le Lettere, 2012.

Rosciate, Alberico da. *Dictionarium iuris tam civilis quam canonici.* Venice, 1581.

Rucellai, Giovanni. *Giovanni Rucellai e il suo Zibaldone,* vol. 1: *Il Zibaldone quaresimale.* Edited by Alessandro Perosa. London: Warburg Institute, 1960.

Sozzini, Mariano Junior. *Consilia.* 5 vols. Venice, 1571.

Sozzini, Mariano and Bartolomeo Sozzini. *Consilia.* 5 vols. Venice, 1579, 1594.

Stapleford, Richard, ed. and trans. *Lorenzo de' Medici at Home: The Inventory of the Palazzo Medici in 1492.* University Park, PA: Penn State University Press, 2013.

Statuta communis Florentiae anno salutis mccccxv. 3 vols. Freiburg [Florence], 1778–83.

Statuti della repubblica fiorentina. 2 vols. Edited by Romolo Caggese. Vol. 1: *Statuto del capitano del popolo degli anni 1322–25.* Florence: Galileana, 1910. Vol. 2: *Statuti del podestà dell'anno 1325.* Florence: Ariani, 1921. Newly edited by Giuliano Pinto, Francesco Salvestrini, and Andrea Zorzi. Florence: Olschki, 1999.

Statuti di Bologna dell'anno 1288. 2 vols. Edited by Gina Fasoli and Pietro Sella. Vatican City, 1939.

Statuto del Comune di Cortona (1325–1380). Edited by Simone Allegria and Valleria Capelli. Florence: Olschki, 2015.

Statuto del comune di Montepulciano (1337). Edited by Ubaldo Morandi. Florence: Le Monnier, 1966.

Statuto di Arezzo (1327). Edited by Giulia Maria Camerani. Florence: Deputazione per la Storia Patria per la Toscana, 1946.

Tasso, Torquato. *Dialoghi.* Edited by Bruno Basale. Milan: Murisa, 1991.

Tasso, Torquato. *I discorsi dell'arte, poetica, Il padre di famiglia, e L'Aminta.* Edited by Angelo Solerti. Turin: G.B. Paravia, 1901.

Toschi, Domenico. *Additiones locupletissimae ad caetera octo volumina.* Lyons, 1670.

Toschi, Domenico. *Practicarum conclusionum iuris in omni foro*. 8 vols. Rome, 1606.

Ubaldi, Angelo degli. *Consilia*. Frankfurt, 1575.

Ubaldi, Angelo degli. *Tractatus de inventario*. In *Tractatus universi iuris*, 29 vols., vol. 8, part 2, fols. 155va–56rb. Venice, 1584.

Ubaldi, Baldo degli. *Commentaria in primam et secundam infortiati partes*. Lyon, 1585.

Ubaldi, Baldo degli. *Consilia*. 5 vols. Venice, 1575.

Ubaldi, Baldo degli. *Opera omnia*. 9 vols. Venice, 1586.

Ubaldi, Baldo degli. *Tractatus de aditione cum inventario*. In *Tractatus universi iuris*, 29 vols., vol. 8, part 2, fol. 323ra–vb. Venice, 1584.

L'ultimo statuto della Repubblica di Siena (1545). Edited by Mario Ascheri. Siena: Accademia Senese degli Intronati, 1993.

Secondary Sources

Ago, Renata. *Gusto for Things: A History of Objects in Seventeenth-Century Rome*. Translated by Bradford Bouley and Corey Tazzara, with Paula Findlen. Chicago: University of Chicago Press, 2013.

Ago, Renata. "Oltre la dote: i beni femminili," in *Il lavoro delle donne*, 164–82. Edited by Angela Groppi. Bari: Laterza, 1996.

Ago, Renata. "Ruoli familiari e statuto giuridico." *Quaderni storici* 88 (April 1995): 111–33.

Albini, Giuliana. "Declassamento sociale e povertà vergognosa: uno sguardo sulla società viscontea," in *La mobilità sociale nel Medioevo italiano*, vol. 2: *Stato e istituzioni (secoli xiv–xv)*, 71–97. Edited by Andrea Gamberini. Rome: Viella, 2017.

Arcangeli, Letizia. "Ragioni di stato e ragioni di famiglia: strategie successorie dell'aristocrazia milanese tra Quattro e Cinquecento (Visconti, Trivulzio, Borromeo)." *Fidéicommis, procédés juridiques et pratiques sociales (Italie-Europe, bas moyen âge–xix siècle, Mélanges de l'École Française de Rome: Italie et Méditerranée modernes et contemporaines* 124 (2012): 447–69.

Ascheri, Mario. "Bartolo da Sassoferrato: il 'suo' *tractatus* consiliare e i suoi *consilia*," in *Diritto medievale e moderno: Problemi del processo, della cultura e delle fonti giuridiche*, 212–23. Rimini: Maggioli, 1991.

Ascheri, Mario. *The Laws of Late Medieval Italy (1000–1500): Foundations for a European Legal System*. Leiden and Boston, MA: Brill, 2013.

Bargagli, Roberta. *Bartolomeo Sozzini: giurista e politico (1436–1506)*. Milan: Giuffrè, 2000.

Baskins, Cristelle. *Cassone Painting: Humanism and Gender in Early Modern Italy*. Cambridge: Cambridge University Press, 1998.

Beckert, Jens. *Inherited Wealth*. Translated by Thomas Dunlap. Princeton: Princeton University Press, 2004.

Beckert, Jens. "The Great Transformation of Embeddedness: Karl Polanyi and the New Economic Sociology," in *Market and Society: The Great Transformation Today*, 38–55. Edited by Chris Hann and Keith Hart. New York: Cambridge University Press, 2009.

Béguin, Katia, Pierre-Charles Pradier, and Elena Avellino. "Nascondere il valore dei titoli pubblici per truccare i bilanci patrimoniali: il caso delle rendite dell'Hotel de Ville (Parigi xvii secolo)." *Quaderni storici* 135, *Questioni di stima* (December 2010): 703–22.

Belk, Russell. "Sharing." *Journal of Consumer Research* 36 (2010): 715–34.

Belk, Russell. "You Are What You Can Access: Sharing and Collaborative Consumption Online." *Journal of Business Research* 67 (2014): 1595–600.

Bellavitis, Anna. "Dare credito, fiducia e responsabilità alle donne (Venezia, sec. xvi)," in *Dare credito alle donne: presenze femminile nell'economia tra medioevo ed età moderna*, 259–67. Edited by Giovanna Petti Balbi and Paola Guglielmotti. Asti: Centro di studi Renato Bordone, 2012.

Bellavitis, Anna. "Dot et richesse des femmes à Venise au XVIe siècle." *Clio: Histoire, femmes et sociétés* 7 (1998): 91–100.

Bellavitis, Anna. *Famille, genre, transmission à Venise au xvie siècle*. Rome: École Française de Rome, 2008.

Bellavitis, Anna and Isabelle Chabot. "A propositio di 'Men and Women in Renaissance Venice' di Stanley Chojnacki." *Quaderni storici* 118 (2005): 203–29.

Bellomo, Manlio. *I fatti e il diritto: tra le certezze e i dubbi dei giuristi medievali (secoli xiii–xiv)*. Rome: Il Cigno, 2000.

Bellomo, Manlio. *La condizione giuridica della donna in Italia*. Turin: Edizioni Rai, 1970.

Bellomo, Manlio. *Problemi di diritto familiare nell'età dei comuni: Beni paterni e 'pars filii'*. Milan: Giuffrè, 1968.

Bellomo, Manlio. *Ricerche sui rapporti patrimoniali tra coniugi: Contributo alla storia della famiglia medievale*. Milan: Giuffrè, 1961.

Bellomo, Manlio. "La struttura patrimoniale della famiglia italiana nel tardo medioevo," in *Marriage, Property, and Succession*, 53–69. Edited by Lloyd Bonfield. Berlin: Duncker & Humblot, 1982.

Bezemer, Kaes. "The Infrastructure of the Early *Ius Commune*: The Formation of *Regulae*, or Its Failure," in *The Creation of the* Ius Commune: *From* Casus *to* Regula, 57–75. Edited by John W. Cairns and Paul J. Du Plessis. Edinburgh: Edinburgh University Press, 2010.

Biow, Douglas. *On the Importance of Being an Individual in Renaissance Italy: Men, Their Professions, and Their Beards*. Philadelphia: University of Pennsylvania Press, 2015.

Biscione, Giuseppe. *Statuti del Comune di Firenze nell'Archivio di State: Tradizione archivistica e ordinamenti*. Rome: Ministero per i Beni e le Attività Culturali, 2009.

Borello, Benedetta. *Il posto di ciascuno: fratelli, sorelle e fratellanze (xvi–xix secoli)*. Rome: Viella, 2016.

Borello, Benedetta. "Prossimi e lontani: fratelli aristocratici a Roma e Siena (secoli xvii–xix)," in *Famiglie: circolazione di beni, circuiti di affetti in età moderna*, 117–40. Edited by Renata Ago and Benedetta Borello. Rome: Viella, 2008.

Borkowski, Andrew and Paul du Plessis. *Textbook on Roman Law*. 3rd ed. Oxford: Oxford University Press, 2005.

Boschetto, Luca. *Leon Battista Alberti e Firenze*. Florence: Olschki, 2000.

Brizio, Elena. "In the Shadow of the Campo: Sienese Women and Their Families (c. 1400–1600)," in *Across the Religious Divide: Women, Property, and Law in the Wider Mediterranean (ca. 1300–1800)*, 122–36. Edited by Jutta Sperling and Shona Kelly Wray. London: Routledge, 2010.

Brucker, Gene. *The Civic World of Early Renaissance Florence*. Princeton: Princeton University Press, 1977.

Brucker, Gene. "Florence and Its University, 1348–1434," in *Action and Conviction in Early Modern Europe: Essays in Memory of E. H. Harbison*, 220–36. Edited by T. K. Rabb and Jerrold E. Seigel. Princeton: Princeton University Press, 1969.

Brucker, Gene. *Florentine Politics and Society, 1343–1378*. Princeton: Princeton University Press, 1962.

Brundage, James A. *Law, Sex, and Christian Society in Medieval Europe*. Chicago: University of Chicago Press, 1987.

Burke, Jill. *Changing Patrons: Social Identity and the Visual Arts in Renaissance Florence*. Philadelphia: University of Pennsylvania Press, 2004.

Busse, Mark and Veronica Strang. "Introduction: Ownership and Appropriation," in *Ownership and Appropriation*, 1–19. Edited by Veronica Strang and Mark Busse. Oxford and New York: Berg, 2011.

Caferro, William. *Contesting the Renaissance*. Malden, MA: Wiley-Blackwell, 2011.

Calabritto, Monica. "A Case of Melancholic Humors and *Dilucida Intervalla*." *Intellectual History Review* 18 (2008): 139–54.

Calabritto, Monica. "Furor melanconico tra teoria e pratica legale." *Studi storici* 51 (2010): 113–35.

Calonaci, Stefano. *Dietro lo scudo incantato: I fedecommessi di famiglia e il trionfo della borghesia fiorentina (1400 ca.–1750)*. Florence: Le Monnier, 2005.

Calonaci, Stefano. "Gli angeli del testamento: Donne fedecommissarie e fedecommittente nella Toscana moderna," in *Nobil donne, monache e cavaliere dell'Ordine di Santo Stefano: Modelli e strategie femminili nella vita pubblica della Toscana granducale*, 79–96. Edited by Marcella Aglietti. Pisa: Edizioni ETS, 2010.

Calvi, Giulia. "Rights and Ties That Bind: Mothers, Children, and the State in Tuscany during the Early Modern Period," in *Kinship in Europe: Approaches to Long-Term Development*, 145–62. Edited by David Warren Sabean, Simon Teuscher, and Jon Mathieu. New York and London: Berghahn, 2007.

Caravale, Mario. "Fedecommesso (storia)." *Enciclopedia del diritto*, vol. 17: 109–114. Milan: Giuffrè, 1968.

Carrier, James G. *Gifts and Commodities: Exchange and Western Capitalism since 1700*. London: Routledge, 1995.

Carsten, Janet. *After Kinship*. Cambridge: Cambridge University Press, 2004.

Carsten, Janet. "Houses in Langkawi: Stable Structures or Mobile Homes?," in *About the House: Lévi-Strauss and Beyond*, 105–28. Edited by Janet Carsten and Stephen Hugh-Jones. Cambridge: Cambridge University Press, 1995.

Casanova, Cesarina. *La famiglia italiana in età moderna*. Rome: Carocci, 1998.

Casey, James. *The History of the Family*. Oxford: Blackwell, 1989.

Cavallar, Osvaldo and Julius Kirshner. *Jurists and Jurisprudence in Medieval Italy: Texts and Contexts.* Toronto: University of Toronto Press, 2020.

Cavanna, Adriano. "Il ruolo del giurista nell'età del diritto comune." *Studia et documenta historiae et iuris* 44 (1978): 95–138.

Cavina, Marco. *Il padre spodestato: l'autorità paterna dall'antichità a oggi.* Bari: Laterza, 2007.

Ceccarelli, Giovanni. "Stime senza probabilità: assicurazione e rischio nella Firenze rinascimentale." *Quaderni storici* 45.135: *Questioni di stima* (December 2010): 651–701.

Chabot, Isabelle. "'Biens de famille': Contrôle des ressources patrimoniales, *gender* et cycle domestique (Italie, XIIIième–XVième siècles)," in *The Household in Late Medieval Cities, Italy and Northwestern Europe Compared,* 89–104. Edited by Myriam Carlier and Tim Soens. Leuven: Garant, 2001.

Chabot, Isabelle. *La dette des familles: femmes, lignage et patrimoine à Florence aux xive et xve siècles.* Rome: École Française de Rome, 2011.

Chabot, Isabelle. "Le gouvernement des pères: l'État florentin et la famille (xive–xve siècles)," in *Florence et la Toscane, xive–xixe siècles: Les dynamiques d'un État italien,* 241–63. Edited by R. Boutier, S. Landi, and O. Rouchon. Rennes: Presses Universitaires de Rennes, 2004.

Chabot, Isabelle. "La loi du lignage: Notes sur le système successoral florentin (XIVe–XVe, XVIIe siècles)." *Clio: Histoire, femmes et sociétés* 7 (1998): 51–72.

Chauvard, Jean-François, Anna Bellavitis, and Paola Lanaro, "De l'usage du fidéicommis à l'âge moderne: État des lieux." *Mélanges de l'École française de Rome, Italie et Méditerranée modernes et contemporaines,* 124.2 (2012): *Fidéicommis: Procédés juridiques et pratiques sociales (Italie-Europe, Mas Moyen Âge–xviiie siècle),* http://journals.openedition.org/mefrim/650.

Chojnacki, Stanley. *Women and Men in Renaissance Venice: Twelve Essays on Patrician Society.* Baltimore, MD: Johns Hopkins University Press, 2000.

Clavero, Bartolome. "Dictum beati: a proposito della cultura del lignaggio." *Quaderni storici* 86 (August 1994): 335–63.

Clementi, Siglinde. "Undivided Brothers: Renouncing Sisters: Family Strategies of Low Nobility in Sixteenth- and Seventeenth-Century Tyrol," in *Gender, Law and Economic Well-Being in Europe from the Fifteenth to the Nineteenth Century: North versus South?,* 149–63. Edited by Anna Bellavitis and Beatrice Zucca Michelotto. Oxford and New York: Routledge, 2018.

Cogné, Alban. "Le fidéicommis: un instrument d'immobilisation des patrimoines? Le cas de la Lombardie durant la période moderne," *Fidéicommis, procédés juridiques et pratiques sociales (Italie-Europe, bas moyen âge–xix siècle, Mélanges de l'École Française de Rome: Italie et Méditerranée modernes et contemporaines* 124 (2012). http://journals/openedition.org/mefrim/925.

Cohn, Samuel K., Jr. *The Cult of Remembrance and the Black Death: Six Renaissance Cities in Central Italy.* Baltimore, MD: Johns Hopkins University Press, 1992.

Cohn, Samuel K., Jr. *Death and Property in Siena, 1200–1800: Strategies for the Afterlife.* Baltimore, MD: Johns Hopkins University Press, 1988.

Cohn, Samuel K., Jr. "Renaissance Attachment to Things: Material Culture in Last Wills and Testaments." *Economic History Review* 65 (2012): 984–1004.

Condorelli, Orazio. "*Prudentiae in iure*: la tradizione dei giuristi medievali (prime ricerche)," in *Phronêsis-Prudentia-Klugheit: Das Wissen des Klugen in Mittelalter, Renaissance und Neuzeit*, 137–201. Edited by Alexander Fidora, Andreas Niederberger, and Mario Scattola. Porto: Fédération Internationale des Instituts dÉtudes Médiévales, 2013.

Contino, Elvira. "Societas e famiglia nel pensiero di Baldo degli Ubaldi." *Rivista di storia del diritto italiano* 82 (2009): 19–92.

Coontz, Stephanie. *The Way We Never Were: American Families and the Nostalgia Trap*. New York: Basic Books, 1992; rev. ed., 2016.

Cooper, J. P. "Patterns of Inheritance and Settlement by Great Landowners from the Fifteenth to the Eighteenth Centuries," in *Family and Inheritance: Rural Society in Western Europe, 1200–1800*, 192–327. Edited by Jack Goody, Joan Thirsk, and E. P. Thompson. Cambridge: Cambridge University Press, 1976.

Cossar, Roisin. *Clerical Households in Late Medieval Italy*. Cambridge, MA and London: Harvard University Press, 2017.

Courtemanche, Andrée. *La richesse des femmes: patrimoines et gestion à Manosque au xive siècle*. Montreal: Bellarmin; Paris: Vrin, 1993.

Crawley, Karen. "The Critical Force of Irony: Reframing Photographs in Cultural Legal Studies," in *Cultural Legal Studies: Law's Popular Cultures and the Metamorphosis of Law*, 183–205. Edited by Cassandra Sharp and Marett Leiboff. London and New York: Routledge, 2016.

Davidsohn, Robert. *Storia di Firenze*, vol. 4, *I primordi della civiltà fiorentina*, part 1, *Impulsi interni, influssi esterni e cultura politica*. Translated from German by Eugenio Dupré-Theseider. Florence: Sansoni, 1973.

Davis, Natalie Zemon. *The Gift in Sixteenth-Century France*. Madison: University of Wisconsin Press, 2000.

Delille, Gérard. *Famille et propriété dans le Royaume de Naples, xve–xixe siècle*. Rome: École Française de Rome, 1985.

Derouet, Bernard. "Dowry: Sharing Inheritance or Exclusion? Timing, Destination, and Contents of Transmission in Late Medieval and Early Modern France," in *Sibling Relations and the Transformations of European Kinship, 1300–1900*, 31–46. Edited by Christopher H. Johnson and David Warren Sabean. New York and Oxford: Berghahn, 2011.

Dizionario biografico degli italiani, vol. 83 (2015), s.v. "Pietro da Perugia," by Paolo Rosso.

Dotti, Marco. "Famiglie, istituzioni e comunità," in *Oikonomia urbana: Uno spaccato di Lodi in età moderna (secoli xvii–xviii)*, 115–74. Edited by Emanuele C. Colombo and Marco Dotti. Milan: Franco Angeli, 2011.

Duby, Georges. *The Early Growth of the European Economy: Warriors and Peasants from the Seventh to the Twelfth Century*. Translated by Howard B. Clarke. Ithaca, NY: Cornell University Press, 1974.

"Dynasty Trusts and the Rule of Perpetuities." *Harvard Law Review* 116 (2003): 2588–609.

Edgerton, Samuel Y. Jr. *Pictures and Punishment: Art and Criminal Prosecution during the Florentine Renaissance*. Ithaca, NY: Cornell University Press, 1985.

Edigati, Daniele. "Ut mulier non circumveniatur: La capacità di agire della donna in età moderna fra *ius commune* e *ius proprium*," in *Nobil donne, monache e cavaliere dell'Ordine di Santo Stefano: Modelli e strategie femminili nella vita pubblica della Toscana granducale*, 59–76. Edited by Marcella Aglietti. Pisa: Edizioni ETS, 2010.

Emigh, Rebecca Jean. *The Undevelopment of Capitalism: Sectors and Markets in Fifteenth-Century Tuscany*. Philadelphia, PA: Temple University Press, 2009.

Epstein, Steven. *Wills and Wealth in Medieval Genoa, 1150–1250*. Cambridge, MA: Harvard University Press, 1984.

Evans, Adrian. B. "Enlightening the Archive: Glimpsing Embodied Consumption Practices in Probate Inventories of Household Possessions." *Historical Geography* 36 (2008): 40–72.

Feci, Simona. "Exceptional Women: Female Merchants and Working Women in Italy in the Early Modern Period," in *Gender, Law and Economic Well-Being in Europe from the Fifteenth to the Nineteenth Century: North versus South?*, 62–76. Edited by Anna Bellavitis and Beatrice Zucca Michelotto. Oxford and New York: Routledge, 2018.

Feci, Simona. *Pesci fuor d'acqua: Donne a Roma in età moderna: diritti e patrimoni*. Rome: Viella, 2004.

Ferraro, Joanne M. *Family and Public Life in Brescia, 1580–1650: The Foundations of Power in the Venetian State*. Cambridge: Cambridge University Press, 1993.

Fisher, Caroline M. "Guardianship and the Rise of the Florentine State, 1368–93," in *Famiglie e poteri in Italia tra medioevo ed età moderna*, 265–82. Edited by Anna Bellavitis and Isabelle Chabot. Rome: École Française, 2009.

Fontaine, Laurence. *L'économie morale: Pauvreté, crédit et confiance dans l'Europe préindustrielle*. Paris: Gallimard, 2008.

Friedman, Lawrence M. *Dead Hands: A Social History of Wills, Trusts, and Inheritance Law*. Stanford, CA: Stanford University Press, 2009.

Frigo, Daniela. *Il padre di famiglia: governo della casa e governo civile nella tradizione dell' 'economica' tra Cinque e Seicento*. Rome: Bulzoni, 1985.

Fubini Leuzzi, Maria. *"Condurre a onore": Famiglia, matrimonio e assistenza a Firenze in età moderna*. Florence: Olschki, 1999.

Fumagalli, Camillo. *Il diritto di fraterna nella giurisprudenza da Accursio alla codificazione*. Turin: Fratelli Bocca, 1912.

Furlotti, Barbara. *A Renaissance Baron and His Possessions: Paolo Giordano I Orsini, Duke of Bracciano (1541–1585)*. Turnhout: Brepols, 2012.

Garlati, Loredana. "La famiglia tra passato e presente," in *Diritto della famiglia*, 1–48. Edited by Salvatore Patti and Maria Giovanna Cubeddu. Milan: Giuffrè, 2011.

Gell, Alfred. "Inter-Tribal Commodity Barter and Reproductive Gift-Exchange in Old Melanesia," in *Barter, Exchange and Value: An Anthropological Approach*, 142–68. Edited by Caroline Humphrey and Stephen Hugh-Jones. Cambridge: Cambridge University Press, 1992.

Goldthwaite, Richard A. *The Building of Renaissance Florence: An Economic and Social History*. Baltimore, MD: Johns Hopkins University Press, 1980.

Goldthwaite, Richard A. *The Economy of Renaissance Florence*. Baltimore, MD: Johns Hopkins University Press, 2009.

Goldthwaite, Richard A. and Tim Carter. *Orpheus in the Marketplace: Jacopo Peri and the Economy of Late Renaissance Florence*. Cambridge, MA: Harvard University Press, 2013.

Goody, Jack. *The European Family*. Oxford: Blackwell, 2000.

Gordley, James. *Foundations of Private Law: Property, Tort, Contract, Unjust Enrichment*. Oxford: Oxford University Press, 2006.

Gordley, James. "*Ius Quaerens Intellectum*: The Method of the Medieval Civilians," in *The Creation of the Ius Commune: From Casus to Regula*, 77–101. Edited by John W. Cairns and Paul J. Du Plessis. Edinburgh: Edinburgh University Press, 2010.

Gottlieb, Beatrice. *Family in the Western World: From the Black Death to the Industrial Age*. Oxford and New York: Oxford University Press, 1993.

Gravela, Marta. *Il corpo della città: politica e parentela a Torino nel tardo Medioevo*. Rome: Viella, 2017.

Gravela, Marta. "Parentela e finanziamento dello stato: Percorsi di mobilità sociale nella Torino del Tre-Quattrocento," in *La mobilità sociale nel Medioevo italiano*, vol. 2: *Stato e istituzioni (secoli xiv–xv)*, 141–63. Edited by Andrea Gamberini. Rome: Viella, 2017.

Greenblatt, Stephen. *Renaissance Self-Fashioning: From More to Shakespeare*. Chicago: University of Chicago Press, 1980.

Gregory, Heather. "Daughters, Dowries and Family in Fifteenth-Century Florence." *Rinascimento* 27 (1987): 217–37.

Grossi, Paolo. *Il dominio e le cose*. Milan: Giuffrè, 1992.

Grossi, Paolo. *Le situazioni reali nell'esperienza giuridica medievale*. Padua: CEDAM, 1968.

Hacke, Daniela. "'Non lo volevo per marito in modo alcuno': Forced Marriages, Generational Conflicts, and the Limits of Patriarchy in Early Modern Venice, c. 1580–1680," in *Time, Space, and Women's Lives in Early Modern Europe*, 203–21. Edited by Anne Jacobson Schutte, Thomas Kuehn, and Silvana Seidel Menchi. Kirksville, MO: Truman State University Press, 2001.

Hankins, James. *Virtue Politics: Soulcraft and Statecraft in Renaissance Italy*. Cambridge, MA: Harvard University Press, 2019.

Hanlon, Gregory. *Human Nature in Rural Tuscany: An Early Modern History*. New York: Palgrave, 2007.

Hardwick, Julie. *Family Business: Litigation and the Political Economies of Daily Life in Early Modern France*. Oxford and New York: Oxford University Press, 2009.

Hardwick, Julie. *The Practice of Patriarchy: Gender and the Politics of Household Authority in Early Modern France*. University Park, PA: Penn State University Press, 1998.

Herlihy, David. "Family," in *Portraits of Medieval and Renaissance Living: Essays in Honor of David Herlihy*, 7–28. Edited by Samuel K. Cohn, Jr. and Steven A. Epstein. Ann Arbor: University of Michigan Press, 1996.

Herlihy, David. "Family and Property in Renaissance Florence," in *The Medieval City*, 3–24. Edited by Harry A. Miskimin, David Herlihy, and A. L. Udovitch. New Haven, CT: Yale University Press, 1977.

Herlihy, David. *Medieval Households*. Cambridge, MA: Harvard University Press, 1985.

Herlihy, David and Christiane Klapisch-Zuber. *Tuscans and Their Families*. New Haven, CT: Yale University Press, 1985.

Hughes-Johnson, Samantha. "Early Medici Patronage and the Confraternity of the Buonuomini of San Martino." *Confraternitas* 22 (2011): 3–25.

Hughes-Johnson, Samantha. "Fashioning Family Honour in Renaissance Florence: The Language of Women's Clothing and Gesture in the Frescoes in the Oratory of the Confraternity of the Buonomini of San Martino in Florence." *Confraternitas* 23.2 (2012): 3–31.

Jansen, Katherine Ludwig. *Peace and Penance in Late Medieval Italy*. Princeton: Princeton University Press, 2018.

Johnson, Tom. "Medieval Law and Materiality: Shipwrecks, Finders, and Property on the Suffolk Coast, ca. 1380–1410." *American Historical Review* 120 (2015): 407–32.

Johnston, David. *The Roman Law of Trusts*. Oxford: Oxford University Press, 1988.

Jordan, William Chester. *Women and Credit in Pre-Industrial and Developing Societies*. Philadelphia: University of Pennsylvania Press, 1993.

Kahn, Victoria. *Rhetoric, Prudence, and Skepticism in the Renaissance*. Ithaca, NY and London: Cornell University Press, 1985.

Kantorowicz, Ernst. *The King's Two Bodies: A Study in Medieval Political Theology*. Princeton: Princeton University Press, 1957.

Kaser, Max. *Roman Private Law*. 2nd ed. Translated by Rolf Dannenbring. Durban: Butterworths, 1968.

Kent, Dale. "The Buonomini di San Martino: Charity for 'the Glory of God, the Honour of the City, and the Commemoration of Myself'," in *Cosimo il Vecchio de' Medici, 1389–1464: Essays in Commemoration of the 600th Anniversary of Cosimo de' Medici's Birth*, 49–67. Edited by Francis Ames-Lewis. Oxford: Clarendon Press, 1992.

Kent, Francis William. *Household and Lineage in Renaissance Florence: The Family Life of the Capponi, Ginori, and Rucellai*. Princeton: Princeton University Press, 1977.

Kirshner, Julius. "Baldus de Ubaldis on Disinheritance: Contexts, Controversies, *Consilia*." *Ius Commune: Zeitschrift für Europäische Rechtsgeschichte* 27 (2000): 119–214.

Kirshner, Julius. "*Consilia* as Authority in Late Medieval Italy: The Case of Florence," in *Legal Consulting in the Civil Law Tradition*, 107–40. Edited by Mario Ascheri, Ingrid Baumgärtner, and Julius Kirshner. Berkeley, CA: Robbins Collection, 1999.

Kirshner, Julius. "Custom, Customary Law and *Ius Commune* in Francesco Guicciardini," in *Bologna nell'età di Carlo V e Guicciardini*, 151–79. Edited by Emilia Pasquini and Paolo Prodi. Bologna: Il Mulino, 2002.

Kirshner, Julius. "Materials for a Gilded Cage: Non-Dotal Assets in Florence, 1300–1500," in *The Family in Italy from Antiquity to the Present*, 184–207. Edited by David I. Kertzer and Richard P. Saller. New Haven, CT: Yale University Press, 1991.

Kirshner, Julius. *Pursuing Honor while Avoiding Sin: The Monte delle Doti of Florence*. Milan: Giuffrè, 1978.

Kirshner, Julius. "The Seven Percent Fund of Renaissance Florence," in *Marriage, Dowry, and Citizenship in Late Medieval and Renaissance Italy*, 114–30. Toronto: University of Toronto Press, 2015.

Kirshner, Julius. "Wives' Claims against Insolvent Husbands in Late Medieval Italy," in *Women of the Medieval World*, 256–303. Edited by Julius Kirshner and Suzanne F. Wemple. Oxford: Blackwell, 1985.

Kirshner, Julius and Anthony Molho. "The Dowry Fund and the Marriage Market." *Journal of Modern History* 50 (1978): 403–38.

Kirshner, Julius and Jacques Pluss. "Two Fourteenth-Century Opinions on Dowries, Paraphernalia and Non-Dotal Goods." *Bulletin of Medieval Canon Law* 9 (1979): 65–77.

Klapisch-Zuber, Christiane. *L'Arbre des familles*. Paris: La Martinière, 2003.

Klapisch-Zuber, Christiane. "Family Trees and the Construction of Kinship in Renaissance Italy," in *Gender, Kinship, Power: A Comparative and Interdisciplinary History*, 101–13. Edited by May Jo Maynes, Ann Weltner, Brigitte Soland, and Ulrike Strasser. London and New York: Routledge, 1996.

Klapisch-Zuber, Christiane. "The Genesis of the Family Tree." *I Tatti Studies in the Italian Renaissance* 4 (1991): 105–29.

Klapisch-Zuber, Christiane and Michel Demonet, "'A uno pane e uno vino': The Rural Tuscan Family at the Beginning of the Fifteenth Century," in *Women, Family, and Ritual in Renaissance Italy*, 36–67. Translated by Lydia G. Cochrane. Chicago: University of Chicago Press, 1985.

Komter, Aafke E. *Social Solidarity and the Gift*. Cambridge: Cambridge University Press, 2005.

Kuehn, Thomas. "Adoption à Florence à la fin du Moyen Age." *Médiévales* 35 (1998): 69–81.

Kuehn, Thomas. "Debt and Bankruptcy in Florence: Statutes and Cases." *Quaderni storici* 137 (August 2011): 355–90.

Kuehn, Thomas. *Emancipation in Late Medieval Florence*. New Brunswick, NJ: Rutgers University Press, 1982.

Kuehn, Thomas. *Family and Gender in Renaissance Italy*, 1300–1600. Cambridge: Cambridge University Press, 2017.

Kuehn, Thomas. "*Fideicommissum* and Family: The Orsini di Bracciano." *Viator* 39.2 (2008): 323–42.

Kuehn, Thomas. *Heirs, Kin, and Creditors in Renaissance Florence*. Cambridge: Cambridge University Press, 2008.

Kuehn, Thomas. "Honor and Conflict in a Fifteenth-Century Florentine Family." *Ricerche storiche* 10 (1980): 287–310.

Kuehn, Thomas. *Illegitimacy in Renaissance Florence*. Ann Arbor: University of Michigan Press, 2002.

Kuehn, Thomas. "Intestate Inheritance as a Family Matter: Ius Commune, Statutes, and Cases from Florence," in *How Nordic Was Nordic Law? – Ten Years After*, 59–80. Edited by Per Andersen, Kirsi Salonen, Helle I. M. Sigh, and Helle Vogt. Copenhagen: DJØF, 2014.

Kuehn, Thomas. *Law, Family, and Women: Toward a Legal Anthropology of Renaissance Italy*. Chicago: University of Chicago Press, 1991.

Kuehn, Thomas. "*Memoria* and Family in Law," in *Art, Memory, and Family in Renaissance Florence*, 262–74. Edited by Giovanni Ciappelli and Patricia Lee Rubin. Cambridge: Cambridge University Press, 2000.

Kuehn, Thomas. "Multorum Fraudibus Occurrere: Litigation and Jurisprudential Interpretation Concerning Fraud and Liability in Quattrocento Florence." *Studi senesi* 93 (1981): 309–50.

Kuehn, Thomas. "'Nemo mortalis cognitus vivit in evo': Moral and Legal Conflicts in a Florence Inheritance Case of 1442," in *The Moral World of the Law*, 113–33. Edited by Peter Coss. Cambridge: Cambridge University Press, 2000.

Kuehn, Thomas. "Person and Gender in the Laws," in *Gender and Society in Renaissance Italy*, 87–106. Edited by Judith C. Brown and Robert C. Davis. London and New York: Longman, 1998.

Kuehn, Thomas. "Protecting Dowries in Law in Renaissance Florence," in *Studies on Florence and the Italian Renaissance in Honour of F. W. Kent*, 199–211. Edited by Peter Howard and Cecilia Hewlett. Turnhout: Brepols, 2016.

Kuehn, Thomas. "Travails of the Widow in Law in Florence at the End of the Fifteenth Century: An Illustrative Case." *Sixteenth Century Journal* 49 (2018): 691–711.

Lanaro, Paola. "La restituzione della dote: il gioco ambiguo della stima tra beni mobili e beni immobili (Venezia tra Cinque e Settecento)." *Quaderni storici* 135, *Questioni di stima* (December 2010): 753–78.

Lasorsa, Saverio. *L'organizzazione dei cambiatori fiorentini nel medio evo*. Berignola: Scienza e Diletto, 1904.

Leach, James. "Knowledge as Kinship: Mutable Essence and the Significance of Transmission on the Rai Coast of Papua New Guinea," in *Kinship and Beyond: The Genealogical Model Reconsidered*, 175–92. Edited by Sandra Bamford and James Leach. New York and Oxford: Berghahn, 2009.

Lee, Alexander. *The Ugly Renaissance: Sex, Greed, Violence and Depravity in an Age of Beauty*. New York: Doubleday, 2013.

Leprai, Stella. "Ai confini del ducato: forme di mobilità sociale nelle comunità dell'Appennino tosco-ligure-emiliano," in *La mobilità sociale nel Medioevo italiano*, vol. 2: *Stato e istituzioni (secoli xiv–xv)*, 337–53. Edited by Andrea Gamberini. Rome: Viella, 2017.

Lepsius, Susanne. *Der Richter und die Zeugen: Eine Untersuchung anhand des Tractatus testimoniorum des Bartolus von Sassoferrato, mit Edition*. Frankfurt am Main: Klostermann, 2003.

Leverotti, Franca. *Famiglie e istituzioni nel medioevo italiano: dal tardo antico al rinascimento*. Rome: Carocci, 2005.

Leverotti, Franca. "Strutture familiari nel tardo medioevo italiano." *Revista d'historia medieval* 10 (1999): 233–68.

Levy, Allison. *House of Secrets: The Many Lives of a Florentine Palazzo*. New York: L. B. Tauris, 2019.

Lindow, James R. *The Renaissance Palace in Florence: Magnificence and Splendour in Fifteenth-Century Italy*. Aldershot: Ashgate, 2007.

Litchfield, R. Burr. *Emergence of a Bureaucracy: The Florentine Patricians, 1530–1790*. Princeton: Princeton University Press, 1986.

Lombardi, Luigi. *Saggio sul diritto giurisprudenziale*. Milan: Giuffrè, 1967.

Longchamps de Berier, Franciszek. *Il fedecommesso universale nel diritto romano classico*. Warsaw: Liber, 1997.

Luongo, Alberto. "Relativamente marginali: la condizione social delle donne nella Gubbio trecentesca." *Archivio storico italiano* 127 (2019): 57–92.

Madero, Marta. "Interpreting the Western Legal Tradition: Reading the Work of Yan Thomas." Translated by Kathleen Guilloux. *Annales: Histoires, sciences sociales* 67 (2012): 103–32.

Marchisello, Andrea. "Il giudice, il diritto, la forza: note sull'esecuzione della sentenza civile in epoca moderna," in *Il diritto come forza, la forza del diritto: le fonti in azione del diritto europeo tra medioevo ed età contemporanea*, 63–79. Edited by Alberto Sciumè. Turin: Giappichelli, 2012.

Mari, Paolo. "Bartolo e la condizione femminile: brevi appunti dalle lecturae bartoliane," in *Bartolo da Sassoferrato nella cultura europea tra Medioevo e Rinascimento*, 239–52. Edited by Victor Crescenzi and Giovanni Rossi. Sassoferrato: Istituto internazionale di Studi Piceni 'Bartolo da Sassoferrato,' 2015.

Martin, John Jeffries. "Inventing Sincerity, Refashioning Prudence: The Discourse of the Individual in Renaissance Europe." *American Historical Review* 102 (1997): 1309–42.

Martin, John Jeffries. *Myths of Renaissance Individualism*. New York: Palgrave Macmillan, 2004.

Martines, Lauro. *Lawyers and Statecraft in Renaissance Florence*. Princeton: Princeton University Press, 1968.

Martines, Lauro. *The Social World of the Florentine Humanists, 1390–1460*. Princeton: Princeton University Press, 1963.

Mattox, Philip. "Domestic Sacral Space in the Florentine Renaissance Palace," in *Approaching the Italian Renaissance Interior: Sources, Methodologies, Debates*, 36–51. Edited by Marta Ajmar-Wollheim, Flora Dennis, and Ann Matchette. Oxford: Blackwell, 2007.

Mauss, Marcel. *The Gift: Forms and Functions of Exchange in Archaic Societies*. Translated by Ian Cunnison. London: Cohen and West, 1966 [1922].

Mayali, Laurent. *Droit savant et coutumes: L'exclusion des filles dotées, xiième–xvème siècles*. Frankfurt: Klostermann, 1987.

Mayali, Laurent. "*Due erunt in carne una* and the Medieval Canonists," in *Iuris Historia: Liber Amicorum Gero Dolezalek*, 161–75. Edited by Vincenzo Colli and Emanuele Conti. Berkeley, CA: Robbins Collection, 2008.

Mazzi, Maria Serena and Sergio Raveggi. *Gli uomini e le cose nelle campagne fiorentine del Quattrocento*. Florence: Olschki, 1983.

McLean, Paul D. and Neha Gondal, "The Circulation of Interpersonal Credit in Renaissance Florence." *European Journal of Sociology* 55 (2014): 135–76.

Mellyn, Elizabeth. *Mad Tuscans and Their Families: A History of Mental Disorder in Early Modern Italy*. Philadelphia: University of Pennsylvania Press, 2014.

Miller, William Ian. *Bloodtaking and Peacemaking: Feud, Law, and Society in Saga Iceland*. Chicago: University of Chicago Press, 1997.

Miller, William Ian. *Eye for an Eye*. Cambridge: Cambridge University Press, 2006.

Miller, William Ian. *Humiliation: And Other Essays on Honor, Social Discomfort, and Violence*. Ithaca, NY: Cornell University Press, 1993.

Molho, Anthony. *Marriage Alliance in Late Medieval Florence*. Cambridge, MA: Harvard University Press, 1994.

Molho, Anthony, Roberto Barducci, Gabriella Battista, and Francesco Donnini. "Genealogy and Marriage Alliance: Memories of Power in Late Medieval Florence," in *Portraits of Medieval and Renaissance Living: Essays in Memory of David Herlihy*, 39–70. Edited by Samuel K. Cohn, Jr. and Steven A. Epstein. Ann Arbor: University of Michigan Press, 1996.

Mongiano, Elisa. "Attività notarile in funzione anti-processuale," in *Hinc publica fides: il notaio e l'amministrazione della giustizia*, Atti del Convegno internazionale di Studi Storici, Genoa 8–9 Ottobre 2004, 185–214. Edited by Vita Piergiovanni. Milan: Giuffrè, 2006.

Monti, Annamaria. "Fedecommessi lombardi: profili giuridici e riflessi private delle dispense senatorie." *Fidéicommis, procédés juridiques et pratiques sociales (Italie-Europe, bas moyen âge–xix siècle, Mélanges de l'École Française de Rome: Italie et Méditerranée modernes et contemporaines 124* (2012). http://journals.openedition.org/mefrim/793.

Morse, Margaret A. "Creating Sacred Space: The Religious Visual Culture of the Renaissance Venetian *Casa*," in *Approaching the Italian Renaissance Interior: Sources, Methodologies, Debates*, 36–51. Edited by Marta Ajmar-Wollheim, Flora Dennis, and Ann Matchette. Oxford: Blackwell, 2007.

Najemy, John. *Corporatism and Consensus in Florentine Electoral Politics*, 1280–1400. Chapel Hill: University of North Carolina Press, 1982.

Najemy, John. *A History of Florence*, 1200–1575. Oxford and Malden, MA: Blackwell, 2006.

Nardi, Paolo. *Mariano Sozzini: giureconsulto senese del Quattrocento*. Milan: Giuffrè, 1974.

Nauta, Lodi. *In Defense of Common Sense: Lorenzo Valla's Humanist Critique of Scholastic Philosophy*. Cambridge, MA: Harvard University Press, 2009.

Niccolai, Franco. *La formazione del diritto successorio negli statuti comunali del territorio lombardo-tosco*. Milan: Giuffrè, 1940.

Orlin, Lena Cowen. "Fictions of the Early Modern English Probate Inventory," in *The Culture of Capitalism: Property, Cities, and Knowledge in Early Modern England*, 51–83. Edited by Henry S. Turner. New York and London: Routledge, 2002.

Ortalli, Gherardo. *La pittura infamante, secoli xii–xvi*, rev. ed. Rome Viella: 2015 [1979].

Padgett, John F. "Economic Credit in Renaissance Florence." webshare .uchicago.edu/users/jpadgett/Public/papers/unpublished/Economic .Credit.post.AJS.pdf.

Padgett, John F. "Open Elite? Social Mobility, Marriage, and Family in Florence, 1282–1494." *Renaissance Quarterly* 63 (2010): 357–411.

Padgett, John F. and Paul D. McLean. "Organizational Invention and Elite Transformation: The Birth of Partnership Systems in Renaissance Florence." *American Journal of Sociology* 111 (2006): 1463–568.

Padovani, Andrea. *Studi storici sulla dottrina delle sostituzioni.* Milan: Giuffrè, 1983.

Park, Katherine. "The Readers of the Florentine Studio according to Communal Fiscal Records (1357–1380, 1413–1446)." *Rinascimento* n.s. 10 (1980): 249–310.

Pedersen, Frederik. "The Family Economy," in *A Cultural History of Marriage*, 6 vols. Edited by Joanne M. Ferraro. Vol. 2: *A Cultural History of Marriage in the Medieval Age*, 97–117. Edited by Joanne M. Ferraro and Frederik Pedersen. London and New York: Bloomsbury, 2020.

Perelló, Carlos Amunátegui. "Problems Concerning *Familia* in Early Rome." *Roman Legal Tradition* 4 (2008): 37–45.

Petti Balbi, Giovanna and Paola Guglielmotti, eds. *Dare credito alle donne: presenze femminile nell'economia tra medioevo ed età moderna.* Asti: Centro di studi Renato Bordone, 2012.

Petti Balbi, Giovanna and Paola Guglielmotti. "*Donna et domina*: pratiche testamentarie e condizione femminile a Genova nel secolo xiv," in *Margini di libertà: testamenti femminili nel medioevo*, 153–82. Edited by Maria Clara Rossi. Sommacompagna: Cierre, 2010.

Piccialuti, Maura. *L'immortalità dei beni: Fedecommessi e primogeniture a Roma nei secoli xvii e xviii.* Rome: Viella, 1999.

Pluss, Jacques Anthony. "Baldus de Ubaldis of Perugia on Dominium over Dotal Property." *Tijdschrift voor Rechtsgeschiedenis* 52 (1984): 399–411.

Polanyi, Karl. *The Great Transformation: The Political and Economic Origins of Our Time.* 2nd ed. Boston, MA: Beacon, 2001; 1st ed., 1944.

Pomata, Gianna "Family and Gender," in *Early Modern Italy*, 69–86. Edited by John A. Marino. New York and Oxford: Oxford University Press, 2002.

Quaglioni, Diego. *"Civilis sapientia": dottrine giuridiche e dottrine politiche fra medioevo ed età moderna.* Rimini: Maggioli, 1989.

di Renzo Villata, Gigliola. "Persone e famiglia nel diritto medioevale e moderno." *Digesto civile*, vol. 13, 4th ed., 457–527. Turin: UTET, 1996.

di Renzo Villata, Gigliola. *La tutela: Indagini sulla scuola dei glossatori.* Milan: Giuffrè 1975.

Riello, Giorgio. "'Things Seen and Unseen': The Material Culture of Early Modern Inventories and Their Representation of Domestic Interiors," in *Early Modern Things: Objects and Their Histories, 1500–1800*, 125–50. Edited by Paula Findlen. New York and London: Routledge, 2013.

Riles, Annelise. "Property as Legal Knowledge: Means and Ends." *Journal of the Royal Anthropological Institute* n.s. 10 (2004): 775–95.

Roick, Matthias. *Pontano's Virtues: Aristotelian Moral and Political Thought in the Renaissance.* London and New York: Bloomsbury, 2017.

Romano, Andrea *Famiglie, successioni e patrimonio familiare nell'Italia medievale e moderna.* Turin: Giappichelli, 1994.

Roover, Raymond de. *The Rise and Decline of the Medici Bank, 1397–1494.* Cambridge, MA: Harvard University Press, 1963.

Rossi, Giovanni. "I fedecommessi nella dottrina e nella prassi giuridica di *ius commune* tra xvi e xvii secolo," in *La famiglia nell'economia europea secc. xiii–xviii*, 175–202. Edited by Simonetta Cavaciocchi. Florence: Firenze University Press, 2009.

Rossolino, Riccardo. *Credito e morte a Palermo nel Seicento*. Naples: Bibliopolis, 2017.

Ruppel, Sophie. "Subordinates, Patrons, and Most Beloved: Sibling Relationships in Seventeenth-Century German Court Society," in *Sibling Relations and the Transformations of European Kinship, 1300–1900*, 85–110. Edited by Christopher H. Johnson and David Warren Sabean. New York and Oxford: Berghahn, 2011.

Sabbatini, Renzo. "Famiglie e potere nella Lucca moderna," in *Famiglie e poteri in Italia tra Medioevo ed età moderna*, 233–61. Edited by Anna Bellavitis and Isabelle Chabot. Rome: École Française de Rome, 2009.

Sabean, David Warren and Simon Teuscher. "Kinship in Europe: A New Approach to Long-Term Development," in *Kinship in Europe: Approaches to Long-Term Development*, 1–32. Edited by David Warren Sabean, Simon Teuscher, and Jon Mathieu. New York and London: Berghahn, 2007.

Sahlins, Marshall. *What Kinship Is and Is Not*. Chicago: University of Chicago Press, 2013.

Santarelli, Umberto. *Mercanti e società tra mercanti: Lezioni di storia del diritto*. Turin: Giappichelli, 1989.

Santarelli, Umberto. *Per la storia del fallimento nelle legislazioni italiane dell'età intermedia*. Padua: CEDAM, 1964.

Sbriccoli, Mario. *L'interpretazione dello Statuto: Contributo allo studio della funzione dei giuristi nell'età comunale*. Milan: Giuffrè, 1969.

Scarabotto, Diane. "Between: The Hybrid Economies of Collaborative Networks." *Journal of Consumer Research* 42 (2015): 152–76.

Schutte, Anne Jacobson. *By Force and Fear: Taking and Breaking Monastic Vows in Early Modern Europe*. Ithaca, NY and London: Cornell University Press, 2011.

Shaw, James E. "Women, Credit, and Dowry in Early Modern Italy," in *Women and Credit in Pre-Industrial Europe*, 173–202. Edited by Elise M. Dermineur. Turnhout: Brepols, 2018.

Sheedy, Anna T. *Bartolus on Social Conditions in the Fourteenth Century*. New York: Columbia University Press, 1942.

Signori, Gabriela. "Similitude, égalité et réciprocité: l'économie matrimoniale dans les sociétés urbaines de l'Empire à la fin du Moyen Âge." *Annales: Histoires, Sciences Sociales* 67 (2012): 657–78.

Smail, Daniel Lord. *Legal Plunder: Households and Debt Collection in Late Medieval Europe*. Cambridge, MA and London: Harvard University Press, 2016.

Smith, Alison A. "Gender, Ownership and Domestic Space: Inventories and Family Archives in Renaissance Verona." *Renaissance Studies* 12 (1998): 375–91.

Snyder, Jon R. *Dissimulation and the Culture of Secrecy in Early Modern Europe*. Berkeley and London: University of California Press, 2009.

Spicciani, Amletto. "The 'Poveri Vergognosi' in Fifteenth-Century Florence," in *Aspects of Poverty in Early Modern Europe*, 119–82. Edited by Thomas Riis. Alphen aan den Rijn: Sijthoff, 1981.

Stanford Encyclopedia of Philosophy, s.v. "Aquinas's Moral, Political, and Legal Philosophy." Revised 2011: http://plato.stanford.edu/entries/aquinas-moral-political.

Stewart, Frank Henderson. *Honor*. Chicago: University of Chicago Press, 1994.

Strathern, Marilyn. "Sharing, Stealing and Borrowing Simultaneously," in *Ownership and Appropriation*, 23–41. Edited by Veronica Strang and Mark Busse. Oxford and New York: Berghahn, 2011.

Tanzini, Lorenzo. *1345, la bancarotta di Firenze: una storia di banchieri, fallimenti e finanza*. Rome: Salerno, 2018.

Tanzini, Lorenzo. *Statuti e legislazione a Firenze dal 1355 al 1415: Lo statuto cittadino del 1409*. Florence: Olschki, 2004.

Terpstra, Nicholas. "Real and Virtual Families: Forms and Dynamics of Fostering and Adoption in Bologna's Early Modern Hospitals," in *Adoption and Fosterage Practices in the Late Medieval and Modern Age*, 143–58. Edited by Maria Clara Rossi and Marina Garbelotti. Rome: Viella, 2015.

Teuscher, Simon. "Flesh and Blood in the Treatises on the Arbor Consanguinitatis (Thirteenth to Sixteenth Centuries)," in *Blood and Kinship: Matter for Metaphor from Ancient Rome to the Present*, 83–104. Edited by Christopher H. Johnson, Bernhard Jussen, David Warren Sabean, and Simon Teuscher. New York and Oxford: Berghahn, 2013.

Thomas, Yan. "Les artifices de la verité en droit commun médiéval." *L'Homme* 175–76 (July–September 2005): 113–30. http://journals.openedition.org/l'homme/29519.

Thomas, Yan. *Fictio legis: La funzione romana e i suoi limiti medievali*. Edited by Michele Spanò. Macerata: Quodlibet, 2016.

Thomas, Yan. "Il padre, la famiglia e la città: figli e figlie davanti alla giurisdizione domestica a Roma," in *Pater familias*, 23–57. Edited by Angiolina Arru. Rome: Biblink, 2002.

Thomas, Yan. *Il valore delle cose*. Macerata: Quodlibet, 2015.

Torre, Angelo. "'Cause pie': riflessioni su lasciti e benefici in antico regime." *Quaderni storici* 154 (April 2017): 155–80.

Treggiari, Ferdinando. "Commentaria (Commentaries on Civil Law), Fourteenth Century, Bartolus a Saxoferrato (1313/14–1357/58)," in *The Formation and Transmission of Western Legal Culture: 150 Books That Made the Law in the Age of Printing*, 40–44. Edited by Serge Dauchy, Georges Martyn, Anthony Musson, Heikki Pihlajanäki, and Adam Wyffels. Cham: Springer, 2016.

Treggiari, Ferdinando. *Minister ultimae voluntatis: Esegesi e sistema nella formazione del testamento fiduciario*, vol. 1: *Le premesse romane e l'età del diritto comune*. Naples: Edizioni Scientifiche Italiane, 2002.

Treggiari, Ferdinando. "La società di fatto: Sondaggi di dottrina giuridica medievale," in *Scritti in onore di Vito Rizzo: Persona, mercato, contratto e rapporti di consumo*, 2235–45. Edited by E. Caterini, L. D. Nella, A. Flamini, L. Mezzasoma, and S. Polidori. Naples: Edizioni Scientifiche Italiane, 2017.

Trexler, Richard C. "Charity and the Defense of Urban Elites in the Italian Communes," in *Dependence in Context in Renaissance Florence*, 61–111. Binghamton: Center for Medieval and Early Renaissance Studies, 1994.

Tria, Luigi. *Il fedecommesso nella legislazione e nella dottrina dal secolo xvi ai giorni nostri*. Milan: Giuffrè, 1945.

Trifone, Romualdo. *Il fedecommesso: Storia dell'istituto dal diritto romano all'inizio del xvi secolo*. Naples: Stabilimento d'Arte Grafiche, 1914.

Tuohy, Thomas. *Herculean Ferrara: Ercole d'Este (1471–1505) and the Invention of a Ducal Capital*. Cambridge: Cambridge University Press, 1996.

Vallario, Angela M. "Death by a Thousand Cuts: The Rule against Perpetuities." *Journal of Legislation* 25 (2015): 141–62.

Vallerani, Massimo. "*Consilia iudicialia*, sapienza giuridica e processo nelle città comunali italiane." *Mélanges de l'École Française de Rome-Moyen Âge* 123 (2011): 129–49.

van Bavel, Bas. *The Invisible Hand? How Market Economies Have Emerged and Declined since AD 500*. New York and Oxford: Oxford University Press, 2016.

Verga, Angelo. *Le comunioni tacite familiari*. Padua: CEDAM, 1930.

Visceglia, Maria Antonietta. *Il bisogno di eternità: i comportamenti aristocratici a Napoli in età moderna*. Naples: Guida, 1988.

Waelkens, Laurent. *Amne Adverso: Roman Legal Heritage in European Culture*. Translated by Line Leys. Leuven: Leuven University Press, 2015.

Waelkens, Laurent. "Medieval Family and Marriage Law: From Actions of Status to Legal Doctrine," in *The Creation of the Ius Commune: From Casus to Regula*, 103–25. Edited by John W. Cairns and Paul J. Du Plessis. Edinburgh: Edinburgh University Press, 2010.

Watson, Alan. *The Law of Succession in the Later Roman Republic*. Oxford: Clarendon Press, 1971.

Weiner, Annette B. *Inalienable Possessions: The Paradox of Keeping-While Giving*. Berkeley: University of California Press, 1992.

Widlok, Thomas. *Anthropology and the Economy of Sharing*. London and New York: Routledge, 2017.

Widlok, Thomas. "Sharing: Allowing Others to Take What Is Valued." *HAU: Journal of Ethnographic Theory* 3 (2013): 11–31.

Wieacker, Franz. *Storia del diritto privato moderno*, 2 vols., vol. 1. Translated by Umberto Santarelli. Milan: Giuffrè, 1980.

Witthoft, Brucia. "Marriage Rituals and Marriage Chests in Quattrocento Florence." *Artibus et Historiae* 3.5 (1982): 43–59.

Zorzoli, Maria Carla. "Della famiglia e del suo patrimonio: riflessioni sull'uso del fedecommesso in lombardia tra cinque e seicento," in *Marriage, Property, and Succession*, 155–213. Edited by Lloyd Bonfield. Berlin: Duncker & Humblot, 1992.

Index

For EU product safety concerns, contact us at Calle de José Abascal, 56–1°, 28003 Madrid, Spain or eugpsr@cambridge.org.

www.ingramcontent.com/pod-product-compliance
Ingram Content Group UK Ltd.
Pitfield, Milton Keynes, MK11 3LW, UK
UKHW020354140625
459647UK00020B/2474

*   9 7 8 1 0 0 9 0 7 3 9 6 7   *